INTRODUCTION
TO ECONOMETRICS

INTRODUCTION TO ECONOMETRICS

Gary Koop

Department of Economics
University of Strathclyde

John Wiley & Sons, Ltd

Other Wiley Editorial Offices

John Wiley & Sons Inc., 111 River Street, Hoboken, NJ 07030, USA

Jossey-Bass, 989 Market Street, San Francisco, CA 94103-1741, USA

Wiley-VCH Verlag GmbH, Boschstr. 12, D-69469 Weinheim, Germany

John Wiley & Sons Australia Ltd, 42 McDougall Street, Milton, Queensland 4064, Australia

John Wiley & Sons (Asia) Pte Ltd, 2 Clementi Loop #02-01, Jin Xing Distripark, Singapore 129809

John Wiley & Sons Canada Ltd, 6045 Freemont Blvd, Mississauga, ONT, L5R 4J3

Wiley also publishes its books in a variety of electronic formats. Some content that appears in print may not be available in electronic books.

Library of Congress Cataloging-in-Publication Data

Koop, Gary.
Introduction to econometrics / Gary Koop.
    p. cm.
Includes bibliographical reference and index.
ISBN 978-0-470-03270-1
1. Econometrics.   I. Title.
HB 139.K63593 2008
330.01′5195–dc22
                                        2007030007

A catalogue record for this book is available from the British Library

ISBN: 9780470032701 (pbk)

Typeset in 11/13pt GARAMOND MT roman by Thomson Digital Noida

Contents

Preface

For many years I have taught econometrics courses to students at various stages of their university careers and with varying backgrounds and interests. There are many competing tensions one faces when teaching to a diverse body of students. One of the most important is the tension between students who just want to use econometrics to work with data and those who want to do further study in econometrics and, thus, want to learn econometric theory. Econometric theory involves knowledge of probability and can use fairly sophisticated mathematical tools. Many of the students who just wish to use econometrics struggle in an econometric theory course. And many of the students wishing to do further study in econometrics find that an undergraduate data analysis course is insufficient preparation.

I believe that students can do good empirical work without a deep knowledge of econometric theory. For instance, regression-based methods can be motivated intuitively as a best-fitting line and interpreted as measuring the effect of explanatory variables on a dependent variable. Since many econometric models for cross-sectional and time series data can be thought of as regressions, I believe one can teach many fields of econometrics intuitively without much theory. For instance, to run a sensible regression, one doesn't need to know the proof of the Gauss–Markov theorem. To work with cointegrated models, one doesn't need to prove the spurious regression problem. This belief underlay my earlier textbooks *Analysis of Economic Data* and *Analysis of Financial Data* (both published by John Wiley & Sons, Ltd). These books, which involve minimal maths and econometric theory, have had some success. But they do not prepare the student well for further study in econometrics. Furthermore, there are some important topics (e.g. panel data, instrumental variable methods, qualitative choice models) that are difficult to motivate intuitively without some econometric theory. These considerations form the main motivation for this book. In it, I attempt to cover a wide range of models used by applied economists. In addition, although I have tried to emphasize intuition rather than proofs, this book does contain the econometric theory necessary to build a bridge to further study of econometrics.

In terms of econometric theory, my belief is that you can go pretty far using a few tools such as the expected value and variance operators and a bit of probability theory. This book only uses such tools (and an appendix explains them for the benefit of the student with no previous knowledge of such tools). One difficult decision I had was whether to use asymptotic theory in this book. Asymptotic theory is widely used by classical econometric theorists. Many students find it to be quite difficult. Knowledge of asymptotic theory is not necessary intuitively to understand econometric methods and do good empirical work. However, some concepts (e.g. instrumental variables estimation) are hard to motivate without some asymptotic theory. In light of these competing considerations, what I have done in this book is put key results using asymptotic theory in appendices to several of the chapters. A student can skip these appendices and still obtain a good understanding of much econometric theory. However, for the student interested in doing further classical econometric study, asymptotic results are available.

One final distinctive characteristic of this book is worth noting. It is common for students to go through weeks or months of lectures learning econometric theory before actually using it in practice. Some students do not like this. When I was a student many years ago, I know I did not – I wanted to get started working with data as soon as possible. Accordingly, I have written this textbook so the student can get started with data work very quickly. The first two chapters offer a non-technical summary of the basic tools of econometrics such as regression and correlation (and the exercises at the end of the chapters provide several datasets). In addition to allowing students to get started quickly in their empirical work, these chapters should give the student an intuitive grasp of what econometrics is for and what regression modeling is all about. This foundation should make the theoretical econometric material, which begins in Chapter 3, more accessible. The website associated with this book contains many datasets (as well as other teaching materials).

I would like to thank Steve Hardman at John Wiley & Sons for his enthusiasm and expert editorial advice. I would also like to thank all my students and, in particular, those at the Universities of Strathclyde and Leicester for their comments and reactions to the lectures that formed the foundation of this book. Many reviewers also offered numerous helpful comments. Most of these were anonymous, but Darryl Holden, Jan Kiviet, and Kevin Reilly offered numerous invaluable suggestions that were incorporated in the book. Finally, I would like to express my deepest gratitude to my wife, Lise, for all the support and encouragement she gave me along the way.

Gary Koop

Author's Note

The author is donating all royalties from the sale of this textbook to IFAW (The Inter-national Fund for Animal Welfare). IFAW works to improve the welfare of

wild and domestic animals throughout the world by reducing commercial exploitation of animals, protecting wildlife habitats, and assisting animals in distress. IFAW also seeks to motivate the public to prevent cruelty to animals and to promote animal welfare and conservation policies that advance the well-being of both animals and people. In addition to supporting all of these projects and programs, IFAW is spending a portion of the royalties earned from the sale of this textbook on the conservation and care of primates.

IFAW has its international headquarters in the USA and offices in 15 countries. More information about IFAW can be found at: www.ifaw.org.

CHAPTER 1

An Overview of Econometrics

1.1   The importance of econometrics

The Duke of Wellington, a British commander of the Napoleonic Wars, once said: 'All the business of war, indeed all the business of life, is to endeavour to find out what you don't know by what you do; that's what I call "guessing what is on the other side of the hill".' This is an apt description of what econometrics is all about.

Economics is full of unanswered questions such as: 'Will a change in interest rates affect the exchange rate?' 'Do the long-term unemployed have a more difficult time getting jobs than the short-term unemployed? 'What is the impact of gas prices on the choice of whether to drive or take the bus to work?'. These are examples of the 'what we don't know' of economics. The 'what we do know' of economics are data. All sorts of agencies (e.g. governments, newspapers, companies even individuals) collect facts that shed light on the 'what we don't know'. Look, for instance, in most newspapers and you will find lots of information about the prices of various assets (e.g. interest rates, exchange rates, stock prices, etc.). Most governments carry out surveys or censuses of many activities of their citizens, and these can, for example, be used to compare the experience of the long-term unemployed with that of the short-term unemployed. Economic researchers have carried out surveys of commuters, and some of the information provided can be used to investigate factors that influence the choice between the private car and public transport.

Wellington knew that one had to appeal to the facts to make a good military decision. The same applies in economics. Without an appeal to the facts (i.e. the data), economic debates can degenerate into a sterile repetition of fixed opinions. Or they can become informal storytelling sessions where economists support their views with their favorite anecdotes. When making military preparations, anyone can 'guess what is on the other side of this hill', but it takes a great commander to combine all the available information and draw the most sensible conclusions. To continue the analogy, the purpose of econometrics is to show the economist how to be a great commander, to use 'what we know' in the most effective manner in order to try and resolve 'what we don't know'. In other words, econometrics shows us how to use data in a sensible and systematic manner to shed light on economic questions.

The purpose of this chapter is to provide you with an understanding of the basic concepts and tools that are used by econometricians. Given the primary role of data in econometrics, it won't surprise you to learn that much of this chapter is about data. We discuss the types of data commonly used by economists and offer a brief discussion about where data are obtained.[1] Following this, we discuss some simple ways of analyzing data (e.g. graphical methods and descriptive statistics) and offer an introduction to some of the basic theoretical tools used by the econometrician (e.g. expected values and variances). These basic concepts and tools are then used in all the remaining chapters of this book.

1.2   Types of economic data

This section introduces the types of data used by economists and defines the notation and terminology associated with them.

1.2.1   Time series data

Macroeconomists and financial economists are often interested in concepts such as gross domestic product (GDP), stock prices, interest rates, exchange rates, etc. Such data are collected at specific points in time. In all of these examples, the data are ordered by time and are referred to as *time series data*. The underlying phenomenon that we are measuring (e.g. GDP, stock prices, interest rates, etc.) is referred to as a *variable*. Time series data can be observed at many frequencies. Commonly used frequencies are: annual (i.e. a variable is observed every year), quarterly (i.e. 4 times a year), monthly, weekly or daily.

In this book, we will use the notation Y_t to indicate an observation on variable Y (e.g. an exchange rate) at time t. A series of data runs from period $t = 1$ to $t = T$. Here, T is used to indicate the total number of time periods covered in a dataset. To give an example, if we were to use monthly time series data from January 1947 to October 1996 on the UK pound/US dollar exchange rate – a period of 598 months – then $t = 1$ would indicate January 1947, $t = 598$ would indicate October 1996 and $T = 598$ would be the total number of months. Hence, Y_1 would be the pound/dollar exchange rate in January 1947, Y_2 would be this exchange rate in February 1947, etc. Time series data are presented in chronological order.

Working with time series data often requires some special tools, which are discussed in Chapters 6 and 7.

1.2.2 Cross-sectional data

In contrast to the above, researchers often work with data that are characterized by individual units. These units might refer to companies, people, or countries. For instance, a financial economist investigating theories relating to portfolio allocation might collect data on the return earned on the stocks of many different companies. With such *cross-sectional* data, the ordering of the data typically does not matter (unlike time series data).

In this book, we use the notation Y_i to indicate an observation on variable Y for individual i. Observations in a cross-sectional dataset run from unit $i = 1$ to N. By convention, N indicates the number of cross-sectional units (e.g. the number of companies surveyed). For instance, a researcher might collect data on the share price of $N = 100$ companies at a certain point in time. In this case, Y_1 will be equal to the share price of the first company, Y_2 will be equal to the share price of the second company, and so on.

It is worthwhile stressing another important distinction between types of data. In the preceding example, the researcher collecting data on share prices will have a number corresponding to each company (e.g. the price of a share of company 1 is $25). This is referred to as *quantitative data*.

However, there are many cases where data do not come in the form of single numbers. For instance, the labour economist, when asking whether or not each surveyed employee belongs to a union, receives either a Yes or a No answer. These answers are referred to as *qualitative data*. Such data arise often in economics when choices are involved (e.g. the choice to buy or not to buy a product, to take public transport or a private car). Econometricians usually convert these qualitative answers into numeric data. For instance, the labor economist might set Yes $= 1$ and No $= 0$. Hence, $Y_1 = 1$ means that the first individual surveyed does belong to a union, and $Y_2 = 0$ means that the second individual does not. When variables can take on only the values 0 or 1, they are referred to as *dummy* (or *binary*) *variables*.

1.2.3 Panel data

Some datasets will have both a time series and a cross-sectional component. Such data are referred to as *panel data*. Economists working on issues related to economic growth often make use of panel data. They might work, for instance, with data for 90 countries for the years 1950–2000 for the variable $Y =$ GDP. Such a dataset would contain the value of GDP for each country in 1950 ($N = 90$ observations), followed by GDP for each country in 1951 (another $N = 90$ observations), and so on. Over a period of T years, there would be TN observations on Y. We will use the notation Y_{it} to indicate an observation on variable Y for country i at time t. Panel datasets are often used by labour economists. For instance, the government often carries out surveys of many people asking them questions about their employment, income, education, etc. From such a survey the labour economist might work with the variable $Y =$ the wage of $N = 1\,000$ individuals for $T = 5$ years.

1.2.4   Obtaining data

All of the data you need in order to understand the basic concepts and to carry out the analyses covered in this book can be downloaded from the website associated with this book. However, in the future you may need to gather your own data for an essay, dissertation, or report. Economic data come from many different sources, and it is hard to offer general comments on the collection of data. Below are a few key points that you should note about common datasets and where to find them.

It is becoming increasingly common for economists to obtain their data over the internet, and many relevant websites now exist from which data can be downloaded. You should be forewarned that the web is a rapidly growing and changing place, so that the information and addresses provided here might soon be outdated. Accordingly, this section is provided only to give an indication of what can be obtained over the internet, and as such is far from complete.

Some of the datasets available on the web are free, but many are not. Most university libraries or computer centres subscribe to various databases that the student can use. You are advised to check with your own university library or computer centre to see what datasets you have access to. Most universities will at a minimum have access to the major datasets collected by the government. For instance, in the UK the Office of National Statistics (ONS) collects all sorts of data, and these are usually available through UK university libraries. The UK Data Archive (http://www.data-archive.ac.uk/) is another useful source. An extremely useful American site is 'Resources for Economists on the Internet' (http://rfe.org). This site contains all sorts of interesting material on a wide range of economic topics and provides links to many different data sources. On this site you can also find links to journal data archives. Many journals encourage their authors to make their data publicly available, and hence, in many cases, you can get data from published academic papers through journal data archives. A good example is the Journal of Applied Econometrics Data Archive (http://www.econ.queensu.ca/jae/).

Another site with useful links is the National Bureau of Economic Research (http://www.nber.org/). One good data source available through this site is the Penn World Table (PWT), which gives macroeconomic data for over 100 countries for many years. We will refer to the PWT below. Most countries also have large panel datasets where large groups of individuals are surveyed every year. In America, the Panel Study of Income Dynamics (http://psidonline.isr.umich.edu/) is a valuable resource for researchers in many fields. In the UK, the comparable panel dataset is the British Household Panel Survey (http://www.iser.essex.ac.uk/ulsc/bhps/).

With regard to financial data, there are many excellent databases of stock prices and accounting information for all sorts of companies for many years. Unfortunately, these tend to be very expensive and, hence, you should see whether your university has a subscription to a financial database. Two of the more popular ones are DataStream by Thompson Financial (http://www.datastream.com/) and Wharton Research Data Services (http://wrds.wharton.upenn.edu/). For free data, a more limited choice of financial data is available through popular internet ports such as Yahoo (http://yahoo.finance.com). The Federal Reserve Bank of St Louis also maintains a free database with a wide variety of data, including some financial time series (http://research.stlouisfed.org/fred2/). The Financial Data Finder (http://www.cob.ohio-state.edu/fin/osudata.htm), provided by the Fisher College of Business at the Ohio State University, is also a useful resource. Many academics also make the datasets they have used available on their websites. For instance, Robert Shiller at Yale University has a website that provides links to many different interesting financial datasets (http://aida.econ.yale.edu/%7Eshiller/index.html). A general point worth stressing is that spending some time searching the web can often be very fruitful.

1.2.5   Data transformations: levels and growth rates

In this book, we will mainly assume that the data of interest, Y, are directly available. However, in practice, it is common to take raw data from one source and then transform it into a different form for empirical analysis. For instance, the financial economist may take raw time series data on the variables X = company earnings and W = number of shares and create a new variable: Y = earnings per share. Here, the transformation would be

$$Y = \frac{X}{W}.$$

The exact nature of the transformation required depends on the problem at hand, so it is hard to offer any general recommendations on data transformation. Some special cases are considered in later chapters. Here, it is useful to introduce some transformations that often arise with time series data.

To motivate this transformation, note that in many cases macroeconomists and financial economists are not interested directly in a variable (e.g. GDP), but rather how it is changing over time. To make things concrete, consider financial economists. In many cases they would not be interested in the price of an asset, but rather in the return that an investor would make from purchase of the asset. This depends on how much the price of the asset will change over time. Suppose, for instance, that the financial economist has annual data on the price of a share in a particular company for 1950–1998 (i.e. 49 years of data), denoted by Y_t for $t = 1 - 49$. In some cases this might be the variable of primary interest. Such a variable is referred to as a level (i.e. we refer to the 'level of the share price'). However, people are often more interested in the growth of the share price. A simple way to measure growth is to take the share price series and calculate a percentage change for each year. The percentage change in the share price between period $t - 1$ and t is calculated according to the formula

$$\% \ change = \frac{Y_t - Y_{t-1}}{Y_{t-1}} \times 100.$$

It is worth stressing that a percentage change always has a timescale associated with it (e.g. the percentage change between period $t - 1$ and t). For instance, with annual data this formula would produce an annual percentage change, with monthly data the formula would produce a monthly percentage change, etc. As will be discussed in later chapters, it is sometimes convenient to take the natural logarithm of variables. The definition and properties of logarithms can be found in Appendix A: Mathematical Basics at the end of this book. Using the properties of logarithms, it can be shown that the percentage change in a variable is approximately

$$\% \text{ change} \approx [\ln(Y_t) - \ln(Y_{t-1})] \times 100.$$

In practice, the '×100' is often dropped, so that, say, 5 % would be 0.05. The percentage change in an asset's price is often referred to as the growth of the price or the change in the price.[2] Changes in variables are often used with macroeconomic variables. For instance, macroeconomists sometimes study GDP growth (instead of the level of GDP) or inflation (which is the change in the price level). Chapters 6 and 7 cover time series econometrics, and in these chapters it is often important to distinguish between the level of a variable and its growth rate.

1.3   Working with data: graphical methods

Once you have your data, it is important for you to summarize it. After all, anybody who reads your work will not be interested in the dozens or, more likely, hundreds or more observations contained in the original raw dataset. Indeed, you can think of the whole field of econometrics as one devoted to the development and dissemination of methods whereby information in datasets is summarized in informative ways. Charts and tables are very useful ways of presenting your data. There are many different types (e.g. bar chart, pie chart, etc.). In this section, we will illustrate a few of the commonly used types of chart. Since most economic data are either in time series or cross-sectional form, we will briefly introduce simple techniques for graphing both types of data.

1.3.1   Time series graphs

Monthly time series data from January 1947 to October 1996 on the UK pound/US dollar exchange rate are plotted in Figure 1.1. Such charts are commonly referred to as *time series graphs*. The dataset contains 598 observations – far too many to be presented as raw numbers for a reader to comprehend. However, a reader can easily capture the main features of the data by looking at the graph. One can see, for instance, the attempt by the UK government to hold the exchange rate fixed until the end of 1971 (apart from large devaluations in September 1949 and November 1967) and the gradual depreciation of the pound as it floated downwards through the middle of the 1970s.

1.3.2   Histograms

With time series data, a graph that shows how a variable evolves over time is often very informative. However, in the case of cross-sectional data, such methods are not appropriate and we must summarize the data in other ways.

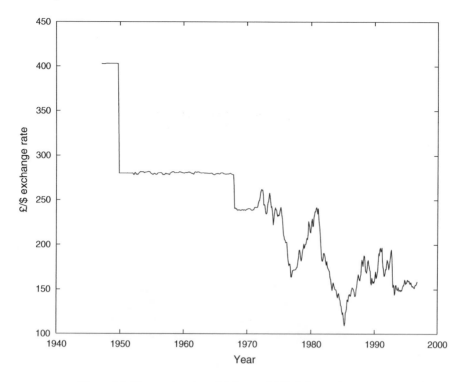

Figure 1.1 Time series plot of UK pound/US dollar exchange rate.

The Penn Word Table allows us to obtain cross-sectional data on real GDP per capita in 1992 for 90 countries. Real GDP per capita in every country has been converted into US dollars using purchasing power parity exchange rates. This allows us to make direct comparisons across countries. One convenient way of summarizing these data is through a *histogram*. To construct a histogram, begin by choosing *class intervals* or *bins* that divide the countries into groups based on their GDP per capita. In our dataset, GDP per person varies from $408 in Chad to $17 945 in the USA. One possible set of class intervals is 0–2 000, 2 001–4 000, 4 001–6 000, 6 001–8 000, 8 001–10 000, 10 001–12 000, 12 001–14 000, 14 001–16 000, and 16 001–18 000 (where all figures are in US dollars). Note that each class interval is $2 000 wide. In other words, the class width for each of our bins is 2 000. For each class interval we can count up the number of countries that have GDP per capita in that interval. For instance, there are seven countries in our dataset with real GDP per capita between $4 001 and $6 000. The number of countries lying in one class interval is referred to as the frequency of that interval. A histogram is a bar chart that plots frequencies against class intervals.

Figure 1.2 is a histogram of our cross-country GDP per capita dataset that uses the class intervals specified in the previous paragraph. Note that, if you do not wish to specify class intervals, any relevant computer software package will do it automatically for you. Most computer packages will also create a frequency table, which we have put into Table 1.1. The frequency table indicates the number of countries belonging to each class interval.

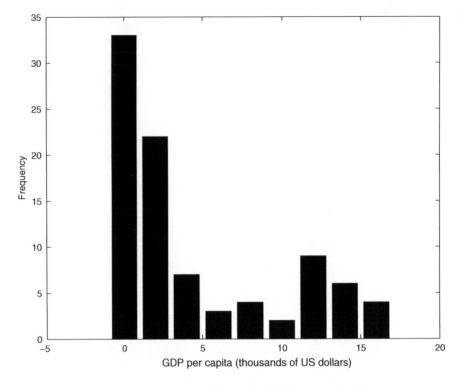

Figure 1.2 Histogram of GDP per capita for 90 countries.

For instance, we can read that there are 33 countries with GDP per capita less than $2 000, 22 countries with GDP per capita above $2 000 but less than $4 000, and so on. The last row indicates that there are four countries with GDP per capita between $16 000 and $18 000.

This same information is graphed in a simple fashion in the histogram in Figure 1.2. Graphing allows for a quick visual summary of the cross-country *distribution* of GDP

Table 1.1 Frequency table for GDP per capita data.

Class interval ($)	Frequency
0–2 000	33
2 001–4 000	22
4 001–6 000	7
6 001–8 000	3
8 001–10 000	4
10 001–12 000	2
12 001–14 000	9
14 001–16 000	6
16 001–18 000	4

per capita. We can see from the histogram that many countries are very poor, but that there is also a 'clump' of countries that are quite rich (e.g. 19 countries have GDP per capita greater than \$12 000). There are relatively few countries in between these poor and rich groups (i.e. few countries fall in the bins between \$6 001 and \$12 000). Researchers often refer to this clumping of countries into poor and rich groups as the 'twin peaks' phenomenon. In other words, if we imagine that the histogram is a mountain range, we can see a peak at the class intervals \$0–\$2 000 and a smaller peak at the class interval \$12 000–\$14 000. These features of the data can be seen easily from the histogram, but would be difficult to comprehend simply by looking at the raw data.

1.3.3   *XY* plots

Economists are often interested in the nature of the relationships between two or more variables. For instance: 'What is the relationship between capital structure (i.e. the division between debt and equity financing) and firm performance (e.g. profit)?', 'Are higher education levels and work experience associated with higher wages among workers in a given industry?', 'Are changes in the money supply a reliable indicator of inflation changes?', 'Do differences in financial regulation explain why some countries are growing faster than others?', etc. All these questions involve two or more different variables. The techniques described previously are suitable for describing the behaviour of only one variable; for instance, the properties of the single variable real GDP per capita are illustrated in Figure 1.2 above. They are not, however, suitable for examining relationships between pairs of variables.

Once we are interested in understanding the nature of the relationships between two or more variables, it becomes harder to use graphs. Beginning in the next chapter, we will discuss regression analysis, which is the most important tool used by economists working with many variables. However, graphical methods can be used to draw out some simple aspects of the relationship between two variables. *XY plots* (also called scatter diagrams) are particularly useful in this regard.

Below you will find a graph of data on deforestation (i.e. the average annual forest loss over the period 1981–1990 expressed as a percentage of total forested area) for 70 tropical countries, along with data on population density (i.e. the number of people per thousand hectares). It is commonly thought that countries with a high population density will likely deforest more quickly than those with low population densities, since high population density may increase the pressure to cut down forests for fuel wood or for agricultural land required to grow more food.

Figure 1.3 is an *XY* plot of these two variables. Each point on the chart represents a particular country. Reading up the *Y* axis (i.e. the vertical axis) gives us the rate of deforestation in that country. Reading across the *X* axis (i.e. the horizontal axis) gives us population density. It is possible to label each point with its corresponding country name. We have not done so here, as labels for 70 countries would clutter the chart and make it difficult to read. However, one country, Nicaragua, has been labeled. Note that

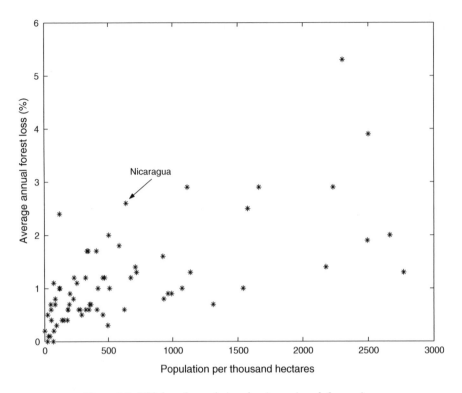

Figure 1.3 *XY* plot of population density against deforestation.

this country has a deforestation rate of 2.6 % per year $(Y = 2.6)$ and a population density of 640 people per thousand hectares $(X = 640)$.

The *XY* plot can be used to give a quick visual impression of the relationship between deforestation and population density. An examination of this graph indicates some support for the idea that a relationship between deforestation and population density does exist. For instance, if we look at countries with a low population density (less than 500 people per hectare, say), almost all of them have very low deforestation rates (less than 1 % per year). If we look at countries with high population densities (e.g. over 1 500 people per thousand hectares), almost all of them have high deforestation rates (more than 2 % per year). This indicates that there may be a positive relationship between population density and deforestation (i.e. high values of one variable tend to be associated with high values of the other, and low values tend to be associated with low values). It is also possible to have a negative relationship between two variables. This might occur, for instance, if we substituted urbanization for population density in an *XY* plot. In this case, high levels of urbanization might be associated with low levels of deforestation since expansion of cities would possibly reduce population pressures in rural areas where forests are located.

It is worth noting that the positive or negative relationships found in the data are only tendencies and, as such, do not hold necessarily for every country. That is, there may be exceptions to the general pattern of an association between high population density and high rates of deforestation. For example, on the *XY* plot we can observe one country with a high population density of roughly 1 300 and a low deforestation rate of 0.7 %. Similarly, low population density can also be associated with high rates of deforestation, as evidenced by one country with a low population density of roughly 150 but a high deforestation rate of almost 2.5 % per year. As economists, we are usually interested in drawing out general patterns or tendencies in the data. However, we should always keep in mind that exceptions (in statistical jargon *outliers*) to these patterns typically exist. In some cases, finding out which countries don't fit the general pattern can be as interesting as the pattern itself.

1.4   Working with data: descriptive statistics and correlation

Graphs have an immediate visual impact that is useful for livening up an essay or report. However, in many cases it is important to be numerically precise. The following chapters of this book will describe common numerical methods for summarizing the relationship between several variables in detail. Here, we discuss briefly a few descriptive statistics for summarizing the properties of a single variable or at most two variables. By way of motivation, we will return to the concept of a distribution illustrated briefly in our discussion of histograms. The concept of a probability distribution is a fundamental one in statistics and we will use it throughout this book. Appendix B: Probability Basics, at the end of this book, formally defines and motivates probability distributions. Here we provide some informal intuition about distributions and ways of summarizing their properties.

In our cross-country dataset, real GDP per capita varies across the 90 countries. This variability can be seen by looking at the histogram in Figure 1.2, which plots the distribution of GDP per capita across countries. Suppose you wanted to summarize the information contained in the histogram numerically. One thing you could do is to present the numbers in the frequency table (see Table 1.1). However, even this table may provide too many numbers to be easily interpretable. Instead it is common to present two simple numbers called the *mean* and *standard deviation*. The mean is the statistical term for the average. Remember that $Y_1, \ldots, Y_N$ can be used to denote the N different observations on our variable. This is referred to as a *sample*. The mathematical formula for the mean is given by

$$\overline{Y} = \frac{\sum_{i=1}^{N} Y_i}{N},$$

where N is referred to as the sample size (here this is the number of countries) and $\sum_{i=1}^{N}$ is the summation operator (i.e. it adds up real GDP per capita for all countries). The summation operator is defined and discussed in Appendix A: Mathematical Basics. In our case, mean GDP per capita is $5 443.80. Throughout this book, we will place a bar over a variable to indicate its mean (i.e. $\overline{Y}$ is the mean of the variable Y, $\overline{X}$ is the mean of the variable X, etc.).

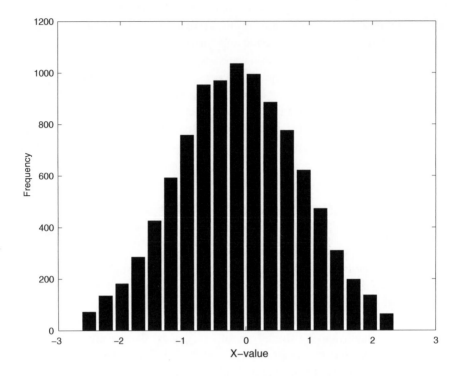

Figure 1.4 Histogram for a bell-shaped distribution.

The concept of the mean is associated with the middle of a distribution. For example, if we look at the previous histogram in Figure 1.2, $5 443.80 lies somewhere in the middle of the distribution. The cross-country distribution of real GDP per capita is quite unusual, having the twin peaks property described earlier. It is more common for distributions of economic variables to have a single peak and to be bell-shaped. Figure 1.4 is a histogram that plots just such a bell-shaped distribution. For such distributions, the mean is located precisely in the middle of the distribution, under the single peak. The leading example of a distribution of this sort is the *normal distribution* (see Appendix B, Definition B.10).

Of course, the mean or average hides a great deal of variability across countries. Other useful summary statistics, which shed light on the cross-country variation in GDP per capita, are the minimum and maximum. For our dataset, minimum GDP per capita is $408 (Chad) and maximum GDP is $17 945 (USA). By looking at the distance between the maximum and minimum, we can see how dispersed the distribution is.

The concept of *dispersion* is quite important in economics and is closely related to the concepts of variability and inequality. For instance, real GDP per capita in 1992 in our dataset varies from $408 to $17 945. If poorer countries were, in the near future, to grow quickly, and richer countries to stagnate, then the dispersion of real GDP per capita in, say, 2012, might be significantly less. It may be the case that the poorest country at this time will have real GDP per capita of $10 000 while the richest country will remain at \$17 945. If this were to happen, then the cross-country distribution of real GDP per capita would be more equal (less dispersed, less variable). Intuitively, the notions of dispersion, variability, and inequality are closely related.

The minimum and maximum, however, can be unreliable guidelines to dispersion. For instance, what if, with the exception of Chad, all the poor countries experienced rapid economic growth between 1992 and 2012 while the richer countries did not grow at all? In this case, cross-country dispersion or inequality would decrease over time. However, since Chad and the USA did not grow, the minimum and maximum would remain at \$408 and \$17 945 respectively. A more common measure of dispersion, which does not suffer from this drawback, is the standard deviation. Its formula is given by

$$s = \sqrt{\frac{(Y_i - \overline{Y})^2}{N - 1}}.$$

Statisticians refer to the square of the standard deviation as the *variance* (s^2), and it is common to see either terminology used. It is important to remember this close relationship between the standard deviation and the variance.

The standard deviation has little direct intuition. In our cross-country GDP dataset, the standard deviation is \$5 369.496 and it is difficult to get a direct feel for what this number means in an absolute sense. However, the standard deviation can be interpreted in a comparative sense. That is, if you compare the standard deviations of two different distributions, the one with the smaller standard deviation will always exhibit less dispersion. In our example, if the poorer countries were to suddenly experience economic growth and the richer countries to stagnate, the standard deviation would decrease over time.

1.4.1 Expected values and variances

In the previous section we talked about means and variances. We should actually have called them *sample* means and sample variances. The word 'sample' is added to emphasize that they are calculated using an actual 'sample' of data. For instance, in our cross-country GDP dataset we took the data we had and calculated exact numbers for $\overline{Y}$ and s. We found these to be \$5 443.80 and \$5 369.496 respectively. These are the sample mean and standard deviation calculated using the dataset at hand.

As another example, suppose we have collected data on the return to holding stock in a company for the past 100 months. We can use these data to calculate the sample mean and sample variance. However, these numbers are calculated on the basis of the historical performance of the company. In finance, we are often interested in predicting future stock returns. By definition, we do not know exactly what these will be, so we need to extend the concepts of means and variances to cases where we do not have a sample of data. Potential investors would be interested in something like a mean and a variance. That is, investors would be interested in the typical return that they might expect. They might also be interested in the risk involved in purchasing the stock. The concept of a typical or *expected value* sounds similar to the ideas we discussed relating to the mean. The concept of riskiness sounds similar to the idea of a variance we discussed above. In short, we need concepts like the sample mean and variance, but for cases where we do not actually have data to calculate them. The relevant concepts are the *population mean* and the *population variance*.

In Appendix B: Probability Basics, we formally define the population mean and variance and discuss their properties. Here, we provide some intuition and definitions. A common way to motivate the distinction between motivating population and sample concepts is through an example. Consider, for instance, the height of every individual in the USA. In the population as a whole there is some average height (the population mean height) and some variance of heights (the population variance). This population mean and variance will be unknown, unless someone actually went out and measured the height of every person in the USA. However, a researcher might have data on the actual heights of 100 people (e.g. a medical researcher might measure the height of each of 100 patients). Using the data for 100 people, the researcher could calculate $\overline{Y}$ and s^2. These are the sample mean and variance and will be actual numbers. The medical researcher could then use these numbers as estimates (or approximations) for what is going on in the country as a whole (i.e. sample means and variances can be used as estimates for population means and variances). This is an important distinction in statistics, and it is important to stress that sample and population concepts are different, with the former being actual numbers calculated using the data at hand and the latter being unobserved.

Perhaps the previous two paragraphs are enough intuitively to motivate the distinction between sample and population means and variances. To see why financial analysts need to know this distinction (and to introduce some notation), let us use our example of potential investors interested in the potential return they might make from buying a stock. Let Y denote next month's return on this stock. From the investors' point of view, Y is unknown. The typical return they might expect is measured by the population mean and is referred to as the expected value. We use the notation $E(Y)$ to denote the expected return (also known as the mean return and often labelled μ). Its name accurately reflects the intuition for this statistical concept. The 'expected value' sheds light on what we expect will occur.

However, the return on a stock is rarely exactly what is expected (i.e. rarely will you find Y to turn out to be exactly $E(Y)$). Stock markets are highly unpredictable – sometimes the return on the stock could be higher than expected, sometimes it could be lower than expected. In other words, there is always risk associated with purchasing a stock. A potential investor will be interested in a measure of this risk. Variance is a common way of measuring this risk. We use the notation $var(Y)$ for this.

Appendix B: Probability Basics describes how to obtain $E(Y)$ and $var(Y)$ given a probability distribution. To give some intuition, here we provide an example from the field of finance. Suppose you are an investor trying to decide whether to buy a stock on the basis of its return next month. You do not know what this return will be. You are quite confident (say, 70 % sure) that the markets will be stable, in which case you will earn a 1 % return. However, you also know there is a 10 % chance the stock market will crash, in which case the stock return will be -10%. There is also a 20 % probability that good news will boost the stock markets and you will get a 5 % return on your stock.

In this example, there are three possible outcomes (good, normal, bad) which are 0.05, 0.01, and -0.10 (i.e. the possible returns are 5, 1, or -10%). We will use the symbol 'Pr' for probability. Thus, $\Pr(Y = 0.05) = 0.20$ says that there is a 20 % chance of obtaining the 5 % return. We can now define the expected return as a weighted average of all the three possible outcomes, where the weights are given as the probability that each occurs:

$$E(Y) = \Pr(Y = 0.05)0.05 + \Pr(Y = 0.01)0.01 + \Pr(Y = -0.10)(-0.10)$$
$$= 0.20 \times 0.05 + 0.70 \times 0.01 + 0.10(-0.10)$$
$$= 0.007$$

In words, the expected return on the stock next month is 0.7 % (i.e. a bit less than 1 %).

In our example, we have assumed that there are only three possible outcomes next month. In general, if there are K possible outcomes (label them $y_1 = 1, 2, \ldots, y_K$), the formula for the expected value is

$$E(Y) = \sum_{i=1}^{K} \Pr(Y = y_i)y_i.$$

The formula for the expected value when the variable is continuous (and, thus, there are an infinite number of possible outcomes) is given in Appendix B, Definition B.8. It has similar intuition but is slightly more complicated.

The formula for $var(Y)$ is also given in Appendix B. Suffice it to note here that it can be calculated by means of the expected value operator using the formula

$$var(Y) = E(Y^2) - [E(Y)]^2.$$

In our financial example, we have already calculated $E(Y) = 0.007$. However, to calculate the variance we still need to calculate $E(Y^2)$. This can be done in the same manner as before, except using Y^2 instead of Y. That is, the general formula, if there are K possible outcomes, is

$$E(Y^2) = \sum_{i=1}^{K} \Pr(Y^2 = y_i^2)y_i^2.$$

In the particular example, the three possible outcomes for Y^2 are $(0.05)^2 = 0.0025$, $(0.01)^2 = 0.0001$, and $(-0.10)^2 = 0.01$. We can plug these into the formula for calculating $E(Y^2)$:

$$E(Y^2) = \Pr(Y^2 = 0.0025) \times 0.0025 + \Pr(Y^2 = 0.0001) \times 0.0001$$
$$+ \Pr(Y^2 = 0.01) \times 0.01$$
$$= 0.20 \times 0.0025 + 0.70 \times 0.0001 + 0.10 \times 0.01$$
$$= 0.00157.$$

We can use this result to obtain

$$var(Y) = E(Y^2) - [E(Y)]^2$$
$$= 0.00157 - (0.007)^2$$
$$= 0.001521.$$

The standard deviation, being the square root of the variance, can be calculated to be 0.039.

To summarize, in the previous section on descriptive statistics we motivated the use of the sample mean and variance, $\overline{Y}$ and s^2, to give the researcher an idea of the average value and dispersion, respectively, in a dataset. In this section, we have motivated their population counterparts, $E(Y)$ and $var(Y)$, as having similar intuition but being relevant for summarizing information about an uncertain outcome (e.g. the return on a stock next month). In the following chapters, we will use the expected value and variance operators extensively, and their formal properties are given in Appendix B. However, it is always important to have an intuitive understanding about what the mean and variance operator are, and the intention of this section is to provide this intuition.

1.4.2   Correlation

The mean and variance are properties of one variable. However, economists are often interested in investigating the nature of the relationship between two (or more) variables. Most of this textbook is about investigating such relationships, and we will develop many different approaches for doing so. Here, we take a first step in this direction by introducing the idea of *correlation*. Correlation is an important way of numerically quantifying the relationship between two variables. In this chapter, we will first describe the theory behind correlation, and then work through a few examples designed to think about the concept in different ways.

Let X and Y be two variables (e.g. population density and deforestation, respectively), and let us also suppose that we have data on $i = 1, \ldots, N$ different units (e.g. countries). The correlation between X and Y is denoted by r and its mathematical formula is

$$r = \frac{\sum_{i=1}^{N}(Y_i - \overline{Y})(X_i - \overline{X})}{\sqrt{\sum_{i=1}^{N}(Y_i - \overline{Y})^2}\sqrt{\sum_{i=1}^{N}(X_i - \overline{X})^2}}.$$

The variables to which r refers are usually clear from the context. However, in some cases we will use subscripts to indicate that r_{XY} is the correlation between variables X and Y, r_{XZ} is the correlation between variables X and Z, etc.

Once you have calculated the correlation between two variables, you will obtain a number (e.g. $r = 0.55$). It is important that you know how to interpret this number. In this section, we will try to develop some intuition about correlation. Firstly, however, let us briefly list some of the numerical properties of correlation.

Properties of correlation

1. r always lies between -1 and 1.
2. Positive values of r indicate a positive correlation between X and Y. Negative values indicate a negative correlation. $r = 0$ indicates that X and Y are uncorrelated.
3. Larger positive values of r indicate stronger positive correlation. $r = 1$ indicates perfect positive correlation. Larger negative values of r indicate stronger negative correlation. $r = -1$ indicates perfect negative correlation.
4. The correlation between Y and X is the same as the correlation between X and Y.
5. The correlation between any variable and itself is 1.

Econometricians use the word 'correlation', in much the same way as the layperson does, as measuring the degree of association or the strength of the relationship between two variables. The following continuation of the deforestation/population density example will serve to illustrate verbal ways of thinking about the concept of correlation.

Example: The correlation between deforestation and population density

Let us suppose that we are interested in investigating the relationship between deforestation and population density. Remember that the data set used to create Figure 1.3 contains these variables for a cross-section of 70 tropical countries. The correlation between deforestation (Y) and population density (X) turns out to be 0.66. Being greater than zero, this number allows us to make statements of the following form:

1. There is a positive relationship (or positive association) between deforestation and population density.
2. Countries with high population densities tend to have high deforestation rates. Countries with low population densities tend to have low deforestation rates. Note that we use the word 'tend' here. A positive correlation does not mean that every country with a high population density necessarily has a high deforestation rate, but, rather, that this is the general tendency. It is possible that a few individual countries do not follow this pattern.
3. Deforestation rates vary across countries, as do population densities. Some countries have high deforestation rates, others have low rates. This high/low cross-country variance in deforestation rates tends to 'match up' with the high/low variance observed in population densities.

All that the preceding statements require is for r to be positive. If r were negative, the opposite of these statements would hold. For instance, high values of X would be associated with low values of Y, etc. It is somewhat more difficult to get an intuitive feel for the exact number of the correlation (e.g. how the correlation 0.66 differs from 0.26). The XY plots discussed below offer some help, but here we will briefly note an important point to which we shall return when we discuss regression. The degree to which deforestation rates vary across countries can be measured numerically using the formula for the standard deviation discussed previously. As mentioned in point 3 in the above example, the fact that deforestation and population density are positively correlated means that their patterns of cross-country variability tend to match up. It turns out that the correlation squared (r^2) measures the proportion of the cross-country variability in deforestation that matches up with, or is explained by, the variance in population density. In other words, correlation is a numerical measure of the degree to which patterns in X and Y correspond. In our population/deforestation example, since $0.66^2 = 0.44$, we can say that 44 % of the cross-country variance in deforestation can be explained by the cross-country variance in population density.

Example: House prices in Windsor, Canada

The file HPRICE.XLS, available on the website associated with this book, contains data relating to $N = 546$ houses sold in Windsor, Canada, in the summer of 1987. It contains the selling price (in Canadian dollars) along with many characteristics for each house. We will use this dataset in future chapters, but for now let us focus on just a few variables. In particular, let us focus on the relationship between $Y =$ the sales price of the house and $X =$ the size of its lot in square feet. The correlation between these two variables is $r_{XY} = 0.54$.

The following statements can be made about house prices in Windsor:

1. Houses with large lots tend to be worth more than those with small lots.
2. There is a positive relationship between lot size and sales price.
3. The variation in lot size accounts for 29 % (i.e. $0.54^2 = 0.29$) of the variability in house prices.

Now let us add a third variable, $Z =$ number of bedrooms. Calculating the correlation between house prices and number of bedrooms, we obtain $r_{YZ} = 0.37$. This result says, as we would expect, that houses with more bedrooms tend to be worth more than houses with fewer bedrooms. Similarly, we can calculate the correlation between number of bedrooms and lot size. This correlation turns out to be $r_{XZ} = 0.15$ and indicates that houses with larger lots also tend to have more bedrooms. However, this correlation is small and, unexpectedly, suggests that the link between lot size and number of bedrooms is quite weak. In other words, you may have expected that houses on larger lots, being bigger, would have more bedrooms than houses on smaller lots. However, the correlation indicates that there is only a weak tendency for this to occur.

The above example allows us to motivate briefly an issue of importance, namely that of *causality*. Researchers are often interested in finding out whether one variable 'causes' another. We will not provide a formal definition of causality here but instead will use the word in its everyday meaning. In this example, it is sensible to use the positive correlation between house price and lot size to reflect a causal relationship. That is, lot size is a variable that directly influences (or causes) house prices. However, house prices do not influence (or cause) lot size. In other words, the direction of causality flows from lot size to house prices, not the other way around.

Another way of thinking about these issues is to ask yourself what would happen if a homeowner were to purchase some adjacent land and thereby increase the lot size of the house. This action would tend to increase the value of the house (i.e. an increase in lot size would cause the price of the house to increase). However, if you reflect on the opposite question, 'Will increasing the price of the house cause lot size to increase?', you will see that the opposite causality does not hold (i.e. house price increases do not cause lot size increases). For instance, if house prices in Windsor were suddenly to rise for some reason (e.g. owing to a boom in the economy), this would not mean that houses in Windsor suddenly acquired bigger lots.

The discussion in the previous paragraph could be repeated with 'lot size' replaced by 'number of bedrooms'. That is, it is reasonable to assume that the positive correlation between $Y =$ house prices and $Z =$ number of bedrooms is due to Z influencing (or causing) Y, rather than the opposite. Note, however, that it is difficult to interpret the positive (but weak) correlation between $X =$ lot size and $Z =$ number of bedrooms as reflecting causality. That is, there is a tendency for houses with many bedrooms to occupy large lots, but this tendency does not imply that the former causes the latter.

One of the most important things in empirical work is knowing how to interpret your results. The house example illustrates this difficulty well. It is not enough just to report a number for a correlation (e.g. $r_{XY} = 0.54$). Interpretation is important too. Interpretation requires a good intuitive knowledge of what a correlation is in addition to a great deal of common sense about the economic phenomenon under study. Given the importance of interpretation in empirical work, the following section will present several examples to show why variables are correlated and how common sense can guide us in interpreting them.

Understanding why variables are correlated

In our deforestation/population density example, we discovered that deforestation and population density are indeed correlated positively, indicating a positive relationship between the two. But what exact form does this relationship take? As discussed above, we often like to think in terms of causality or influence, and it may indeed be the case that correlation and causality are closely related. For instance, the finding that population density and deforestation are correlated could mean that the former directly causes the latter. Similarly, the finding of a positive correlation between education levels and wages could be interpreted as meaning that more education does directly influence the wage one earns. However, as the following examples demonstrate, the interpretation that correlation implies causality is not always necessarily an accurate one.

Example: Correlation does not necessarily imply causality

It is widely accepted that cigarette smoking causes lung cancer. Let us assume that we have collected data from many people on (a) the number of cigarettes each person smokes per week (X) and (b) whether they have ever had or now have lung cancer (Y). Since smoking causes cancer, we would undoubtedly find that $r_{XY} > 0$; that is, that people who smoked tend to have higher rates of lung cancer than non-smokers. Here, the positive correlation between X and Y indicates direct causality.

Now suppose that we also have data on the same people, measuring the amount of alcohol they drink in a typical week. Let us call this variable Z. In practice it is the case that heavy drinkers also tend to smoke, and hence $r_{XZ} > 0$. This correlation does not mean that cigarette smoking also causes people to drink. Rather it probably reflects some underlying psychological or social attitude: people who smoke often tend to drink as well. Thus, a correlation between two variables does not necessarily mean that one causes the other. It may be the case that an underlying third variable is responsible.

Now consider the correlation between lung cancer and drinking. Since people who smoke tend to get lung cancer more, and people who smoke also tend to drink more, it is not unreasonable to expect that lung cancer rates will be higher among heavy drinkers (i.e. $r_{YZ} > 0$). Note that this positive correlation does not imply that alcohol consumption causes lung cancer. Rather, it is cigarette smoking that causes cancer, but smoking and drinking are related to some underlying psychological or social attitude. This example serves to indicate the kind of complicated patterns of causality that occur in practice and how care must be taken when trying to relate the concepts of correlation and causality.

Another important distinction is that between direct (or immediate) and indirect (or proximate) causality. Recall that, in our deforestation/population density example, population density (X) and deforestation (Y) were found to be positively correlated (i.e. $r_{XY} > 0$). One reason for this positive correlation is that high population pressures in rural areas cause farmers to cut down forests to clear new land in order to grow food. It is this latter ongoing process of agricultural expansion that directly causes deforestation. If we calculated the correlation between deforestation and agricultural expansion (Z), we would find $r_{YZ} > 0$. In this case, population density would be an indirect cause and agricultural expansion a direct cause of deforestation. In other words, we can say that X (population pressures) causes Z (agricultural expansion), which in turn causes Y (deforestation). Such a pattern of causality is consistent with $r_{XY} > 0$ and $r_{YZ} > 0$. In our house price example, however, it is likely that the positive correlations we observed reflect direct causality. For instance, having a larger lot is considered by most people to be a good thing in and of itself, so that increasing the lot size should directly increase the value of a house. There is no other intervening variable here, and hence we say that the causality is direct.

The general message that should be taken from these examples is that correlations can be very suggestive but cannot on their own establish causality. In the smoking/cancer example above, the finding of a positive correlation between smoking and lung cancer, in conjunction with medical evidence on the manner in which substances in cigarettes trigger changes in the human body, has convinced most people that smoking causes cancer. In the house price example, common sense tells us that the variable 'number of bedrooms' directly influences house prices. In economics, the concept of correlation can be used in conjunction with common sense or a convincing economic theory to establish causality.

Understanding correlation through XY plots

Intuition about the meaning of correlations can also be obtained from the XY plots. Recall that, when interpreting Figure 1.3, we discussed positive and negative relationships based on whether the XY plots exhibited a general upward or downward slope. If two variables are correlated, then an XY plot of one against the other will exhibit such patterns. For instance, the XY plot of population density against deforestation exhibits an upward sloping pattern (see Figure 1.3). This plot implies that these two variables should be positively correlated, and we find that this is indeed the case from the correlation $r = 0.66$. The important point here is that positive correlation is associated with upward sloping patterns in the XY plot, and negative correlation is associated with downward sloping patterns. All the intuition we developed about XY plots in the previous section can now be used to develop intuition about correlation.

Figure 1.5 uses the Windsor house price dataset to produce an XY plot of $X =$ lot size against $Y =$ house price. Recall that the correlation between these two variables was calculated as $r_{XY} = 0.54$, which is a positive number. This positive (upward sloping) relationship between lot size and house price can clearly be seen in Figure 1.5. That is, houses with small lots (i.e. small X-axis values) also tend to have small prices (i.e. small Y-axis values). Conversely, houses with large lots tend to have high prices.

The previous discussion relates mainly to the sign of the correlation. However, XY plots can also be used to develop intuition about how to interpret the magnitude of a correlation, as the following examples illustrate. Figure 1.6 is an XY plot of two perfectly correlated variables (i.e. $r = 1$). They do not correspond to any actual economic data, but were simulated on the computer. All the points lie exactly on a straight line.

At the other extreme, Figure 1.7 is an XY plot of two completely uncorrelated variables ($r = 0$). Note that the points are randomly scattered over the entire graph. Real-world datasets (e.g. in Figure 1.3 or 1.5) tend to be between the two extremes.

We have illustrated these points about correlation using positively correlated variables. Plots for negative correlation exhibit downward (instead of upward) sloping patterns, but otherwise the same sorts of pattern noted above hold for them. These figures illustrate one way of thinking about correlation: correlation indicates how well a straight line can

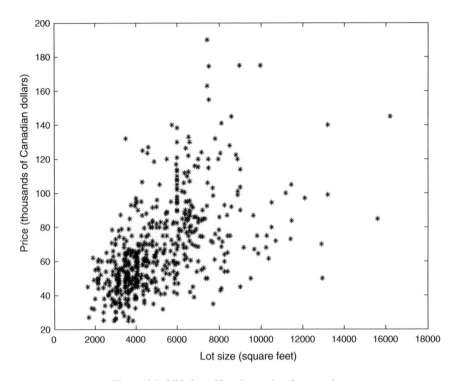

Figure 1.5 *XY* plot of lot size against house price.

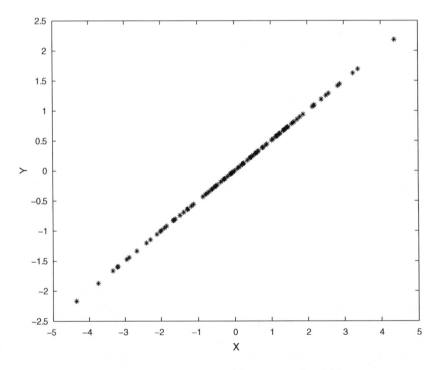

Figure 1.6 *XY* plot of two perfectly correlated variables.

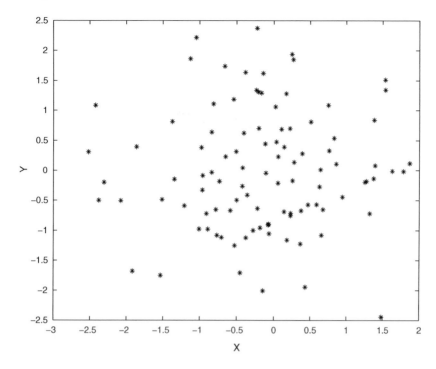

Figure 1.7 *XY* plot of uncorrelated variables.

be fitted through an *XY* plot. Variables that are strongly correlated have observations that fit on or close to a straight line. Variables that are weakly correlated have observations that are more scattered in an *XY* plot.

Correlation between several variables

Correlation is a property that relates two variables. Frequently, however, researchers must work with several variables. For instance, house prices depend on the lot size, number of bedrooms, number of bathrooms and many other characteristics of the house. As we will see in subsequent chapters, regression is the most appropriate tool for use if the analysis contains more than two variables. However, it is also not unusual for empirical researchers, when working with several variables, to calculate the correlation between each pair. Note that there are many correlations when the number of variables is large. For instance, if we have three variables, X, Y, and Z, then there are three possible correlations (i.e. r_{XY}, r_{XZ}, and r_{YZ}). However, if we add a fourth variable, W, the number increases to six (i.e. r_{XY}, r_{XZ}, r_{XW}, r_{YZ}, r_{YW}, and r_{ZW}). In general, for M different variables there will be $\frac{M(M-1)}{2}$ possible correlations. A convenient way of ordering all these correlations is to construct a matrix or table, as illustrated by the following example.

Using data on three variables labelled X, Y, and Z, we calculate the *correlation matrix* in Table 1.2.

To explain the interpretation of a correlation matrix, note that the number 0.318 is r_{XY} since it appears in the column labelled X and the row labelled Y. Similarly,

Table 1.2   A correlation matrix.

	X	Y	Z
X	1.000		
Y	0.318	1.000	
Z	−0.131	0.097	1.000

$r_{XZ} = -0.131$ and $r_{YZ} = 0.097$. Note that the 1.000 values in the correlation matrix indicate that any variable is perfectly correlated with itself, and the upper right-hand corner of the matrix is left blank since it would be identical to the lower left-hand corner (e.g. since $r_{XY} = r_{YX}$).

1.4.3   Population Correlations and Covariances

Previously we discussed means and variances and distinguished between sample and population variants. For instance, the sample mean was denoted by $\overline{Y}$ and was the average calculated using the data at hand. The population mean was denoted by $E(Y)$ (or μ) and called the expected value. It was a more theoretical concept. We motivated it with an example where Y was next month's return on a stock. This is not known exactly, but financial analysts are often able to predict what they would expect the return to be. This is $E(Y)$. However, there is uncertainty associated with the analyst's prediction, and this is measured through the (population) variance, denoted $var(Y)$.

The same sample/population distinction holds with correlations. We will use the notation $corr(X, Y)$ to denote the *population correlation* (remember r is our notation for the sample correlation). A formal definition of the population correlation is given in Appendix B: Probability Basics, Definition B.8. Here, we try informally to motivate why this concept might be useful using a financial example. Consider a portfolio consisting of the shares of two companies with returns X and Y. The expected return of the portfolio depends on the expected returns of the two individual stocks (i.e. $E(X)$ and $E(Y)$). What is the risk of this portfolio? The risk of an individual stock can be related to its variance. However, with a portfolio of stocks the correlation between their returns is also important. The financial analyst is, thus, interested in $corr(X, Y)$ when evaluating the riskiness of a portfolio.

To illustrate the previous point, suppose an investor is interested in investing over the summer months in the shares of two companies: an umbrella manufacturer and an ice cream maker. Sales of these two companies are susceptible to the weather. If it is a hot, sunny summer, then ice cream makers do well (and owners of their stock make large returns). But if the summer is rainy, sales are very poor for the ice cream makers (and owners of their stock make small or negative returns). Hence, it seems like shares in the ice cream company are very risky. Shares in the umbrella manufacturer are also very risky – but for exactly the opposite reasons. Sunny summers are bad for umbrella sales, whereas rainy summers ensure good sales.

However, the overall portfolio is much less risky than the individual stocks. Whenever one of the stocks does poorly, the other does well. In a rainy summer, investors will earn a good return on the part of their portfolio in umbrella stocks but a bad return on the part in ice cream stocks. In a sunny summer, the opposite will occur. Hence, the investors' portfolios will be quite safe — earning an adequate return regardless of the weather.

In statistical language, the previous example shows how the correlation between the returns on the shares in the two companies is a crucial factor in assessing the riskiness of a portfolio. In our example, this correlation was negative (i.e. whenever one stock made a good return, the other made a bad return). In practice, of course, the correlations between the returns in shares of two different companies may be positive or negative.

The previous discussion is meant to motivate why correlation is an important concept for the financial economist. To develop a formula for exactly what the population correlation is requires us to take a slight detour and introduce the concept of a *covariance*. Covariance is defined as

$$cov(X, Y) = E(XY) - E(X)E(Y).$$

Previously, we have illustrated how expected values are calculated (and Appendix B provides a formal definition) and $E(X)$ and $E(Y)$ can be calculated as described above. To calculate $E(XY)$, the same formula is used, except that the variable is XY. The population correlation is the covariance normalized so as to have the same properties as the sample correlation (see the Properties of Correlation list near the beginning of this section and replace r with $corr(X, Y)$). It has the following formula:

$$corr(X, Y) = \frac{cov(X, Y)}{\sqrt{var(X)var(Y)}}.$$

Knowledge of this exact formula is only occasionally required in this textbook. However, it is crucial to have some intuition about correlation and how it depends on the variances and covariances of two variables.

As with means and variances, it is common for sample concepts to be used as estimates of population concepts. Thus, to return to our ice cream/umbrella example, the portfolio manager would be interested in knowing $corr(X, Y)$: the population correlation between the stock returns in the two companies. The portfolio manager might collect data from the last 20 summers on stock returns for the two companies and use these data to calculate r: the sample correlation. The sample correlation could then be used as an estimate of $corr(X, Y)$.

1.5   Chapter summary

1. Economic data come in many forms. Common types are time series, cross-sectional, and panel data.
2. Economic data can be obtained from many sources. The internet is becoming an increasingly valuable repository for many datasets.
3. Simple graphical techniques, including histograms and XY plots, are useful ways of summarizing the information in a dataset.
4. Many numerical summaries can be used. The most important are the mean, a measure of the location of a distribution, and the standard deviation, a measure of how spread out or dispersed a distribution is.
5. If Y is a variable that could have many outcomes, then the expected value, $E(Y)$, is a measure of the typical or expected outcome and the variance, $var(Y)$, is a measure of the dispersion of possible outcomes.
6. Correlation is a numerical measure of the relationship or association between two variables.
7. Correlation can also be interpreted graphically by means of XY plots. That is, the sign of the correlation relates to the slope of a best-fitting line through an XY plot. The magnitude of the correlation relates to how scattered the data points are around the best fitting line.
8. There are many reasons why two variables might be correlated with each other. However, correlation does not necessarily imply causality between two variables.
9. $corr(X, Y)$ is the population correlation and is a useful concept when talking about many issues in economics and finance (e.g. portfolio management).

Exercises

All datasets mentioned below are available on the website associated with this book.

1. (a) File INCOME.XLS contains data on the natural logarithm of personal income and consumption in the USA from 1954$Q1^3$ to 1994$Q2$. Make one time series graph that contains both of these variables.
   (b) Transform the logged personal income data to growth rates. Remember that the percentage change in personal income between period $t - 1$ and t is approximately $[\ln(Y_t) - \ln(Y_{t-1})] \times 100$ and the data provided in INCOME.XLS are already logged. Make a time series graph of the series you have created.
2. (a) Recreate the histogram in Figure 1.2 using the dataset GDPPC.XLS.

    (b) Create histograms using different class intervals. For instance, begin by letting your software package choose default values and see what you get, then try values of your own.

3. The file FOREST.XLS contains data on both the percentage increase in cropland from 1980 to 1990 and on the percentage increase in pasture land over the same period. Construct and interpret XY plots of these two variables (one at a time) against deforestation. Does there seem to be a positive relationship between deforestation and expansion of pasture land? How about between deforestation and the expansion of cropland?

4. Construct and interpret descriptive statistics for the pasture change and cropland change variables in FOREST.XLS.

5. (a) Using the data in HPRICE.XLS, calculate and interpret the mean, standard deviation, minimum, and maximum of $Y =$ house price, $X =$ lot size, and $Z =$ number of bedrooms.

    (b) Verify that the correlation between X and Y is the same as given in the example in this chapter. Repeat for X and Z, then for Y and Z.

    (c) Now add a new variable, $W =$ number of bathrooms. Calculate the mean of W.

    (d) Calculate and interpret the correlation between W and Y. Discuss to what extent it can be said that W causes Y.

    (e) Repeat part (d) for W and X and then for W and Z.

6. People with a university education tend to hold higher-paying jobs than those with fewer educational qualifications. This could be due to the fact that a university education provides important skills that employers value highly. Alternatively, it could be the case that smart people tend to go to university and that employers want to hire smart people (i.e. a university degree is of no interest in and of itself to employers). Suppose you have data on $Y =$ income, $X =$ number number of years of schooling, and $Z =$ the results of an intelligence test of many people, and that you have calculated r_{XY}, r_{XZ}, and r_{YZ}. In practice, what signs would you expect these correlations to have? Assuming the correlations do have the signs you expect, can you tell which of the two stories in the paragraph above is correct?

7. The file EXCHAP1.XLS contains four variables: Y, $X1$, $X2$, and $X3$.

    (a) Calculate the correlation between Y and $X1$. Repeat for Y and $X2$ and for Y and $X3$.

    (b) Create an XY plot involving Y and $X1$. Repeat for Y and $X2$ and for Y and $X3$.

    (c) Interpret your results for (a) and (b).

8. (a) Using the data in FOREST.XLS, calculate and interpret a correlation matrix involving deforestation, population density, change in pasture, and change in cropland.

    (b) Repeat part (a) using the following variables in the dataset HPRICE.XLS: house price, lot size, number of bedrooms, number of bathrooms, and number of storeys. How many individual correlations have you calculated?

Endnotes

1. This book (like most comparable textbooks) is about analyzing data (not obtaining data). There are so many possible places from which data can be obtained, with each economic problem having its own data requirements, that it is not possible to offer more than a superficial discussion of obtaining data in this book.
2. The return that an investor earns on owning a share is its change in price plus dividends paid. Thus, the percentage change calculated here can be interpreted as the return (exclusive of dividends). Alternatively, adding dividends in to calculate the return involves a simple change to this formula.
3. The Q notation denotes the quarter of the year in which the observation occurs. For instance, $1954Q1$ means the first quarter (January to March) of 1954.

CHAPTER 2

A Non-technical Introduction to Regression

2.1 Introduction

The idea of a model is a fundamental one in econometrics. Rather than provide an abstract definition of what a model is, in this chapter we make the concept of a model concrete by introducing the most commonly used model in econometrics: the linear regression model. This model is important in and of itself. Furthermore, many more complicated models can be interpreted as extensions of the regression model. For this reason, it is important that the econometrician know the regression model well. The strategy we will adopt in this textbook is to begin with a non-technical discussion of regression. By 'technical' we mean that minimal mathematics will be used and concepts will be explained intuitively, without providing a thorough theoretical development using the tools of probability. Then, in Chapter 3, we will go through the regression model again, but in a more rigorous fashion, and formal derivations will be provided using probability theory. The justification for this strategy is twofold. Firstly, after reading this non-technical introduction to regression, you should be able to get started in actually doing some empirical work on the computer using datasets. In fact, for cross-sectional datasets, which do not suffer from any of the complications discussed in Chapter 5, the present chapter will tell you most of what you need to know to do empirical work in practice. Thus, you do not have to wait until a great deal of theoretical material is covered before beginning to work with data. You can get started now. Secondly, after reading this chapter, it is hoped that you will get familiar with the regression model. Thus, in the next chapter, you can begin to learn econometric theory in a familiar context. I always find it easiest to learn new statistical concepts in a familiar, concrete context, and I think many students do as well. I hope that the present chapter will make the regression model familiar and, thus, make the new material in later chapters easier to understand.

2.2   The simple regression model

Regression is the most important tool applied economists use to understand the relationship among two or more variables. It is particularly useful for the common case where there are many variables and the interactions between them are complex. This chapter begins with a discussion of the simple regression model. This model involves only two variables instead of the many variables that arise in most economic problems. We will begin with it because the simple regression model allows us to develop the basic regression concepts using some graphs. Furthermore, multiple regression (i.e. regression when we have more than two variables) concepts are the same as, or are simple extensions of, simple regression counterparts.

2.2.1   Regression as a best-fitting line

To illustrate these concepts in a practical context, we will consider a microeconomic application.[1] Our dataset contains the costs of production (measured in millions of dollars) for 123 electric utility companies in the USA in 1970. Researchers are often interested in cost functions or, more broadly, in understanding the factors that affect costs. The costs incurred by an electric utility company can potentially depend on many factors. One of the most important of these is undoubtedly the output of the company. We would expect companies that are producing more electricity also to be incurring higher costs (e.g. because they have to buy more fuel to generate the electricity). Hence, in addition to costs, our dataset includes information on the output of each company (measured as millions of kilowatt hours of electricity produced). Figure 2.1 is an XY plot of these two variables: costs and output. That is, each point in Figure 2.1 represents a particular company. From any point, reading down to the X axis gives the amount of output produced by the company, and reading across to the Y axis gives the costs incurred by the company. This is an example of an economic problem (i.e. how output affects costs in the electric utility industry) and a dataset that can be used for investigating this problem.

An XY plot such as Figure 2.1 can often shed light on the relationship between two variables. However, graphs provide only an informal picture of such relationships, and it is usually desirable to provide precise numerical measures. This is one thing the regression model can do. For instance, from Figure 2.1 we can see that companies with higher output tend also to have higher costs. However, the microeconomist might want to know what the marginal costs are in this industry (i.e. by how much costs will change if output is increased). For this, precise numerical answers are required. Regression provides such answers.

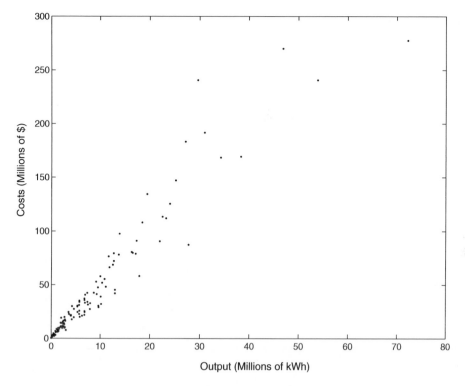

Figure 2.1 *XY* plot of output versus costs.

The linear regression model begins by assuming a linear relationship between two variables, Y and X (e.g. cost and output). Any straight line relationship can be written as

$$Y = \alpha + \beta X,$$

where α is the intercept of the line and β is its slope. For the reader unfamiliar with these concepts, Appendix A: Mathematical Basics at the end of the book discusses the equation of a straight line. This equation is referred to as the *regression line*. If we knew what α and β were, then we would know what the relationship between Y and X was. In practice, of course, we do not know α and β. Furthermore, even if our regression model, which posits a linear relationship between Y and X, were true, in the real world we would never find that our data points lie precisely on a straight line. Factors such as measurement error mean that individual data points might lie close to but not exactly on a straight line.

For instance, suppose costs of production (Y) depend on output (X) in the following manner: $Y = 2 + 5X$ (i.e. $\alpha = 2$ and $\beta = 5$). If X is 1 (i.e. output is one million kilowatt hours), this model says the costs of the firm should be $Y = 2 + 5 \times 1 = 7$ (i.e. costs should be seven million dollars). But not every firm with output of one million kilowatt hours will have costs of exactly seven million dollars. Some firms may be more efficient than others so may produce the same amount of output at less cost. Furthermore, the regression model is very likely missing some important variables that may affect costs. Costs of production depend not only on output produced but also on the price of the inputs used. For instance, if firm A can hire employees at a lower wage than firm B, then firm A will have lower costs than firm B even if both firms are producing the same amount of electricity. For these kinds of reason, even if $Y = 2 + 5X$ is an accurate description of the true relationship between Y and X, it will not be the case that every data point lies exactly on the line. Thus, we add an error, ε, to create the *regression model*:

$$Y = \alpha + \beta X + \varepsilon.$$

In future chapters, we will see how the properties of ε are crucial to deriving our econometric results. However, in the present non-technical introduction, you can think of the error intuitively as allowing for the actual costs of production of the firm to be a bit different from what the regression line says they should be.

Let us now introduce some jargon and additional intuition about the regression model. The variable on the left-hand side of the regression equation, Y, is referred to as the *dependent variable*, X is called the *explanatory variable* (or independent variable), and α and β are called *coefficients*. As this terminology suggests, it is common to assume that the explanatory variable explains (or influences or causes) the dependent variable, and the coefficient β measures the influence of X on Y.

At this stage, it is worthwhile digressing to discuss the issue of why one variable is chosen as the dependent variable and another as the explanatory variable. In Chapter 1 we discussed causality in the section Understanding Why Variables are Correlated. A key idea of that section is summarized in the phrase 'correlation does not necessarily imply causality'. Similar issues hold with respect to regression, and it must be emphasized that great care has to be taken when interpreting regression results as reflecting causality. In an ideal situation it will clearly be the case that the explanatory variable causes the dependent variable. However, this ideal situation does not always arise. When will it be reasonable to interpret regression results as reflecting causality? In many cases the economic theory you use will tell you. For instance, microeconomic theory can be used to derive the cost function. This theory says that the cost function depends on outputs and the prices of inputs. Thus, the economic theory says that costs should be the dependent variable and output and input prices the explanatory variables. In other cases, common sense may tell you which variable causes another. For instance, in Chapter 1 we used a dataset containing the sales price of many houses and the characteristics of the houses (e.g. number of bedrooms). Here, common sense tells us that the number of bedrooms should be the explanatory variable and the price of the house the dependent variable. The number of bedrooms will influence the price of the house (e.g. if you add an extra bedroom to your house this will cause it to rise in price). The reverse causality does not make sense. For instance, house prices have been going up in many countries in recent years and many people have seen the value of their houses go up. This has not 'caused' them to have more bedrooms.

However, in some cases it is not clear which variable influences or causes which. Does wage inflation cause price inflation since firms pass through wage increases to their customers in the form of higher prices? Or does price inflation cause wage inflation since workers bargain for higher wages to keep up with inflation? Both possibilities make sense. So in a regression involving the two variables wage inflation and price inflation it is unclear which should be the dependent variable and which the explanatory variable. In the latter chapters of this book, we will discuss some cases such as this, where it is unclear which variable should be the dependent variable and which the explanatory variable. At this point, you should note that great care has to be taken in interpreting regression results as implying causality.

Now let us return to the regression model. In light of the error, ε, and the fact that we do not know what α and β are, the first problem in regression analysis is how we can figure approximately, or *estimate*, what α and β are. Using a common notational convention, we will call these estimates $\widehat{\alpha}$ and $\widehat{\beta}$. That is, α and β are the true unknown regression coefficients and $\widehat{\alpha}$ and $\widehat{\beta}$ are estimates of them. Estimation is one of the most important activities of the econometrician. Here, we try to illustrate estimation in the regression model in a simple intuitive way using a graph. In future chapters, we will discuss estimation in the regression model in a more formal manner.

Consider Figure 2.2, which is an XY plot of output versus costs of production for 123 electric utility companies with a straight line drawn through the points. This straight line is an example of a regression line. There are many straight lines that could have been drawn in Figure 2.2. Why was this particular one chosen? The answer is that this

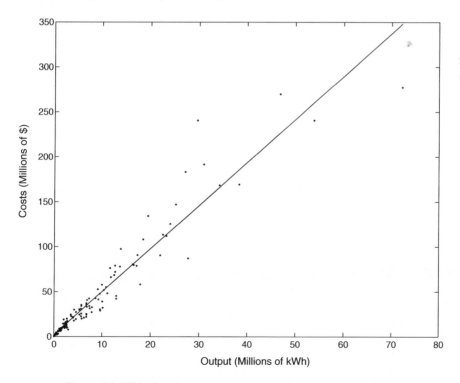

Figure 2.2 XY plot of output versus costs with fitted regression line.

is the line that fits the best and, thus, best captures the relationship between output and costs. This answer raises the question of what is meant by the 'best-fitting' line. Before we answer this question, a reminder of some notation from Chapter 1 is required. So far we have been using the generic notation Y (or X) to denote the dependent (or explanatory) variable. We have data on each variable for many units of observation (i.e. for many electric utility companies). We will call the unit of observation the 'individual', although, in an application, the 'individual' could be a firm, a country, or anything else on which we have data. We will let N denote the number of observations and let subscripts indicate the particular observation. So, for instance, Y_1 indicates the dependent variable for the first individual, X_4 the explanatory variable for the fourth individual, etc. We will let i denote a generic individual so that Y_i for $i = 1, \ldots, N$ indicates all of our observations for the dependent variable. The regression line for each individual is written as

$$Y_i = \alpha + \beta X_i + \varepsilon_i.$$

We now make a distinction between errors and *residuals*. The error is defined as the distance between a particular data point and the true regression line. Mathematically, we can rearrange the regression model to write the error as

$$\varepsilon_i = Y_i - \alpha - \beta X_i.$$

However, if we replace α and β with their estimates, we get a straight line that is generally a little different from the true regression line. The deviations from this estimated regression line are called residuals. We will use the notation $\widehat{\varepsilon}$ when we refer to residuals. That is, the residuals are given by

$$\widehat{\varepsilon}_i = Y_i - \widehat{\alpha} - \widehat{\beta} X_i.$$

There is an error and a residual for every individual. In Figure 2.2, the residual will be the distance between the actual data point and the fitted regression line. The *fitted regression line* is

$$\widehat{Y}_i = \widehat{\alpha} + \widehat{\beta} X_i.$$

Now let us return to the question of how good estimates of α and β can be found. In Figure 2.2 it is not possible to find a single line that passes through all the data points. Any line we use will yield residuals for each individual. A regression line that fits well will make these residuals as small as possible. The usual way of measuring the size of the residuals is by means of the *sum of squared residuals* (SSR), which can be written in the following different (equivalent) ways:

$$SSR = \sum_{i=1}^{N} \widehat{\varepsilon}_i^2$$

$$= \sum_{i=1}^{N} \left(Y_i - \widehat{\alpha} - \widehat{\beta} X_i \right)^2$$

$$= \sum_{i=1}^{N} \left(Y_i - \widehat{Y}_i \right)^2.$$

The previous equations use the summation operator. The reader unfamiliar with it is referred to Appendix A: Mathematical Basics at the end of the book.

To obtain the best-fitting straight line, we want to find the values of $\widehat{\alpha}$ and $\widehat{\beta}$ that make SSR as small as possible. As we will see in subsequent chapters, the solution to the problem 'find values of $\widehat{\alpha}$ and $\widehat{\beta}$ that minimize SSR' can be obtained using some simple mathematics. For now, note only that standard spreadsheets (e.g. Excel) or econometrics software packages (e.g. PC-Give, E-views, Stata, or Microfit) will calculate $\widehat{\alpha}$ and $\widehat{\beta}$. These estimates are referred to as *ordinary least squares* (OLS) estimates. For the dataset used to construct Figures 2.1 and 2.2, the OLS estimates are $\widehat{\alpha} = 2.19$ and $\widehat{\beta} = 4.79$. Thus, the equation of the straight line in Figure 2.2 is

$$\widehat{Y}_i = 2.19 + 4.79X_i.$$

2.2.2   Interpreting OLS estimates

Above we have described how you would obtain OLS estimates of α and β. We now turn to their interpretation. The OLS estimate of the intercept in the regression model can be interpreted as the predicted value of the dependent variable when the explanatory variable equals zero. That is, if you plug $X_i = 0$ into the equation for the fitted regression line $\widehat{Y}_i = \widehat{\alpha} + \widehat{\beta}X_i$, you obtain $\widehat{Y}_i = \widehat{\alpha}$. Often this does not have an interesting economic interpretation. For instance, in our example, the intercept is the cost of production for an electric utility company with no output. This is not a very interesting concept since all of our companies are producing something.[2]

The estimate of the slope coefficient, $\widehat{\beta}$, is typically of most interest to the economist. This coefficient is the slope of the best-fitting straight line through an XY plot such as Figure 2.2. Another interpretation of $\widehat{\beta}$ is obtained by differentiating the fitted regression line with respect to the explanatory variable:

$$\frac{d\widehat{Y}_i}{dX_i} = \widehat{\beta}.$$

Even if you do not know differentiation, the intuition of the previous expression is not difficult to see. Derivatives measure how much Y changes when X is changed by a small (marginal) amount. Hence, $\widehat{\beta}$ can be interpreted as the marginal effect of X on Y. It is a measure of how much the explanatory variable influences the dependent variable. To be more precise, we can interpret $\widehat{\beta}$ as a measure of how much Y tends to change when X is changed by one unit. The definition of 'unit' in the previous sentence depends on the particular dataset being studied. For our example involving the costs of production in the electric utility industry, we found $\widehat{\beta} = 4.79$. This is a measure of how much costs tend to change when output changes by one unit. Since costs are measured in terms of millions of dollars and output is measured in terms of millions of kilowatt hours of electricity produced, we can interpret our estimate of $\widehat{\beta} = 4.79$ as saying: if output is increased by one million kilowatt hours (i.e. a change of one unit in the explanatory variable), costs will tend to increase by $4 790 000.

2.2.3   Measuring the fit of a regression model

In the preceding discussion we learned how to calculate and interpret regression coefficients. We explained that OLS estimation of a regression line means finding the 'best-fitting' line in the sense that it minimizes the SSR. However, it is possible that the 'best' fit is not a very good fit at all. Hence, it is desirable to have some measure of fit (i.e. a measure of how good the best-fitting line is). The most common measure of fit is referred to as the R^2.

Since residuals measure how far the data point of a particular individual lies from the regression line, an examination of the residuals can be very informative about the fit of a regression line. However, there are N residuals and, for most datasets, there are just too many residuals to be easily included in a report. There is a need for one single number that summarizes all the information in the residuals. This is what R^2 is.

From Chapter 1 (or see Appendix B: Probability Basics at the end of this book), recall that variance is a measure of dispersion or variability of the data. The variance of any variable can be estimated by

$$var(Y) = \frac{\sum_{i=1}^{N}(Y_i - \overline{Y})^2}{N-1},$$

where $\overline{Y} = \frac{\sum_{i=1}^{N} Y_i}{N}$ is the mean, or average value, of the variable. Here, we define a closely related concept, the total sum of squares or TSS:

$$TSS = \sum_{i=1}^{N}(Y_i - \overline{Y})^2,$$

which can be seen to be proportional to the variance. Loosely speaking, the $N-1$ term in the denominator of $var(Y)$ will cancel out with another $N-1$ in our final formula for R^2, and hence we ignore it. Thus, you can think of TSS as being a measure of the variability of Y. The regression model seeks to explain the variability of Y using the explanatory variable X. It can be shown that the total variability of Y can be broken down into two parts as

$$TSS = RSS + SSR,$$

where RSS is the regression sum of squares, a measure of the explanation provided by the regression model. RSS is given by

$$RSS = \sum_{i=1}^{N}\left(\widehat{Y}_i - \overline{Y}\right)^2.$$

In terms of our electric utility example we can say that costs of production vary across firms (as measured by *TSS*). This variation can be broken down into the part that can be explained by the fact that different firms are producing different amounts of electricity (as measured by *RSS*) and the part that cannot be explained and hence is simply left as a residual (as measured by *SSR*).

The measure of fit uses these concepts and is defined as

$$R^2 = \frac{RSS}{TSS}$$

or, equivalently,

$$R^2 = 1 - \frac{SSR}{TSS}.$$

Intuitively, the R^2 measures the proportion of the total variance of Y that can be explained by X. Note that *TSS*, *RSS* and *SSR* are all sums of squared numbers and, hence, are all non-negative. Because *TSS* is the sum of *RSS* and *SSR*, this implies that $TSS \geq RSS$ and $TSS \geq SSR$. Using these facts, it can be seen that $0 \leq R^2 \leq 1$.

Further intuition about this measure of fit can be obtained by noting that small values of *SSR* indicate that the residuals are small and, hence, that the regression model is fitting well (i.e. the data points are near the fitted regression line $\widehat{\alpha} + \widehat{\beta}X$). A regression line that fits all the data points perfectly in the XY plot will have no errors, and hence $SSR = 0$ and $R^2 = 1$. Looking at the formula above, you can see that values of R^2 near 1 imply a good fit and that $R^2 = 1$ implies a perfect fit. In sum, high values of R^2 imply a good fit and low values imply a bad fit.

An alternative source of intuition is provided by the *RSS*. *RSS* measures how much of the variation in Y the explanatory variables explain. If *RSS* is near *TSS*, then the explanatory variables account for almost all of the variability and the fit will be a good one. Looking at the previous formula, you can see that the R^2 is near 1 in this case.

In the regression of Y =cost of production on X =output for the 123 electric utility companies, $R^2 = 0.92$. This number can be interpreted as saying that 92 % of the variation in costs across companies can be explained by the variation in output.

2.2.4   Basic statistical concepts in the regression model

The coefficients α and β measure the relationship between Y and X. However, as we have stressed above, we do not know what this relationship is and, hence, have to use estimates, $\widehat{\alpha}$ and $\widehat{\beta}$. This raises the question of how accurate these estimates are. The most common way of assessing how is through *confidence intervals*. Closely related to the confidence interval is the concept of a *hypothesis test*. In this section, we provide some intuition for what confidence intervals and hypothesis tests are and show how they can be used in practice. Chapter 3 provides a more formal discussion and derives many of the formulae introduced in this section.

OLS provides us with point estimates for α and β (e.g. $\widehat{\beta} = 4.79$ is the point estimate of β in the regression of costs of production on output using our electric utility industry dataset). You can think of a point estimate as your best guess of what β is. Confidence intervals provide interval estimates that give the range in which you can be highly confident β must lie. Such intervals can be used to make statements that reflect the uncertainty we may have about the value of β (e.g. 'We are confident that β is greater than 4.53 and less than 5.05'). We can obtain different confidence intervals corresponding to different levels of confidence. For instance, in the case of a 95 % confidence interval we can say 'We are 95 % confident that β lies in the interval', in the case of a 90 % confidence interval we can say 'We are 90 % confident that β lies in the interval', and so on. The degree of confidence we have in a chosen interval (e.g. 95 %) is referred to as the *confidence level*. In the next chapter, we will actually derive the formula used for calculating a confidence interval. For empirical practice, any relevant computer package will calculate confidence intervals for you. Thus, the intuition provided in this paragraph should be enough to get you started working with confidence intervals. For instance, for the electric utility dataset, the 95 % confidence interval for β is [4.53, 5.05]. This can be expressed as: 'We are 95 % confident that the marginal effect of output on costs is at least 4.53 and at most 5.05'. Thus far we have talked about the confidence interval for β. Confidence intervals for α (or indeed any coefficient in any model) can be also be interpreted in the same way.

Hypothesis testing is another exercise commonly carried out by the empirical economist. As with confidence intervals, we will defer discussion of the statistical theory that underlies hypothesis testing until Chapter 3. Instead we will focus on the practical details of how to carry out hypothesis tests and interpret the results. Classical hypothesis testing involves specifying a hypothesis to test. This is referred to as the *null hypothesis*, and is labeled H_0. It is compared with an *alternative hypothesis*, labeled H_1. In the simple regression model, a common hypothesis test is whether $\beta = 0$. If $\beta = 0$, then the explanatory variable has no explanatory power whatsoever. If you think of the kinds of question of interest to economists (e.g. 'Does education increase an individual's earning potential?', 'Will a certain advertising strategy increase sales?', 'Will a new government training scheme lower unemployment?', etc.), you will see that many are of the form 'Does the explanatory variable have an effect on the dependent variable?' or, equivalently, 'Is $\beta \neq 0$ in the regression of Y on X?'. The purpose of the hypothesis test of $\beta = 0$ is to answer this question. Formally, we say that this is a test of H_0: $\beta = 0$ against H_1: $\beta \neq 0$.

It is worth noting that hypothesis testing and confidence intervals are closely related. In fact, one way of testing whether $\beta = 0$ is to look at the confidence interval for β and see whether it contains zero. If it does not, then we can, to introduce some statistical jargon, 'reject the hypothesis that $\beta = 0$' or conclude 'X has significant explanatory power for Y' or 'β is significantly different from zero' or 'β is statistically significant'. If the confidence interval does include zero, then we change the word 'reject' to 'accept' and 'has significant explanatory power' to 'does not have significant explanatory power', and so on. This confidence interval approach to hypothesis testing is exactly equivalent to the formal approach to hypothesis testing discussed below.

Just as confidence intervals came with various levels of confidence (e.g. 95 % is the usual choice), hypothesis tests come with various *levels of significance*. If you use the confidence interval approach to hypothesis testing, then the level of significance is 100 % minus the confidence level. That is, if a 95 % confidence interval does not include zero, then you may say 'I reject the hypothesis that $\beta = 0$ at the 5 % level of significance' (i.e. 100 %−95 % = 5 %). If you had used a 90 % confidence interval (and found it did not contain zero), then you would say: 'I reject the hypothesis that $\beta = 0$ at the 10 % level of significance'.

The standard way of carrying out a hypothesis is to begin by specifying a hypothesis to test and choosing a significance level. In the simple regression model, this will usually be H_0: $\beta = 0$ and the 5 % level of significance. Then one calculates a test statistic and compares it with a *critical value*, a concept we will formally discuss in Chapter 3. In the case of testing whether $\beta = 0$, the test statistic is known as a *t-statistic* (or *t*-ratio or *t*-stat). It is calculated as

$$t = \frac{\widehat{\beta}}{s_b},$$

where s_b will be explained later. Suffice it to note here that s_b is called the *standard error* of $\widehat{\beta}$ (i.e. it is the standard deviation[3] of $\widehat{\beta}$) and is calculated in any relevant computer software package. The idea underlying hypothesis testing is that we accept H_0 if the calculated value of the test statistic is consistent with what could plausibly happen if H_0 were true. If H_0 is true and $\beta = 0$, then we will expect $\widehat{\beta}$ to be small, so if $\widehat{\beta}$ is large this is evidence against H_0. Formally, the issue is whether $\widehat{\beta}$ is small or large relative to its standard deviation. This accounts for the inclusion of s_b in the *t*-statistic. The question arises as to what we mean by 'large' and 'small' *t*-statistics. In a formal statistical sense, this test statistic is large or small relative to a critical value taken from statistical tables of the Student *t*-distribution. We will define and discuss these points in the next chapter. However, for a great deal of empirical practice it suffices to note that most relevant computer packages print out the *P-value* for this test (and for other tests). If the *P*-value is provided, then statistical tables are unnecessary. The *P*-value is the level of significance at which you can reject H_0 using your dataset. So if you have decided to use the 5 % level of significance and your software package calculates a *P*-value of 0.05, then you can reject H_0. Furthermore, if the *P*-value is less than 0.05, then you can also reject H_0. This follows from the fact that, if you can reject a hypothesis at a given level of significance (say, 4 %), then you can also reject it at any higher level of significance (say, 5 %).

Students often want to interpret the *P*-value as measuring the probability that $\beta = 0$. Thus, if the *P*-value is less than 0.05, one could say 'There is less than a 5 % probability that $\beta = 0$ and, since this is very small, I can reject the hypothesis that $\beta = 0$'. This is not formally correct: the *P*-value is *not* the probability that $\beta = 0$. However, you can think in this way if you want some informal intuition to help motivate why small values of the *P*-value lead you to reject H_0.

To summarize, when you are doing empirical work and are interested in testing H_0: $\beta = 0$, computer packages will produce the *P*-value for the test of this hypothesis:

1. If the P-value is less than 5 % (written as 0.05 by the computer), then the t-statistic is 'large' and we conclude that $\beta \neq 0$.
2. If the P-value is greater than or equal to 5 %, then the t-statistic is 'small' and we conclude that $\beta = 0$.

The preceding test used the 5 % level of significance. However, if we were to replace the figure 5 % in the above expressions with 1 % (or 10 %), our hypothesis test would be carried out at the 1 % (or 10 %) level of significance.

Computer packages typically provide the following information about β (or any coefficient):

- $\widehat{\beta}$, the OLS point estimate, or best guess, of what β is;
- the 95 % confidence interval, which gives the interval in which we are 95 % confident β will lie;
- the standard deviation (or standard error) of $\widehat{\beta}$, s_b, which is a measure of how accurate $\widehat{\beta}$ is (s_b is also a key component in the mathematical formula for the confidence interval and the test statistic for testing H_0: $\beta = 0$);
- the test statistic, t, for testing H_0: $\beta = 0$;
- the P-value for testing H_0: $\beta = 0$.

2.2.5 Hypothesis testing involving R^2: The F-statistic

Most computer packages that include regression also print out results for the test of the hypothesis H_0: $R^2 = 0$. Recall that R^2 is a measure of how well the regression line fits the data or, equivalently, of the proportion of the variability of Y that can be explained by X. If $R^2 = 0$, then X does not have any explanatory power for Y. The test of the hypothesis $R^2 = 0$ can therefore be interpreted as a test of whether the regression explains anything at all. For the case of simple regression, this test is equivalent to a test of $\beta = 0$. However, for multiple regression (which we will discuss shortly), the test of $R^2 = 0$ will be different than tests of whether a regression coefficient equals zero.

The strategy and intuition involved in testing $R^2 = 0$ proceed along the same lines as above. That is, the computer software calculates a test statistic that you must then compare with a critical value. Alternatively, most software will also calculate a P-value that directly gives a measure of the plausibility of the null hypothesis H_0: $R^2 = 0$ against the alternative hypothesis H_1: $R^2 \neq 0$.

In this case, the appropriate test statistic is called the F-statistic and is calculated as

$$F = \frac{(N-2)R^2}{1 - R^2}.$$

The appropriate statistical table for obtaining the critical value is the one for the F-distribution (we will explain this distribution in a subsequent chapter) which accounts for the name 'F- statistic', although it is worth noting that the test statistic we have labelled F is only one in an entire class of test statistics that take their critical values from the F-distribution.

Table 2.1 Simple regression results using electric utility industry dataset.

Variable	Coefficient	Standard error	t-stat	P-value	95 % confidence interval
Intercept	2.19	1.88	1.16	0.25	$[-1.53, 5.91]$
Output	4.79	0.13	36.36	0.00^{*}	$[4.53, 5.05]$

*By 0.00 we mean zero to two decimal places. The number produced by the computer package is 5.4×10^{-67}.

In a similar fashion to our previous discussion about testing whether $\beta = 0$, here we can say that 'large' values of the test statistic indicate that $R^2 \neq 0$, while 'small' values indicate that $R^2 = 0$. The P-value can be used to decide what is 'large' and what is 'small' (i.e. to decide whether R^2 is significantly different from zero or not). The test is performed according to the same strategy as described for our test of whether $\beta = 0$:

1. If the P-value for the F-test is less than 5 % (i.e. 0.05), we conclude that $R^2 \neq 0$.
2. If the P-value for the F-test is greater than or equal to 5 % , we conclude that $R^2 = 0$.

The previous strategy provides a statistical test with a 5 % level of significance. To carry out a test at the 1 % level of significance, merely replace 5 % (0.05) with 1 % (0.01) in the preceding sentences. Other levels of significance (e.g. 10 %) can be calculated in an analogous manner.

Example: Cost of production in the electric utility industry

To summarize the material so far, consider our example where $Y =$ costs of production and $X =$ output of electricity by 123 electric utility companies. Table 2.1 presents regression results in the form in which they would be produced by most software packages.

Furthermore, $R^2 = 0.92$ and the P-value for testing H_0: $R^2 = 0$ is 0.00. The column labeled 'Coefficient' presents the OLS estimates, $\widehat{\alpha}$ and $\widehat{\beta}$, while the column labeled 'Standard error' presents the standard deviations of $\widehat{\alpha}$ and $\widehat{\beta}$. The column labeled 't-stat' presents the t-statistics for testing the hypotheses H_0: $\alpha = 0$ (in the row labeled 'Intercept') and H_0: $\beta = 0$ (in the row labeled 'Output'), while the column labeled 'P-value' presents the P-values corresponding to these hypothesis tests. The last column contains 95 % confidence intervals for α and β.

By way of summary of the material so far, it is worthwhile illustrating how the results presented above might be written up in a report. A typical report would include the presentation of the statistical material in Table 2.1, followed by a discussion of the economic interpretation of the results. Finally, statistical information (e.g. confidence intervals and hypothesis tests) would be presented. The report might go as follows:

Table 2.1 presents results from an OLS regression using the electric industry dataset (in a report you would insert details about your data here). Since we are interested in investigating how different output choices by firms influence their costs of production, we select costs of production as our dependent variable and output as the explanatory variable. The table reveals that the estimated coefficient on output is 4.79, which suggests that electric utility firms with higher levels of output tend to have higher costs of production. In particular, increasing output by one million kilowatt hours tends to increase costs by \$4 790 000.

It can be observed that the marginal effect of output on costs is strongly statistically significant, since the P-value is very small (much smaller, say, than 1 %). An examination of the 95 % confidence interval shows that we can be quite confident that increasing output by one million kilowatt hours is associated with an increase in costs of at least \$4.53 million and at most \$5.05 million. An examination of the R^2 reinforces the view that output provides a large part of the explanation for why costs vary across utilities. In particular, 92 % of the variability in costs of production across firms can be explained by different output levels. The P-value for the F-statistic is much smaller than 1 %, indicating significance of the R^2 at the 1 % level.

2.3   The multiple regression model

So far, we have discussed simple regression which investigates the relationship between two variables: the dependent variable, Y, and the explanatory variable, X. However, most analyses in economics involve many variables. Multiple regression extends simple regression to the case where there are many explanatory variables.

The basic underlying ideas and intuition for multiple regression are the same as for simple regression. To be precise, for simple regression we went through the following elements:

1. The development of graphical intuition for regression techniques as the fitting of a straight line through an XY plot.
2. The introduction of the regression coefficient as measuring a marginal effect.
3. The description of the OLS estimate as a best-fitting line (in terms of minimizing the sum of squared residuals) through an XY plot.
4. The introduction of R^2 as a measure of fit of a regression model.
5. The introduction of statistical techniques such as confidence intervals and hypothesis tests.

With some exceptions (highlighted below), these five elements do not differ for the multiple regression model. However, there are differences in interpretation of coefficients, and, with many explanatory variables, important issues relating to how they should be chosen arise. Many of these ideas are best illustrated through an empirical example and, accordingly, we use the house price dataset first introduced in Chapter 1.[4]

> **Example: Explaining house prices**
>
> Much research in applied microeconomics and marketing focuses on the pricing of goods. One common approach involves building a model in which the price of a good depends on the characteristics of that good. Our dataset contains data on an application of this so-called hedonic pricing approach to the housing market. It contains data on $N = 546$ houses sold in Windsor, Canada. Our dependent variable, Y, is the sale price of the house in Canadian dollars. The price of a house is affected by many characteristics of the house (and our dataset contains eleven explanatory variables). Here, we focus on the following four explanatory variables:
>
> - $X_1 =$ the lot size of the property (in square feet);
> - $X_2 =$ the number of bedrooms;
> - $X_3 =$ the number of bathrooms;
> - $X_4 =$ the number of storeys (excluding the basement).

2.3.1   Ordinary least squares estimation of the multiple regression model

The multiple regression model with k explanatory variables is written as

$$Y_i = \alpha + \beta_1 X_{1i} + \beta_2 X_{2i} + \cdots + \beta_k X_{ki} + \varepsilon_i,$$

where, as before, we are using i subscripts to denote individual observations and $i = 1, \ldots, N$. For simple regression, we estimated α and β. With multiple regression we now have to estimate α and $\beta_1, \ldots, \beta_k$. However, the strategy for finding estimates of all these coefficients is exactly the same as for the simple regression model. That is, we define the sum of squared residuals:

$$SSR = \sum_{i=1}^{N} \left(Y_i - \widehat{\alpha} - \widehat{\beta}_1 X_{1i} - \widehat{\beta}_2 X_{2i} - \cdots - \widehat{\beta}_k X_{ki} \right)^2.$$

The OLS estimates are found by choosing the values of $\widehat{\alpha}$ and $\widehat{\beta}_1, \widehat{\beta}_2, \ldots, \widehat{\beta}_k$ that minimize the SSR. Conceptually, this is a straightforward mathematical problem, but the resulting formulae are complicated and are not listed here. Computer software packages will calculate OLS estimates automatically.

2.3.2   Statistical aspects of multiple regression

The statistical aspects of multiple regression are basically the same as for simple regression. In particular, the R^2 is still a measure of fit and is calculated in the same way.

Note, however, that it should be interpreted as a measure of the explanatory power of all the explanatory variables together rather than as just the one explanatory variable in the simple regression model. Similarly, the F-statistic for testing if $R^2 = 0$ has a slightly different formula (the $N - 2$ in its formula is replaced by $N - k - 1$), but you can still look at its P-value to carry out the test of this hypothesis. If we find that $R^2 \neq 0$, then we can say that 'The explanatory variables in the regression, taken together, help explain the dependent variable', whereas if we find that $R^2 = 0$, we can say that 'The explanatory variables are not significant and do not provide any explanatory power for the dependent variable'.

The general formulae for calculating confidence intervals for the regression coefficients and for testing whether they are equal to zero are the same as in the simple regression case. However, the actual numbers that comprise the formulae (e.g. s_b) are calculated in a slightly more complicated way. Nevertheless, the practical intuition remains unchanged. In other words, a 95 % confidence interval will provide an interval estimate such that you can say that 'I am 95 % confident that the coefficient lies in the 95 % confidence interval'. If the P-value for a hypothesis test that a coefficient equals zero is less than 0.05, we can conclude that the relevant explanatory variable is significant at the 5 % level. It is worth stressing that there is now a P-value and a confidence interval associated with each of the coefficients, α and $\beta_1, \ldots, \beta_k$. However, from the point of view of a researcher wishing to interpret computer output for use in a report, the statistical aspects of multiple regression are essentially the same as for simple regression.

2.3.3 Interpreting OLS estimates in the multiple regression model

It is in the interpretation of OLS estimates that some subtle (and important) distinctions exist between the simple and multiple regression cases. This section will provide a few ways of thinking about or interpreting coefficients in the multiple regression model. Before we begin, it is important to be clear about the notation we will use. When we speak of a property that holds generally for any of the coefficients, we will denote the coefficient by β_j (i.e. the coefficient on the jth explanatory variable, where j could be any number between 1 and k). When we wish to talk about a specific coefficient, we will give an exact number for j (e.g. β_2 has $j = 2$ and is the coefficient on the second explanatory variable).

In the simple regression case we saw how β could be interpreted as a marginal effect (i.e. as a measure of the effect that a change in X has on Y or as a measure of the influence of X on Y). In multiple regression, β_j still can be interpreted as a marginal effect, but in a slightly different way. In particular, β_j is the marginal effect of X_j on Y, *holding all other explanatory variables constant*. The preceding sentence is of critical importance to the correct interpretation of regression results. For this reason, we will spend some time illustrating precisely what we mean by it, by way of consideration of our house price example.

Example: **Explaining house prices (continued)**

The table below contains results from the regression of $Y =$ house sale price on $X_1 =$ lot size, $X_2 =$ number of bedrooms, $X_3 =$ number of bathrooms, and $X_4 =$ number of storeys.

Furthermore, $R^2 = 0.54$ and the P-value for testing $H_0 : R^2 = 0$ is 0.00.

The first column lists the explanatory variables. In this example there are four of them (plus the intercept). Each row contains the same information as in the table for the simple regression model (i.e. the OLS estimate of the relevant coefficient followed by its standard deviation, t-statistic, P-value for testing whether $\beta_j = 0$, and the 95 % confidence interval for the coefficient).

It is common to present regression results in a table such as Table 2.2. An alternative way of presenting much the same information is to write out the fitted regression line with t-statistics (or standard errors or P-values) in parentheses underneath the coefficients:

$$\widehat{Y} = \underset{(-1.11)}{-4\,009.55} + \underset{(14.70)}{5.43}\,X_1 + \underset{(2.33)}{2\,824.61}\,X_2 + \underset{(9.86)}{17\,105.17}\,X_3 + \underset{(7.57)}{7\,634.90}\,X_4.$$

As an example, consider the coefficient for the first explanatory variable, lot size. It can be seen that $\widehat{\beta}_1 = 5.43$. Below are some (very similar) ways of stating what this value means.

1. 'An extra square foot of lot size will tend to add another \$5.43 onto the price of a house, *ceteris paribus*'.[5]
2. If we consider houses with the same number of bedrooms, bathrooms, and storeys, an extra square foot of lot size will tend to add another \$5.43 onto the price of the house'.

Table 2.2 Multiple regression results using house price dataset.

Variable	Coefficient	Standard error	t-stat	P-value	95 % confidence interval
Intercept	−4 009.55	3 603.11	−1.11	0.27	[−11 087.3, 3 068.25]
Lot size	5.43	0.37	14.70	0.00	[4.70, 6.15]
Number of bedrooms	2 824.61	1 214.81	2.33	0.02	[438.30, 5 210.93]
Number of bathrooms	17 105.17	17 34.43	9.86	0.00	[13 698.12, 20 512.22]
Number of storeys	7 634.90	1 007.97	7.57	0.00	[5 654.87, 9 614.92]

It is worth expanding on the motivation for the last expression. We cannot simply say that 'Houses with bigger lots are worth more' since this is not the case (e.g. some nice houses on small lots will be worth more than poor houses on large lots). However, we can say that 'If we consider houses that vary in lot size but are comparable in other respects, those with larger lots tend to be worth more'. The expression above explicitly incorporates the qualification 'but are comparable in other respects'. We did not have to include this qualification with simple regression. There are many different ways to express the interpretation of these coefficients. However, the general point we wish to make is as follows: in the case of simple regression we can say that 'β measures the influence of X on Y'; in multiple regression we say that 'β_j measures the influence of X_j on Y, all other explanatory variables being equal'.

The coefficients on the other explanatory variables can be interpreted in analogous ways. Since $\widehat{\beta}_2 = 2\,824.61$, we can say that 'If we consider comparable houses (e.g. those with 5 000 square foot lots, two bathrooms, and two storeys), those with three bedrooms tend to be worth \$2 842.61 more than those with two bedrooms'. Since, $\widehat{\beta}_3 = 17\,105.17$, we can say that 'Houses with an extra bathroom tend to be worth \$17 105.17 more, *ceteris paribus*'. Since $\widehat{\beta}_4 = 7634.90$, we might say that 'If we compare houses that are similar in all other respects, those with an extra storey tend to be worth \$7 634.90 more'.

The statistical properties of the regression coefficients can be interpreted in the same way as for simple regression. For instance, since the P-values for all of the explanatory variables (except the intercept) are less than 0.05, we can say that 'The coefficients $\beta_1, \beta_2, \beta_3$, and β_4 are statistically significant at the 5 % level', or, equivalently, 'We can reject the four separate hypotheses that any of the coefficients is zero at the 5 % level of significance'. By way of another example, let us consider the 95 % confidence interval for β_2, which is $[438.2761, 5210.931]$. This information might be presented as: 'Our point estimate indicates that the marginal effect of number of bedrooms on house prices is \$2 842.61, but this is only an estimate and so may not be precisely true. The 95 % confidence interval indicates that we can only be confident that this marginal effect lies somewhere between \$438.28 and \$5 210.93'.

The hypothesis test of whether $R^2 = 0$ yields a P-value of much less than 5 %, indicating that X_1, X_2, X_3, and X_4 jointly have statistically significant explanatory power for the dependent variable. In fact, variations in lot size and the number of bedrooms, bathrooms, and storeys account for 54 % of the variability in house prices.

2.3.4   Which explanatory variables to choose in a multiple regression model?

This section discusses several issues of importance for empirical practice. These all relate to the question of which explanatory variables should be chosen in a multiple regression model. As we will see below (and offer formal proofs in a subsequent chapter) there are two important considerations that pull in opposite directions. One is that it is good to include all variables that help explain the dependent variable. This consideration suggests that you should include as many explanatory variables as possible. The second is that including irrelevant variables (i.e. ones that are statistically insignificant) can reduce the statistical significance of all the explanatory variables. This consideration suggests that you should include as few explanatory variables as possible. Playing off these two competing considerations is an important aspect of any empirical exercise. Hypothesis testing procedures can offer a great deal of help. That is, if a hypothesis test indicates that an explanatory variable is insignificant, then it can be deleted from the regression model.

We begin by discussing why it is crucial not to exclude important explanatory variables. To place our discussion in a practical context, we return to the empirical example where the dependent variable is house price and potential explanatory variables are house characteristics. Previously (see Table 2.2.), we ran a multiple regression with four explanatory variables. Let us compare this with the results from a simple regression of $Y = $ sale price on $X = $ number of bedrooms. OLS estimation of this simple regression model yields the following fitted regression line:

$$\widehat{Y} = 28\,773.43 + 13\,269.98X.$$

Since $\widehat{\beta} = 13\,269.98$ in this simple regression, we are able to make the statement: 'The marginal effect of number of bedrooms on house prices is \$13 269.98' or 'Houses with an extra bedroom tend to cost \$13 269.98 more'. You should contrast these statements with the ones made with multiple regression. For the simple regression we have left out the *ceteris paribus* conditions that are implicit in the part of the sentence (which we used when discussing Table 2.2 results) 'If we consider comparable houses (e.g. those with 5000 square foot lots, two bathrooms, and two storeys). . .'.

Note that the estimated coefficient on the explanatory variable 'number of bedrooms' in the simple regression is much higher than for the multiple regression (remember that $\widehat{\beta}_2 = 2\,824.61$ in the multiple regression). Why is this the case? To answer this question, first imagine that friends in Windsor wanted to build an extra bedroom in their house and asked you, the economist, how much that extra bedroom would add to the value of the house. Would you use the simple or the multiple regression result to answer this question?

The simple regression here contains data only on house price and number of bedrooms. You can think of it as observing all the houses and concluding that those with more bedrooms tend to be more expensive (e.g. those with three bedrooms tend to be worth \$13 269.98 more than those with two bedrooms). However, this does not necessarily mean that adding an extra bedroom to the house will raise its price by \$13 269.98. The reason is that there are many factors other than the number of bedrooms that potentially influence house prices. Furthermore, these factors may be correlated with each other (i.e. in practice, big houses tend to have more bedrooms, more bathrooms, more storeys, and larger lot size, so all these characteristics will be correlated with one another). To investigate the possibility, let us consider the correlation matrix of all the variables in the dataset. In the multiple regression model used to create Table 2.2, we have five variables (the dependent variable and four explanatory variables). Correlation measures the association between two variables. With five variables it can be confirmed that there are ten possible correlations (e.g. the correlation between house price and lot size, the

Table 2.3 Correlation matrix for house price dataset.

	Price	Lot size	# bedrooms	# bathrooms	# storeys
Price	1				
Lot size	0.54	1			
Number of bedrooms	0.37	0.15	1		
Number of bathrooms	0.52	0.19	0.37	1	
Number of storeys	0.42	0.08	0.41	0.32	1

correlation between lot size and number of bedrooms, etc.). As discussed in Chapter 1, if you put all the correlations in a table, then you obtain a so-called correlation matrix. For our dataset we have Table 2.3

You read across the appropriate row and down the appropriate column to find the correlation between any desired pair of variables. For instance, 0.32 is the correlation between number of bathrooms and number of storeys. Note that the correlation between any variable and itself is 1, which accounts for the 1s that go across the diagonal of the table. Furthermore, the upper right-hand section of the table is left blank since it would be identical to the lower left-hand section (e.g. the correlation between lot size and number of bedrooms is the same as the correlation between number of bedrooms and lot size).

Since all the elements of the correlation matrix are positive, it follows that each pair of variables are positively correlated with each other (e.g. the correlation between the number of bathrooms and the number of bedrooms is 0.37, indicating that houses with more bathrooms also tend to have more bedrooms). In cases like this, simple regression cannot disentangle the influences of the individual variables on house prices. Therefore, when the simple regression method examines all the houses and notes that those with more bedrooms cost more, this does not necessarily mean that bedrooms are adding value to the house. Buyers may really be valuing bathrooms or lot size over bedrooms. Suppose, for instance, that it is bathrooms that people really value. Houses with more bathrooms tend to be big houses which tend to have more bedrooms. The simple regression model simply looks at house price and number of bedrooms and sees that those with more bedrooms tend to be worth more. What it does not realize is that it is really the number of bathrooms that people value. Thus, if you advise your friends that an extra bedroom is worth \$13 269.98, you may be seriously misleading them. In essence, in the simple regression model, we leave out important explanatory variables such as lot size, the number of bathrooms, and the number of storeys. The simple regression combines the contribution of all these factors together and allocates it to the only explanatory variable it can: bedrooms. Hence, $\widehat{\beta}$ is very big.

In contrast, multiple regression allows us to disentangle the individual contributions of the four explanatory variables. The figure of $\widehat{\beta}_2 = 2\,824.61$ comes closer to being a genuine measure of the effect of adding an extra bedroom. By presenting this figure to your friend, you can be confident that you are not making the error above. That is, you can be sure that it is more likely to be the bedroom that is adding the value – and that you are not confounding the contributions of the various explanatory variables.

These problems relate to a statistical issue called *omitted variables bias*. In Chapter 4, we will develop the statistical theory necessary formally to explain what this means.

Informally, however, we can say that, if we omit explanatory variables that should be present in the regression and if these omitted variables are correlated with those that are included, then the coefficients on the included variables will be wrong. In the previous example, the simple regression of $Y =$ sale price on $X =$ number of bedrooms omitted many variables that were important for explaining house prices (e.g. lot size, number of bathrooms, etc.). These omitted variables were also correlated with number of bedrooms. Hence, the simple regression coefficient estimate $\widehat{\beta} = 13\,269.98$ is unreliable owing to omitted variables bias.

One practical consequence of omitted variables bias is that you should always try to include all those explanatory variables that could affect the dependent variable. Unfortunately, in practice, this is rarely possible. House prices, for instance, depend on many other explanatory variables than those found in our dataset (e.g. the state of repair of the house, how pleasant the neighbors are, cupboard and storage space, whether the house has hardwood floors, the quality of the garden, etc.). In practice, it is usually difficult to get data on all the explanatory variables you would want (e.g. how do you measure 'pleasantness of the neighbors'?). You will virtually always have omitted variables and there is little that can be done about it – other than to hope that the omitted variables do not have much explanatory power and that they are not correlated with the explanatory variables included in the analysis.

The previous paragraphs provide a justification for working with as many explanatory variables as possible. However, there is a counterargument to be made for using as few explanatory variables as possible. It can be shown that the inclusion of irrelevant variables decreases the accuracy of the estimation of all the coefficients (even the ones that are not irrelevant). This decrease in accuracy will be reflected in overly large confidence intervals and P-values.

How should we trade off the benefits of including many variables (i.e. reducing the risk of omitted variables bias) with the costs of possibly including irrelevant variables (i.e. reducing the accuracy of estimation)? A common practice is to begin with as many explanatory variables as possible, then discard those that are not statistically significant (and then rerun the regression with the new set of explanatory variables).

2.3.5 Multicollinearity

Multicollinearity is another issue that the empirical researcher should be aware of. It is a problem that arises if some or all of the explanatory variables are highly correlated with one another. If it is present, the regression model has difficulty telling which explanatory variables are influencing the dependent variable. A multicollinearity problem reveals itself through low t-statistics and therefore high P-values. In these cases you may conclude that coefficients are insignificant and hence should be dropped from the regression. In an extreme case it is possible for you to find that all the coefficients are insignificant using t-statistics, while the R^2 is quite large and significant. Intuitively, this means that the explanatory variables together provide a great deal of explanatory power, but that multicollinearity makes it impossible for the regression to decide which particular explanatory variables are providing the explanation.

There is not too much that can be done to correct this problem other than to drop out some of the highly correlated variables from the regression. However, there are many cases when you would not want to do so. For instance, in our house price example, if number of bedrooms and number of bathrooms had been found to be highly correlated, multicollinearity would be a problem. But you may hesitate to throw out one of these variables since common sense indicates that both of them influence house prices. The following example illustrates a case where a multicollinearity problem exists and how to correct for it by omitting an explanatory variable.

Example: The effect of interest rates on the exchange rate

Suppose you want to examine the effect of interest rate policy on the exchange rate. One way would be to select an exchange rate (e.g. the £/$ rate) as the dependent variable and run a regression of it on the interest rate. But there are many possible interest rates that could be used as explanatory variables (e.g. the bank prime rate, the Treasury bill rate, etc.). These interest rates are very similar to one another and will be highly correlated. If you include more than one of them you will likely run into a multicollinearity problem. The solution to this problem is clear: include only one of the interest rates. Since the various interest rates are essentially measures of the same phenomenon, common sense says that throwing out all but one of the interest rate variables will not cause any loss in explanatory power and will address the multicollinearity problem.

Note that multicollinearity involves correlations between explanatory variables, not between an explanatory variable and the dependent variable (indeed, we want our explanatory variables to be highly correlated with the dependent variable). For it to be a problem, the correlations between variables must be extremely high (i.e. very close to $+1$ or -1). If we return to the house pricing example, we can see that the explanatory variables are moderately correlated with one another (e.g. some correlations are around 0.3 or 0.4). However, this moderate correlation does not lead to a multicollinearity problem since all the coefficients are significantly different from zero (see the P-values in Table 2.2).

2.3.6   Multiple regression with dummy variables

The variables in the examples above were always quantitative. For instance, house prices were measured in dollars, and electricity output was measured in millions of kilowatt hours. However, some of the data economists use are qualitative (i.e. they are not numbers). For instance, a labor economist might survey many workers, and one of the questions asked might be: 'Do you belong to a union?'. The answer to this ('Yes' or 'No') is qualitative. Or the labor economist might ask the gender of each surveyed worker. Once again, the answer ('Male' or 'Female') is qualitative. Dummy variables are a way of turning qualitative explanatory variables into quantitative explanatory variables. Once the variables are quantitative, then multiple regression techniques can be used. Formally, a dummy variable is a variable that can take on only two values, 0 or 1.

Example: Explaining house prices (continued)

Previously, we worked through an extended example that investigated the factors influencing housing prices in Windsor, Canada. Recall that the explanatory variables we used were all quantitative (e.g. lot size of property measured in square feet, the number of bathrooms, etc.). However, there are other possible factors influencing house prices that are not directly quantitative. Examples include the presence of a driveway, air conditioning, a recreation room, a basement, and gas central heating. All these variables are Yes/No qualitative variables (e.g. Yes = the house has a driveway/No = the house does not have a driveway).

In order to carry out a regression analysis using these explanatory variables, we first need to transform them into dummy variables by changing the Yes/No into 1/0. Using the letter D to indicate dummy explanatory variables, we can employ the following definition:

- $D_1 = 1$ if the house has a driveway ($= 0$ if it does not).
- $D_2 = 1$ if the house has a recreation room ($= 0$ if not).
- $D_3 = 1$ if the house has a basement ($= 0$ if not).
- $D_4 = 1$ if the house has gas central heating ($= 0$ if not).
- $D_5 = 1$ if the house has air conditioning ($= 0$ if not).

As with any variable, we can put an additional subscript on to denote a particular observation. For instance, if the ith house has a driveway, a basement, and gas central heating, but no air conditioning and no recreation room, we would have $D_{1i} = 1, D_{2i} = 0, D_{3i} = 1, D_{4i} = 1$, and $D_{5i} = 0$.[6]

Once qualitative explanatory variables have been transformed into dummy variables, regression can be carried out in the standard way and all the theory and intuition discussed above can be used. Hence, in terms of statistical issues (e.g. OLS estimation, confidence intervals, hypothesis testing, etc.) dummy explanatory variables do not raise any new considerations. However, in terms of interpretation of the regression coefficient, the presence of dummy explanatory variables does raise some new issues, and hence a brief discussion of them is warranted.

Let us begin by considering a simple regression model with one dummy explanatory variable, D:

$$Y_i = \alpha + \beta D_i + \varepsilon_i$$

for $i = 1, \ldots, N$ observations. If we carry out OLS estimation of the above regression model, we obtain $\widehat{\alpha}$ and $\widehat{\beta}$ and can write the fitted regression line as

$$\widehat{Y}_i = \widehat{\alpha} + \widehat{\beta} D_i.$$

Since D_i is either 0 or 1, we either have $\widehat{Y}_i = \widehat{\alpha}$ or $\widehat{Y}_i = \widehat{\alpha} + \widehat{\beta}$. An example will serve to illustrate how this fact can be used to interpret regression results with dummy explanatory variables.

Example: Explaining house prices (continued)

The following fitted regression line is obtained from a regression of Y = house prices on D = air conditioning dummy using our house price dataset:

$$\widehat{Y}_i = 59\,884.85 + 25\,995.74 D_i.$$

How can we interpret these numbers? We can, of course, use the same marginal effect intuition as for any simple regression model. That is, we can say that $\widehat{\beta}$ is a measure of how much the dependent variable tends to change when the explanatory variable is changed by one unit. However, with the present dummy explanatory variable, a 'one unit' change implies a change from 'no air conditioner' to 'having an air conditioner'. That is, we can say 'Houses with an air conditioner tend to be worth $25\,996 more than houses without an air conditioner'.

However, there is another, closely related, way of thinking about regression results when the explanatory variable is a dummy. In the case of houses without air conditioning $D_i = 0$ and hence $\widehat{Y}_i = 59\,884.85$. In other words, our regression model finds that houses without air conditioning are worth on average $59\,885 (rounding to the nearest dollar). In the case of houses with air conditioning, $D_i = 1$ and the regression model finds that $\widehat{Y}_i = 59\,884.85 + 25\,995.74 = 85\,880.59$. Thus, houses with air conditioning are worth on average $85\,881. This is one attractive way of presenting the information provided by the regression.

To provide more intuition, note that, if we had not carried out a regression but simply calculated the average price for houses with air conditioning, we would have found this to be $85\,881. If we had then calculated the average price for houses without air conditioning, we would have found them to be worth $59\,885. That is, we would have found exactly the same results as in the regression analysis.

Remember, however, the previous discussion of the omitted variables bias. The simple regression in this example is omitting many important explanatory variables. We definitely cannot use the results of this simple regression to make statements like 'Adding an air conditioner to your house will raise its value from $59\,885 to $85\,881'. Since air conditioners cost a few hundred (or at most a few thousand) dollars, the previous statement is clearly ridiculous. In practice, you should use multiple regression and use more explanatory variables. This leads us to consider the question of how to interpret dummy variables in multiple regression. A multiple regression model with several dummy explanatory variables can be written as

$$Y_i = \alpha + \beta_1 D_{1i} + \cdots + \beta_k D_{ki} + \varepsilon_i$$

for $i = 1, \ldots, N$ observations. OLS estimation of this regression model and statistical analysis of the results can be carried out in the standard way. To aid in interpretation, we return to the house price example.

Example: Explaining house prices (continued)

Consider the case where we have two dummy explanatory variables, $D_1 = 1$ if the house has a driveway ($= 0$ if not) and $D_2 = 1$ if the house has a recreation room ($= 0$ if not). These dummy variables implicitly classify the houses in the dataset into four different groups, as we will see when we interpret the following fitted regression line:

$$\widehat{Y}_i = 47\,099.08 + 21\,159.91D_{1i} + 16\,023.69D_{2i}.$$

Putting in either 0 or 1 values for the dummy variables (and rounding to the nearest dollar), we obtain the fitted values for Y for the four categories of houses:

1. Houses with a driveway and recreation room ($D_1 = 1$ and $D_2 = 1$) have $\widehat{Y}_i = 47\,099 + 21\,160 + 16\,024 = \$84,283.$
2. Houses with a driveway but no recreation room ($D_1 = 1$ and $D_2 = 0$) have $\widehat{Y}_i = 47\,099 + 21\,160 = \$68\,259.$
3. Houses with a recreation room but no driveway ($D_1 = 0$ and $D_2 = 1$) have $\widehat{Y}_i = 47\,099 + 16\,024 = \$63,123.$
4. Houses with no driveway and no recreation room ($D_1 = 0$ and $D_2 = 0$) have $\widehat{Y}_i = \$47,099.$

   In short, multiple regression with dummy variables may be used to classify the houses into different groups and to find average house prices for each group.

In practice, you may often have a mix of different types of explanatory variable. The simplest such case is one where there is one dummy variable (D) and one regular non-dummy explanatory variable (X) in a regression:

$$Y_i = \alpha + \beta_1 D_i + \beta_2 X_i + \varepsilon_i.$$

The interpretation of results from such a regression can be illustrated in the context of an example.

Example: Explaining house prices (continued)

If we regress $Y =$ house price on $D =$ air conditioner dummy and $X =$ lot size, we obtain $\widehat{\alpha} = 32\,693$, $\widehat{\beta}_1 = 20\,175$, and $\widehat{\beta}_2 = 5.638$. Above we noted that the dummy can take on only the values 0 or 1, and demonstrated that the fitted value for Y can take on a different value for each group of houses. Hence, regression results could be interpreted as revealing the average price of a house in each possible group. Here, things are not quite so simple since we obtain a fitted regression line of

$$\widehat{Y}_i = \widehat{\alpha} + \widehat{\beta}_1 + \widehat{\beta}_2 X_i = 52\,868 + 5.638X_i$$

if $D_i = 1$ (i.e. the ith house has an air conditioner) and

$$\widehat{Y}_i = \widehat{\alpha} + \widehat{\beta}_2 X_i = 32\,693 + 5.638 X_i$$

if $D_i = 0$ (i.e. the house does not have an air conditioner). In other words, there are two different regression lines depending on whether the house has an air conditioner or not. Contrast this point with the discussion in the example above where we had only one dummy explanatory variable. In that case, the regression implied that the average price of the house differed between houses with and without air conditioners. Here, we are saying a wholly different regression line exists.

Note, however, that the two regression lines have the same slope and only differ in their intercepts. This is a property of multiple regression models that have both dummy and regular explanatory variables: the dummy variables define different categories of observations (e.g. different groups of houses) and these different categories have different intercepts in their regression lines. However, all categories have the same slope, and thus the marginal effect of X on Y is the same for all observations. Should you wish your different categories to have different intercepts and different slopes, then you should interact your dummy and non-dummy explanatory variables. To understand what is meant by this, consider the following regression model:

$$Y_i = \alpha + \beta_1 D_i + \beta_2 X_i + \beta_3 Z_i + \varepsilon_i,$$

where D and X are dummy and non-dummy explanatory variables, as above. However, here we have added a new variable Z into the regression, and we define $Z = DX$.

How do we interpret results from a regression of Y on D, X, and Z? This question can be answered by noting that Z_i is either 0 (for observations with $D_i = 0$) or X_i (for observations with $D_i = 1$). If, as before, we consider the fitted regression lines for individuals with $D_i = 0$ and $D_i = 1$, we obtain the following:

- If $D_i = 0$, then $\widehat{Y}_i = \widehat{\alpha} + \widehat{\beta}_2 X_i$.
- If $D_i = 1$, then $\widehat{Y}_i = \left(\widehat{\alpha} + \widehat{\beta}_1\right) + \left(\widehat{\beta}_2 + \widehat{\beta}_3\right) X_i$.

In other words, two different regression lines corresponding to $D = 0$ and $D = 1$ exist and have different intercepts and different slopes. One implication is that the marginal effect of X on Y is different for observations with $D_i = 0$ than with $D_i = 1$.

Example: Explaining house prices (continued)

If we regress $Y =$ house price on three explanatory variables: $D =$ air conditioner dummy, $X =$ lot size, and $Z = DX$, we obtain $\widehat{\alpha} = 35\,684$, $\widehat{\beta}_1 = 7\,613$, $\widehat{\beta}_2 = 5.02$, and $\widehat{\beta}_3 = 2.25$. This implies that the marginal effect of lot size on housing is 7.27 (i.e. adding an extra square foot of lot size is associated with a \$7.27 increase in house prices) for houses with air conditioners and only \$5.02 for houses without. Furthermore, since the *P*-value corresponding to β_3 is 0.02, the difference in marginal effects is statistically significant. This finding indicates, that increasing lot size will tend to add more to the value of a house if it has an air conditioner than if it does not.

2.3.7 What if the dependent variable is a dummy?

Thus far, we have focused on the case where the explanatory variables can be dummies. However, in some cases the dependent variable may be a dummy. For instance, a transportation economist might be interested in investigating individual choice between public transport and the private automobile. An empirical analysis might involve collecting data from many different individuals about their transport habits. Potential explanatory variables would include: commuting time, individual income, and so on. The dependent variable, however, would be qualitative (e.g. each individual may say 'Yes, I take my car to work' or 'No, I do not take my car to work'), and the economist would have to create a dummy dependent variable. This case will be discussed in Chapter 9. At this stage it is only worth stressing that standard OLS regression methods are sometimes used when your dependent variable is a dummy. However, estimators known as probit and logit are more attractive choices.

2.4 Chapter summary

This chapter has presented a non-technical overview of regression methods. Future chapters will provide theoretical derivations relating to many of the issues and concepts discussed in this chapter. However, it is important to have a good intuitive understanding of the regression model before proceeding with theoretical material. Furthermore, after reading this non-technical introduction to regression, you should be able to get started in actually doing some empirical work (at least with cross-sectional data). In future chapters, we will often refer to this one (e.g. when referring to how coefficients should be interpreted).

The major points covered in this chapter include:

1. Simple regression quantifies the effect of an explanatory variable, X, on a dependent variable, Y, through a regression line $Y = \alpha + \beta X$.
2. Estimation of α and β involves choosing estimates which produces the best-fitting line through an XY graph. These are called ordinary least squares (OLS) estimates, are labeled $\widehat{\alpha}$ and $\widehat{\beta}$, and are obtained by minimizing the sum of squared residuals (*SSR*).

3. Simple regression coefficients should be interpreted as marginal effects (i.e. as measures of the effect on Y of a small change in X).

4. R^2 is a measure of how well the regression line fits the data.

5. The confidence interval provides an interval estimate of any coefficient (e.g. an interval for β in which you can be confident β lies).

6. A hypothesis test of whether $\beta = 0$ can be used to find out whether the explanatory variable belongs in the regression. A hypothesis test can either be done by comparing a test statistic (i.e. the t-stat) with a critical value taken from statistical tables or by examining the P-value. If the P-value for the hypothesis test of whether $\beta = 0$ is less than 0.05, then you can reject the hypothesis at the 5 % level of significance.

7. The multiple regression model has more than one explanatory variable. The basic intuition of all concepts in this model (e.g. OLS estimates, confidence intervals, etc.) is the same as for the simple regression model. However, with multiple regression the interpretation of regression coefficients is subject to *ceteris paribus* conditions. For instance, β_j measures the marginal effect of X_j on Y, *holding the other explanatory variables constant*.

8. If important explanatory variables are omitted from the regression, the estimated coefficients can be misleading, a condition known as omitted variables bias. The problem gets worse if the omitted variables are strongly correlated with the included explanatory variables.

9. If the explanatory variables are highly correlated with one another, coefficient estimates and statistical tests may be misleading. This is referred to as the multicollinearity problem.

10. In empirical work, we often have dummy explanatory variables (i.e. variables that take on values of 0 or 1). The statistical techniques associated with the use of dummy explanatory variables are exactly the same as with non-dummy explanatory variables.

11. A regression involving only dummy explanatory variables implicitly classifies the observations into various groups (e.g. houses with air conditioners and houses without). Interpretation of results is aided by careful consideration of what the groups are.

12. A regression involving dummy and non-dummy explanatory variables implicitly classifies the observations into groups and says that each group will have a regression line with a different intercept. All these regression lines have the same slope.

13. A regression involving dummy, non-dummy, and interaction (i.e. dummy times non-dummy variables) explanatory variables implicitly classifies the observations into groups and says that each group will have a different regression line with a different intercept and slope.

Exercises

The data for these questions are provided on the website associated with this book.

1. In this chapter, we illustrated simple regression using an example involving costs of production in the electric utility industry for 123 electric utility companies in the USA in 1970 (dataset ELECTRIC.XLS). Table 2.1 presents results from a regression of costs on output. The complete dataset contains the cost and output variables as well as some additional ones:

   - Y = costs of production (measured in millions of dollars per year);
   - X_1 = output (measured in thousands of kilowatt hours per year);
   - X_2 = price of labour (measured in dollars per worker per year);
   - X_3 = price of capital (measured in dollars per unit of capital per year);
   - X_4 = price of fuel (measured in dollars per million BTUs).

   (a) Run a regression of Y on X_1, X_2, X_3, and X_4 and interpret your results.
   (b) Compare the results you obtained in part (a) with those in Table 2.1 and discuss the issue of omitted variables bias.
   (c) What are the confidence intervals for each of the coefficients? How are these interpreted?
   (d) Discuss the statistical significance of the coefficients. Are there explanatory variables that can be dropped?

2. Dataset FOREST.XLS contains data for 70 tropical countries on deforestation rates, population density, and the changes in cropland and pasture land. Population density is measured as the number of people per thousand hectares, while the other variables are all annual percentage changes averaged over the years 1981–1990. Using deforestation as the dependent variable, carry out a multiple regression analysis of this dataset, addressing the issues raised in this chapter. You should:

   (a) Run the regression and interpret the coefficient estimates you obtain.
   (b) Discuss the statistical significance of the coefficients. Are there explanatory variables that can be dropped?
   (c) Discuss the fit of the regression.
   (d) Calculate a correlation matrix. Through consideration of this and your regression results, discuss the issue of multicollinearity.

3. The dataset WAGEDISC.XLS contains data on $N = 100$ employees in a particular occupation. Suppose that interest centres on investigating the factors that explain salary differences in this occupation with a view to addressing the issue of sex discrimination in this occupation. The dataset contains the following variables:

   - Y = salary (measured in thousands of dollars);

- $X_1 =$ education level (measured in years of schooling);
- $X_2 =$ experience level (measured in years of employment);
- $D =$ dummy for gender ($= 1$ for male, $= 0$ for female).

(a) Calculate and discuss descriptive statistics for this dataset. For instance, what is the mean salary?

(b) Calculate the mean salary for female employees and male employees separately. Compare.

(c) Run a simple regression of Y on D. Is the slope coefficient in this regression statistically significant? Compare your regression result with your finding in (b). Can you use these findings to conclude that women are discriminated against in this occupation?

(d) Run a multiple regression of Y on X_1, X_2, and D. Write a short report outlining your findings and addressing the issue of wage discrimination in this occupation. Are your results statistically significant?

(e) Compare your results in part (d) with part (c). Why do they differ? Hint: calculate a correlation matrix for all the explanatory variables and think about what the correlations mean.

(f) Construct a new variable $Z = DX_2$ and run a regression of Y on X_1, X_2, D, and Z. Is Z statistically significant? How would the short report you wrote in part (d) change? Explain in words what the coefficient on Z measures.

Endnotes

1. This dataset, ELECTRIC.XLS, is available on the website associated with this book.
2. One of the few examples of an intercept having an economic interpretation is the regression implied by the capital asset pricing model (CAPM) in financial economics. If capital markets are perfect, then its intercept should be zero. Thus, for the CAPM it is of interest to estimate α and see if it really is near zero.
3. We remind the reader that the standard deviation is the square root of the variance, see Appendix B: Probability Basics for more detail.
4. This dataset, HPRICE.XLS, is available on the website associated with this book.
5. *Ceteris paribus* is a Latin phrase meaning 'all else being equal'. It is commonly used in economics.
6. These variables (and several others) are in dataset HPRICE.XLS available on the website associated with this book.

CHAPTER 3

The Econometrics of the Simple Regression Model

3.1 Introduction

In the preceding chapter, we introduced the multiple regression model with k explanatory variables which can be written as

$$Y_i = \alpha + \beta_1 X_{1i} + \beta_2 X_{2i} + \cdots + \beta_k X_{ki} + \varepsilon_i,$$

where i subscripts denote individual observations and we have $i = 1, \ldots, N$ observations. As we have seen, this model can be used to estimate the effect that the explanatory variables, $X_1, \ldots, X_k$, have on the dependent variable, Y. Previously, we presented a non-technical introduction to the multiple regression model where the OLS estimator was motivated as being a good one since it minimized the sum of squared residuals. We also introduced the concepts of a confidence interval and a hypothesis test based on this OLS estimator. However, our motivation for these was informal and we did not actually derive them. In this chapter, we provide such derivations. In order to do so, we use probability theory. An introduction to probability is given in Appendix B: Probability Basics at the end of this book, and the reader unfamiliar with probability should refer to this.

In econometrics, we are always dealing with uncertainty. We are uncertain what the regression coefficients, $\alpha, \beta_1, \ldots, \beta_k$ are (and, hence, have to estimate them). We are uncertain whether a particular hypothesis (e.g. $\beta_j = 0$) is true (and, hence, have to derive hypothesis testing procedures). We are uncertain about what future values of Y might be (and, hence, have to derive procedures for forecasting). Probability provides us with a language and a formal structure for dealing with uncertainty. In this chapter we show how probability is used with the regression model.

To draw out the basic ideas in the simplest fashion, we will work with the simple regression model without an intercept

$$Y_i = \beta X_i + \varepsilon_i.$$

Results (e.g. confidence intervals) for the multiple regression model are very similar and have the same intuitive motivation, but are messier. Hence, we will not provide them in this chapter in order to focus on the main statistical concepts in as simple a framework as possible.

3.2   A review of basic concepts in probability in the context of the regression model

Econometricians begin by assuming that Y is a random variable.[1] They do this since they view any model, including the regression model, as providing a description about what probable values for the dependent variable are. To make this concept more concrete, consider the example (discussed in the preceding chapters) where Y is the price of a house and X is a house characteristic (e.g. X is lot size). Consider what would happen if you knew X but did not know Y. Say you knew that $X = 5\,000$ square feet (a typical value in our dataset) for a particular house. This would not be enough information to tell you exactly the price of the house. Just knowing the size of a house is not enough to tell you precisely what the price of the house will be. Thus, Y is uncertain. However, it is not completely uncertain. A house with $X = 5\,000$ might sell for roughly $70\,000 or $60\,000 or $50\,000 (which are typical values in our dataset), but it will not sell for $1\,000 (far too cheap) or $1\,000\,000 (far too expensive). Econometricians use probability to summarize which are plausible and which are implausible values for the house.

A probability density function (or p.d.f., see Appendix B, Definition B.7, for further details) is used for summarizing what is known about any random variable. Figure 3.1 is a graph of what the p.d.f. for Y might be for our house price example. It summarizes the range of plausible values that Y might take when $X = 5\,000$. Figure 3.1 is an example of a normal distribution (see Appendix B, Definition B.10). This is the most commonly-used distribution in econometrics. Notice that Figure 3.1 is a bell-shaped curve. The curve is highest for the most plausible values that the house price might take. That is, it is highest around $50\,000, $60\,000, and $70\,000 (which are house price values that often occur in the dataset). It is lowest for extreme, implausible values of the house price (e.g. $1\,000 and $200\,000). In Chapter 1 we intuitively introduced the ideas of a mean (or expected value) and variance (see also Appendix B, Definition B.8). Remember that we motivated the mean as the 'average' or 'typical' value of a variable and the variance as being a measure of how dispersed a variable is. The exact shape of any normal distribution depends on its

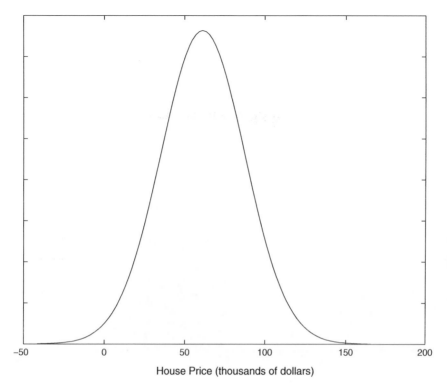

Figure 3.1 Normal p.d.f. of house price of a house with a lot size =5 000 square feet.

mean and its variance. The notation that says 'Y is a random variable that has a normal p.d.f. with mean μ and variance σ^2 is[2]

$$Y \sim N(\mu, \sigma^2).$$

Figure 3.1 has been drawn with $\mu = 61.153$ (i.e. \$61 153 is the mean, or average, value for a house with a lot size of 5 000 square feet) and $\sigma^2 = 683.812$. The latter is a measure of dispersion, of the range of plausible values for a house with a lot size of 5 000 square feet, but beyond this statement we have not provided much intuition yet for how σ^2 is interpreted.

We have said that p.d.f.s are a formal way of summarizing the uncertainty we have about a random variable such as house price. This arises since areas under the curve defined by the p.d.f. are probabilities. This is illustrated in Figure 3.2 which is the same as Figure 3.1 except that the area under the curve between the points 60 and 100 is shaded in. The shaded area is the probability that the house is worth between \$60 000 and \$100 000. In this example, this probability is 45 % and can be written as $\Pr(60 \leq Y \leq 100) = 0.45$. This can be calculated using statistical tables (or most econometrics software packages

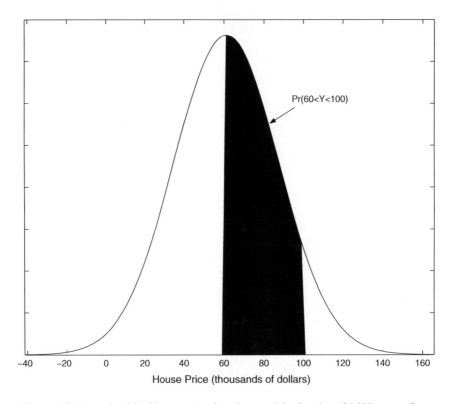

Figure 3.2 Normal p.d.f. of house price for a house with a lot size of 5 000 square feet.

can calculate it). Note that, by definition, the entire area under any p.d.f. is 1. Hence, the area of any region under the p.d.f. will be a number less than 1. This is sensible since probabilities all must be between 0 and 1. You cannot have the probability of an event occurring being 120 % or −6 %!

As a digression (which will also allow us to review some important tools in probability and statistics), it is worth briefly describing the use of statistical tables for the normal distribution. The table for this distribution is given at the back of this book. However, it is just a single table. How can we use just one table when there is a normal p.d.f. for every value of μ and σ^2? The answer is that the table provided is for the so-called *standard normal distribution* which is $N(0,1)$. Knowledge of probabilities for the $N(0,1)$ is enough to figure out probabilities for the $N(\mu, \sigma^2)$ for any μ and σ^2. To see why this is true, suppose $Y \sim N(\mu, \sigma^2)$ and consider a new random variable

$$Z = \frac{Y - \mu}{\sigma}.$$

In this book we repeatedly use the properties of the expected value and variance operators. Here, we use them to work out the properties of Z. We have intuitively motivated these operators in Chapter 1 and we refer the reader to theorem B.2 in Appendix B for some of their key properties. Since μ and σ^2 are the mean and variance of Y, we can write $E(Y) = \mu$ and $var(Y) = \sigma^2$. What are the mean and variance of Z? Since μ and σ^2 are not random variables, we can use theorem B.2, part 1, to say

$$
\begin{aligned}
E(Z) &= E\left(\frac{Y - \mu}{\sigma}\right) \\
&= \frac{E(Y - \mu)}{\sigma} \\
&= \frac{E(Y) - \mu}{\sigma} \\
&= \frac{\mu - \mu}{\sigma} = 0.
\end{aligned}
$$

Similarly, theorem B.2, parts 2 and 3, can be used to derive

$$
\begin{aligned}
var(Z) &= var\left(\frac{Y - \mu}{\sigma}\right) \\
&= \frac{var(Y - \mu)}{\sigma^2} \\
&= \frac{var(Y)}{\sigma^2} = \frac{\sigma^2}{\sigma^2} = 1.
\end{aligned}
$$

Thus, Z is $N(0, 1)$ and we can use the statistical tables at the end of this book to figure our probabilities relating to it. Note that Z is often referred to as a *Z-score*. The strategy used to construct Z is a common one.

As an example of how the Z-score is used, let us consider the shaded area under the normal p.d.f. in Figure 3.2. We have already said that $Y \sim N(61.153, 683.812)$. The shaded area is $\Pr(60 \leq Y \leq 100)$ and this is what we want to calculate. However, we do not have statistical tables for the $N(61.153, 683.812)$ distribution. Hence, we want to try and transform the problem into one involving the Z-score so that we can use the $N(0, 1)$ distribution (which we do have a table for). We can do this as follows (using the properties of the inequality operator):

$$
\begin{aligned}
\Pr(60 &\leq Y \leq 100) \\
&= \Pr\left(\frac{60 - \mu}{\sigma} \leq \frac{Y - \mu}{\sigma} \leq \frac{100 - \mu}{\sigma}\right) \\
&= \Pr\left(\frac{60 - 61.153}{\sqrt{683.812}} \leq \frac{Y - 61.153}{\sqrt{683.812}} \leq \frac{100 - 61.153}{\sqrt{683.812}}\right) \\
&= \Pr(-0.04 \leq Z \leq 1.49).
\end{aligned}
$$

We have now transformed the problem to one involving the standard normal distribution and we can use the normal statistical tables to calculate $\Pr(-0.04 \le Z \le 1.49) = 0.45$. If you are having trouble seeing this, note that we can break the area under the curve into two parts as $\Pr(-0.04 \le Z \le 1.49) = \Pr(-0.04 \le Z \le 0) + \Pr(0 \le Z \le 1.49)$. The table tells us directly that $\Pr(0 \le Z \le 1.49) = 0.4319$. Since the normal is symmetric, $\Pr(-0.04 \le Z \le 0) = \Pr(0 \le Z \le 0.04)$, and the table gives this to be 0.0160. Adding these two probabilities together gives 0.4479 (which we have rounded to 0.45 above).

To summarize, our goal is to derive properties of the OLS estimator, confidence intervals, and hypothesis tests. To this end, we have begun by assuming Y to be a random variable with a normal distribution. We have used this as a way of introducing the idea of a p.d.f., showing how p.d.f.s can be used to summarize our uncertainty about Y (i.e. we can use statistical tables to calculate the probability that Y lies in any region). This has also allowed us to do some derivations with the expected value and variance operators. Since a great deal of this book will involve working with probability and manipulating the expected value and variance operators, the reader who is having difficulty with the derivations we have done so far should spend some time looking at Appendix B: Probability Basics.

3.3   The classical assumptions for the regression model

The previous section introduced the idea that Y was a random variable and the basic language and tools we will use (e.g. the normal distribution and the expected value and variance operators). So far we have said nothing about estimation of β nor about confidence intervals and hypothesis tests. In order to do this, we have to provide a set of assumptions that formally defines the regression model. These assumptions are the standard benchmark for beginning study of the regression model and are referred to as the *classical assumptions*. Remember that we have $Y_1, Y_2, \ldots, Y_N$ observations on our dependent variable. Thinking in terms of probability, each of these will be the realization of a random variable. A set of assumptions that fully defines the p.d.f. for all these observations defines a model. The classical assumptions define a linear regression model.

The classical assumptions are as follows (for each of $i = 1, \ldots, N$ observations):

1. $E(Y_i) = \beta X_i$.
2. $var(Y_i) = \sigma^2$.
3. $cov(Y_i, Y_j) = 0$ for $i \ne j$.
4. Y_i is normally distributed.
5. X_i is fixed. It is not a random variable.

Compact notation for the classical assumptions is

$$Y_i \text{ is } N(\beta X_i, \sigma^2),$$

for $i = 1, \ldots, N$ and Y_i and Y_j are uncorrelated with one another if $i \ne j$.

In Chapter 2, we motivated the regression model as fitting a straight-line through an XY plot. The classical assumptions formalize this, and it is worthwhile discussing the intuition for each of the classical assumptions. The first assumption, $E(Y_i) = \beta X_i$, captures the linearity assumption. Remember that we are working with the simplest possible regression model (without an intercept), which accounts for the fact that there is no α in this expression. In the multiple regression model, the assumption $E(Y_i) = \beta X_i$ will be replaced with $E(Y_i) = \alpha + \beta_1 X_{1i} + \beta_2 X_{2i} + \cdots + \beta_k X_{ki}$. In words, the assumption implies that we expect Y_i to lie on the regression line. Of course, when looking at an actual dataset, it will be very unusual for Y_i to lie exactly on the regression line, but the assumption is saying that on average it will do so. Some observations will lie above the line, some below, but on average they will match the regression line. This is sensible intuition consistent with how we motivated regression in Chapter 2.

The second assumption is that all observations have the same variance. In Chapter 5, we will discuss relaxing this assumption. Perhaps it is best understood through an example that shows when it is violated. Consider our example where the dependent variable is the price of a house and the explanatory variable is its lot size. In our dataset there will be big houses (i.e. those with large lot size) and small houses. Suppose the small houses are all very similar to one another (e.g. they are all small bungalows built to the same specifications). If this is the case, then the small houses would all have roughly the same price. That is, if there were dozens of identical small houses being sold, buyers would quickly learn that the going rate was, say, $30 000, and no buyer would pay much more and no seller accept much less than this price. Thus, the variability of the price of small houses would be small (i.e. $var(Y)$ is small for small houses). Suppose the big houses were much more diverse. Then big house prices would vary much more (i.e. $var(Y)$ is large for big houses). This story illustrates a case where assumption 2 would be violated. We would not have $var(Y_i)$ being the same for every house: it would differ between big and small houses. Assumption 2, which is referred to as *homoskedasticity*, rules out this possibility. When assumption 2 is violated, we have *heteroskedasticity*, a topic which will be discussed in Chapter 5.

The third assumption is that different observations are uncorrelated with one another. This can be seen if you remember that

$$corr(Y_i, Y_j) = \frac{cov(Y_i, Y_j)}{\sqrt{var(Y_i)var(Y_j)}}$$

and, thus, $cov(Y_i, Y_j) = 0$ implies $corr(Y_i, Y_j) = 0$. This assumption is usually reasonable with cross-sectional data. Consider, for instance, survey data (e.g. surveys of workers' wages and their characteristics). Surveys often proceed by randomly selecting workers and then asking them questions. The fact that the workers are randomly selected ensures uncorrelatedness of their responses. As we will see, with time series data assumption 3 is not sensible. For instance, in studies of the unemployment rate, the fact that economic activity goes up and down only gradually (i.e. owing to business cycle effects) means that the unemployment rate in 1996 is correlated with the unemployment rate in 1997. If

1996 was a time of low unemployment, then it is probably the case that 1997 also was. This means the unemployment rate is correlated over time. In Chapter 5, we will show how to relax assumption 3.

The fourth assumption, that Y is normally distributed, is harder to motivate. Suffice it to note that, in many empirical applications, normality is a reasonable assumption. Furthermore, asymptotic theory can be used to relax this assumption. Asymptotic theory is discussed in Appendix C at the end of the book, and several of the chapters (including this one) have appendices that explain how asymptotic theory can be used to relax normality assumptions used in different models.

The final assumption is that the explanatory variable is fixed and is not a random variable. In the experimental sciences, this is a reasonable assumption. The experimenter sets up the experiment (i.e. chooses values for the explanatory variable) and then observes the outcome. Because the values for the explanatory variable are simply selected, X is not a random variable. Economics research is not usually an experimental science, and hence assumption 5 may not be reasonable in many contexts. In the Appendix to this chapter, we show how asymptotic theory can be used to replace assumption 5 with the assumption that X_i is a random variable that is uncorrelated with the error in the regression. Under this assumption, all the results based on OLS estimation derived in this chapter can be shown to still hold. However, if X_i is a random variable that is correlated with the error, then OLS results no longer hold. In Chapter 5, we discuss this case and show how OLS should no longer be used (instead something called the instrumental variables estimator should be).

We have written the classical assumptions in terms of what they say about Y_i. Many econometricians prefer to think in terms of the regression errors and express the classical assumptions in terms of them. Using the properties of the expected value, variance, and covariance operators, the following can be shown to be an equivalent way of writing the classical assumptions:

1. $E(\varepsilon_i) = 0$. Mean zero errors.
2. $var(\varepsilon_i) = E(\varepsilon_i^2) = \sigma^2$. Constant variance errors (homoskedasticity).
3. $cov(\varepsilon_i, \varepsilon_j) = 0$ for $i \neq j$. Errors are uncorrelated with one another.
4. ε_i is normally distributed.
5. X_i is fixed. It is not a random variable.

Note that the result $var(\varepsilon_i) = E(\varepsilon_i^2)$ is one we use in several derivations in this book. It arises from the definition of variance $var(\varepsilon_i) = E(\varepsilon_i^2) - [E(\varepsilon_i)]^2$ and the fact that errors have mean zero (i.e. $E(\varepsilon_i) = 0$). An intuitive understanding of the implications of these assumptions proceeds in a similar fashion to our previous discussion. For instance, assumption 1 formalizes a point made with Figure 2.2. in Chapter 2. Any straight-line fit through an XY plot does not exactly go through all the data points, and hence errors are made. Some errors are positive, some are negative, but on average the errors have mean zero. In terms of an XY plot, assumption 2 says that errors will exhibit the same dispersion (i.e. the same variance) for all different values of X. In terms of a survey, assumption 3 says any error I make in filling out my survey form is unrelated to any error you make in filling out your survey form (a reasonable assumption with survey data). Assumption 4 is less intuitive but can be relaxed using asymptotic theory. Assumption 5 is probably most suited for the experimental sciences, but is a good place to start for the econometrician. It, too, can be relaxed using asymptotic theory (provided the explanatory variable is uncorrelated with the error).

3.4 Properties of the ordinary least-squares estimator of β

In Chapter 2, we introduced the OLS estimator as one that produced the best-fitting line through an XY plot. In terms of the simple regression model (without intercept)

$$Y_i = \beta X_i + \varepsilon_i,$$

the OLS estimator is chosen to minimize the sum of squared residuals:

$$SSR = \sum_{i=1}^{N} \varepsilon_i^2.$$

In Chapter 2, the formula for the OLS estimator was not given. Finding the value of β that minimizes SSR is a straightforward calculus problem. The solution is given by

$$\widehat{\beta} = \frac{\sum_{i=1}^{N} X_i Y_i}{\sum_{i=1}^{N} X_i^2}.$$

By definition, the OLS estimator has one nice property: it produces a fitted regression line that fits best in the sense of making the sum of squared residuals as small as possible. However, it has some other attractive properties. In order to show these properties, and in order to establish some results that we will use to construct confidence intervals and do hypothesis tests, it is important to derive the distribution of the OLS estimator.

The first thing to note is that $\widehat{\beta}$ is a random variable. Its formula depends on Y_i for $i = 1, \ldots, N$ which are all normal random variables. Furthermore, the classical assumptions have X_i for $i = 1, \ldots, N$ being fixed (not random variables). Hence, an examination of the formula for $\widehat{\beta}$ indicates that it is a linear function of normal random variables. Definition B.10 in Appendix B contains a result that can be summarized as saying 'linear combinations of normal random variables are normal'. This result can be used to say that $\widehat{\beta}$ is a normal random variable. Normal random variables are characterized by a mean and variance. Thus, if we can figure out the mean and variance of $\widehat{\beta}$, we can fully characterize its probability distribution. Why do we want to know this? As we will see, the distribution of $\widehat{\beta}$ is used to derive the confidence intervals and hypothesis testing procedures we discussed in Chapter 2.

Before deriving the mean and variance of $\widehat{\beta}$, we first derive an alternative way of writing the OLS estimator that we will use in several future derivations. For future reference, we will label this as equation (*). The following derivation replaces Y_i with what the regression model says it is (i.e. $X_i\beta + \varepsilon_i$) in the formula for $\widehat{\beta}$ and then rearranges terms:

$$\widehat{\beta} = \frac{\sum X_i Y_i}{\sum X_i^2} = \frac{\sum X_i(X_i\beta + \varepsilon_i)}{\sum X_i^2} \qquad (*)$$

$$= \beta + \frac{\sum X_i \varepsilon_i}{\sum X_i^2}.$$

This formula says that $\widehat{\beta}$ can be written as that which we are trying to estimate (i.e. β), plus a term involving the explanatory variables and errors. Since it depends on the unknown errors, this is not an expression that is useful for evaluating the OLS estimator in practice. However, it is useful in many theoretical derivations.

Property 1: The expected value of the OLS estimator is β:

$$E\left(\widehat{\beta}\right) = \beta.$$

Proof:

$$E(\widehat{\beta}) = E\left(\beta + \frac{\sum X_i \varepsilon_i}{\sum X_i^2}\right)$$

$$= \beta + E\left(\frac{\sum X_i \varepsilon_i}{\sum X_i^2}\right)$$

$$= \beta + \frac{1}{\sum X_i^2} E\left(\sum X_i \varepsilon_i\right)$$

$$= \beta + \frac{1}{\sum X_i^2} \sum X_i E(\varepsilon_i)$$

$$= \beta.$$

The proof uses equation (*), the properties of the expected value operator, and assumption 1 (i.e. that errors have mean zero). If you do not see where each line comes from, you should refer to Appendix B, Theorem B.2. Remember β and X_i are assumed not to be random and, hence, can be treated as constants in the derivation.

Property 1 is an attractive one. Any estimator will, as its name suggests, only be an estimate of β. So we cannot expect $\widehat{\beta}$ to be precisely equal to β. However, property 1 tells us that, on average, $\widehat{\beta}$ will be precisely equal to β. Sometimes the OLS estimate will be high, other times low, but on average it will be correct.

Property 1 allows us to introduce another important concept: unbiasedness. An estimator is *unbiased* if its expected value is equal to the thing being estimated. Here, since $E(\widehat{\beta}) = \beta$, we can say that $\widehat{\beta}$ is an unbiased estimator of β. Unbiasedness is a desirable property and econometricians usually seek to find estimators that are unbiased. In contrast, a biased estimator is one with an expected value not equalling what is being estimated.

Property 2: The variance of the OLS estimator under the classical assumptions is

$$var(\widehat{\beta}) = \frac{\sigma^2}{\sum X_i^2}.$$

Proof:

$$var(\widehat{\beta}) = var\left(\beta + \frac{\sum X_i \varepsilon_i}{\sum X_i^2}\right)$$

$$= var\left(\frac{\sum X_i \varepsilon_i}{\sum X_i^2}\right)$$

$$= \left(\frac{1}{\sum X_i^2}\right)^2 var\left(\sum X_i \varepsilon_i\right)$$

$$= \left(\frac{1}{\sum X_i^2}\right)^2 \sum X_i^2 var(\varepsilon_i)$$

$$= \left(\frac{1}{\sum X_i^2}\right)^2 \sigma^2 \sum X_i^2$$

$$= \frac{\sigma^2}{\sum X_i^2}.$$

The proof uses equation (*), the properties of the variance operator, and assumption 2 (i.e. that errors have a constant variance, σ^2). The properties of the variance operator are given in Appendix B, Theorem B.2. Remember β and X_i are assumed not to be random and, hence, can be treated as constants.

Property 2 quantifies the variability of the random variable, $\widehat{\beta}$. For an unbiased estimator such as $\widehat{\beta}$, having a low variability is a good thing. Remember that we said $\widehat{\beta}$ is an estimate and thus sometimes will be too high, other times too low, but on average it will be correct. Intuitively, it is better if it is *a little* too high or *a little* too low rather than *a lot* too high or *a lot* too low. An estimator with a small variance will exhibit the first property (i.e. be only a little too high or low).

As we have seen in Chapter 2, next to the OLS estimates, computer packages will present their standard errors. These standard errors are $\sqrt{var(\widehat{\beta})}$.

It is worth noting that, with any econometric problem, there are always several estimators that you might use. For instance, exercise 2 at the end of this chapter provides five different estimators in a particular set-up. As another example, for the simple regression model (without intercept) it can be shown that the following is an unbiased estimator of β:

$$\widetilde{\beta} = \frac{\sum_{i=1}^{N} Y_i}{\sum_{i=1}^{N} X_i},$$

provided $\sum_{i=1}^{N} X_i \neq 0$. Why is the OLS estimator used instead of $\widetilde{\beta}$? It can be shown that this estimator has a larger variance than $\widehat{\beta}$ (see exercise 3). Thus, when faced with two different unbiased estimators, you should choose the one with the smallest variance. As a bit of jargon, an estimator is said to be *efficient* relative to another if it has a smaller variance.

Combining properties 1 and 2 along with the fact that $\widehat{\beta}$ has a normal distribution leads to property 3.

Property 3: The distribution of the OLS estimator under classical assumptions takes the following form:

$$\widehat{\beta} \quad \text{is} \quad N\left(\beta, \frac{\sigma^2}{\sum X_i^2}\right).$$

Property 3 is important since, as we will see shortly, it can be used to derive confidence intervals and hypothesis tests.

Figure 3.3 gives an example of what the p.d.f. of $\widehat{\beta}$ might look like. Remember that a p.d.f. summarizes the uncertainty in a random variable. Regions where the p.d.f. is highest are the most likely regions where the random variable would be. Figure 3.3 is calculated assuming $\widehat{\beta}$ is $N(2, 1)$, and it can be seen that the bell-shaped curve is highest at its

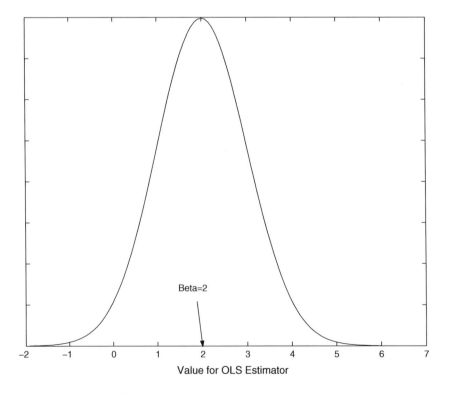

Figure 3.3 The p.d.f. of the OLS estimator.

mean, $\beta = 2$. Hence, it is most likely that $\widehat{\beta}$ will be near its true value, 2. However, remembering that areas under the curve measure the probabilities associated with various intervals, it can be seen that there is appreciable probability that $\widehat{\beta}$ will be near 1 or 3. For instance, using normal statistical tables, we can calculate $\Pr(1.0 \leq \widehat{\beta} \leq 3.0) = 0.68$, so there is a 68 % probability that $\widehat{\beta}$ will be within 1.0 of the true value, $\beta = 2$, and $\Pr(0 \leq \widehat{\beta} \leq 1) = 0.14$, so there is a 14 % chance $\widehat{\beta}$ will lie between 0 and 1.

To illustrate the concept of efficiency and the role of the variance in choosing between two estimators, suppose $\widehat{\beta}$ is $N(2, 1)$ and we have another unbiased estimator, $\widetilde{\beta}$, which is $N(2, 4)$. Thus, this new estimator is also unbiased since $E(\widetilde{\beta}) = 2$ (which is the true value for β in this illustration), but it has a larger variance than the OLS estimator since $var(\widetilde{\beta}) = 4$. The p.d.f.s of $\widehat{\beta}$ and $\widetilde{\beta}$ are plotted in Figure 3.4. It can be seen that, since $var(\widetilde{\beta}) > var(\widehat{\beta})$, the p.d.f. of the new estimator is more dispersed than that of the OLS estimator. Both estimators are unbiased, and thus on average the estimates they provide are correct. However, the new estimator is much more likely to provide an estimate that is greatly above or below the true value of $\beta = 2$. For instance, with the OLS estimator, it is very unlikely to get a negative estimate since $\Pr(\widehat{\beta} \leq 0) = 0.02$. However, with the new estimator, $\Pr(\widetilde{\beta} \leq 0) = 0.16$, and thus there is a much larger chance of obtaining a negative estimate.

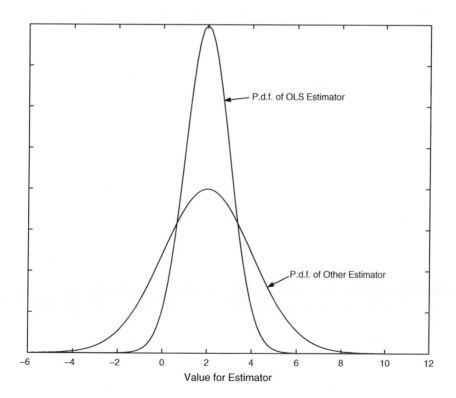

Figure 3.4 The p.d.f.s of the OLS estimator and a less efficient estimator.

Thus far we have shown that the OLS estimator is unbiased and has a certain variance. We have motivated unbiasedness as a desirable property but a high variance as an undesirable one. When choosing between estimators, it is good to choose an unbiased one with as small a variance as possible. In general, this is a hard thing to do. It may be hard to prove that estimators are unbiased, and, even if you can, it may be impossible to find an estimator that always has a smaller variance than its competitor. However, in the regression model under the classical assumptions, choosing the best estimator is quite easy owing to the following important theorem.

Property 4: The Gauss–Markov theorem.

In the regression model, if the classical assumptions hold, then OLS is the best, linear unbiased estimator. This is often shortened to 'OLS is BLUE', where B stands for best (in the sense of having smallest variance), L stands for linear (in the sense that the estimator is a linear function of the observations of the dependent variable, Y), U stands for unbiased, and E stands for estimator.

The proof of this theorem is provided in the Appendix to this chapter. One thing worth noting is that the proof uses the first, second, third, and fifth of the classical assumptions, but not the fourth (i.e. the assumption of normal errors). Thus, OLS is BLUE even if errors are not normal.

You may think we have now offered adequate justification for why OLS is a good estimator under the classical assumptions. It is the estimator that minimizes the sum of squared residuals, it is unbiased, and it has a smaller variance than any other linear unbiased estimator. However, we will offer one more justification for using OLS since this allows us to introduce an important concept in econometrics: *maximum likelihood estimation*.

The classical assumptions say that Y_i is $N(\beta X_i, \sigma^2)$. The problem of estimation is to figure out what plausible values of β and σ^2 are. We will return to a discussion of σ^2 shortly, for now let us focus on β. The choice of β determines the mean of the normal distribution. In Figure 3.1 we plotted a normal distribution for Y = the price of a house with a lot size of 5 000 square feet. Previously, we explained how to interpret Figure 3.1. We said it was a summary of our uncertainty about the price of such a house. That is, it said the price of the house was likely to be approximately \$60 000 (i.e. the mean was \$61 153), but that a fair amount of probability was associated with values up to \$100 000 or as low as \$20 000. How do we know whether this is a reasonable summary of uncertainty about what the price of such a house might be? The answer is that we can look at the prices that houses with a lot size of roughly 5 000 square feet sold for. In our dataset, houses with this size lot did indeed tend to sell for roughly \$60 000, but there were many that sold for less or more than this. In statistical language, Figure 3.1 was a reasonable one for our dataset since the distribution of the random variable Y allocated most of its probability in regions where the observed values of Y actually occurred.[3] This idea – that the p.d.f. you specify for Y should match up with what actually occurs – is the intuition for maximum likelihood estimation.

To motivate maximum likelihood estimation in a slightly different way, consider Figure 3.5. Since Y_i is $N(\beta X_i, \sigma^2)$, different values of β imply different normal distributions for Y. Figure 3.5 plots three normal distributions for three different choices for β

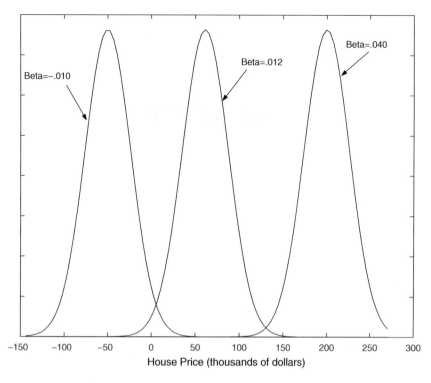

Figure 3.5 Three possible normal p.d.f.s of house price for a house with a lot size of 5 000 square feet.

with $X_i = 5\,000$. They were generated with $\beta = -0.010, 0.012$, and 0.040. Which one should be chosen as the estimate of β? Which one is the most reasonable representation of the uncertainty in the price of a house with a lot size of 5 000 square feet? The first p.d.f. (obtained using $\beta = -0.010$) allocates almost all of its probability to negative values for the house price (the mean of this distribution is $-\$50\,000$). This is clearly nonsensical. The third p.d.f. (obtained using $\beta = 0.040$) is not as obviously nonsensical but allocates too much probability to very high house prices (the mean of this distribution is $\$200\,000$). It implies that it is almost certain that the house price will be greater than $\$150\,000$ which is clearly out of line with the observations in this dataset. The second p.d.f. (obtained using $\beta = 0.012$) is the same as one presented in Figure 3.1, and we have already argued that it presents a much more reasonable picture of the uncertainty that exists about the price of a house (with a lot size of 5 000). Thus, if faced with these three choices for β , 0.012 is the most likely value. $\beta = 0.012$ should be chosen as the esti-mate in this example. This is what the maximum likelihood estimator does. It looks over every possible value for β and chooses the one that leads to the most plausible (most 'likely') distribution for the dependent variable.

Formally, maximum likelihood estimation involves maximizing the *likelihood function*. The likelihood function is the joint probability density function for all the observations. Under the classical assumptions, we have $Y_1, \ldots, Y_N$ all being normal random variables, each with mean βX_i and variance σ^2, and they are uncorrelated with each other. If we let $p(Y_i|X_i, \beta)$ denote the p.d.f. of each random variable, where the inclusion of X_i, β makes explicit that the p.d.f. depends on the value of the explanatory variable and β, then the joint p.d.f. of all the observations can be written as

$$p(Y_1, \ldots, Y_N) = \prod_{i=1}^{N} p(Y_i|X_i, \beta).$$

This result follows from the fact that a joint p.d.f. is simply the product of each of the individual p.d.f.s if the random variables are independent of one another. The classical assumptions say that our random variables are uncorrelated with one another, which, for normal random variables, implies they are independent of one another (independence is defined in Appendix B, Definition B.4). Once we plug the observed data (e.g. the observed prices and the values for lot size for the 546 houses in our example) into $p(Y_1, \ldots, Y_N)$, then we obtain the likelihood function which we label $L(\beta)$. We have written it as a function of β to make explicit that it depends on β and this is what we want to estimate. For readers unfamiliar with the probability theory underlying these results, Appendix B provides a discussion of the relevant material (see especially Definition B.9).

Maximum likelihood estimation involves selecting the value for β that maximizes $L(\beta)$. As we will see, the idea of maximum likelihood can be used with any model, not just the regression model. For the regression model, maximum likelihood estimation is particularly simple owing to the following property.

Property 5: The maximum likelihood estimator of β is the OLS estimator (under the classical assumptions).

Proof: Using the formula for the normal p.d.f. (see Appendix B, Definition B.10), we obtain

$$p(Y_i|X_i, \beta) = \frac{1}{\sqrt{2\pi\sigma^2}} \exp\left[-\frac{1}{2\sigma^2}(Y_i - \beta X_i)^2\right].$$

The likelihood function is the product of this p.d.f. over every observation. Using the properties of the exponential function, this can be calculated as

$$L(\beta) = \prod_{i=1}^{N} \frac{1}{\sqrt{2\pi\sigma^2}} \exp\left[-\frac{1}{2\sigma^2}(Y_i - \beta X_i)^2\right]$$

$$= \frac{1}{(2\pi\sigma^2)^{\frac{N}{2}}} \exp\left[-\frac{1}{2\sigma^2}\sum_{i=1}^{N}(Y_i - \beta X_i)^2\right].$$

We need to find the value for β that maximizes this likelihood function. This may look complicated, but it is not if one trick is used. The trick is to work with the log of the likelihood function. It turns out that, for many models, the log of the likelihood function is much easier to work with than the likelihood function itself. Furthermore, the maximum of the log likelihood function will be exactly the same as the maximum of the likelihood function.[4] In this case, the log of the likelihood function, which we denote as $l(\beta)$, is

$$l(\beta) = \ln[L(\beta)]$$

$$= \ln\left\{\frac{1}{(2\pi\sigma^2)^{\frac{N}{2}}}\exp\left[-\frac{1}{2\sigma^2}\sum_{i=1}^{N}(Y_i - \beta X_i)^2\right]\right\}$$

$$= \ln\left\{\frac{1}{(2\pi\sigma^2)^{\frac{N}{2}}}\right\} - \frac{1}{2\sigma^2}\sum_{i=1}^{N}(Y_i - \beta X_i)^2.$$

You can use calculus to find the value of β that maximizes $l(\beta)$. However, you do not need to do so. If you inspect the expression for $l(\beta)$, you can see that β appears only in the term $\sum_{i=1}^{N}(Y_i - \beta X_i)^2$. Owing to the negative term multiplying it (i.e. $-\frac{1}{2\sigma^2}$), in order to make $l(\beta)$ as large as possible, we must make $\sum_{i=1}^{N}(Y_i - \beta X_i)^2$ as small as possible. But this is the sum of squared errors from Chapter 2 (which becomes the *SSR* when we replace β with an estimate). There we said that the OLS estimator minimized this. Now we are saying that the maximum likelihood estimator also should minimize the sum of squared errors. Therefore, the two estimators must be equivalent to one another. Thus, our result is proven. For the linear regression model (under the classical assumptions), the maximum likelihood estimator is the OLS estimator. This provides us with yet another reason for saying OLS is a good estimator for β.

3.5 Deriving a confidence interval for β

We have justified in several ways why the OLS estimator, $\widehat{\beta}$, is a good estimator (under the classical assumptions). However, it is useful to know how accurate the estimates provided by OLS are. As we have seen in Chapter 2, confidence intervals shed light on this issue. Confidence intervals provide interval estimates that give a range in which one is highly confident that β must lie. In Chapter 2, we described how confidence intervals should be interpreted in an empirical exercise. However, we did not show how they are derived and did not provide the formula for the confidence interval. In this section we will do so. As a first step we will do so assuming the error variance, σ^2, is known. We will discuss relaxing this assumption later. The basic strategy outlined in this section can be summarized as follows: Make a probability statement involving $\widehat{\beta}$. This will depend on β. Then rearrange this probability statement so that β is isolated in between two inequality signs. The result will be the confidence interval. This basic strategy can be used with any model and with parameters other than β.

The derivation of the confidence interval begins by using property 3 (i.e. that $\widehat{\beta}$ is normal with mean β and a particular variance) to construct a Z-score (see Section 3.1):

$$Z = \frac{\widehat{\beta} - E(\widehat{\beta})}{\sqrt{var(\widehat{\beta})}} = \frac{\widehat{\beta} - \beta}{\sqrt{\frac{\sigma^2}{\sum X_i^2}}}.$$

Remember that Z-scores standardize variables to have mean 0 and variance 1. Thus, Z is $N(0, 1)$ and we can use statistical tables for the normal distribution to make probability statements. For instance,

$$\Pr[-1.96 \leq Z \leq 1.96] = 0.95.$$

Note that the confidence interval we are deriving is based on a 95 % probability statement and, for this reason, is a 95 % confidence interval. To derive the confidence interval, rearrange the inequalities to put β in the middle:

$$\Pr\left[-1.96 \leq \frac{\widehat{\beta} - \beta}{\sqrt{\frac{\sigma^2}{\sum X_i^2}}} \leq 1.96\right]$$

$$= \Pr\left[-1.96\sqrt{\frac{\sigma^2}{\sum X_i^2}} \leq \widehat{\beta} - \beta \leq 1.96\sqrt{\frac{\sigma^2}{\sum X_i^2}}\right]$$

$$= \Pr\left[\widehat{\beta} - 1.96\sqrt{\frac{\sigma^2}{\sum X_i^2}} \leq \beta \leq \widehat{\beta} + 1.96\sqrt{\frac{\sigma^2}{\sum X_i^2}}\right]$$

$$= 0.95.$$

Note that $\widehat{\beta}$ is a random variable, but the classical interpretation of econometrics says that β is not a random variable. Hence, the preceding equation cannot be interpreted as a probability statement for β and we do not call it a 'probability interval' but rather a 'confidence interval'.

Thus, we have derived a 95 % confidence interval for β under the classical assumptions (and assuming σ^2 is known) as

$$\widehat{\beta} - 1.96\sqrt{\frac{\sigma^2}{\sum X_i^2}} \leq \beta \leq \widehat{\beta} + 1.96\sqrt{\frac{\sigma^2}{\sum X_i^2}}.$$

Alternative ways of writing this confidence interval are

$$\widehat{\beta} \pm 1.96\sqrt{\frac{\sigma^2}{\sum X_i^2}}$$

or

$$\left[\widehat{\beta} - 1.96\sqrt{\frac{\sigma^2}{\sum X_i^2}}, \widehat{\beta} + 1.96\sqrt{\frac{\sigma^2}{\sum X_i^2}}\right].$$

The '95 %' is referred to as the confidence level. Other confidence levels can be handled by beginning with a different probability (e.g. 90 %) and taking a different number from normal tables. For instance, the derivation of a 90 % confidence interval would begin with the same Z-score and use the normal tables to find that $\Pr[-1.64 \leq Z \leq 1.64] = 0.90$. The result will be the same confidence interval formula with the one exception that the '1.96s' will be replaced by '1.64s' in the previous equations.

For empirical practice, this formula for the confidence interval typically cannot be used since the error variance, σ^2, is unknown. We will shortly discuss how it can be replaced with an estimate and the implications of doing so.

3.6   Hypothesis tests about β

As in the derivation of a confidence interval, we will begin by assuming σ^2 to be known and discuss relaxing this assumption later. In Chapter 2, we described hypothesis testing in a non-technical fashion, with a focus on issues of relevance for empirical practice. Most computer packages print out information for the test of the hypothesis that $\beta = 0$, and thus we described that test in detail in Chapter 2. Here we provide formal details.

To emphasise that hypothesis testing procedures can be used for any hypothesis in any model, here we will list the general steps in any hypothesis test along with the specific derivations relevant for hypothesis tests about β:

- Step 1: Specify a hypothesis, H_0.
  Hypotheses involving β can be written as $H_0 : \beta = \beta_0$ (where β_0 is known, usually $\beta_0 = 0$).
- Step 2: Specify a test statistic.
  For the hypothesis specified in step 1, a common test statistic is

$$Z = \frac{\widehat{\beta} - \beta}{\sqrt{\frac{\sigma^2}{\sum X_i^2}}}.$$

- Step 3: Figure out the distribution of the test statistic, assuming H_0 is true.
  As discussed in the derivation of the confidence interval:

$$Z = \frac{\widehat{\beta} - \beta_0}{\sqrt{\frac{\sigma^2}{\sum X_i^2}}} \text{ is } N(0, 1).$$

- Step 4: Choose a level of significance.
  We will make the common choice of 5 % (i.e. 0.05).
- Step 5: Use steps 3 and 4 to obtain a critical value.

Since Z is $N(0, 1)$ and $\Pr[-1.96 \leq Z \leq 1.96] = 0.95$, the critical value is 1.96. Note that the probability statement used to derive the critical value is 0.95 which is one minus the level of significance.

- Step 6: Calculate your test statistic from step 2 and compare with the critical value from step 5. Reject H_0 if the absolute value of the test statistic is greater than the critical value (else accept H_0).

Here this strategy amounts to rejecting H_0 if $|Z| > 1.96$.

The intuition underlying hypothesis testing procedures was described in Chapter 2. Briefly, the econometrician accepts H_0 if the calculated value of the test statistic is consistent with what could plausibly happen if H_0 were true. Formally, this means we derive the distribution of the test statistic assuming H_0 is true (step 3). We can use this to make probability statements such as $\Pr[-1.96 \leq Z \leq 1.96] = 0.95$. In other words, this means 'if H_0 is true, then we are almost positive (i.e. there is a 95 % probability) that Z will lie between -1.96 and 1.96.' If the calculated value of Z does not lie in this interval, then we take this as evidence that H_0 is not true and reject the hypothesis that $\beta = \beta_0$.

3.7 Modifications to statistical procedures when σ^2 is unknown

The previous derivations of the confidence interval and hypothesis testing procedure assumed σ^2 to be known. In empirical work, we rarely (if ever) know what σ^2 is, and hence the question arises as to what should be done when it is unknown. The answer is to replace it with an estimate. However, by doing so, one alteration of our previous derivations is required. In this section, we describe how σ^2 can be estimated and discuss this alteration.

The commonly used estimator for σ^2 is referred to as s^2. In order to motivate its formula, we remind the reader that the OLS residuals are given by

$$\widehat{\varepsilon}_i = Y_i - \widehat{\beta} X_i.$$

The OLS estimator of σ^2 is given by

$$s^2 = \frac{\sum \widehat{\varepsilon}_i^2}{N - 1}.$$

It can be shown that this is an unbiased estimator, and hence

$$E(s^2) = \sigma^2.$$

The proof of the previous statements is not provided since it involves probability theory that goes (slightly) beyond what is used elsewhere in this textbook. Nevertheless, the intuition for why s^2 is a good estimator of σ^2 is not hard to provide. Remember that, under the classical assumptions, we are assuming $E(\varepsilon_i^2) = \sigma^2$ which suggests that ε_i^2 might be a good estimator for σ^2. But we have N different errors, so why not use all of them in an estimator? This suggests using the average of the errors squared as an estimator for σ^2:

$$\frac{\sum \varepsilon_i^2}{N}.$$

Unfortunately, this estimator is not operational, since we do not observe ε_i. However, we can replace the errors with residuals, and thus obtain an estimator of

$$\frac{\sum \widehat{\varepsilon}_i^2}{N}.$$

This, in fact, can be shown to be the maximum likelihood estimator of σ^2 (see exercise 4 at the end of this chapter). The unbiased OLS estimator is almost equal to this expression. The slight difference (i.e. replacing N with $N-1$) is necessary to ensure that s^2 is an unbiased estimator. When we move from simple regression to multiple regression, the formula for s^2 changes slightly. If the multiple regression contains k explanatory variables and an intercept, then

$$s^2 = \frac{\sum \widehat{\varepsilon}_i^2}{N-k-1} = \frac{SSR}{N-k-1}.$$

In order to derive a confidence interval for β when σ^2 is unknown, we can simply replace the σ^2 with s^2 in the previous formulae. The derivation does not change, except that the distribution used to derive the probability statements is no longer normal. Rather it follows a Student t distribution. This distribution is explained in Appendix B, Definition B.12. It is very similar to the normal distribution, having the same bell shape as Figure 3.1. Just as with the normal, when one constructs a Z-score, the resulting variable has mean 0 and variance 1. One slight difference from the normal is that the statistical tables for the Student t distribution depend on its so-called *degrees of freedom*. For the purposes of this textbook, you do not have to understand what 'degrees of freedom' means. The key thing to note is it is something easy to calculate and tells you which row of the Student t statistical tables to look in (Appendix B, Definition B.12 has an example that shows you how to read Student t statistical tables).

To understand these points, remember that a first step in the derivation of the confidence interval was to say

$$Z = \frac{\widehat{\beta} - \beta}{\sqrt{\frac{\sigma^2}{\sum X_i^2}}} \text{ is } N(0,1).$$

When we replace σ^2 with s^2, this statement becomes

$$Z = \frac{\widehat{\beta} - \beta}{\sqrt{\frac{s^2}{\sum X_i^2}}} \text{ is } t_{N-1},$$

where t_{N-1} is the Student t distribution with $N - 1$ degrees of freedom. We now must use Student t statistical tables instead of the normal tables, and the value for $N - 1$ tells you what row in the Student t tables should be used.

As an example, suppose we have $N = 22$. With σ^2 known, we used the normal statistical tables to find $\Pr[-1.96 \leq Z \leq 1.96] = 0.95$, from which we derived the 95 % confidence interval:

$$\widehat{\beta} \pm 1.96\sqrt{\frac{\sigma^2}{\sum X_i^2}}.$$

With σ^2 unknown and replaced with s^2, we have to look in the t_{20} row of the Student t statis- tical tables. From this we find $\Pr[-2.08 \leq Z \leq 2.08] = 0.95$, from which we can derive the 95 % confidence interval

$$\widehat{\beta} \pm 2.08\sqrt{\frac{s^2}{\sum X_i^2}}.$$

Just as with confidence intervals, hypothesis testing about β when σ^2 is unknown involves taking the preceding formulae, which were calculated assuming σ^2 to be known, and replacing σ^2 with s^2. Critical values must be obtained from the Student t statistical tables, instead of the normal. That is, assuming σ^2 to be known, we had the test statistic

$$Z = \frac{\widehat{\beta} - \beta_0}{\sqrt{\frac{\sigma^2}{\sum X_i^2}}},$$

which was $N(0, 1)$. Now (with σ^2 unknown) we have the test statistic

$$t = \frac{\widehat{\beta} - \beta_0}{\sqrt{\frac{s^2}{\sum X_i^2}}},$$

which is t_{N-1}, where t_{N-1} is the Student t distribution with $N - 1$ degrees of freedom. In Chapter 2, we referred to this test statistic as the t-statistic (or the t-ratio). This terminology is adopted since the test statistic has a Student-t distribution. To be consistent with this terminology, we have called this statistic t instead of Z.

To continue our example, suppose we have $N = 22$. With σ^2 known, we used the normal statistical tables to find $\Pr[-1.96 \leq Z \leq 1.96] = 0.95$, from which we obtained the critical value of 1.96 which was relevant for a hypothesis test with a 5 % level of significance. With σ^2 unknown and replaced with s^2, we have to look in the row of the Student t statistical tables for 21 degrees of freedom. From this we find $\Pr[-2.08 \leq t \leq 2.08] = 0.95$, from which we obtain the critical value of 2.08.

This completes our description of how the test of $H_0: \beta = \beta_0$ can be carried out. However, we remind the reader that all relevant computer packages now present P-values for testing $H_0 : \beta = 0$. This means you do not need to look up critical values in statistical tables. Remember that the *P*-value equals the smallest level of significance at which you can reject H_0. Hence, if you are using a 5 % level of significance, you can reject H_0 if the *P*-value is less than 0.05.

3.8 Chapter summary

This chapter has presented an introduction to the statistical methods that are used by econometricians. It showed how econometricians make probabilistic assumptions about how the data are generated. These assumptions are then used to derive properties of estimators, confidence intervals, and hypothesis testing procedures. In order to keep the derivations simple, we worked with the simple regression model (without an intercept). Results for the multiple regression model are intuitively similar, but the derivations are messier. The expected value and variance operators were the major tools used in this chapter.

The major points and derivations covered in this chapter include:

1. The manner in which the normal distribution (which is characterized by a mean and variance) is used in the context of the simple regression model.
2. The introduction of the classical assumptions, from which all else in this chapter is derived.
3. The properties of the OLS estimator, including a proof that it is unbiased and a derivation of its distribution $\left(\text{i.e. } \widehat{\beta} \text{ is } N\left(\beta, \frac{\sigma^2}{\sum X_i^2}\right) \right)$.
4. The Gauss–Markov theorem which says OLS is BLUE under the classical assumptions.
5. The introduction of maximum likelihood estimation, including a proof that the maximum likelihood estimator of β is equivalent to the OLS estimator.
6. The derivation of a confidence interval for β (assuming σ^2 is known).
7. The derivation of a test of the hypothesis that $\beta = 0$ (assuming σ^2 is known).
8. The OLS estimator of σ^2.
9. How the confidence interval and hypothesis test are modified when σ^2 is unknown.
10. An appendix to this chapter providing an introduction to asymptotic theory in the regression model. Asymptotic theory is used to investigate the properties of estimators as $N \rightarrow \infty$.
11. Asymptotic theory can be used to relax the classical assumptions that the errors are normally distributed and that the explanatory variable is fixed. Provided the explanatory variable is uncorrelated with the error, $\widehat{\beta}$ is asymptotically normal, and thus the confidence intervals and hypothesis testing procedures derived in the body of the chapter are still approximately valid.

Exercises

We remind the reader that Appendix B: Probability Basics provides a review of concepts and definitions used in these exercises.

1. This exercise offers some practice at using statistical tables. See Appendix B, Definitions B.10–B.13 for definitions of distributions and more examples.

   (a) Suppose $X \sim N(-10, 16)$. Calculate $\Pr(X \leq -14)$.
   (b) Suppose you have a test statistic, X, that under H_0, has a chi-square distribution with 20 degrees of freedom. In your dataset, the test statistic is calculated to be 30. Do you reject H_0 at the 5 % level of significance? Do you reject H_0 at the 10 % level of significance?
   (c) Suppose you have a test statistic, X, that, under a certain hypothesis H_0 has a t_{10} distribution. Using your dataset, the test statistic is calculated to be 3.0. Do you reject H_0 at the 5 % level of significance? Do you reject H_0 at the 1 % level of significance?
   (d) Suppose you have a test statistic, X, that, under a certain hypothesis H_0 has an $F_{2,60}$ distribution. In your dataset, the test statistic is calculated to be 20. Do you reject H_0 at the 5 % level of significance?

2. Let Y_i for $i = 1, \ldots, N$ be a random sample from a probability distribution with mean μ and variance 1 (i.e. $E(Y_i) = \mu$ and $var(Y_i) = 1$ for $i = 1, \ldots, N$). Interest centres on estimating μ, and five different estimators are considered:

$$\widehat{\mu}_1 = \frac{\sum_{i=1}^N Y_i}{N},$$

$$\widehat{\mu}_2 = \frac{Y_1 + Y_N}{2},$$

$$\widehat{\mu}_3 = \frac{1}{2}\left[\frac{\sum_{i=1}^{N_1} Y_i}{N_1} + \frac{\sum_{i=N_1+1}^N Y_i}{N - N_1}\right], \text{ where } 1 < N_1 < N,$$

$$\widehat{\mu}_4 = \frac{\sum_{i=1}^N Y_i}{N - 1},$$

$$\widehat{\mu}_5 = Y_1 + \frac{\sum_{i=2}^N Y_i}{N - 1}.$$

   (a) Which of these are unbiased estimators for μ?
   (b) The term 'asymptotically unbiased' means that an estimator becomes unbiased as N goes to ∞. Which of these is an asymptotically unbiased estimator of μ?
   (c) Derive the variance of each of the estimators that you found to be unbiased in part (a).

(d) Use the concept of efficiency and your results from part (c) to discuss which estimator is best.

(e) Show that the set-up in this question is equivalent to the linear regression model with only an intercept (or equivalently, the simple regression model discussed in this chapter with $X_i = 1$ for $i = 1, \ldots, N$), where μ plays the role of the intercept (and the error variance in the regression model is set to 1).

(f) Using part (e), what does the Gauss–Markov theorem say is the best linear unbiased estimator for μ?

3. The simple linear regression model is given by

$$Y_i = \beta X_i + \varepsilon_i.$$

Assume that the classical assumptions hold.

(a) Consider an estimator for β:

$$\widetilde{\beta} = \frac{\sum Y_i}{\sum X_i}.$$

Is this an unbiased estimator for β?

(b) Calculate $var(\widetilde{\beta})$.

(c) Compare $\widetilde{\beta}$ with the OLS estimator $\widehat{\beta}$. Use the concept of efficiency and your results from the previous parts of the question to discuss which estimator you think is best. Hint: To simplify the derivations, you may use the following result:

$$\frac{1}{\sum X_i^2} < \frac{N}{\left(\sum X_i\right)^2}.$$

4. In the body of the chapter, we used the classical assumptions to derive the maximum likelihood estimator for β, assuming that σ^2 was known. This question asks you to extend these results to the case where σ^2 is unknown.

(a) What is the likelihood function, $L(\beta, \sigma^2)$, that treats both β and σ^2 as being unknown?

(b) Show that the maximum likelihood estimator of β is still $\widehat{\beta}$, the OLS estimator, and that the maximum likelihood estimator for σ^2, which we denote by $\widehat{\sigma}^2$, is

$$\widehat{\sigma}^2 = \frac{\sum \widehat{\varepsilon}_i^2}{N},$$

where $\widehat{\varepsilon}_i$ for $i = 1, \ldots, N$ are the OLS residuals.

(c) Use the fact that the OLS estimator of σ^2 (i.e. s^2) is unbiased to show that $\widehat{\sigma}^2$ is a biased estimator of σ^2. Show that the bias of $\widehat{\sigma}^2$ disappears as $N \to \infty$. Note that this implies $\widehat{\sigma}^2$ is asymptotically unbiased (see exercise 2 for a definition of this term).

5. Let Y_i for $i = 1, \ldots, N$ be a random sample from a normal probability distribution with mean μ and variance 1 (i.e. $E(Y_i) = \mu$ and $var(Y_i) = 1$ for $i = 1, \ldots, N$). Exercise 2 provides five different estimators for μ. Derive a 95 % confidence interval for μ for each of these estimators. Can the Gauss–Markov theorem be used to tell you which of these confidence intervals is narrower than the others?

Appendix 1: Proof of the Gauss–Markov theorem

Suppose we are working with the simple regression model (without intercept) and the classical assumptions hold. We want to find the estimator with minimum variance among the group of all estimators that are unbiased and linear in the dependent variable. Let us call an estimator that is linear and unbiased β^*. Since it is linear in the observations of the dependent variable, it must have the form

$$\beta^* = c_1 Y_1 + \cdots + c_N Y_N$$

for constants $c_1, \ldots, c_N$. Since β^* is unbiased, it must have $E(\beta^*) = \beta$. Using the properties of the expected value operator and the first and fifth of the classical assumptions, we can derive

$$\begin{aligned} E(\beta^*) &= E(c_1 Y_1 + \cdots + c_N Y_N) \\ &= c_1 E(Y_1) + \cdots + c_N E(Y_N) \\ &= c_1 \beta X_1 + \cdots + c_N \beta X_N \\ &= \beta \sum_{i=1}^{N} c_i X_i. \end{aligned}$$

An examination of this expression suggests that, for β^* to be unbiased we must have $\sum_{i=1}^{N} c_i X_i = 1$.

The variance of β^* can be calculated using the properties of the variance operator and the second and third of the classical assumptions:

$$\begin{aligned} var(\beta^*) &= var(c_1 Y_1 + \cdots + c_N Y_N) \\ &= c_1^2 var(Y_1) + \cdots + c_N^2 var(Y_N) \\ &= c_1^2 \sigma^2 + \cdots + c_N^2 \sigma^2 \\ &= \sigma^2 \sum_{i=1}^{N} c_i^2. \end{aligned}$$

Using these expressions, the question of finding the linear unbiased estimator that has minimum variance becomes a straightforward (albeit slightly messy) calculus problem.

That is, we want to choose $c_1, \ldots, c_N$ to minimize $\sigma^2 \sum_{i=1}^{N} c_i^2$, subject to the constraint that $\sum_{i=1}^{N} c_i X_i = 1$. This is a constrained optimization problem that can be solved using standard approaches (e.g. Lagrangian methods can be used). The solution turns out to be

$$c_j = \frac{X_j}{\sum_{i=1}^{N} X_i^2},$$

for $j = 1, \ldots, N$. Plugging this into the expression for β^*, we obtain

$$\begin{aligned}
\beta^* &= c_1 Y_1 + \ldots + c_N Y_N \\
&= \frac{X_1 Y_1}{\sum X_i^2} + \ldots + \frac{X_N Y_N}{\sum X_i^2} \\
&= \frac{\sum X_i Y_i}{\sum X_i^2} = \widehat{\beta}.
\end{aligned}$$

In other words, the linear unbiased estimator with minimum variance is the OLS estimator.

Appendix 2: Using asymptotic theory in the simple regression model

In the body of the text, we worked out the properties of the OLS estimator and derived confidence intervals and hypothesis testing procedures under the classical assumptions. One of the classical assumptions was that Y_i (or, equivalently, ε_i) was normally distributed. In this appendix, we show how asymptotic theory can be used to relax this assumption. Formally, we will do all derivations in this appendix without assuming the errors are normal. In fact, we will not make any assumptions about what the p.d.f. of the errors is. In empirical practice, we rarely know that our errors are normally distributed, so the ability to relax the normality assumption is important. We will use asymptotic methods which are based on what happens as sample size goes to infinity. An introduction to these is given in Appendix C at the end of this book, and the reader is referred to Appendix C for definitions of key concepts. We will show that the OLS estimator is consistent and that its asymptotic distribution is normal. Remember that our derivations of confidence intervals and hypothesis tests began with the fact that $\widehat{\beta}$ was $N\left(\beta, \frac{\sigma^2}{\sum X_i^2}\right)$. Here we will end up with a similar distributional result, except that it holds approximately. This can be used to derive (approximate) confidence intervals and hypothesis tests in exactly the same manner as in the body of the chapter. Thus, even if we do not assume the errors are normally distributed, we end up with the same confidence intervals and hypothesis testing procedures as we obtained before. Thus, in a sense, we can say that the normality assumption does not matter; we do not need it. However, it is important to note that the results derived in this appendix are asymptotic. Formally, they only hold when $N \to \infty$. In practice of course, the econometrician does not have an infinite sample size, but might only have $N = 50$ or 100 or $1\,000$. Therefore, when working with data, asymptotic results should always be treated as approximate.

Asymptotic theory also allows us to free up another of the classical assumptions: the one that says that X_i is not a random variable. In this appendix, we will assume that X_i is an independent and identically distributed (i.i.d.) random variable that is independent of the errors. We will denote the mean of X_i by μ_X and the variance of X_i by σ_X^2. All the remaining classical assumptions still hold.

In the chapter we worked with the OLS estimator

$$\widehat{\beta} = \frac{\sum_{i=1}^{N} X_i Y_i}{\sum_{i=1}^{N} X_i^2}$$

and we derived another way of writing it:

$$\widehat{\beta} = \beta + \frac{\sum X_i \varepsilon_i}{\sum X_i^2}. \qquad (*)$$

We use this expression in the following derivation.

Property 1: $\widehat{\beta}$ is a consistent estimator of β.

Proof:

$$\text{plim}(\widehat{\beta}) = \text{plim}\left(\beta + \frac{\sum X_i \varepsilon_i}{\sum X_i^2}\right)$$

$$= \beta + \text{plim}\left(\frac{\sum X_i \varepsilon_i}{\sum X_i^2}\right) \text{by Slutsky's theorem}$$

$$= \beta + \text{plim}\left(\frac{\frac{1}{N}\sum X_i \varepsilon_i}{\frac{1}{N}\sum X_i^2}\right)$$

$$= \beta + \frac{\text{plim}\left(\frac{1}{N}\sum X_i \varepsilon_i\right)}{\text{plim}\left(\frac{1}{N}\sum X_i^2\right)} \text{ by Slutsky's theorem.}$$

We can now use a law of large numbers (LLN) (see Appendix C) to figure out plim $\left(\frac{1}{N}\sum X_i \varepsilon_i\right)$. Remember that the basic idea of an LLN can be summarized in the phrase 'averages converge to expected values'. Note that expressions such as $\frac{1}{N}\sum X_i \varepsilon_i$ are averages, which suggests that the use of an LLN is appropriate. In the LLN in Appendix C, we used the notation Z_i. If we set $Z_i = X_i \varepsilon_i$, it can be confirmed that this definition for Z_i satisfies the conditions for using the LLN. Thus, it follows that

$$\text{plim}\left(\frac{1}{N}\sum X_i \varepsilon_i\right) = E(X_i \varepsilon_i) = 0,$$

where the last equals sign arises since the errors and explanatory variables are assumed to be independent of one another. Since zero divided by a positive number is still zero (i.e.

$\frac{1}{N}\sum X_i^2$ will be positive since squared numbers are positive), the proof is basically established and we can say $\text{plim}(\widehat{\beta}) = \beta$. However, for completeness, we also derive the denominator in the final expression for $\text{plim}(\widehat{\beta})$. The LLN can be used to say $\text{plim}\left(\frac{1}{N}\sum X_i^2\right) = E(X_i^2)$. Remember that the definition of the variance is $\text{var}(X_i) = E(X_i^2) - [E(X_i)]^2$. We can arrange this expression as $E(X_i^2) = \text{var}(X_i) + [E(X_i)]^2 = \sigma_X^2 + \mu_X^2$. Hence,

$$\text{plim}(\widehat{\beta}) = \beta + \frac{0}{\sigma_X^2 + \mu_X^2} = \beta,$$

and consistency is proven.

Property 2: The OLS estimator is asymptotically normal. As $N \to \infty$ we have

$$\sqrt{N}(\widehat{\beta} - \beta) \quad \text{is} \quad N\left(0, \frac{\sigma^2}{\sigma_X^2 + \mu_X^2}\right).$$

Proof:

Equation (*) can be written as

$$\sqrt{N}(\widehat{\beta} - \beta) = \sqrt{N}\frac{\sum X_i \varepsilon_i}{\sum X_i^2} = \sqrt{N}\frac{\frac{1}{N}\sum X_i \varepsilon_i}{\frac{1}{N}\sum X_i^2}.$$

Note that we have multiplied the top and bottom of the fraction by $\frac{1}{N}$ Multiplying the top and bottom of a fraction by the same thing does not change it. But now both top and bottom are written as averages, and so we can use our tools of asymptotic theory. The central limit theorem (CLT) (see Appendix C) can be used to say that the top of the fraction is asymptotically normal. That is, as $N \to \infty$,

$$\sqrt{N}\frac{1}{N}\sum X_i \varepsilon_i \quad \text{is} \quad N(0, \text{var}(X_i \varepsilon_i)).$$

Using the definition of the variance, the properties of the expected value operator (remember we have assumed X_i and ε_i are independent of one another, and hence we can use Appendix B, Theorem B.2), the fact that errors have mean zero, and (derived in the proof of property 1) the relationship $E(X_i^2) = \sigma_X^2 + \mu_X^2$, we obtain

$$\begin{aligned} \text{var}(X_i \varepsilon_i) &= E(X_i^2 \varepsilon_i^2) - [E(X_i \varepsilon_i)]^2 \\ &= E(X_i^2)E(\varepsilon_i^2) - [E(X_i)E(\varepsilon_i)]^2 \\ &= (\sigma_X^2 + \mu_X^2)\sigma^2 - [\mu_X 0]^2 \\ &= (\sigma_X^2 + \mu_X^2)\sigma^2. \end{aligned}$$

We have already shown (in our derivation of property 1) that

$$\text{plim}\left(\frac{1}{N}\sum X_i^2\right) = (\sigma_X^2 + \mu_X^2).$$

Using Cramer's theorem, we can combine the result from the CLT with the forms for $var(X_i\varepsilon_i)$ and $\text{plim}\left(\frac{1}{N}\sum X_i^2\right)$ to obtain

$$\sqrt{N}(\widehat{\beta} - \beta) \text{ converges to } N\left(0, \frac{(\sigma_X^2 + \mu_X^2)\sigma^2}{(\sigma_X^2 + \mu_X^2)^2}\right).$$

Cancelling out the common factor in the variance,

$$\sqrt{N}(\widehat{\beta} - \beta) \text{ converges to } N\left(0, \frac{\sigma^2}{(\sigma_X^2 + \mu_X^2)}\right)$$

and property 2 is proven.

Using the asymptotic results in practice

Property 2 tells us that, as $N \to \infty$, $\sqrt{N}(\widehat{\beta} - \beta)$ converges to a normal distribution. It is likely that, if N is large, this result will hold approximately. Thus, using the properties of the expected value and variance operators, we can rearrange property 2 to produce the following approximate result:

$$\widehat{\beta} \quad \text{is} \quad N\left(\beta, \frac{\sigma^2}{N(\sigma_X^2 + \mu_X^2)}\right).$$

The trouble with using this in practice is that $(\sigma_X^2 + \mu_X^2)$ is not known. However, we do know that $\text{plim}\left(\frac{1}{N}\sum X_i^2\right) = \sigma_X^2 + \mu_X^2$. Thus, $\frac{1}{N}\sum X_i^2$ is a consistent estimator of $\sigma_X^2 + \mu_X^2$. Plugging in this estimator, we obtain the approximate result

$$\widehat{\beta} \quad \text{is} \quad N\left(\beta, \frac{\sigma^2}{\sum X_i^2}\right).$$

But this is exactly the result we started with when deriving confidence intervals and hypothesis tests under the classical assumptions! Hence, all the derivations we performed in the body of the chapter hold (approximately). There is no point in repeating these derivations here. Rather, we end this appendix by repeating the key result: if we relax the assumptions of normality of errors, we get exactly the same confidence intervals and hypothesis tests as were derived under the classical assumptions (but here they hold approximately).

Endnotes

1. See Appendix B, Definition B.3, for a definition of a random variable.
2. A common notation is to use the Greek letters μ and σ^2 for mean and variance.
3. In probability theory, we work with random variables (e.g. Y) as well as realizations of random variables (i.e. the observed value of Y). In this book, to keep the notation simple, we use the same notation for both. The context will make clear which is being referred to.
4. This follows from a general mathematical rule: the value for x that maximizes a function $f(x)$ will be exactly the same as the value that maximizes $g[f(x)]$, where $g[.]$ is any increasing function.

CHAPTER 4

The Econometrics of the Multiple Regression Model

4.1 Introduction

In Chapter 2, we introduced the multiple regression model with k explanatory variables:

$$Y_i = \alpha + \beta_1 X_{1i} + \beta_2 X_{2i} + \cdots + \beta_k X_{ki} + \varepsilon_i,$$

where, as before, we are using i subscripts to denote individual observations and $i = 1, \ldots, N$. In Chapter 2, this model was discussed in a non-technical manner, focusing on how to interpret output produced by computer software packages. We discussed interpretation of regression coefficients, confidence intervals, hypothesis testing procedures, and a popular measure of fit, R^2. In addition, problems that arise with multiple regression, such as multicollinearity and omitted variables bias, were introduced. In short, Chapter 2 covered most of what you would need to know to do empirical work with the multiple regression model. Why, then, do we add another chapter on this model? A first reason is that the discussion in Chapter 2 was informal and non-technical. Formal exposition using some mathematics does provide additional insight beyond that given by informal discussions. Secondly, there are some issues that were difficult to discuss without using some probability theory. After Chapter 3, the reader should have knowledge of and familiarity with this theory.

In this chapter, we provide a more rigorous discussion of many of the topics covered in Chapter 2, especially issues relating to the choice of explanatory variables (e.g. omitted variables bias and multicollinearity). Some of the new issues discussed relate to hypothesis testing. In Chapter 3, we discussed hypothesis testing in the simple regression model. But all the hypotheses tested there involved one thing (e.g. testing whether the single coefficient equals zero using a t-statistic or whether the $R^2 = 0$ using an F-statistic). In the multiple regression model there are many other hypotheses (often involving several coefficients) that the researcher may want to test. Thus, in this chapter, we describe two additional approaches to hypothesis testing. The first of these involves F-statistics and is useful for testing multiple hypotheses about the regression coefficients. The second, likelihood ratio testing, can also be used to test multiple hypotheses about the regression coefficients, but has much wider applicability. Likelihood ratio testing can be used with a wide variety of models. We will introduce it here (in the context of the familiar regression model), but use it in several other places in this book. Finally, this chapter discusses selection of the appropriate functional form of a regression.

4.2   Basic results for the multiple regression model

In Chapter 3 we derived theoretical results using the simple regression model with classical assumptions. These are basically the same when we move to the multiple regression model

$$Y_i = \alpha + \beta_1 X_{1i} + \beta_2 X_{2i} + \cdots + \beta_k X_{ki} + \varepsilon_i.$$

The classical assumptions are as follows:

1. $E(\varepsilon_i) = 0$. Mean zero errors.
2. $var(\varepsilon_i) = E(\varepsilon_i^2) = \sigma^2$. Constant variance errors (homoskedasticity).
3. $cov(\varepsilon_i, \varepsilon_j) = 0$ for $i \neq j$. ε_i and ε_j are uncorrelated with one another.
4. ε_i is normally distributed.
5. $X_{1i}, \ldots, X_{ki}$ are fixed. They are not random variables.

Statistical results using the multiple regression model are basically the same as for the simple regression model. For instance, OLS is still unbiased and confidence intervals and hypothesis tests are derived in the same way. The Gauss–Markov theorem still says that, under the classical assumptions, OLS is the best linear unbiased estimator. The formulae do get messier,[1] but the basic insights and intuition are the same. For instance, with an intercept and two explanatory variables, we have

$$Y_i = \alpha + \beta_1 X_{1i} + \beta_2 X_{2i} + \varepsilon_i.$$

The OLS estimator is the one that minimizes the sum of squared residuals and turns out to be

$$\widehat{\beta}_1 = \frac{\left(\sum x_{1i} y_i\right)\left(\sum x_{2i}^2\right) - \left(\sum x_{2i} y_i\right)\left(\sum x_{1i} x_{2i}\right)}{\left(\sum x_{1i}^2\right)\left(\sum x_{2i}^2\right) - \left(\sum x_{1i} x_{2i}\right)^2},$$

$$\widehat{\beta}_2 = \frac{\left(\sum x_{2i} y_i\right)\left(\sum x_{1i}^2\right) - \left(\sum x_{1i} y_i\right)\left(\sum x_{1i} x_{2i}\right)}{\left(\sum x_{1i}^2\right)\left(\sum x_{2i}^2\right) - \left(\sum x_{1i} x_{2i}\right)^2},$$

$$\widehat{\alpha} = \overline{Y} - \widehat{\beta}_1 \overline{X}_1 - \widehat{\beta}_2 \overline{X}_2,$$

where variables with bars over them are means (e.g. $\overline{X}_2 = \frac{\Sigma X_{2i}}{N}$) and lower-case letters indicate deviations from means. That is,

$$y_i = Y_i - \overline{Y},$$
$$x_{1i} = X_{1i} - \overline{X}_1,$$
$$x_{2i} = X_{2i} - \overline{X}_2.$$

You can see how, even with two explanatory variables, the formulae are very cumbersome. With more explanatory variables, they become even more complicated. Nevertheless, the basic interpretation of the coefficients remains simple (i.e. 'β_j is the marginal effect of the jth explanatory variable on Y, holding all the other explanatory variables constant'). Confidence intervals and hypothesis testing procedures can be constructed as in Chapter 3 (the formulae differ slightly, but have exactly the same interpretation). It can be shown that OLS is unbiased (e.g. $E(\widehat{\beta}_j) = \beta_j$ for $j = 1, 2, 3$), etc. For these reasons, we do not repeat all the derivations we performed in Chapter 3.

There are some minor differences that are worth recording here. Firstly, the unbiased estimator for σ^2 has a slightly different formula to that in Chapter 3:

$$s^2 = \frac{\sum \widehat{\varepsilon}_i^2}{N - k - 1},$$

where

$$\widehat{\varepsilon}_i = Y_i - \widehat{\alpha} - \widehat{\beta}_1 X_{1i} - \cdots - \widehat{\beta}_k X_{ki}$$

are the OLS residuals from the multiple regression.

In the case where $k = 2$, the variance of the OLS estimators can be calculated as

$$var\left(\widehat{\beta}_1\right) = \frac{\sigma^2}{(1 - r^2) \sum x_{1i}^2},$$

$$var\left(\widehat{\beta}_2\right) = \frac{\sigma^2}{(1 - r^2) \sum x_{2i}^2},$$

where r is the correlation between X_1 and X_2. Just as with the simple regression model, in practice we replace σ^2 with s^2. This variance is used in the derivations of confidence intervals and hypothesis testing procedures. As an example (and a review), we will repeat the steps for how a t-test for whether $\beta_2 = 0$ can be done in the case where $k = 2$, even though the derivations are basically identical to those in Chapter 3. We begin with the case where σ^2 is known:

- Step 1: Specify a hypothesis, H_0.
  In our case, the hypothesis is $H_0\colon \beta_2 = 0$.
- Step 2: Specify a test statistic.
  For the hypothesis specified in step 1, a common test statistic is

$$Z = \frac{\widehat{\beta}_2 - \beta_2}{\sqrt{var\left(\widehat{\beta}_2\right)}} = \frac{\widehat{\beta}_2 - \beta_2}{\sqrt{\frac{\sigma^2}{(1-r^2)\sum x_{2i}^2}}}.$$

- Step 3: Figure out the distribution of the test statistic, assuming H_0 is true.
  Using the same derivation as in Chapter 3,

$$Z = \frac{\widehat{\beta}_2}{\sqrt{\frac{\sigma^2}{(1-r^2)\sum x_{2i}^2}}} \quad \text{is} \quad N(0,1).$$

- Step 4: Choose a level of significance.
  We will make the common choice of 5 % (i.e. 0.05).
- Step 5: Use steps 3 and 4 to obtain a critical value.
  Since Z is $N(0,1)$ and $\Pr[-1.96 \le Z \le 1.96] = 0.95$, the critical value is 1.96. Note that the probability statement used to derive the critical value is 0.95 which is 1 minus the level of significance.
- Step 6: Calculate your test statistic from step 2 and compare with the critical value from step 5. Reject H_0 if the absolute value of the test statistic is greater than the critical value (else accept H_0).
  Here this strategy amounts to rejecting H_0 if $|Z| > 1.96$.

As in Chapter 3, in order to derive a hypothesis testing procedure when σ^2 is unknown, we can simply replace the σ^2 with s^2 in the previous formulae. The derivation does not change, except that the distribution used to derive the probability statement is no longer normal. Rather it is a Student t distribution. That is, when we replace σ^2 with s^2 and use the Student t distribution, the key equation in step 3 becomes

$$t = \frac{\widehat{\beta}_2}{\sqrt{\frac{s^2}{(1-r^2)\sum x_{2i}^2}}} \quad \text{is} \quad t_{N-k-1}$$

where t_{N-k-1} is the Student t distribution with $N - k - 1$ degrees of freedom.

Thus, we end up with a t-statistic for testing $H_0\colon \beta_2 = 0$. Its formula is slightly different to the one derived in Chapter 3, and the critical value for the test will be taken from a different row of the Student t statistical tables. But all the steps in the derivations are the same.

From Chapter 2 you will remember the most popular measure of model fit, R^2. With multiple regression, it has the same definition as before:

$$R^2 = 1 - \frac{SSR}{TSS} = 1 - \frac{\sum \widehat{\varepsilon}_i^2}{\sum (Y_i - \overline{Y})^2},$$

and can be interpreted as the proportion of the variability of the dependent variable that can be explained by the explanatory variables.

However, there is one issue that arises when using R^2 in multiple regression and necessitates the introduction of a modified version of R^2 that is called *adjusted* R^2 and denoted by $\overline{R}^2$. This issue is that adding new explanatory variables to a model will always increase the R^2 even if the new variables are insignificant. Why is this so? R^2 is a measure of fit. By adding a new explanatory variable, there is no way fit can be made worse. After all, the regression could always set the coefficient on the new variable to zero and achieve exactly the same fit as before. In general, the fit gets better by adding a new explanatory variable. More formally, OLS proceeds by finding the coefficient values that yield the smallest SSR. By adding a new explanatory variable, OLS has one extra dimension for choosing the minimum values of SSR, which means the SSR gets smaller and, thus, R^2 gets larger.

As we have seen in Chapter 2, one way of deciding which explanatory variables belong in a regression is to use hypothesis testing procedures, deleting variables that are insignificant and including those that are significant. It is tempting to think that another way of deciding which explanatory variables belong is to use R^2 and to include explanatory variables that increase the fit of the model. The line of argument in the preceding paragraph says that this is not a good strategy as it would lead to including every potential explanatory variable regardless of whether it is significant. Therefore, R^2 should not be used to decide whether to add a new variable to a regression. However, there is a measure closely related to R^2 that is calculated in econometric computer packages and is occasionally used to choose explanatory variables. This measure is $\overline{R}^2$. It is similar to R^2 but does not always rise when new explanatory variables are added. If you add a new variable and $\overline{R}^2$ increases, you can be confident this new variable should be included as an explanatory variable in the regression. If you have two regressions (with the same dependent variable but different explanatory variables), then the one with the higher $\overline{R}^2$ is the better one.

Adjusted R^2 is defined as

$$\overline{R}^2 = 1 - \frac{\frac{SSR}{N-k-1}}{\frac{TSS}{N-1}} = 1 - \frac{s^2}{\frac{1}{N-1}\sum (Y_i - \overline{Y})^2}.$$

Note that s^2 is the estimate of σ^2 and $\frac{1}{N-1}\Sigma(Y_i - \overline{Y})^2$ is the sample variance, so $\overline{R}^2$ includes a fraction that measures the size of the variance of the errors relative to the variance of the dependent variable. Hence, it has a similar motivation to R^2. But it cannot be interpreted simply as reflecting the proportion of the variability of the dependent variable that can be explained by the explanatory variables. Nevertheless, for reasons we will not prove here, it does not necessarily increase when new explanatory variables are added and is sometimes used as a model selection device.

In summary, there are two measures of fit that are commonly used in empirical work: R^2 and $\overline{R}^2$. Each has advantages and disadvantages. R^2 has a nice simple interpretation as a measure of the proportion of the variation in the dependent variable that is explained by the explanatory variables, but it cannot be used for choosing between models. $\overline{R}^2$ does not have this nice interpretation but can be used for choosing between models.

4.3   Issues relating to the choice of explanatory variables

In Chapter 2, several issues relating to the question of which explanatory variables should be chosen in a multiple regression model were discussed. One issue was that it was good to include all variables that help explain the dependent variable. This consideration suggests you should include as many explanatory variables as possible. The second is that including irrelevant variables (i.e. ones with no explanatory power) will lead to less precise estimates. This consideration suggests you should include as few explanatory variables as possible. In Chapter 2 it was argued that playing off these two competing considerations is an important aspect of any empirical exercise. Hypothesis testing procedures can offer a great deal of help with this. That is, if a hypothesis test indicates an explanatory variable is insignificant, then it can be deleted from the regression model. However, we offered only an informal discussion of why these two issues pulled in the directions they did. In this section, we go through some formal derivations to justify our informal discussion of Chapter 2 and provide further insight into these issues.

A third issue discussed in Chapter 2 was multicollinearity. This is a problem that arises when the explanatory variables are strongly correlated with one another. For this issue, too, we provide formal derivations to tighten up and go beyond the informal discussion of Chapter 2.

4.3.1   Omitted variables bias

To show what happens when you omit an explanatory variable that should be included, we will assume that the true model is the multiple regression model with two explanatory variables:

$$Y_i = \alpha + \beta_1 X_{1i} + \beta_2 X_{2i} + \varepsilon_i,$$

and the classical assumptions hold. The results from the section above show that the correct OLS estimate you should be using is

$$\widehat{\beta}_1 = \frac{\left(\sum x_{1i} y_i\right)\left(\sum x_{2i}^2\right) - \left(\sum x_{2i} y_i\right)\left(\sum x_{1i} x_{2i}\right)}{\left(\sum x_{1i}^2\right)\left(\sum x_{2i}^2\right) - \left(\sum x_{1i} x_{2i}\right)^2},$$

where we remind the reader that variables with small letters are denoting deviations from means.

Suppose, however, that you mistakenly omit the second explanatory variable from the regression and instead work with

$$Y_i = \alpha + \beta_1 X_{1i} + \varepsilon_i.$$

A simple extension of the derivations of Chapter 3 can be used to show that the OLS estimator for β_1 is

$$\tilde{\beta}_1 = \frac{\sum x_{1i} y_i}{\sum x_{1i}^2},$$

and we are labeling this estimator of β_1 as $\tilde{\beta}_1$ to distinguish it from the correct OLS estimator. Of course, $\tilde{\beta}_1$ and $\hat{\beta}_1$ are different from one another, which is a strong warning signal that we are doing something wrong by omitting an explanatory variable that should be included. In fact, it turns out that $\tilde{\beta}_1$ is biased.

In order to show that $\tilde{\beta}_1$ is biased, we need some preliminary calculations. Firstly, note that

$$\overline{Y} = \frac{\sum Y_i}{N} = \frac{\sum(\alpha + \beta_1 X_{1i} + \beta_2 X_{2i} + \varepsilon_i)}{N}$$
$$= \alpha + \beta_1 \overline{X}_1 + \beta_2 \overline{X}_2 + \overline{\varepsilon}.$$

Secondly, we can use this equation to write

$$y_i = Y_i - \overline{Y}$$
$$= (\alpha + \beta_1 X_{1i} + \beta_2 X_{2i} + \varepsilon_i) - (\alpha + \beta_1 \overline{X}_1 + \beta_2 \overline{X}_2 + \overline{\varepsilon})$$
$$= \beta_1 x_{1i} + \beta_2 x_{2i} + \varepsilon_i - \overline{\varepsilon}.$$

Thirdly, we can substitute y_i by this expression into the formula for $\tilde{\beta}_1$:

$$\tilde{\beta}_1 = \frac{\sum x_{1i}(\beta_1 x_{1i} + \beta_2 x_{2i} + \varepsilon_i - \overline{\varepsilon})}{\sum x_{1i}^2}$$
$$= \frac{\beta_1 \sum x_{1i}^2}{\sum x_{1i}^2} + \frac{\beta_2 \sum x_{1i} x_{2i}}{\sum x_{1i}^2} + \frac{\sum x_{1i}(\varepsilon_i - \overline{\varepsilon})}{\sum x_{1i}^2}$$
$$= \beta_1 + \frac{\beta_2 \sum x_{1i} x_{2i}}{\sum x_{1i}^2} + \frac{\sum x_{1i}(\varepsilon_i - \overline{\varepsilon})}{\sum x_{1i}^2}.$$

Finally, we can establish the biasedness of $\tilde{\beta}_1$ by taking the expected value of both sides of this equation:

$$E\left(\tilde{\beta}_1\right) = E\left(\beta_1 + \frac{\beta_2 \sum x_{1i}x_{2i}}{\sum x_{1i}^2} + \frac{\sum x_{1i}(\varepsilon_i - \bar{\varepsilon})}{\sum x_{1i}^2}\right)$$
$$= \beta_1 + \frac{\beta_2 \sum x_{1i}x_{2i}}{\sum x_{1i}^2},$$

where the derivation above uses the fact that the expected values of constants are the constants (and, remember, the classical assumptions imply the explanatory variables are constant) and the expected values of the errors are zero. Thus, $E(\tilde{\beta}_1) \neq \beta_1$, and, if we omit an explanatory variable in the regression that should be included, we obtain a biased estimate of the coefficient on the included explanatory variable. This is referred to as omitted variables bias. Although we have derived it in the case where the true model contains two explanatory variables, it holds in models with any number of explanatory models. Omitted variables bias even occurs in the more complicated models we will discuss in future chapters. Thus, it is quite important in any model not to omit important explanatory variables that should be included.

To provide some more insight into the problem of omitted variables bias, it is worthwhile examining the previous equation more closely. It can be seen that omitted variables bias does not exist if either $\beta_2 = 0$ or $\frac{\sum x_{1i}x_{2i}}{\sum x_{1i}^2} = 0$. The first of these cases is not very interesting since, if $\beta_2 = 0$, then X_2 does not belong in the true regression to begin with, and thus an important explanatory variable is not being omitted. The second case provides more insight since $\frac{\sum x_{1i}x_{2i}}{\sum x_{1i}^2}$ is closely related to the correlation between X_1 and X_2 (which we will call r). In fact, if you look at the equation for r in Chapter 1, you can see that $\frac{\sum x_{1i}x_{2i}}{\sum x_{1i}^2} = 0$ if $r = 0$. Thus, the problem of omitted variables does not arise if the omitted explanatory variable is uncorrelated with the included explanatory variable. This result was discussed in Chapter 2, but now we have proved it.

Note also that $\frac{\sum x_{1i}x_{2i}}{\sum x_{1i}^2} > 0$ if $r > 0$ and $\frac{\sum x_{1i}x_{2i}}{\sum x_{1i}^2} < 0$ if $r < 0$. Thus, we can use our derivations to talk about the sign of the omitted variables bias. If $\beta_2 > 0$, then we can say 'if the omitted explanatory variable is positively correlated with the included explanatory variable, then the coefficient on the included explanatory variable will be upward biased'. Or, if $\beta_2 < 0$, then we can say 'if the omitted explanatory variable is positively correlated with the included explanatory variable, then the coefficient on the included explanatory variable will be downward biased'.

Since we do not know what β_2 is, such statements have to be used with caution. Nevertheless, this kind of result can be useful when interpreting empirical results. Consider for instance, our housing dataset where the dependent variable was the price of a house and the explanatory variables consisted of housing characteristics including the size of the lot the house was on. A common house-selling cliche is that the three most important house characteristics are 'location, location, and location'. Let $X_1 =$ lot size and $X_2 =$ desirability of location. Suppose (as is common in many empirical studies of house prices), that we do not have data on X_2. In this case, we would likely run into the problem of omitted variables bias since we do not have a 'desirability of location' explanatory variable that is sure to be important. We would expect the effect of this variable on house price to be positive (i.e. $\beta_2 > 0$). We would also expect desirability of location to be positively associated with lot size (i.e. desirable neighborhoods usually have big houses on big lots) and, thus, $\frac{\sum x_{1i}x_{2i}}{\sum x_{1i}^2} > 0$. We could use these facts to argue that the coefficient on X_1 is likely to be upward biased.

4.3.2 Inclusion of irrelevant explanatory variables

Now let us flip the role of the two models discussed in the previous section so that

$$Y_i = \alpha + \beta_1 X_{1i} + \varepsilon_i$$

is the true model (and the classical assumptions hold), but you mistakenly include an irrelevant variable and work with

$$Y_i = \alpha + \beta_1 X_{1i} + \beta_2 X_{2i} + \varepsilon_i.$$

This implies that you use

$$\widetilde{\beta}_1 = \frac{\left(\sum x_{1i}y_i\right)\left(\sum x_{2i}^2\right) - \left(\sum x_{2i}y_i\right)\left(\sum x_{1i}x_{2i}\right)}{\left(\sum x_{1i}^2\right)\left(\sum x_{2i}^2\right) - \left(\sum x_{1i}x_{2i}\right)^2}$$

when you should have been using

$$\widehat{\beta}_1 = \frac{\sum x_{1i}y_i}{\sum x_{1i}^2}.$$

The Gauss–Markov theorem tells us that $\widehat{\beta}_1$ is the best linear unbiased estimator. Thus, it has a smaller variance than any other unbiased estimator. If we can show that $\widetilde{\beta}_1$ is unbiased, then we can call on the Gauss–Markov theorem to tell us that $var(\widetilde{\beta}_1) > var(\widehat{\beta}_1)$, which proves that including irrelevant explanatory variables will lead to less precise estimates.

Thus, it is important to prove $\widetilde{\beta}_1$ to be unbiased. The proof proceeds as follows. First, a derivation nearly identical to the one in the previous section establishes that

$$y_i = Y_i - \overline{Y} = \beta_1 x_{1i} + (\varepsilon_i - \overline{\varepsilon}).$$

Placing this expression for y_i into the formula for $\tilde{\beta}_1$ yields

$$\tilde{\beta}_1 = \frac{\left(\sum x_{1i}[\beta_1 x_{1i} + (\varepsilon_i - \bar{\varepsilon})]\right)\left(\sum x_{2i}^2\right) - \left(\sum x_{2i}[\beta_1 x_{1i} + (\varepsilon_i - \bar{\varepsilon})]\right)\left(\sum x_{1i}x_{2i}\right)}{\left(\sum x_{1i}^2\right)\left(\sum x_{2i}^2\right) - \left(\sum x_{1i}x_{2i}\right)^2}$$

$$= \frac{\beta_1\left[\left(\sum x_{1i}^2\right)\left(\sum x_{2i}^2\right) - \left(\sum x_{1i}x_{2i}\right)^2\right]}{\left(\sum x_{1i}^2\right)\left(\sum x_{2i}^2\right) - \left(\sum x_{1i}x_{2i}\right)^2}$$

$$+ \frac{\left(\sum x_{1i}(\varepsilon_i - \bar{\varepsilon})\right)\left(\sum x_{2i}^2\right) - \left(\sum x_{2i}(\varepsilon_i - \bar{\varepsilon})\right)\left(\sum x_{1i}x_{2i}\right)}{\left(\sum x_{1i}^2\right)\left(\sum x_{2i}^2\right) - \left(\sum x_{1i}x_{2i}\right)^2}$$

$$= \beta_1 + \frac{\left(\sum x_{1i}(\varepsilon_i - \bar{\varepsilon})\right)\left(\sum x_{2i}^2\right) - \left(\sum x_{2i}(\varepsilon_i - \bar{\varepsilon})\right)\left(\sum x_{1i}x_{2i}\right)}{\left(\sum x_{1i}^2\right)\left(\sum x_{2i}^2\right) - \left(\sum x_{1i}x_{2i}\right)^2}.$$

Taking expected values of both sides of this equation:

$$E\left(\tilde{\beta}_1\right) = E\left[\beta_1 + \frac{\left(\sum x_{1i}(\varepsilon_i - \bar{\varepsilon})\right)\left(\sum x_{2i}^2\right) - \left(\sum x_{2i}(\varepsilon_i - \bar{\varepsilon})\right)\left(\sum x_{1i}x_{2i}\right)}{\left(\sum x_{1i}^2\right)\left(\sum x_{2i}^2\right) - \left(\sum x_{1i}x_{2i}\right)^2}\right]$$

$$= \beta_1 + E\left[\frac{\left(\sum x_{1i}(\varepsilon_i - \bar{\varepsilon})\right)\left(\sum x_{2i}^2\right) - \left(\sum x_{2i}(\varepsilon_i - \bar{\varepsilon})\right)\left(\sum x_{1i}x_{2i}\right)}{\left(\sum x_{1i}^2\right)\left(\sum x_{2i}^2\right) - \left(\sum x_{1i}x_{2i}\right)^2}\right]$$

$$= \beta_1,$$

where the final line in the equation can be derived using the fact that the expected values of the errors are zero and the explanatory variables are assumed to be fixed. Thus, including irrelevant variables does not cause OLS estimates to be biased, but (via the Gauss–Markov theorem) it does mean that the resulting estimates will be less precise than they could be.

We remind the reader that the message of the omitted variables bias is that you should always try to include all those explanatory variables that could affect the dependent variable. The message of the present section is that you should always try to not include irrelevant variables, since this will decrease the accuracy of the estimation of all the coefficients (even the ones that are not irrelevant). In practice, you should begin with as many explanatory variables as possible, then use hypothesis testing procedures to discard those that are irrelevant (and then rerun the regression with the new set of explanatory variables).

4.3.3   Multicollinearity

A final issue related to the choice of explanatory variables is multicollinearity. This topic was discussed in an intuitive manner in Chapter 2. Remember that multicollinearity is said to occur if the explanatory variables are very highly correlated with one another.

Informally speaking, if two variables are highly correlated, they contain roughly the same information. The OLS estimator has trouble estimating two separate marginal effects for two such highly correlated variables, and the individual coefficients end up being imprecisely estimated (even though the two explanatory variables may jointly have considerable explanatory power). The most common solution to multicollinearity is to drop one of the highly correlated explanatory variables. These points were made in Chapter 2. In this section, we offer a few additional technical details to see why these problems arise.

In Section 4.2 we presented the variances of the OLS estimators in the multiple regression model with two explanatory variables:

$$var\left(\widehat{\beta}_1\right) = \frac{s^2}{(1 - r^2)\sum x_{1i}^2},$$

$$var\left(\widehat{\beta}_2\right) = \frac{s^2}{(1 - r^2)\sum x_{2i}^2}.$$

These variances figure crucially in many derivations (e.g. the derivations of hypothesis testing procedures and confidence intervals). Note that the correlation between the two explanatory variables, r, appears in the formulae. In the extreme case of perfect multicollinearity ($r = 1$ or $r = -1$), these variances cannot be calculated (i.e. to calculate them would involve dividing by zero). In practice, this means that the computer will instantly detect a perfect multicollinearity problem by giving an error message.

It is rare to get a case of perfect multicollinearity, and, if you do, the computer will reveal the problem by giving an error message. Much more common is to have explanatory variables that are strongly, but not perfectly, correlated with one another. That is, it is common to have r being near 1 or -1. Note that these cases imply $(1 - r^2)$ will be near zero and, thus, the variances of $\widehat{\beta}_1$ and $\widehat{\beta}_2$ will become very large. If you look back on Chapters 2 and 3, you can see how these variances feed into the formulae for both confidence intervals and t-statistics.[2] The statistical results in those earlier chapters related to the simple regression model, but, as emphasized at the beginning of this chapter, very similar formulae hold for the multiple regression model. For instance, the t-statistic for testing $H_0: \beta_2 = 0$ is

$$t = \frac{\widehat{\beta}_2}{\sqrt{var\left(\widehat{\beta}_2\right)}}.$$

An examination of such formulae will convince you that, if multicollinearity occurs and the variances of $\widehat{\beta}_1$ and $\widehat{\beta}_2$ become very large, then t-statistics will become small and confidence intervals will become wide. Thus, we have formally shown how multicollinearity causes inaccurate estimates and hypothesis tests will tend to indicate that coefficients such as β_1 and β_2 are insignificant.

Note, however, that multicollinearity might have no effect on R^2. To make this point most clearly, we can rewrite its formula as

$$R^2 = 1 - \frac{SSR}{TSS} = 1 - \frac{(N - k - 1)s^2}{TSS}.$$

The correlation between the two explanatory variables does not appear in this formula. It is possible for the regression to fit very well (i.e. for s^2 to be small) even if multicollinearity is present.

Thus, we have shown the common symptoms of a multicollinearity problem: some or all explanatory variables appear to be insignificant, even though the model is fitting well (has a high R^2). We have derived our results using a multiple regression model with two variables, but the same sort of derivations and results hold with more explanatory variables. There are quite sophisticated methods for investigating if multicollinearity is a problem. However, in most empirical work, a careful examination of a correlation matrix for the explanatory variables is adequate. That is, if you find the correlation between any two of your explanatory variables to be very high, then you are facing a multicollinearity problem. This advice does not define what we mean by a correlation being 'high'. There is no hard and fast rule. As a rough guideline, if you find $|r| > 0.9$ for any pair of explanatory variables, then you probably have a multicollinearity problem. As discussed in Chapter 2, the usual solution to a multicollinearity problem is to drop one of the highly correlated variables. The reader is referred to this earlier discussion for an example and further discussion.

4.4 Hypothesis testing in the multiple regression model

In the previous section, we derived some results for the multiple regression model with two explanatory variables. In this section, we will return to the general form for the multiple regression model:

$$Y_i = \alpha + \beta_1 X_{1i} + \beta_2 X_{2i} + \cdots + \beta_k X_{ki} + \varepsilon_i.$$

The classical assumptions are assumed to hold. As we have seen, testing whether individual explanatory variables have explanatory power involves doing a t-test of $H_0: \beta_j = 0$ (where β_j denotes any of the coefficients). However, there are many times when the researcher is interested in tests involving more than one of the coefficients. Two approaches are discussed in this section. The first of these, F-tests, are suitable for testing hypotheses involving any number of linear combinations of regression coefficients. The second, likelihood ratio tests, can do the same, but can also be used for non-linear restrictions and can be used with models other than the regression model.

4.4.1 *F*-tests

In Chapter 2, we presented a test for whether $R^2 = 0$ to see whether the explanatory variables jointly have explanatory power. This is equivalent to a test of the hypothesis

$$H_0 : \beta_1 = \cdots = \beta_k = 0.$$

Note that this hypothesis involves many restrictions (i.e. $\beta_1 = 0$, $\beta_2 = 0$, $\beta_3 = 0$, etc., up to β_k), so falls in the set-up discussed in this section. It is worth stressing that testing the hypothesis $H_0 : \beta_1 = \cdots = \beta_k = 0$ is not the same as testing the k individual hypotheses $H_0 : \beta_1 = 0$ and $H_0 : \beta_2 = 0$ to $H_0 : \beta_k = 0$.

In Chapter 2, we introduced an *F*-statistic for testing this hypothesis. For the multiple regression model with k explanatory variables and an intercept, this has the form

$$F = \frac{R^2}{1 - R^2} \frac{N - k - 1}{k}.$$

Remember, when testing, you work out the distribution of your test statistic assuming H_0 is true. Then you get a critical value for the test from the resulting distribution. In this case, F has an $F_{k, N-k-1}$ distribution. Statistical tables for the *F*-distribution are provided at the end of this textbook and Appendix B gives relevant definitions and examples of how statistical tables can be read. Alternatively, computer packages (like Excel, Stata or PC Give) will provide *P*-values for this test. Remember that, if the *P*-value is less than 0.05, then you reject H_0 at the 5 % level of significance.

This is an example of an *F*-test. However, *F*-tests can be used with many other hypotheses. Formally, *F*-tests can be used for any hypothesis that can be written as a linear combination of the regression coefficients. To illustrate what is meant by this, we provide some examples for the multiple regression model with three explanatory variables. To introduce some terminology, we will refer to the original multiple regression model as the *unrestricted model*. We will refer to the regression with the restrictions implied by the hypothesis imposed as the *restricted model*.

Thus, the unrestricted model is

$$Y_i = \alpha + \beta_1 X_{1i} + \beta_2 X_{2i} + \beta_3 X_{3i} + \varepsilon_i.$$

An example of a hypothesis one might test using an *F*-test is

$$H_0 : \beta_1 = \beta_2 = 0.$$

Note that this hypothesis involves two restrictions (i.e. $\beta_1 = 0$ and $\beta_2 = 0$) and they are linear functions. That is, any linear function of the regression coefficients can be written as $a\beta_1 + b\beta_2 + c\beta_3 = d$ for constants a, b, c, and d. Zero restrictions such as $\beta_2 = 0$ are thus linear functions (e.g. $\beta_2 = 0$ has $a = c = d = 0$, $b = 1$).

The resulting restricted model is

$$Y_i = \alpha + \beta_3 X_{3i} + \varepsilon_i.$$

F-tests can also be used to test more general hypotheses such as

$$H_0: \beta_1 = 0, \beta_2 + \beta_3 = 1.$$

Noting that the second restriction can be written as $\beta_2 = 1 - \beta_3$, we can write the restricted model as

$$Y_i - X_{2i} = \alpha + \beta_3(X_{3i} - X_{2i}) + \varepsilon_i.$$

This restricted model is just a simple regression with the dependent variable being $Y - X_2$, an intercept, and $(X_3 - X_2)$ being the explanatory variable.

In general, you can show that for any set of linear restrictions on the unrestricted model you can write out a new restricted model that is still a linear regression model but with diff- erent dependent and/or explanatory variables. For testing such hypotheses, the following test statistic can be used:

$$F = \frac{(SSR_R - SSR_{UR})/q}{SSR_{UR}/(N - k - 1)},$$

where SSR is the familiar sum of squared residuals and the subscripts UR and R distinguish between the SSR from the 'unrestricted' and 'restricted' regression models. The number of restrictions being tested is q (e.g. $q = 2$ in the examples above). Since $SSR_R > SSR_{UR}$ (i.e. the model with fewer restrictions can always achieve the lower SSR), it can be seen that F is positive. Large values of F indicate that H_0 is incorrect. We must work out its distribution in order to obtain a critical value to determine how 'large' F must be in order to reject H_0. That is, as with any hypothesis test, you calculate the test statistic (here F) and compare it with a critical value. If F is greater than the critical value, you reject H_0 (else you accept H_0). We will not provide this derivation here. It turns out that F is distributed as $F_{q,N-k-1}$. In other words, critical values should be obtained from the F-distribution with q degrees of freedom in the numerator and $N - k - 1$ degrees of freedom in the denominator. In practice, the more sophisticated econometrics packages will provide you with a P-value for any test you do.

The F-statistic is sometimes written in terms of unrestricted and restricted values for R^2 as follows:

$$F = \frac{(R_{UR}^2 - R_R^2)/q}{(1 - R_{UR}^2)/(N - k - 1)}.$$

Note, however, that this is only correct if the dependent variables in the restricted and unrestricted regression models are the same. For instance, you cannot use this form for the F-statistic for testing $\beta_1 = 0, \beta_2 + \beta_3 = 1$.

4.4.2 Likelihood ratio tests

When motivating why the OLS estimator was a good one, we introduced the idea of maximum likelihood estimation. We can also use the maximum likelihood approach to do hypothesis testing. The *likelihood ratio test* is slightly more complicated than the F-test or t-test, but it has one large advantage: likelihood ratio testing can be done in a much wider variety of contexts. F-tests are only useful for testing hypotheses involving regression coefficients. Likelihood ratio testing can be done in any model. However, in this section, we define and explain likelihood ratio testing in the multiple regression model to provide insight in a familiar context.

In Chapter 3 we derived the likelihood function for the simple regression model. This can be extended to the case of multiple regression:

$$L\left(\alpha,\beta_1,\ldots,\beta_k,\sigma^2\right) = \prod_{i=1}^{N} \frac{1}{\sqrt{2\pi\sigma^2}} \exp\left[-\frac{1}{2\sigma^2}\left(Y_i - \alpha - \beta_1 X_{1i} - \cdots - \beta_k X_{ki}\right)^2\right]$$

$$= \frac{1}{(2\pi\sigma^2)^{\frac{N}{2}}} \exp\left[-\frac{1}{2\sigma^2}\sum_{i=1}^{N}(Y_i - \alpha - \beta_1 X_{1i} - \cdots - \beta_k X_{ki})^2\right].$$

Proofs similar to those provided in Chapter 3 can be done to show that the maximum likelihood estimator (MLE) for the regression coefficients is simply the OLS estimator (we denote these estimates as $\widehat{\alpha},\widehat{\beta}_1,\ldots,\widehat{\beta}_k$) and the MLE of σ^2 is

$$\widehat{\sigma}^2 = \frac{\sum\left(Y_i - \widehat{\alpha} - \widehat{\beta}_1 X_{1i} - \cdots - \widehat{\beta}_k X_{ki}\right)^2}{N}$$

$$= \frac{\sum\widehat{\varepsilon}_i^2}{N}.$$

As in the previous section, we distinguish between a restricted and an unrestricted model. Therefore, we will put 'U' superscripts on the estimates in the unrestricted multiple regression model, and thus

$$L\left(\widehat{\alpha}^{\mathrm{U}},\widehat{\beta}_1^{\mathrm{U}},\cdots,\widehat{\beta}_k^{\mathrm{U}},\widehat{\sigma}^{2\mathrm{U}}\right)$$

is the value of the likelihood function at the unrestricted MLEs.

Suppose the hypothesis being tested involves restrictions on the regression coefficients. The previous section gives a few examples of the types of hypotheses we have in mind (e.g. $H_0: \beta_1 = \cdots = \beta_k = 0$ or $H_0: \beta_1 = 0, \beta_2 + \beta_3 = 1$). We have seen that, if the hypothesis involves a linear restriction on the coefficients, then the restricted model can be written as a new regression model with different dependent and/or explanatory variables. Thus, OLS on the new restricted regression will provide us with the maximum likelihood estimates of the coefficients in the restricted model. Using 'R' superscripts to denote the restricted model, we can obtain the likelihood function evaluated at the restricted MLE:

$$L\left(\widehat{\alpha}^{R}, \widehat{\beta}_{1}^{R}, \ldots, \widehat{\beta}_{k}^{R}, \widehat{\sigma}^{2R}\right).$$

To illustrate this point, consider the multiple regression model with three explanatory variables and suppose we want to test the hypothesis

$$H_0\colon \beta_1 = 0, \beta_2 + \beta_3 = 1.$$

In the previous section, we showed that, if we imposed the restrictions in H_0, we obtain the restricted model

$$Y_i - X_{2i} = \alpha + \beta_3(X_{3i} - X_{2i}) + \varepsilon_i.$$

OLS estimation of this simple regression model will yield $\widehat{\alpha}^{R}$ and $\widehat{\beta}_{3}^{R}$. But what are $\widehat{\beta}_{1}^{R}$ and $\widehat{\beta}_{2}^{R}$? The restrictions in H_0 can be used to say $\widehat{\beta}_{1}^{R} = 0$ and $\widehat{\beta}_{2}^{R} = 1 - \widehat{\beta}_{3}^{R}$. Thus, provided the restrictions on the coefficients are linear, we can obtain restricted MLEs by running an OLS regression on an appropriately transformed model. Likelihood ratio testing also works with non-linear hypotheses, such as $H_0\colon \beta_1 = \beta_2^3, \beta_3 = \frac{1}{\beta_2}$ or, in general, $H_0\colon g(\beta_1, \ldots, \beta_k) = 0$, where $g(\cdot)$ is a set of up to k non-linear functions. However, with non-linear restrictions on the coefficients, the restricted model is no longer a linear regression model. Techniques for estimating non-linear regression models will be discussed only cursorily in this textbook in the following section (although most econometric software packages will allow you to do non-linear regression in a straightforward manner).

The previous material shows how you can obtain an unrestricted and restricted MLE whenever H_0 involves linear restrictions on the regression coefficients. How can this information be used to carry out a test of H_0? It turns out that the likelihood ratio can be used to do this. The *likelihood ratio* is defined as

$$\lambda = \frac{L\left(\widehat{\alpha}^{R}, \widehat{\beta}_{1}^{R}, \cdots, \widehat{\beta}_{k}^{R}, \widehat{\sigma}^{2R}\right)}{L\left(\widehat{\alpha}^{U}, \widehat{\beta}_{1}^{U}, \cdots, \widehat{\beta}_{k}^{U}, \widehat{\sigma}^{2U}\right)}.$$

Remember that the general strategy for any hypothesis test is to choose a test statistic and then derive its distribution, assuming H_0 is true. This distribution can then be used to obtain critical values (or P-values) for the test. With likelihood ratio testing, the test statistic used is $-2\ln(\lambda)$. It turns out that the distribution of this test statistic is approximately[3] chi-square:

$$-2\ln(\lambda) \sim \chi_{q}^{2},$$

where q is the number of restrictions being imposed under H_0.

Rather remarkably, it turns out that $-2\ln(\lambda)$ is approximately chi-square in any case where you are testing a hypothesis that restricts a model. Thus, likelihood ratio testing is a very general approach that can be used with any class of models (not just regression models). We will use likelihood ratio testing in later chapters in this textbook. There are also two closely related tests called the *Wald test* and the *Lagrange multiplier test*. These are not that hard to use in practice, but the relevant derivation and explanation is slightly more difficult than the likelihood ratio test. For this reason, discussion of the Wald and Lagrange multiplier tests is relegated to an appendix to this chapter.

We will not provide a proof that $-2\ln(\lambda)$ has an approximate chi-square distribution. Rather we will provide some intuition for why this test is a sensible one and show how it is used in practice. The basic idea underlying likelihood ratio testing is that imposing a restriction will lead to a lower likelihood function. After all, maximum likelihood estimation involves maximizing a function. Mathematically, you can always find a higher maximum if you are free to search over all coefficient values than if you are constrained by the imposition of a restriction. For this reason, it will always be the case that $L\left(\widehat{\alpha}^{R}, \widehat{\beta}_{1}^{R}, \dots, \widehat{\beta}_{k}^{R}, \widehat{\sigma}^{2R}\right) \leq L\left(\widehat{\alpha}^{U}, \widehat{\beta}_{1}^{U}, \dots, \widehat{\beta}_{k}^{U}, \widehat{\sigma}^{2U}\right)$ and, thus, that $0 \leq \lambda \leq 1$. However, if H_0 is true and the restrictions are correct, then it should be the case that λ is very near to 1 (and, thus, the test statistic, $-2\ln(\lambda)$, should be small). On the other hand, if the restrictions are incorrect, then imposing them will cause a large reduction in the likelihood function and λ should become small (and, thus, $-2\ln(\lambda)$, should be big). As with any test statistic, a critical value should be used to decide whether the test statistic is 'big' and, thus, whether H_0 should be rejected. In this case, the critical value must be taken from the chi-square statistical tables.

These points can be illustrated in the case of the simple regression model (with known variance and no intercept) which has a single coefficient, β. The unrestricted likelihood function is written as $L(\beta)$. Consider testing the hypothesis $H_0: \beta = 0$. Under this hypothesis the restricted likelihood function is $L(\beta = 0)$. Figure 4.1 plots an example of a likelihood function. The MLE is the value for β that yields the highest value for the likelihood function. Thus, it lies directly beneath the highest point on the curve and is labeled 'MLE' in the figure. The value for the likelihood function at this point is labeled $L(\beta = \text{MLE})$. By definition, this is the highest value that the likelihood function could be. At the point $\beta = 0$, the likelihood function is slightly lower. This point is labeled $L(\beta = 0)$ in the graph. The likelihood ratio is

$$\lambda = \frac{L(\beta = 0)}{L(\beta = \text{MLE})}.$$

Even if the true value of β is zero, you would not expect the MLE to be precisely zero since an estimate will virtually never be the same as the truth. So, in this case, the fact that the MLE is not zero is not enough to reject $H_0: \beta = 0$. In this case it turns out that $\lambda = 0.773$ and the test statistic $-2\ln(\lambda) = 0.515$. Since one restriction is being imposed under H_0, we must take the critical value for the test from the χ_1^2 distribution. If we use the 5 % level of significance, the critical value is 3.84. Since $0.515 < 3.84$, we accept the null hypothesis and conclude that $\beta = 0$.

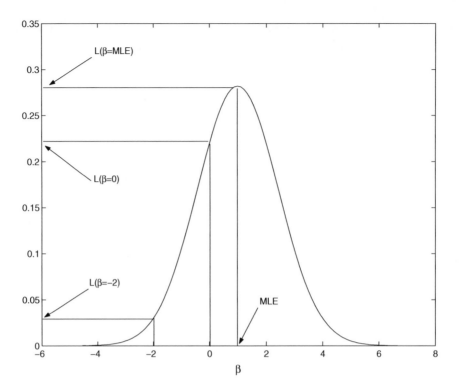

Figure 4.1 A likelihood function.

Now consider testing the hypothesis $H_0: \beta = -2$. Under this hypothesis the restricted likelihood function is $L(\beta = -2)$ which is also labeled as such in Figure 4.1. The value for the likelihood function at this point is much lower than at the MLE. In this case, the likelihood ratio is:

$$\lambda = \frac{L(\beta = -2)}{L(\beta = \text{MLE})} = \frac{0.031}{0.282} = 0.110.$$

Using this likelihood ratio, the test statistic is $-2\ln(\lambda) = 4.416$. Since the 5 % critical value is 3.84, we can reject the hypothesis that $\beta = -2$.

When calculating the likelihood ratio, you can always directly evaluate the likelihood function at the unrestricted and restricted MLEs. However, it is worth noting that, for the multiple regression model, the likelihood ratio can be written in a simpler form. In general, the likelihood function for a multiple regression model evaluated at either the unrestricted or restricted MLE can be written as

$$L\left(\widehat{\alpha}, \widehat{\beta}_1, \ldots, \widehat{\beta}_k, \widehat{\sigma}^2\right) = \frac{1}{\left(2\pi\widehat{\sigma}^2\right)^{\frac{N}{2}}} \exp\left[-\frac{1}{2\widehat{\sigma}^2} \sum_{i=1}^{N}\left(Y_i - \widehat{\alpha} - \widehat{\beta}_1 X_{1i} - \cdots - \widehat{\beta}_k X_{ki}\right)^2\right].$$

However, if you recall the form for $\widehat{\sigma}^2$, you can see that the whole term in the square brackets in the exponential reduces to a constant (i.e. $-\frac{N}{2}$) which will always cancel out in any likelihood ratio calculation. The only part of the likelihood function that matters when calculating the likelihood ratio is thus

$$L\left(\widehat{\alpha}, \widehat{\beta}_1, \ldots, \widehat{\beta}_k, \widehat{\sigma}^2\right) \propto \frac{1}{(\widehat{\sigma}^2)^{\frac{N}{2}}}$$

$$\propto \frac{1}{(SSR)^{\frac{N}{2}}},$$

where, as before,

$$SSR = \sum \widehat{\varepsilon}_i^2$$

is the sum of squared residuals. If we now add 'U' and 'R' subscripts to denote unrestricted and restricted models, we can write the likelihood ratio as:

$$\lambda = \frac{\frac{1}{(SSR^R)^{\frac{N}{2}}}}{\frac{1}{(SSR^U)^{\frac{N}{2}}}} = \left(\frac{SSR^U}{SSR^R}\right)^{\frac{N}{2}}.$$

Thus, the likelihood ratio can be evaluated using the sum of squared residuals from the restricted and unrestricted regression models. Since we have shown above how OLS regression methods can be used to estimate the unrestricted and restricted models, it follows that λ can be easily calculated in any econometrics software package.

4.5 Choice of functional form in the multiple regression model

4.5.1 Non-linearity in regression

So far, we have worked with the linear version of the multiple regression model:

$$Y_i = \alpha + \beta_1 X_{1i} + \cdots + \beta_k X_{ki} + \varepsilon_i.$$

However, sometimes you may think the relationship between your explanatory and dependent variables is non-linear:

$$Y_i = f(X_{1i}, \ldots, X_{ki}, \alpha, \beta_1, \ldots, \beta_k) + \varepsilon_i,$$

where $f(\cdot)$ is some non-linear function of the explanatory variables and coefficients. Note that we have given these coefficients the same names, $\alpha, \beta_1, \ldots, \beta_k$, as in the linear regression model, but they can play a quite different role and are not necessarily interpreted as intercept and slope coefficients.

Maximum likelihood is commonly used to estimate such non-linear regression models. That is, if the errors are assumed to satisfy the classical assumptions, then the likelihood function can be written as

$$L(\alpha, \beta_1, \dots, \beta_k) = \prod_{i=1}^{N} \frac{1}{\sqrt{2\pi\sigma^2}} \exp\left[-\frac{1}{2\sigma^2} f(X_{1i}, \dots, X_{ki}, \alpha, \beta_1, \dots, \beta_k)^2\right].$$

The maximum likelihood estimators are those that maximize this function. However, unlike with the linear regression model, it is in general impossible to obtain a closed-form solution. That is, you cannot take first derivatives of $L(\alpha, \beta_1, \dots, \beta_k)$, set them to zero, and then solve to obtain expressions for $\widehat{\alpha}, \widehat{\beta}_1, \dots, \widehat{\beta}_k$ that can easily be evaluated. Instead, maximum likelihood estimation of non-linear regression models is done by getting the computer to use a *numerical optimization algorithm*. To explain what this is would involve a long, technical digression that will not be provided in this textbook.[4] Suffice it to note here that most econometric software packages can estimate non-linear regression models.

Non-linear regression methods are rarely used in econometrics since, in many cases, a non-linear function can be transformed into a linear one and then linear regression techniques can be used. To use standard linear regression techniques, the requirement is that the regression function must be linear in the coefficients, not the explanatory variables. As an example, the commonly-used Cobb–Douglas production function relates output, Y, to various inputs, $X_1, \dots, X_k$, in the following manner:

$$Y_i = \alpha_1 X_{1i}^{\beta_2} X_{2i}^{\beta_3} \dots X_{ki}^{\beta_k}.$$

But if we take logs of both sides of this equation, we obtain

$$\ln(Y_i) = \alpha + \beta_1 \ln(X_{1i}) + \dots + \beta_k \ln(X_{ki}),$$

where $\alpha = \ln(\alpha_1)$. Adding an error to this equation, we obtain a linear multiple regression model of the sort we have discussed in detail in this book, except that the dependent variable is $\ln(Y)$ and the explanatory variables are $\ln(X_1), \dots, \ln(X_k)$. Thus, you can run a regression of the logged dependent variable on logs of the explanatory variables and all of the results we have derived thus far will hold. For instance, if the errors satisfy the classical assumptions, then the Gauss–Markov theorem tells us that OLS is BLUE, confidence intervals and hypothesis testing procedures can be done using the formulae derived previously, etc. This regression is often referred to as *log-linear* since it is linear in the logs of the variables.

One reason that taking logs of variables is popular is that the interpretation of coefficients is very simple. Remember that, in Chapter 2, we explained that any regression coefficient can be interpreted as 'if X_j increases by one unit, then Y will tend to increase by β_j units (holding all other explanatory variables constant)'. That is, the interpretation of regression coefficients was in terms of the units (e.g. \$, weeks, tons, etc.) that the variables are measured in. However, when both the dependent and jth explanatory variables are logged, then the units do not matter. In particular, the regression coefficient is interpreted as an *elasticity*: 'if X_j increases by one per cent, then Y will tend to increase by β_j per cent (holding all other explanatory variables constant)'. Note that instead of 'units' we are now referring to percentage changes, regardless of what the explanatory and dependent variables are.

Taking logs of variables is a common transformation, although care has to be taken since the log of zero or a negative number is not defined. Thus, if you try to calculate $\ln(X_1)$ where X_1 is a variable that can take on negative values, then the computer software will produce an error message. Therefore, you should avoid logging variables that have zeros or negative values. However, there is nothing wrong with having an equation where some of the explanatory variables are logged and others are not.

The log-linear regression model is a popular one, but a huge variety of possible non-linear forms exist that still result in a regression model that is linear in (suitably transformed) variables. For instance, in labour economics it is common to work with a regression where the dependent variable is log wages of each individual and the explanatory variables are years of schooling (X_1) and years of work experience (X_2) of the individual:

$$\ln(Y_i) = \alpha + \beta_1 X_{1i} + \beta_2 X_{2i} + \varepsilon_i.$$

Since the dependent variable is logged, this regression is already non-linear. However, it is linear in transformations of the variables, and hence our familiar regression methods can still be used. Note that in this case, where the dependent variable is logged but the explanatory variables are not, coefficients such as β_1 can be interpreted as 'if X_1 increases by one unit, then the dependent variable increases by β_1 per cent (holding other explanatory variables constant)'.

As an extension of this example, note that it is often thought that experience has a non-linear effect on wages. For instance, for new workers, additional experience means they learn their jobs better and better, resulting in a higher wage. However, at some point workers learn their job as well as they ever will and additional years of experience will not further improve their productivity and wages. A simple way to allow for this kind of relationship is to define a new explanatory variable, experience-squared, in the regression and work with

$$\ln(Y_i) = \alpha + \beta_1 X_{1i} + \beta_3 X_{2i}^2 + \varepsilon_i.$$

Once again, although the dependent and one of the explanatory variables are non-linear transformations of the original data (i.e. the log and quadratic transformations), this regression is still linear in its dependent and explanatory variables, and hence all the regression methods we have discussed in this and previous chapters can be used.

Another interesting non-linear transformation allows for interactions between explanatory variables. Take, for instance, the multiple regression model with two explanatory variables:

$$Y_i = \alpha + \beta_1 X_{1i} + \beta_2 X_{2i} + \varepsilon_i.$$

Consider what happens when a third explanatory variable, $X_1 X_2$, is added:

$$Y_i = \alpha + \beta_1 X_{1i} + \beta_2 X_{2i} + \beta_3 X_{1i} X_{2i} + \varepsilon_i.$$

There are no new statistical issues, this is just a regression with three explanatory variables instead of the original two. It is the interpretation that is interesting. What is the marginal effect of X_1 on Y (holding other explanatory variables constant)? In the regression that excludes the interaction term, this marginal effect is β_1. However, the regression that includes the interaction term can be written as

$$Y_i = \alpha + [\beta_1 + \beta_3 X_{2i}] X_{1i} + \beta_2 X_{2i} + \varepsilon_i.$$

Hence, the marginal effect of X_1 on Y is now $[\beta_1 + \beta_3 X_{2i}]$. The marginal effect is not a constant, but rather varies with X_2. Similar derivations can be carried out to show that the marginal effect of X_2 on Y becomes $[\beta_2 + \beta_3 X_{1i}]$. It is common to present such a marginal effect evaluated at the mean of the data (i.e. $[\beta_2 + \beta_3 \overline{X}_1]$ is often presented).

To see why allowing for such interaction effects is useful, consider the case where you are interested in estimating the effect of education on wages. You might run a regression using the following variables:

- Y = log wage;
- X_1 = years of schooling;
- X_2 = score on an intelligence test.

In the regression without the interaction term, the marginal effect of X_1 on Y is β_1 (this is called 'the return to schooling'). This return to schooling is the same for everyone. However, in the regression with the interaction term, the return to schooling is $[\beta_1 + \beta_3 X_{2i}]$. Such a model allows us to investigate whether the return to schooling is different for different people, and, in particular, whether intelligent students benefit more or less from schooling than the less intelligent. Note that in the regression without the interaction term, there is no way in which to investigate this hypothesis.

4.5.2   How to decide which non-linear form?

In the previous section, we showed how a wide variety of non-linear functions relating explanatory variables to a dependent variable can be accommodated without leaving the familiar framework of the multiple regression model. This raises the question of how to decide which particular non-linear form to choose. It can be hard to decide which non-linear form is appropriate since there are so many possibilities to choose from. In this section, we provide a few pieces of advice.

The basic issues relating to selecting a particular non-linear form are the same as those relating to the choice of explanatory variables discussed earlier in this chapter. For instance, suppose you are interested in whether you should work with

$$Y_i = \alpha + \beta_1 X_{1i} + \varepsilon_i$$

or

$$Y_i = \alpha + \beta_1 X_{1i} + \beta_2 X_{2i} + \varepsilon_i.$$

This decision can be made by using hypothesis testing procedures. In this case, a t-test of $H_0: \beta_2 = 0$ can be performed in the second regression. If β_2 is found to be insignificant, then you would work with the first regression. Alternatively, you can run both regressions and obtain the $\overline{R}^2$ for each. The one with the highest $\overline{R}^2$ can be selected as the preferred regression. These pieces of advice hold true regardless of whether X_2 is simply another explanatory variable or $X_2 = X_1^2$ or $X_2 = \ln(X_1)$ or $X_2 = \frac{1}{X_1}$ or any other non-linear function of X_1.

The other issues discussed in this chapter relating to choice of explanatory variables are also relevant. In the example above, suppose that the correct model includes a non-linear explanatory variable $X_2 = X_1^2$ and you omit it and simply run the regression model with X_1 being the only explanatory variable. Then you are omitting a significant explanatory variable and will run into the problem of omitted variables bias. Multicollinearity can also be a worry when investigating non-linearity since often X_1 is strongly correlated with non-linear functions of X_1. In general, the best advice is that you should experiment with many different regressions with different non-linear transformations of the variables and use hypothesis testing procedures or $\overline{R}^2$ to decide between them.

The previous advice about $\overline{R}^2$ needs to be qualified in the case where it is the dependent variable that is being transformed. You can only use $\overline{R}^2$ to compare models involving non–linear transformations of the explanatory variables. You cannot use it to compare models that transform the dependent variable in different ways. Remember that the formulae for R^2 and $\overline{R}^2$ all depend on a term relating to $var(Y)$ (i.e. $\frac{1}{N-1}\Sigma(Y_i - \overline{Y})^2$ is an estimate of this variance). When choosing between two regressions with different dependent variables, $var(Y)$ is a completely different (and non-comparable) concept. In order to use $\overline{R}^2$ for choosing a model, all models must have the same Y.

As an example, suppose you want to choose between the following two models:

$$Y_i = \alpha + \beta_1 X_{1i} + \varepsilon_i$$

and

$$\ln(Y_i) = \alpha + \beta_1 X_{1i} + \varepsilon_i.$$

In this case, you cannot use $\overline{R}^2$ to decide which of these models to use. On the other hand, if you were interested in choosing between

$$Y_i = \alpha + \beta_1 X_{1i} + \varepsilon_i$$

and

$$Y_i = \alpha + \beta_1 \ln(X_{1i}) + \varepsilon_i,$$

you could use $\overline{R}^2$. In fact, in the latter case, use of $\overline{R}^2$ to decide whether the explanatory variable should be logged or not could be the best strategy. An alternative strategy would involve working with the regression model

$$Y_i = \alpha + \beta_1 X_{1i} + \beta_2 \ln(X_{1i}) + \varepsilon_i,$$

and using t-tests to decide whether β_1 and/or β_2 are significant. However, this alternative strategy might run into multicollinearity problems since X_1 and $\ln(X_1)$ are often highly correlated.

To discuss the question of what to do when you are interested in choosing between different non-linear transformations of the dependent variable would involve statistical methods beyond the scope of this textbook. However, there is one important special case for which it is worth describing a test. This test can be used to answer the question: "Should we use a linear or log-linear regression?" The two models we wish to choose between are

$$Y_i = \alpha + \beta_1 X_{1i} + \cdots + \beta_k X_{ki} + \varepsilon_i$$

and

$$\ln(Y_i) = \alpha + \beta_1 \ln(X_{1i}) + \cdots + \beta_k \ln(X_{ki}) + \varepsilon_i.$$

We will refer to the first of these as the linear regression and the second as the log-linear regression. Actually, it does not matter whether all the explanatory variables in the second equation are logged or not. The key issue is that in the second equation the dependent variable is logged and in the first it is not.

The problem with comparing these two models arises since the dependent variables are not directly comparable. However, it turns out that a new variable

$$Y_i^* = \frac{Y_i}{\widetilde{Y}},$$

where $\widetilde{Y}$ is the geometric mean (i.e. $\widetilde{Y} = (Y_1 Y_2 \ldots Y_N)^{\frac{1}{N}}$) can be used to create new dependent variables that are comparable. We will not offer a formal proof, but it can be shown that the following test procedure is a correct one.

Begin by running the linear and log-linear regressions, except using Y^* and $\ln(Y^*)$ as dependent variables. Let SSR_{LIN} and SSR_{LOG} be the sums of squared residuals for these two models. Let us suppose first that $SSR_{LIN} > SSR_{LOG}$ (i.e. the linear regression has a larger sum of squared residuals). A test statistic for the hypothesis that the linear and log linear regressions fit the data equally as well as each other is

$$LL_1 = \frac{1}{2N} \ln\left(\frac{SSR_{LIN}}{SSR_{LOG}}\right).$$

As with any test statistic, its distribution, assuming the null hypothesis is true, must be derived in order to obtain critical values. In this case, it turns out that this distribution is χ_1^2. Hence, using the chi-square statistical tables, it can be confirmed that the 5 % critical value for this test is 3.841. Hence, in practice, you would calculate LL_1 and, if it is greater than 3.841, you would reject the hypothesis that there is no difference between the linear and log-linear regressions and conclude that the log-linear specification is to be preferred. On the other hand, if LL_1 is less than 3.841, you would fail to reject the hypothesis that there is no difference between the linear and log-linear regressions. In this case, you could work with either regression.

The previous discussion assumed $SSR_{LIN} > SSR_{LOG}$. If this does not happen, then the test proceeds with the roles of the linear and log-linear models reversed. That is, if $SSR_{LOG} > SSR_{LIN}$, the test statistic becomes

$$LL_2 = \frac{1}{2N} \ln\left(\frac{SSR_{LOG}}{SSR_{LIN}}\right).$$

This test statistic also has a χ_1^2 distribution, and hence, for a test with a 5 % level of significance, you would calculate LL_2 and, if it is greater than 3.841, you would reject the hypothesis that there is no difference between the linear and log-linear regressions and conclude that the linear specification is to be preferred. On the other hand, if LL_2 is less than 3.841, you would fail to reject the hypothesis that there is no difference between the linear and log-linear regressions and you could work with either regression.

4.6 Chapter summary

In this chapter, we have given a thorough discussion of many issues relating to the multiple regression model. Some of the material of this chapter simply repeated topics covered in Chapter 2, but at a greater level of technical detail. Other material is new. In particular, we discussed issues relating to the choice of explanatory variables (i.e. omitted variables bias, the impact of including irrelevant variables, and multicollinearity). The discussion of omitted variables bias emphasized the importance of including all potential explanatory variables in a regression. The discussion on irrelevant explanatory variables emphasized the importance of excluding irrelevant variables. In order to balance these two competing considerations, hypothesis testing procedures can be used. This motivated the present chapter to provide additional material on hypothesis testing. *F*-tests are useful for testing multiple hypotheses about regression coefficients. Likelihood ratio tests can also be used to test multiple hypotheses about the regression coefficients, but have much wider applicability. The appendix to this chapter discussed two further approaches: Wald and Lagrange Multiplier testing. Finally, this chapter discussed selection of the appropriate functional form of a regression. We showed how many non-linear relationships can be written in the form of a standard linear multiple regression model involving non-linear transformations of the variables. There is nothing new econometrically with such regressions. All of our previous derivations (in respect to hypothesis tests or the fact that OLS is BLUE) apply even if the variables in a regression model are non-linear transformations of the original variables. For empirical practice, we advised experimenting with various regression involving various non-linear transformations of the variables and using hypothesis testing procedures or the adjusted R^2 to choose between them. Care has to be taken when choosing between models that have different non-linear transformations of the dependent variable. The chapter ended with a test for whether the dependent variable should be logged or not.

Exercises

The data for these questions is provided on the website associated with this book.

1. For the multiple regression model with two explanatory variables, derive 95 % confidence intervals for β_1 and β_2. Note: you will find results in Section 4.2 useful when answering this question.
2. In the body of the chapter, the topic of omitted variables was discussed and we used the notation $\widehat{\beta}_1$ to denote the OLS estimate of β_1 in the true model and $\widetilde{\beta}_1$ to denote the OLS estimate of β_1 in the incorrect model with the omitted variable. Can you tell whether $var\left(\widetilde{\beta}_1\right)$ is larger or smaller than $var\left(\widehat{\beta}_1\right)$?
3. Suppose you want to carry out a likelihood ratio test of $H_0: \beta = 0$ in the simple regression model

$$Y_i = \alpha + \beta X_i + \varepsilon_i,$$

which obeys the classical assumptions.

 (a) What are the restricted and unrestricted regression models for testing this hypothesis?
 (b) What are the maximum likelihood estimates in the restricted and unrestricted models?
 (c) Using your results for part (b), derive the likelihood ratio, λ.
 (d) Discuss the relationship between testing H_0 using $-2\ln(\lambda)$ as a test statistic as opposed to using the conventional t-statistic.

4. In Chapter 2, we used a dataset on $N = 546$ houses sold in Windsor, Canada. The dependent variable, Y, is the sale price of the house in Canadian dollars. The explanatory variables were:

 - $X_1 =$ the lot size of the property (in square feet);
 - $X_2 =$ the number of bedrooms;
 - $X_3 =$ the number of bathrooms;
 - $X_4 =$ the number of storeys (excluding the basement);

- $D_1 = 1$ if the house has a driveway ($= 0$ if it does not);
- $D_2 = 1$ if the house has a recreation room ($= 0$ if not);
- $D_3 = 1$ if the house has a basement ($= 0$ if not);
- $D_4 = 1$ if the house has gas central heating ($= 0$ if not);
- $D_5 = 1$ if the house has air conditioning ($= 0$ if not).

(a) Test the hypothesis that the coefficients on the dummy variables are all jointly equal to zero using an F-test and a likelihood ratio test.

(b) Test whether the dependent variable should be logged or not.

(c) Based on your answer to parts (a) and (b), choose the linear regression you prefer and then add squares of X_1, X_2, X_3, and X_4 in order to investigate whether the relationship between any of these explanatory variables and the dependent variable is non-linear. Is there any evidence of such non-linearity in this dataset? Use hypothesis testing procedures to justify your answer.

(d) Now experiment with adding various interaction terms to your regression (e.g. experiment with adding new explanatory variables such as X_1X_2, X_3X_4, etc.). Is there any evidence for such interaction effects in this dataset? Use hypothesis testing procedures to justify your answers.

(e) Based on your answers to the previous parts of this question, choose a final regression model that you prefer (and explain why you prefer it). Provide a written interpretation of the results from this regression in the manner you would do in a report. Include a careful discussion of the marginal effect of each explanatory variable on the dependent variable.

5. Chapter 2 contains three empirical questions. For each of the three datasets, experiment with various regressions in order to select a preferred regression using a process similar to that in question 4. Write a short report summarizing the results of these regressions and provide a discussion of why omitted variables bias, inclusion of irrelevant explanatory variables, and multicollinearity are (or are not) problems to be worried about in your empirical work.

Appendix: Wald and Lagrange multiplier tests

In the body of the chapter, likelihood ratio testing was described. This is a powerful testing tool that can be used in virtually any situation. However, there are two other tests that are commonly used: Wald and Lagrange multiplier tests. To explain them properly would require statistical theory and mathematical tools (especially matrix algebra) beyond that used in this textbook. However, many econometrics software packages contain Wald and Lagrange multiplier tests and many research papers use these methods. Accordingly, it is worthwhile offering at least a brief description of what these are so that you can understand computer output and relevant research papers.

A drawback of the likelihood ratio test is that you need to estimate both the restricted and the unrestricted model. Typically, this is a very minor drawback. As we have seen, if the restrictions are linear, then the restricted model can be written as a new regression model that can easily be estimated. However, if the restrictions are non-linear, then it can be more difficult to estimate the restricted model. In contrast to this, there are some cases where it is hard to estimate the unrestricted model, but the restricted model is easy. The advantage of the Wald test is that only the unrestricted model needs to be estimated. The advantage of the Lagrange multiplier test is that only the restricted model needs to be estimated. To avoid the use of matrix algebra and more sophisticated statistical methods, we will illustrate these test procedures in simple cases.

We will illustrate the Wald test in the multiple regression model where there is a single restriction on the coefficients being tested: $H_0: g(\alpha, \beta_1, \beta_2, \ldots, \beta_k) = c$ for some function $g(\cdot)$ and some constant c. The extension to the case of more than one restriction is conceptually similar but mathematically more difficult. Estimation of the unrestricted multiple regression model provides the unrestricted MLEs: $\widehat{\alpha}^U, \widehat{\beta}_1^U, \ldots, \widehat{\beta}_k^U$. The intuition underlying the Wald test is that, if H_0 is true, then the estimates should be close to satisfying the restriction. That is, it should be the case that $g(\widehat{\alpha}^U, \widehat{\beta}_1^U, \ldots, \widehat{\beta}_k^U)$ is not too different from c. The Wald test statistic is based on measuring whether $g(\widehat{\alpha}^U, \widehat{\beta}_1^U, \ldots, \widehat{\beta}_k^U) - c$ is small. As with the t-statistic, it formalizes the idea of 'small' as being 'small relative to the uncertainty in the estimator as measured by its variance (or standard deviation)'. The Wald test statistic is

$$W = \frac{\left[g\left(\widehat{\alpha}^U, \widehat{\beta}_1^U, \ldots, \widehat{\beta}_k^U\right) - c \right]^2}{var\left[g\left(\widehat{\alpha}^U, \widehat{\beta}_1^U, \ldots, \widehat{\beta}_k^U\right) \right]}.$$

We have already explained how the numerator of W can be calculated, but the denominator is more difficult. $var[g(\widehat{\alpha}^U, \widehat{\beta}_1^U, \ldots, \widehat{\beta}_k^U)]$ is the variance of $g(\widehat{\alpha}^U, \widehat{\beta}_1^U, \ldots, \widehat{\beta}_k^U)$ (or an estimate of it). In simple cases, this can easily be obtained. Suppose, for instance, that $g(\widehat{\alpha}^U, \widehat{\beta}_1^U, \ldots, \widehat{\beta}_k^U) = \widehat{\beta}_1^U + \widehat{\beta}_2^U$. Using the properties of the variance operator,

$$var\left(\widehat{\beta}_1^U + \widehat{\beta}_2^U\right) = var\left(\widehat{\beta}_1^U\right) + var\left(\widehat{\beta}_2^U\right) + 2\,cov\left(\widehat{\beta}_1^U, \widehat{\beta}_2^U\right).$$

The variances and covariances of OLS estimates are routinely calculated in econometrics software packages, so can easily be obtained. For the multiple regression model with two explanatory variables, the formulae for $var(\widehat{\beta}_1^U)$ and $var(\widehat{\beta}_2^U)$ are presented at the beginning of this chapter. However, in cases where the restriction is not a linear function of the coefficients, obtaining $var[g(\widehat{\alpha}^U, \widehat{\beta}_1^U, \ldots, \widehat{\beta}_k^U)]$ involves more complicated statistical methods, so we will note only that most econometrics software packages will calculate it for you.

As with any test statistic, we must derive the distribution of the Wald statistic assuming H_0 is true. This distribution can then be used to obtain critical values (or P-values) for the test. As with the likelihood ratio test, the distribution of this test statistic is approximately (i.e. asymptotically) chi-square:

$$W \sim \chi_q^2,$$

where q is the number of restrictions being imposed under H_0 ($q = 1$ in the example in this appendix).

We will illustrate the Lagrange multiplier test in the case where the unrestricted model is a simple regression model with a single coefficient, β, and the restricted model is defined by: $H_0: \beta = c$. The Lagrange multiplier test involves estimation only of the restricted model. Here, this is done in a trivial sense by setting $\widehat{\beta}^R = c$. The test can be motivated by noting that, if H_0 is true, then the restricted MLE should not be too far from the unrestricted MLEs (i.e. c should not be too far from $\widehat{\beta}$, the OLS estimate). However, basic calculus tells us that, at the maximum of the likelihood function (or indeed any function), the first derivative (i.e. the slope) is zero. Thus, if H_0 is true, the derivative of the likelihood function evaluated at $\widehat{\beta}^R$ should be close to zero.

This intuition is embodied in the Lagrange multiplier statistic which takes the form

$$LM = \frac{\left[\dfrac{d \ln L\left(\widehat{\beta}^R\right)}{d\widehat{\beta}^R} \right]^2}{I\left(\widehat{\beta}^R\right)}.$$

This test statistic provides a formal answer to the intuitive question 'how far away from zero does the slope of the likelihood function become if we impose the restriction?'. The numerator is a direct measure of this slope. However, as with most test statistics, we want a measure of its size relative to its uncertainty. The denominator of LM measures this uncertainty. $I(\cdot)$ denotes something called the *information matrix*. To explain and derive what the information matrix is would require too much additional statistical theory, so here we note only that it can be interpreted as related to the variance of the first derivative of the likelihood function.

The LM statistic has a distribution that is approximately (i.e. asymptotically) chi-square:

$$LM \sim \chi_q^2,$$

where q is the number of restrictions being imposed under H_0 ($q = 1$ in the definitions in this appendix).

The likelihood ratio, Wald and Lagrange multiplier test statistics are asymptotically equivalent. That is, as sample size goes to infinity, they will become the same as one another. The choice of which one to use depends largely on whether the unrestricted or restricted model is difficult to measure. In the case of testing non-linear restrictions on regression coefficients, the Wald test is often used since it can be difficult to measure a regression model with non-linear restrictions imposed. In future chapters, we will discuss extensions of the classical assumptions (e.g. one extension is called heteroskedasticity). The unrestricted model will thus not satisfy the classical assumptions and (depending on the exact model) might be hard to estimate. However, the usual way of testing extensions is to set up a null hypothesis where they do not exist. In other words, H_0 imposes the classical assumptions. In this case, estimating the restricted model is very simple and Lagrange multiplier tests are often used.

In this textbook, we are not using enough mathematics, statistical theory, and matrix algebra to offer a thorough derivation and discussion of Wald and Lagrange multiplier tests. Nevertheless, the material in this appendix should be enough for you to use these tests in practice if you are working with an econometrics software package that allows for their calculation. Furthermore, you should be able to read and understand research papers that use these approaches to testing.

Endnotes

1. This is why, in more advanced textbooks, matrix algebra is used with the multiple regression model. Matrix algebra allows derivations involving the multiple regression model to be done in a compact and efficient way.
2. Remember that, in Chapter 2, the standard error was labeled s_b which is a common notation for $\sqrt{var(\widehat{\beta})}$.
3. The reason this distribution is approximate is that it only holds exactly when sample size becomes infinite. In the body of this textbook, we do not use asymptotic theory. However, the appendices to several chapters in this book include asymptotic results, and Appendix C at the end of the book introduces the basic concepts in asymptotic theory.
4. Most advanced econometrics textbooks (e.g. *Econometric Theory and Methods* by R. Davidson and J. MacKinnon, published by Oxford University Press) will have a discussion of numerical optimization algorithms.

CHAPTER 5

The Multiple Regression Model: Freeing Up the Classical Assumptions

5.1 Introduction

Thus far, we have discussed the regression model under the classical assumptions. Some or all of these assumptions were crucial for many of the derivations of the previous chapters. The derivation of the OLS estimator did not require these assumptions. All it involved was the assumption of a linear relationship between the dependent and explanatory variables and was derived as a best-fitting line that minimized the sum of square residuals. However, to show that the OLS estimator had desirable properties did require assumptions (e.g. the proof of the Gauss–Markov theorem which says that OLS is BLUE required all of the classical assumptions except for the assumption of normal errors). Furthermore, derivation of confidence intervals and all hypothesis testing procedures required all of the classical assumptions. In short, statistical derivations require assumptions, and, thus far, we have offered a thorough discussion of the results that follow from a useful, benchmark, set of assumptions which we called the classical assumptions.

However, in any empirical exercise, it is possible that some or all of the classical assumptions are false. Thus, it is important to check if the classical assumptions are true (using hypothesis testing procedures) and to develop applicable estimators that are applicable if tests indicate some of the classical assumptions are false. The purpose of this chapter is to provide discussion of these issues. It begins with a general discussion of the theory, before considering some special cases. These cases fall into two general categories.

The first category relates to the use of the so-called *generalized least-squares (or GLS) estimator*, and the topics of *heteroskedasticity* and *autocorrelated errors* will be discussed. The second category relates to the use of the so-called *instrumental variables (IV) estimator*.

5.2   Basic theoretical results

In previous chapters, we derived theoretical results using the multiple regression model

$$Y_i = \alpha + \beta_1 X_{1i} + \cdots + \beta_k X_{ki} + \varepsilon_i.$$

The classical assumptions were assumed to hold:

1. $E(\varepsilon_i) = 0$. Mean zero errors.
2. $var(\varepsilon_i) = \sigma^2$. Constant variance errors.
3. $cov(\varepsilon_i, \varepsilon_j) = 0$ for $i \neq j$. ε_i and ε_j are uncorrelated with one another.
4. ε_i is normally distributed.
5. The explanatory variables are fixed. They are not random variables.

Assumption 1 implies that you are working with the correct regression model. It implies that

$$E(Y_i) = \alpha + \beta_1 X_{1i} + \cdots + \beta_k X_{ki}.$$

If you have made the incorrect choice of explanatory variables, then this assumption will be incorrect. But we have already (in Chapters 2 and 4) discussed how to choose explanatory variables. Hence, we will not discuss freeing up this assumption in this chapter.

Assumption 4 can be relaxed (approximately) by using asymptotic theory. Asymptotic theory derives what happens when sample size goes to infinity, the idea being that, if we can figure out what happens to things like confidence intervals and hypothesis testing procedures for infinite N, we can then use these as approximate results for real datasets when N is not too small. In the body of the chapters of this textbook, we do not use asymptotic theory. We do provide some asymptotic results in appendices throughout the book and many details are provided there (see, in particular, Appendix C at the end of the book and Appendix 2 to Chapter 3). However, even if you do not read these appendices, it is useful to have some general intuition that, in the regression model, asymptotic results are the same as those derived assuming normal errors. For instance, in Chapter 3, for the simple regression model, we used the classical assumptions to work out that the OLS estimator had a normal distribution:

$$\widehat{\beta} \text{ is } N\left(\beta, \frac{\sigma^2}{\sum X_i^2}\right).$$

We then used this result to derive confidence intervals and hypothesis testing procedures. However, even if the errors do not have a normal distribution, asymptotic results can be used to prove that $\widehat{\beta}$ is approximately $N(\beta, \frac{\sigma^2}{\sum X^2})$. Thus, the confidence intervals and hypothesis testing procedures derived in Chapter 3 still hold approximately even without assumption 4. For this reason, we will not discuss assumption 4 in this chapter.

It is also worth noting that maximum likelihood estimators can be developed for errors other than the normal. For instance, financial economists often work with asset returns (e.g. stock returns) and regression models involving them often exhibit non-normal errors. In particular, errors in financial regressions often appear to have fat tails (i.e. it is more common to get large movements in asset returns than would be suggested by the normal distribution). The Student t distribution has fatter tails than the normal. Hence, a financial economist could work with a regression model where all the classical assumptions hold except that the errors are assumed to have a Student t distribution. This assumption allows us to derive a likelihood function and obtain a maximum likelihood estimator. The likelihood function will not be the same as the one derived assuming normal errors in Chapter 3, but the same general strategy for obtaining the maximum likelihood estimator will hold. Of course, there is a huge variety of possible error distributions, and hence a huge variety of likelihood functions. For this reason, we will not attempt to go through every possible case. But we note that, in general, any error distribution can be accommodated within the maximum likelihood approach.

We have said that we will not discuss assumptions 1 and 4 in this chapter. This leaves us with assumptions 2, 3, and 5. We will begin with a discussion of assumptions 2 and 3 (a discussion of assumption 5 will follow when we introduce the instrumental variables estimator). As we will see, when assumptions 2 and 3 are violated we can work with something called the GLS estimator. We will consider two special cases: heteroskedasticity (which is a violation of assumption 2) and autocorrelated errors (which are a violation of assumption 3).

Before we proceed with our discussion of heteroskedasticity, we give the following overview of the main results and general strategy we will adopt when dealing with violations of either assumption 2 or 3:

- Under the classical assumptions, the Gauss–Markov theorem says that 'OLS is BLUE'. But if assumptions 2 and 3 are violated, this no longer holds. It turns out that OLS is still unbiased, but is no longer 'best' (i.e. no longer minimum variance).
- Many of our derivations use the following strategy: we transform the original regression model to create a new model that does satisfy the classical assumptions.
- We know that OLS on this transformed model will be BLUE. And, hence, we can simply use all the theory we worked out for the OLS estimator in Chapter 3 (except that the theory will now hold for the transformed model).
- The OLS estimator using such a transformed model is called the generalized least-squares (GLS) estimator.

Note that, by following this strategy, we can minimize the number of new proofs and derivations that are required. We can just reuse all our old proofs and derivations. That is, all proofs derived before under the classical assumptions can be used for our transformed models (since they will satisfy the classical assumptions).

As in Chapter 3, we will discuss most of the basic econometric results in the context of the simple regression model (without an intercept). This will greatly simplify the mathematics. Intuitively similar (but mathematically more complicated) derivations can be done for the multiple regression model.

5.3   Heteroskedasticity

Assumption 2 says that the regression errors all have the same error variance. This is referred to as *homoskedasticity*. To explain the implications of this assumption, consider the house price dataset used in several examples in this book. The error measures whether a house is under- or overpriced relative to similar houses (i.e. the regression line captures the main pattern in the data, the error measures how far above or below this line a house is). Of course, homoskedasticity does not say that the error will be the same for every house, only that the errors are all drawn from the same distribution. Roughly speaking, this says that the magnitudes of the under- or overpricing tend to be the same for all kinds of house. This may be reasonable. But it is possible, for example, that small houses tend to have less dispersed errors than large houses. This might occur if small houses tended to be very similar to one another (e.g. if a large tract of nearly identical small bungalows were built), whereas larger houses are very different from one another. In this case, the sellers of a small house would be less likely to under- or overprice their house (e.g. the sellers can get a good idea of the true value of their house by looking at the price of any of the other small bungalows that sold recently). The sellers of a large house, with few other similar houses to compare with, are more likely to under- or overprice their house. In this case, the assumption that the error variance for small and large houses is the same is unrealistic.

Heteroskedasticity occurs when the error variance differs across observations. A general way of allowing for heteroskedasticity is to replace assumption 2 with[1]

$$var(\varepsilon_i) = \sigma^2 \omega_i^2$$

for $i = 1, \ldots, N$. Note that ω_i^2 has an i subscript, indicating that the variance of the error can be different for every observation.

5.3.1   Some theoretical results assuming $\sigma^2 \omega_i^2$ is known

In this section, we discuss the properties of the OLS estimator and derive a new estimator of β for the case where the error variances are known. Of course, in practice, we will rarely know what the error variances are. Hence, in future sections we will discuss how to proceed when the error variances have to be estimated.

What are the properties of the OLS estimator if heteroskedasticity is present?

Remember that we are working with the simple regression model

$$Y_i = \beta X_i + \varepsilon_i$$

where all the classical assumptions hold, except for assumption 2. We now have heteroskedasticity. In Chapter 3, we showed how the OLS estimator can be written in various ways:

$$\widehat{\beta} = \frac{\sum X_i Y_i}{\sum X_i^2} = \beta + \frac{\sum X_i \varepsilon_i}{\sum X_i^2}.$$

Before, under the classical assumptions, we proved

$$\widehat{\beta} \text{ is } N\left(\beta, \frac{\sigma^2}{\sum X_i^2}\right),$$

which we used to derive confidence intervals and hypothesis testing procedures.

How are these results altered if heteroskedasticity is present? Many of the derivations of Chapter 3 are completely unaffected by the presence of heteroskedasticity. The error variance did not appear in our proof of the unbiasedness of the OLS estimator or when we showed that $\widehat{\beta}$ was normal. Hence, those proofs are unaffected by the presence of heteroskedasticity. We will not repeat the derivations here but simply state that OLS is still unbiased (i.e. $E(\widehat{\beta}) = \beta$) and it is normally distributed even if the errors exhibit heteroskedasticity.

However, the variance of the OLS estimator is affected by the presence of heteroskedasticity. In particular, under the present assumptions (i.e. the classical assumptions except that heteroskedasticity is now present):

$$var(\widehat{\beta}) = \frac{\sigma^2 \sum X_i^2 \omega_i^2}{\left(\sum X_i^2\right)^2}.$$

The proof, which uses various properties of the variance operators (see Appendix B, Theorem B.2) and the expression for $\widehat{\beta}$ given in equation (*) in Chapter 3 is

$$var(\widehat{\beta}) = var\left(\beta + \frac{\sum X_i \varepsilon_i}{\sum X_i^2}\right)$$

$$= var\left(\frac{\sum X_i \varepsilon_i}{\sum X_i^2}\right)$$

$$= \frac{1}{\left(\sum X_i^2\right)^2} var\left(\sum X_i \varepsilon_i\right)$$

$$= \frac{1}{\left(\sum X_i^2\right)^2} \sum X_i^2 var(\varepsilon_i)$$

$$= \frac{\sigma^2}{\left(\sum X_i^2\right)^2} \sum X_i^2 \omega_i^2.$$

This formula is a bit messy, but for an understanding of the theory, the key point is that, if heteroskedasticity is present, the variance of the OLS estimator is different from what it was under the classical assumptions. For empirical practice, the key point is that, if heteroskedasticity is present and you ignore it and simply use the OLS estimator in a software package, the software package will use the incorrect formula for $var\big(\widehat{\beta}\big)$. That is, the software package will use the formula that obtains under the classical assumptions, where it should be using $var\big(\widehat{\beta}\big) = \frac{\sigma^2 \Sigma X_i^2 \omega_i^2}{\left(\Sigma X_i^2\right)^2}$. Since $var\big(\widehat{\beta}\big)$ enters the formula for confidence intervals and test statistics, every confidence interval you present and every hypothesis test you do will be incorrect!

To repeat these important points, OLS is still unbiased if heteroskedasticity is present (so as an estimate it may be okay), but everything else (confidence intervals, hypothesis tests, etc.) will be incorrect. The only case where using OLS is acceptable is if the computer is using the correct $var\big(\widehat{\beta}\big) = \frac{\sigma^2 \Sigma X_i^2 \omega_i^2}{\left(\Sigma X_i^2\right)^2}$ formula. This is a point we will return to later when we define and discuss something called a heteroskedasticity consistent estimator. In practice, the problems with the OLS estimator mean that many work with a different estimator: the generalized least-squares estimator.

The generalized least-squares estimator under heteroskedasticity

Here we adopt the strategy outlined in Section 5.2. Remember that the basic idea underlying this strategy is to transform the model which suffers from heteroskedasticity and create a new model that does obey classical assumptions.

The original regression model is (for $i = 1, \ldots, N$)

$$Y_i = \beta X_i + \varepsilon_i,$$

where the errors are assumed to be heteroskedastic (but otherwise satisfy the classical assumptions). Consider a transformed model where we divide both sides of the regression equation by ω_i:

$$\frac{Y_i}{\omega_i} = \beta \frac{X_i}{\omega_i} + \frac{\varepsilon_i}{\omega_i}$$

or (to make the notation more compact)

$$Y_i^* = \beta X_i^* + \varepsilon_i^*,$$

where $Y_i^* = \frac{Y_i}{\omega_i}$, $X_i^* = \frac{X_i}{\omega_i}$, and $\varepsilon_i^* = \frac{\varepsilon_i}{\omega_i}$.

It can be verified that the transformed model satisfies the classical assumptions. In particular, the properties of the expected value operator (see Appendix B, Theorem B.2) immediately imply that the transformed errors satisfy assumptions 1 and 3.

Assumption 2 (homoskedastic errors) can be proved as follows:

$$var(\varepsilon_i^*) = var\left(\frac{\varepsilon_i}{\omega_i}\right)$$

$$= \frac{1}{\omega_i^2} var(\varepsilon_i)$$

$$= \frac{\sigma^2 \omega_i^2}{\omega_i^2} = \sigma^2.$$

The important thing to stress is that we have now shown that the transformed model satisfies the classical assumptions. Hence, all our OLS results (using the transformed model with Y^* as the dependent variable and X^* as the explanatory variable) can be used to say OLS (on the transformed model) is BLUE, OLS confidence intervals and hypothesis testing procedures (using the transformed model) are correct, etc.

The previous reasoning suggests that using OLS with transformed data provides a good estimator. The resulting estimator is an example of a generalized least-squares estimator. Writing out the formula for the OLS estimator using the transformed variables, we obtain

$$\widehat{\beta}_{\mathrm{GLS}} = \frac{\sum X_i^* Y_i^*}{\sum X_i^{*2}},$$

where we have added a GLS subscript to make clear that this is the GLS estimator (and not the OLS estimator using the original, non-transformed data, which we have labeled $\widehat{\beta}$). We can write the GLS estimator in terms of the original data as

$$\widehat{\beta}_{\mathrm{GLS}} = \frac{\sum \frac{X_i}{\omega_i} \frac{Y_i}{\omega_i}}{\sum \left(\frac{X_i}{\omega_i}\right)^2} = \frac{\sum \frac{X_i Y_i}{\omega_i^2}}{\sum \frac{X_i^2}{\omega_i^2}}$$

To provide some intuition, note that the GLS estimator in the heteroskedastic case is sometimes called the *weighted least-squares* estimator. Each observation of each variable is 'weighted' with weights inversely proportional to the standard deviation of the error. Thus, observations with large error variances (i.e. the less reliable data) receive less weight in the estimator, and observations with small error variances (i.e. the more reliable data) receive more weight. In contrast to the OLS estimator, which treats unreliable and reliable observations in the same manner, the OLS has the sensible property that more reliable observations are given more weight in the estimator.

Note that we are still working with the simple regression model, but the extension to multiple regression is immediate. The GLS estimator can be obtained by dividing every explanatory variable and the dependent variable by ω_i and then doing OLS on the transformed variables.

Since GLS is equivalent to OLS on a transformed model, we can use all our OLS results from previous chapters (and apply them to the transformed model). For instance, all the results in Chapter 3 can be used, except that you plug X_i^* and Y_i^* into all the formulae instead of X_i and Y_i into all the formulae. Therefore, since the transformed model satisfies the classical assumptions, we can immediately draw on our old results to say

$$\widehat{\beta}_{\text{GLS}} \text{ is } N\left(\beta, \frac{\sigma^2}{\sum X_i^{*2}}\right).$$

Thus, under the current assumptions, GLS is unbiased with

$$var(\widehat{\beta}_{\text{GLS}}) = \frac{\sigma^2}{\sum X_i^{*2}}$$
$$= \frac{\sigma^2}{\sum\left(\frac{X_i^2}{\omega_i^2}\right)}.$$

Remembering that the variance of the OLS estimator is $var(\widehat{\beta}) = \frac{\sigma^2 \sum X_i^2 \omega_i^2}{\left(\sum X_i^2\right)^2}$ when heteroskedasticity is present, it can be seen that the variance of the GLS estimator is different.

Furthermore, the Gauss–Markov theorem tells us that, under the classical assumptions, OLS is BLUE. Here we have $\widehat{\beta}_{\text{GLS}}$ being equivalent to OLS estimation of a transformed model that does satisfy the classical assumptions. Hence, under heteroskedasticity, it follows immediately that $\widehat{\beta}_{\text{GLS}}$ is BLUE. An implication of this is that

$$var(\widehat{\beta}_{\text{GLS}}) \leq var(\widehat{\beta}),$$

where $\widehat{\beta}$ is OLS using the original (not transformed) data. Thus, it follows that GLS is a better estimator than OLS. Both are unbiased, but GLS has a smaller variance (i.e. it is more efficient).

The fact that

$$\widehat{\beta}_{\text{GLS}} \text{ is } N\left(\beta, \frac{\sigma^2}{\sum X_i^{*2}}\right)$$

can be used to derive confidence intervals and hypothesis tests exactly as before. We will not repeat this material since the formulae are the same as before, except for X_i^* and Y_i^* replacing X_i and Y_i.

5.3.2 Heteroskedasticity: Estimation when error variances are unknown

The derivations above assumed that ω_i^2 is known. In practice, it will usually be the case that ω_i^2 is unknown. In this case, there are two strategies that can be adopted. If it is possible to find an estimate of ω_i^2, then this estimate can be plugged into the formula for the GLS estimator. In practice, this is usually done by transforming the model using one of the explanatory variables in a manner we will describe shortly. Alternatively, a *heteroskedasticity consistent estimator* (HCE) can be used. In this section, we will explain these two approaches.

Doing GLS by transforming the model

In many cases, the heteroskedasticity can be related to an explanatory variable. Hence, it is common to use the multiple regression model

$$Y_i = \alpha + \beta_1 X_{1i} + \cdots + \beta_k X_{ki} + \varepsilon_i$$

under the classical assumptions, except that

$$var(\varepsilon_i) = \sigma^2 \omega_i^2 = \sigma^2 f(Z_i),$$

where Z is an explanatory variable and $f(\cdot)$ is a positive function. Note that $f(\cdot)$ has to be positive since variances are positive, and so it is common to set

$$f(Z_i) = Z_i^2$$

or

$$f(Z_i) = \frac{1}{Z_i^2}.$$

The first of these captures the idea that 'the error variances vary directly with an explanatory variable', while the second captures the idea that 'the error variances vary inversely with an explanatory variable'. In the house price example above, we speculated that larger houses might have larger error variances. If this is so, then it makes sense to set $f(Z_i) = Z_i^2$, where Z_i is a measure of the size of a house. Other popular functions include $f(Z_i) = \exp(Z_i)$ or $f(Z_i) = \exp(-Z_i)$ for error variances that vary directly and inversely, respectively, with Z_i. It is common for researchers to experiment with different choices for Z, and usually it will be one of $X_1, \ldots, X_k$.

Assuming that you are able to find a Z, how can GLS be done? Remember that, under heteroskedasticity, GLS says we should transform our data as

$$\frac{Y_i}{\omega_i} = \alpha \left(\frac{1}{\omega_i} \right) + \beta_1 \frac{X_{1i}}{\omega_i} + \cdots + \beta_k \frac{X_{ki}}{\omega_i} + \frac{\varepsilon_i}{\omega_i}$$

and then use OLS on the transformed model. Since $\omega_i^2 = f(Z_i)$, we can do this transformation.

Consider the case where $f(Z_i) = Z_i^2$ (so that the error variances vary directly with Z). In this case, the transformed model becomes

$$\frac{Y_i}{Z_i} = \alpha \left(\frac{1}{Z_i} \right) + \beta_1 \frac{X_{1i}}{Z_i} + \cdots + \beta_k \frac{X_{ki}}{Z_i} + \frac{\varepsilon_i}{Z_i}.$$

Thus, the GLS estimator can be obtained by dividing all your variables by Z_i and then doing OLS using these new variables. It is important to note that this model still has the same slope coefficients. That is, the β_k in the transformed regression is the same as the β_k in the original regression and still has the same interpretation as being the marginal effect of X_k on Y (holding the other explanatory variables constant). Note that you cannot divide by zero and, hence, you cannot use this transformation for a variable that has $Z_i = 0$ for any observation. This rules out the use of this transformation with dummy variables. However, if the heteroskedasticity is characterized by $f(Z_i) = \exp(Z_i)$ then zero values of Z_i are acceptable.

Now consider the case where $f(Z_i) = \frac{1}{Z_i^2}$ (so that the error variances vary inversely with Z). In this case, the transformed model becomes

$$Y_i Z_i = \alpha Z_i + \beta_1 X_{1i} Z_i + \cdots + \beta_k X_{ki} Z_i + \varepsilon_i Z_i$$

and the GLS estimator can be obtained by multiplying all your variables by Z_i and then doing OLS using these new variables.

As an empirical tip, often you do not know which of your explanatory variables Z should be or whether the error variances vary directly or inversely with it. In this case, you should try various choices for Z (often trying every possible explanatory variable is sensible) and experiment with dividing and multiplying all your variables by each choice. The heteroskedasticity tests we will describe shortly can be useful in seeing if heteroskedasticity of any sort is present, and, if so, whether you can correct it by transforming the model. The idea is that, if heteroskedasticity tests indicate that heteroskedasticity is present in the original regression, then you should experiment with various transformations of the variables. If heteroskedasticity tests indicate it is not present in one of the transformed models, then you have successfully found a transformation that will solve the heteroskedasticity problem.

As another empirical tip, it is common for cross-sectional datasets to suffer from heteroskedasticity. However, taking logs of variables often seems to correct the heteroskedasticity problem. The log-linear model was discussed in Chapter 4, Section 4.5. In that section, we said that log-linear models had some advantages and showed how to do a hypothesis test for whether the log-linear model should be preferred to the linear one. The ability, in some datasets, of the logarithmic transformation to eliminate heteroskedasticity is another reason that the log-linear model is popular in empirical work.

The heteroskedasticity consistent estimator

If your dataset suffers from heteroskedasticity, it is desirable to use GLS. As we have seen, in many cases this can be done by suitably transforming a multiple regression model and then using OLS on this transformed model. However, in some cases, it can be difficult or impossible to find a suitable transformation. For instance, above we showed how, if the error variances are directly related to a variable Z, then dividing all variables by Z yields an appropriate transformation. But what if you cannot find such a Z? What if it is not a single Z, but rather two or more explanatory variables that affect the error variance? In these cases, doing GLS using the methods described above is impossible.

If you cannot do GLS, it is worth remembering that OLS is still unbiased and is an adequate second-best estimator. But we have seen how the variance formula we derived under the classical assumptions no longer holds, and, if we use this variance formula, confidence intervals and hypothesis testing procedures will be incorrect. The correct variance formula is

$$var(\widehat{\beta}) = \frac{\sigma^2 \sum X_i^2 \omega_i^2}{\left(\sum X_i^2\right)^2}.$$

So one thing you can do is use the OLS estimator, but use this correct formula to calculate the variance. The problem with this strategy is that we do not know $\sigma^2 \omega_i^2$. The solution is to replace it with a estimate. Informally to motivate where this estimate comes from, remember that

$$var(\varepsilon_i) = E(\varepsilon_i^2) = \sigma^2 \omega_i^2.$$

However, the OLS estimator will provide residuals

$$\widehat{\varepsilon}_i^2$$

for $i = 1, \ldots, N$. Since $\widehat{\beta}$ is unbiased, it follows that $\widehat{\varepsilon}_i$ is an unbiased estimate of ε_i. Now, of course, $\widehat{\varepsilon}_i^2$ is not the same as ε_i^2 and nor is it the same as $E(\varepsilon_i^2)$, but it does seem sensible that $\widehat{\varepsilon}_i^2$ will be a good estimator of $E(\varepsilon_i^2)$ (and, thus, $\sigma^2 \omega_i^2$). This is in fact the case.

Thus, an estimate of $var(\widehat{\beta})$ is

$$\widehat{var(\widehat{\beta})} = \frac{\sum X_i^2 \widehat{\varepsilon}_i^2}{\left(\sum X_i^2\right)^2}.$$

This can be used in the formulae for confidence intervals and hypothesis testing procedures to obtain valid statistical procedures. This is an example of a *heteroskedasticity consistent estimator* (HCE). Many popular econometrics software packages (e.g. Stata or PC Give) will calculate HCEs for you (so you do not actually have to write a program that evaluates $\widehat{var(\widehat{\beta})}$).

In summary, if you find it difficult to transform the model to do GLS and eliminate the heteroskedasticity problem, you can still use OLS, but must use the correct formula for $var(\widehat{\beta})$. This is what a HCE will do. The advantage of this approach is clear. HCEs are easy to calculate (at least if you have a good econometrics software package), and you do not need to know the form that the heteroskedasticity takes. The disadvantage of using an HCE is that OLS is not as efficient as the GLS estimator (i.e. it will have a larger variance). This means that estimates will tend to be less precise, confidence intervals will tend to be a bit wider, and *t*-tests will be more likely to indicate that a variable is insignificant.

Other estimators

The two approaches outlined above are the most common ways of treating a heteroskedasticity problem. However, it is worth noting that other estimators are possible, and some econometrics software packages allow for their use. To explain them in detail would require technical derivations beyond those used in this book. Nevertheless, some knowledge of the basic ideas should be enough for you to use them in practice.

In our discussion of heteroskedasticity consistent estimation, we showed how OLS residuals can be used as estimates of error variances. But these estimates can be plugged into the original formula for the GLS estimator. The result is often called the feasible GLS estimator. This works best if heteroskedasticity is of a known form (e.g. you have $var(\varepsilon_i) = \sigma^2 \omega_i^2 = \sigma^2 f(Z_i)$). In this case, there are methods to obtain estimates, $\widehat{\omega}_i^2$, that can be used to produce the feasible GLS estimator:

$$\widehat{\beta}_{\text{FGLS}} = \frac{\sum \frac{X_i Y_i}{\widehat{\omega}_i^2}}{\sum \frac{X_i^2}{\widehat{\omega}_i^2}}.$$

and an estimated version of the variance of this estimator.

Similarly, if heteroskedasticity is of a known form, maximum likelihood estimation can be carried out. Typically, this will involve using non-linear maximization methods, something we do not discuss in this book. Nevertheless, a good computer package will do this for you automatically.

5.3.3   Testing for heteroskedasticity

If heteroskedasticity is not present, then OLS is fine (it is BLUE). But if it is present, you should use GLS (or a HCE). Thus, it is important to know if heteroskedasticity is present. There are many tests for heteroskedasticity, and in this section we will describe several of the most common ones.

Goldfeld–Quandt test

The Goldfeld–Quandt test is good for the case where you suspect heteroskedasticity depends on an explanatory variable, Z, which will often be one of $X_1, \ldots, X_k$. The basic idea underlying this test is that, if you divide your data into high Z and low Z parts and run two separate regressions, then they should have different error variances if heteroskedasticity is present. The test involves the following steps:

1. Order the data by the magnitude of Z (i.e. the first observation will be the one with the lowest value of Z, the second observation will have the second lowest, etc.).
2. Omit the middle d observations (there is no hard and fast rule to choose d, but a common choice is $d = 0.2N$).
3. Run two separate regressions, one using the observations with low values for Z, the other using observations with high Z.
4. Calculate the sum of squares residuals (SSR) for each of the two regressions (call them SSR_{LOW} and SSR_{HIGH}).
5. Calculate the Goldfeld–Quandt test statistic which is

$$GQ = \frac{SSR_{\text{HIGH}}}{SSR_{\text{LOW}}}.$$

Under the hypothesis of homoskedasticity, GQ has an $F_{0.5(N-d-2k-2),0.5(N-d-2k-2)}$ distribution, and hence statistical tables for the F-distribution can be used to get a critical value. You reject homoskedasticity (and, thus, conclude heteroskedasticity is present) if GQ is greater than the critical value. This test is useful if you want to do GLS estimation by transforming the model since, if you find heteroskedasticity to be present for a particular choice for Z, then you can use this choice to transform the model. To be precise, the transformed model becomes

$$\frac{Y_i}{Z_i} = \alpha\left(\frac{1}{Z_i}\right) + \beta_1 \frac{X_{1i}}{Z_i} + \cdots + \beta_k \frac{X_{ki}}{Z_i} + \frac{\varepsilon_i}{Z_i}.$$

This test is good for testing whether the error variances vary directly with Z (e.g. in our house price dataset, it would imply 'large houses tend to have larger error variances'). If you suspect that the error variances vary inversely with Z (e.g. 'large houses tend to have smaller error variances'), then the test works in reverse. That is, you would reverse the ordering of the data in step 1 (this will be equivalent to ordering the data by the magnitude of $\frac{1}{Z}$) and, if the Goldfeld–Quandt test indicates heteroskedasticity, would work with the transformed model

$$Y_i Z_i = \alpha Z_i + \beta_1 X_{1i} Z_i + \cdots + \beta_k X_{ki} Z_i + \varepsilon_i Z_i.$$

Note that you should always test for heteroskedasticity in any transformed model you work with. If you still find that heteroskedasticity exists in your transformed model, then you cannot do OLS on it and claim that it is a GLS estimator. Such a transformation has not succeeded in fixing up the heteroskedasticity problem and you should experiment with other transformations. If you fail to find an appropriate transformation that fixes up the heteroskedasticity problem, use a HCE.

In practice, you will usually want to try various choices for Z. Consider the house price dataset where two explanatory variables are $X_1 =$ lot size and $X_2 =$ number of bedrooms. It could be that heteroskedasticity is associated with lot size or the number of bedrooms (or both, or neither). Suppose there is heteroskedasticity and it is associated only with lot size. Then a Goldfeld–Quandt test using $Z = X_1$ (or $Z = \frac{1}{X_1}$) should correctly indicate heteroskedasticity is present. However, if you mistakenly use $Z = X_2$, the test would probably incorrectly find that there is no heteroskedasticity. Thus, unless you are extremely confident that heteroskedasticity (if it exists) is associated with a particular variable, you should do several Goldfeld–Quandt tests using every variable (and the inverse of every variable).

The Breusch–Pagan test

The Goldfeld–Quandt test is a good one if a logical choice of a single Z suggests itself or if heteroskedasticity is related to a single variable and you are patient enough to experiment with different choices for Z. The Breusch–Pagan test is good if there are several possible explanatory variables that might influence the error variance, so that

$$var(\varepsilon_i) = \sigma^2 f(\gamma_0 + \gamma_1 Z_{1i} + \cdots + \gamma_p Z_{pi}),$$

where $f(.)$ is a positive function. This captures the idea that the error variance might depend on any or all of the variables $Z_1, \ldots, Z_p$ (which will usually be the same as the explanatory variables in the regression itself). The test of heteroskedasticity is based on the hypothesis that $\gamma_1 = \gamma_2 = \cdots = \gamma_p = 0$ since, in this case, $Z_1, \ldots, Z_p$ do not enter the error variance. A likelihood ratio test of $H_0 : \gamma_1 = \gamma_2 = \cdots = \gamma_p = 0$ can be obtained. The Breusch–Pagan test is closely related to this likelihood ratio test. It is a Lagrange multiplier test (see the appendix to Chapter 4) that has the advantage that it only requires OLS estimation of two equations. We will not derive this test, but only describe how to implement it in practice.

The Breusch–Pagan test involves the following steps:

- Run OLS on the original regression (ignoring heteroskedasticity) and obtain the residuals, $\widehat{\varepsilon}_i$, and using the residuals calculate

$$\widehat{\sigma}^2 = \frac{\sum \widehat{\varepsilon}_i^2}{N}.$$

- Run a second OLS regression of the equation

$$\frac{\widehat{\varepsilon}_i^2}{\widehat{\sigma}^2} = \gamma_0 + \gamma_1 Z_i + \cdots + \gamma_p Z_{pi} + v_i.$$

- Calculate the Breusch–Pagan test statistic using the regression sum of squares $(R.S.S)^2$ from this second regression:

$$BP = \frac{R.S.S}{2}.$$

- This test statistic has a chi-square distribution with p degrees of freedom $\chi^2(p)$, which can be used to get a critical value.

The White test for heteroskedasticity

The White test for heteroskedasticity is similar to the Breusch–Pagan test, except it runs a different second regression and uses a slightly different test statistic. As with the Breusch–Pagan test, you begin by running an OLS regression on the original variables. The residuals (squared) from this regression are then used in a second regression. In this second regression, the explanatory variables that might relate to the heteroskedasticity are often the same as those in the Breusch–Pagan test. Alternatively, sometimes squares and cross-products of these explanatory variables are added. The White test involves the following steps:

- Run OLS on the original regression (ignoring heteroskedasticity) and obtain the residuals, $\widehat{\varepsilon}_i$.
- Run a second OLS regression of the equation

$$\widehat{\varepsilon}_i^2 = \gamma_0 + \gamma_1 Z_{1i} + \cdots + \gamma_p Z_{pi} + v_i$$

and obtain the R^2 from this regression.

- Calculate the White test statistic

$$W = NR^2.$$

- This test statistic has a chi-square distribution with p degrees of freedom $\chi^2(p)$.

We stress that $Z_1, \ldots, Z_p$ can be any variables, but it is common for them to be based on the explanatory variables. Hence, you could just set $Z_1 = X_1, \ldots, Z_k = X_k$. However, with the White test, squares and cross-products of the explanatory variables are often used. For instance, if you have two explanatory variables, X_1 and X_2, you could set $Z_1 = X_1, Z_2 = X_2, Z_3 = X_1^2, Z_4 = X_2^2$, and $Z_5 = X_1 X_2$.

An advantage of the Breusch–Pagan and White tests is that they need only be done once. You simply choose the set of variables that might be causing heteroskedasticity (usually these are the same as the explanatory variables in the original regression). A disadvantage is that, if the test indicates that heteroskedasticity is present, it does not offer much guidance on how you should try and transform the model to do GLS. All you know is that heteroskedasticity is present and is related to one (or several) of the variables $Z_1, \ldots, Z_p$. Note that these advantages/disadvantages are the exact opposite of the Goldfeld–Quandt test. The Goldfeld–Quandt test requires selection of a single Z (or doing many tests with many choices of Z). However, if you can find one Z that is related to the heteroskedasticity, this will suggest how you should transform the model to do GLS.

5.3.4 Recommendations for empirical practice

If you think you might have a heteroskedasticity problem, begin by doing some heteroskedasticity tests:

- If your tests indicate heteroskedasticity is present, see if you can transform the model to get rid of heteroskedasticity.
- Sometimes simple things (e.g. logging some or all of your variables) will be enough to fix the heteroskedasticity problem (see Section 5 of Chapter 4 for a discussion of how to interpret coefficients when some or all variables are logged).
- Sometimes multiplying or dividing all your explanatory variables by some variable (Z) is enough to fix the problem.
- Note: every time you try such a transformation you must do heteroskedasticity tests to check if it has fixed the problem. For this purpose, the White and Breusch–Pagan tests are best.
- If you cannot find a transformation that fixes the heteroskedasticity problem, then use an HCE.
- Remember: if heteroskedasticity is present, then hypothesis tests will be incorrect. So wait until after you have corrected the problem (or are using a HCE) before doing hypothesis testing (e.g. to find out which of your explanatory variables are insignificant).

Example: Explaining cross-country patterns of education expenditure

Education economists are interested in figuring out why some countries spend more on education than others. In order to investigate this question, we have a data-set containing observations for 38 countries on three variables:

- EDUC = government expenditure on education (millions of US dollars);
- GDP = gross domestic product (millions of US dollars);
- POP = population (millions of people).

Suppose you are interested in running a regression of EDUC on GDP and POP, but are worried that heteroskedasticity might be present. The purpose of this empirical example is to show how you might proceed, focusing on the Goldfeld–Quandt test. The Goldfeld–Quandt test requires the reordering of all variables according to a variable we labeled Z, and then the data must be divided into two parts, omitting the middle d observations. In this example, we try different choices for Z but always set $d = 8$. Remember that the GQ test statistic has an $F_{0.5(N-d-2k-2),0.5(N-d-2k-2)}$ distribution, which for this application is $F_{12,12}$. Using the F-statistic tables, the 5% critical value is 2.69.

Firstly, we try a Goldfeld–Quandt test with $Z = $ POP and find that $GQ = 0.51$, much less than the critical value. Thus, there does not seem to be heteroskedasticity that is directly related to the population variable. Next, we try a Goldfeld–Quandt test with $Z = \frac{1}{\text{POP}}$ and find that $GQ = 1.96$, which is also less than the critical value.[3] Thus, the test fails to reject the hypothesis of no heteroskedasticity. So there does not seem to be heteroskedasticity that is inversely related to population either.

We have established that there is no evidence of heteroskedasticity associated with the population variable. But what about the GDP variable? When we set $Z = $ GDP, it turns out that $GQ = 11.64$, much more than the critical value. Hence, we accept the hypothesis that heteroskedasticity is present and is associated with GDP.

The next step is to see if we can transform the model to eliminate the heteroskedasticity problem. The fact that the Goldfeld–Quandt tests indicate that the heteroskedasticity is associated with GDP suggests we should transform the model by dividing all the variables by GDP. Hence, the dependent variable will now be $\frac{\text{EDUC}}{\text{GDP}}$ and the explanatory variables will be $\frac{1}{\text{GDP}}$, $\frac{\text{GDP}}{\text{GDP}}$, and $\frac{\text{POP}}{\text{GDP}}$. Note that $\frac{\text{GDP}}{\text{GDP}}$ is 1, so that this explanatory variable is the intercept in the model. Carrying out a Goldfeld–Quandt test on this regression (still ordering using $Z = $ GDP) yields $GQ = 0.71$ which is less than the critical value. Hence, we have evidence that heteroskedasticity is not a problem in this transformed regression.[4] OLS estimation of this transformed model will thus be equivalent to GLS estimation.

The transformed model should be used to present final results in an empirical project. Remember that the regression coefficients are unaffected by the transformation. That is, if

$$\text{EDUC} = \alpha + \beta_1 \text{GDP} + \beta_2 \text{POP}$$

is the original regression line, then the transformed model will yield a regression line of

$$\frac{\text{EDUC}}{\text{GDP}} = \alpha \frac{1}{\text{GDP}} + \beta_1 \frac{\text{GDP}}{\text{GDP}} + \beta_2 \frac{\text{POP}}{\text{GDP}}$$

$$= \alpha \frac{1}{\text{GDP}} + \beta_1 + \beta_2 \frac{\text{POP}}{\text{GDP}}.$$

However, the coefficients are still α, β_1, and β_2 and still have the same interpretation. For instance, β_2 is still the marginal effect of population on education (holding other explanatory variables constant). Note that β_1 (the marginal effect of GDP on education) will be the intercept in the transformed model.

Example: Explaining house prices

In previous chapters, we used OLS methods for a dataset on $N = 546$ houses sold in Windsor, Canada. The dependent variable, Y, is the sale price of the house in Canadian dollars. The explanatory variables were:

- X_1 = the lot size of the property (in square feet);
- X_2 = the number of bedrooms;
- X_3 = the number of bathrooms;
- X_4 = the number of storeys (excluding the basement);
- $D_1 = 1$ if the house has a driveway ($= 0$ if it does not);
- $D_2 = 1$ if the house has a recreation room ($= 0$ if not);
- $D_3 = 1$ if the house has a basement ($= 0$ if not);
- $D_4 = 1$ if the house has gas central heating ($= 0$ if not);
- $D_5 = 1$ if the house has air conditioning ($= 0$ if not).

Goldfeld–Quandt tests could be used with this dataset, but many tests would have to be done and some lead to complications (e.g. how does one order data for the GQ test using a dummy variable? How does one transform a model using a dummy variable?). Accordingly, we will investigate the Breusch–Pagan and White tests in this example. These require the selection of variables that might be related to the error variance (labeled $Z_1, \ldots, Z_p$ above). If we set these variables to be the same as the explanatory variables in the original regression, we find $BP = 112.93$ and $W = 44.97$. Critical values for both of these tests are taken from the $\chi^2(9)$ distribution. The 5 % critical value is 16.92. Since both the test statistics are greater than the critical value, both of these tests indicate that heteroskedasticity exists in this dataset. Thus, although the OLS estimates presented in Chapter 2 for this dataset were unbiased, the confidence intervals and hypothesis tests were incorrect.

At this stage, it is important to experiment with different transformations to try and eliminate the heteroskedasticity problem. If a suitable transformation cannot be found, then a heteroskedasticity consistent estimator should be used. Fortunately, with this dataset, a simple transformation works. If we take logs of all variables except for the dummies (since the log of zero is undefined, you cannot take the log of a dummy variable), we obtain a log-linear specification. In Chapter 4, Section 4.5 we discussed log-linear models and their interpretation. In the log-linear regression, the values for the two heteroskedasticity tests are $BP = 12.96$ and $W = 11.45$. The 5 % critical value for both tests is still 16.92 and hence both tests fail to reject the hypothesis of homoskedasticity. Thus, the log transformation has solved the heteroskedasticity problem in this example.

5.4   The regression model with autocorrelated errors

Assumption 3 of the classical assumptions says that regression errors for different observations are uncorrelated with one another. This is usually a reasonable assumption with cross-sectional data. However, with time series data it may be unreasonable. With time series variables, observations at one point in time often tend to be highly correlated with nearby observations. For instance, in macroeconomic applications the fact that a business cycle exists means that variables tend to go through periods when they are unusually high (e.g. economic growth can be high for periods of several years in expansions), as well as periods when they are unusually low (e.g. economic growth can be low or even negative for long periods in recessions). The correlation between observations can feed through into correlation between different errors and we can have a violation of assumption 3.

Since such problems typically occur with time series data, we will use our time series notation of $t = 1, \ldots, T$ to denote observations (rather than $i = 1, \ldots, N$). In Chapters 6 and 7, we will discuss time series methods in detail. With time series variables, some specialized methods are required and it is not necessarily acceptable to simply run a regression model with your variables. Nevertheless, as a first step in learning time series methods, in this section we will assume that it is acceptable to work with a multiple regression model:

$$Y_t = \alpha + \beta_1 X_{1t} + \cdots + \beta_k X_{kt} + \varepsilon_t.$$

All the classical assumptions are assumed to hold except that $cov(\varepsilon_t, \varepsilon_{t-s}) \neq 0$ for some $s \neq 0$. For instance, if $s = 1$, then the regression error in one period is correlated with the error in the previous period.

In this section, we will be considering an important topic called *autocorrelation* which implies $cov(\varepsilon_t, \varepsilon_{t-s}) \neq 0$. In deriving results, we will use the same line of reasoning as we did in our discussion of heteroskedasticity. Remember that, under the classical assumptions, the Gauss–Markov theorem says 'OLS is BLUE'. But if assumption 3 is violated, this no longer holds. OLS is still unbiased but is no longer 'best' (i.e. it no longer has the smallest variance). This suggests the need for a GLS estimator. We derive this by using an appropriate transformation of the regression model which yields a new model that does satisfy classical assumptions. We know OLS (on this transformed model) will be BLUE. Hence, we can draw on all the theory we worked out for the OLS estimator under the classical assumption to derive properties of the estimator, confidence intervals, hypothesis testing procedures, etc. All of these previous derivations will hold – except they will hold for the transformed model. The OLS estimator using such a transformed model is a GLS estimator.

5.4.1 Properties of autocorrelated errors

We will work with the multiple regression model under the classical assumptions, with the exception that the errors follow an *autoregressive process of order 1 (AR(1))*:

$$\varepsilon_t = \rho\varepsilon_{t-1} + u_t,$$

where it is u_t that satisfies the classical assumptions. So $E(u_t) = 0$, $var(u_t) = \sigma_u^2$, and $cov(u_t, u_{t-s}) = 0$ (for $s \neq 0$). Note that we have put a subscript on this variance, σ_u^2, to make explicit this is the variance of u_t (as opposed to the variance of the regression error). We also assume $-1 < \rho < 1$. To preview material in future chapters, this restriction ensures *stationarity* of the errors and means you do not have to worry about problems relating to *unit roots* and *cointegration* (definitions of which will be provided in Chapters 6 and 7).

We will focus on the AR(1) case, but note that the *AR(p) errors* case is a simple extension:

$$\varepsilon_t = \rho_1\varepsilon_{t-1} + \rho_2\varepsilon_{t-2} + \cdots + \rho_p\varepsilon_{t-p} + u_t.$$

The classical assumptions are written in terms of the regression errors, ε_t, and not the new errors, u_t. We know the properties of the latter but not those of the former. Hence, we must begin by working out the properties of the regression errors, ε_t. The chief properties of relevance of any set of random variables are means, variances, and covariances, and we will derive all of these for the regression errors in this section. To do these derivations, it is convenient to write the AR(1) errors in a different way. The standard way of deriving the properties of the AR(1) model is to assume it holds at all points in time: starting at time $-\infty$ and going forward into the future to time $+\infty$. The economist observes this process for time $t = 1, \ldots, T$. The AR(1) specification holds at every point in time, so we can write

$$\varepsilon_{t-s} = \rho\varepsilon_{t-s-1} + u_{t-s},$$

for any t and s. We can set $s = 1$ and use this result to replace the ε_{t-1} that appears on the right-hand side of the original AR(1) equation. If we do this, an ε_{t-2} appears on the right-hand side. However, we can set $s = 2$ in the immediately preceding equation to obtain an expression for ε_{t-2} that can be used in the original AR(1) equation. If we repeatedly replace any regression error on the right-hand side of the original AR(1) equation, we can eventually express the right-hand side in terms of $u_t, u_{t-1}, \ldots$. The following equations show how this is done:

$$
\begin{aligned}
\varepsilon_t &= \rho\varepsilon_{t-1} + u_t \\
&= \rho\left(\rho\varepsilon_{t-2} + u_{t-1}\right) + u_t \\
&= \rho^2\varepsilon_{t-2} + \rho u_{t-1} + u_t \\
&= \rho^3\varepsilon_{t-3} + \rho^2 u_{t-2} + \rho u_{t-1} + u_t \\
&= \ldots \\
&= u_t + \rho u_{t-1} + \rho^2 u_{t-2} + \rho^3 u_{t-3} + \ldots \\
&= \sum_{i=0}^{\infty} \rho^i u_{t-i}
\end{aligned}
$$

This expression can be used to show that the regression errors have mean zero:

$$
\begin{aligned}
E(\varepsilon_t) &= E\left(\sum_{i=0}^{\infty} \rho^i u_{t-i}\right) \\
&= 0,
\end{aligned}
$$

since $E(u_{t-i}) = 0$ for any point in time.

Derivation of the variances and covariances are slightly more complicated, involving knowledge of a mathematical result for infinite sums. This result says that, if c is a number less than 1 in absolute value, then

$$
\sum_{i=0}^{\infty} c^i = \frac{1}{1-c}.
$$

Using the properties of the variance operator (see Appendix B, Theorem B.2), and remembering that u_t satisfies the classical assumptions, we can derive

$$
\begin{aligned}
var(\varepsilon_t) &= var\left(\sum_{i=0}^{\infty} \rho^i u_{t-i}\right) \\
&= \sum_{i=0}^{\infty} \rho^{2i} var(u_{t-i}) \\
&= \sigma_u^2 \sum_{i=0}^{\infty} \rho^{2i} \\
&= \frac{\sigma_u^2}{1-\rho^2},
\end{aligned}
$$

where the last equal sign uses the infinite sum result with $c = \rho^2$. The key thing about the formula for $var(\varepsilon_t)$ is that it is a constant (i.e. it is the same for every time period). Hence, autocorrelated errors are homoskedastic.

Derivation of the covariances between any two regression errors is a bit messier, but involves only the previous expression for the regression errors and the properties of the expected value operator. That is, using the definition of the covariance operator and noting that we have proved $E(\varepsilon_t) = 0$, we can write

$$cov(\varepsilon_t, \varepsilon_{t-s}) = E(\varepsilon_t \varepsilon_{t-s}) - E(\varepsilon_t) E(\varepsilon_{t-s})$$
$$= E(\varepsilon_t \varepsilon_{t-s})$$
$$= E\left[\left(\sum_{i=0}^{\infty} \rho^i u_{t-i}\right)\left(\sum_{i=0}^{\infty} \rho^i u_{t-s-i}\right)\right].$$

We now have to multiply out the product inside the expected value operator in the last equation. This may look a bit messy, but we can use the fact that $cov(u_t, u_{t-s}) = E(u_t, u_{t-s}) = 0$ (for $s \neq 0$) to delete the vast majority of the terms. For instance, u_t appears in the first bracket but not the second. Thus, any term involving u_t can be deleted since such terms will always be of the form $E(u_t u_{t-j})$ for different positive values for j (and these all will equal zero). Deleting such terms, we have

$$cov(\varepsilon_t, \varepsilon_{t-s}) = E(\rho^s u_{t-s}^2 + \rho^{s+1} u_{t-s-1}^2 + \cdots)$$

$$= E\left(\sum_{i=0}^{\infty} \rho^{s+2i} u_{t-s-i}^2\right)$$

$$= \sum_{i=0}^{\infty} \rho^{s+2i} E(u_{t-s-i}^2)$$

$$= \sigma_u^2 \sum_{i=0}^{\infty} \rho^{s+2i}$$

$$= \sigma_u^2 \rho^s \sum_{i=0}^{\infty} \rho^{2i}$$

$$= \frac{\sigma_u^2 \rho^s}{1 - \rho^2}$$

$$= \rho^s var(\varepsilon_t).$$

The details of these derivations are somewhat messy, but the basic idea arising from them is simple: since $cov(\varepsilon_t, \varepsilon_{t-s}) \neq 0$, the classical assumptions do not hold, and thus we cannot call on the Gauss–Markov theorem to say OLS is BLUE. We have to find a GLS estimator that is BLUE. Before we do so, it is worth noting some implications of the previous derivations. Note first that the derivations above depend crucially on the fact that $|\rho| < 1$. That is, the infinite sum result we have used in the variance and covariance calculation does not hold if $|\rho| \geq 1$. Results we derived as intermediate steps such as $var(\varepsilon_t) = \sigma_u^2 \sum_{i=0}^{\infty} \rho^{2i}$ do still hold if $|\rho| \geq 1$. However, in this case, $var(\varepsilon_t)$ is becoming infinite. We will return to these issues in later chapters on time series when we discuss the issue of non-stationarity. In the present chapter, we always assume $|\rho| < 1$. In this case, it can be seen that the regression errors are becoming less and less correlated as time passes. To see this, compare $cov(\varepsilon_t, \varepsilon_{t-1}) = \rho var(\varepsilon_t)$ and $cov(\varepsilon_t, \varepsilon_{t-2}) = \rho^2 var(\varepsilon_t)$. If ρ is positive and less than 1, it must be the case that $\rho > \rho^2$, and hence $cov(\varepsilon_t, \varepsilon_{t-1}) > cov(\varepsilon_t, \varepsilon_{t-2})$. As s becomes large, ρ^s goes to zero, and hence $cov(\varepsilon_t, \varepsilon_{t-s})$ will go to zero for sufficiently large s. This property is characteristic of many time series datasets (particularly in macroeconomics). That is, there is often a strong correlation between the regression error in the present period and the previous one, but this slowly dies out when you consider the correlation between this period and ones in the more distant past. This type of property characterizes all stationary autoregressive processes, not just the AR(1) process.

5.4.2   The GLS estimator for the regression model with autocorrelated errors

We have now established that the multiple regression model with autocorrelated errors violates the classical assumptions. You can confirm that the proof that OLS is unbiased, provided in Chapter 3, is unaffected by the presence of autocorrelated errors. Hence, OLS is still unbiased. However, it is no longer the best estimator. An appropriate GLS estimator will be unbiased and have a smaller variance. Remember that GLS can be interpreted as OLS on a suitably transformed model. In the case of AR(1) errors, the appropriate transformation is referred to as 'quasi-differencing'. To explain what this means, consider the multiple regression model

$$Y_t = \alpha + \beta_1 X_{1t} + \cdots + \beta_k X_{kt} + \varepsilon_t.$$

This model will hold for every time period, so we can take it at period $t - 1$ and multiply both sides of the equation by ρ:

$$\rho Y_{t-1} = \rho\alpha + \rho\beta_1 X_{1t-1} + \cdots + \rho\beta_k X_{kt-1} + \rho\varepsilon_{t-1}.$$

If we subtract this equation from the original multiple regression equation, we obtain

$$Y_t - \rho Y_{t-1} = \alpha - \rho\alpha + \beta_1(X_{1t} - \rho X_{1t-1})$$
$$+ \cdots + \beta_k(X_{kt} - \rho X_{kt-1}) + \varepsilon_t - \rho\varepsilon_{t-1}$$

which we can write as

$$Y_t^* = \alpha^* + \beta_1 X_{1t}^* + \cdots + \beta_k X_{kt}^* + u_t.$$

However, u_t becomes the error in this new regression and it satisfies the classical assumptions. Hence, OLS on this transformed model will be BLUE. This is the GLS estimator for the multiple regression model with autocorrelated errors. The Gauss–Markov theorem tells us that this estimator will have a smaller variance than OLS.

Note that the GLS estimator involves running a regression of Y^* on $X_1^*, \ldots, X_k^*$. The variables in this regression are 'quasi-differenced':

$$Y_t^* = Y_t - \rho Y_{t-1},$$
$$X_{1t}^* = (X_{1t} - \rho X_{1t-1}),$$

etc.

The case with $\rho = 1$ (which we will consider in Chapters 6 and 7) is called 'differenced'. The present transformation is not quite the same, so we say 'quasi-differenced'.

One (relatively minor) issue arises. If our original data are from $t = 1, \ldots, T$, then $Y_1^* = Y_1 - \rho Y_0$ will involve Y_0 (and the same issue arises for the explanatory variables). But we do not observe *initial conditions* such as Y_0. There are many ways of treating initial conditions. The most common, simplest, strategy (which we will adopt in this book) is to work with data from $t = 2, \ldots, T$ and use $t = 1$ values for variables as initial conditions. This solves the problem but, in a sense, involves the loss of an observation. There are more sophisticated methods such as maximum likelihood estimation that do not involve such a loss.

Thus, if we knew ρ, we could quasi-difference the data and do OLS using the transformed data. The resulting estimator (which is a GLS estimator) is the best linear unbiased estimator. Confidence intervals and hypothesis testing procedures can be derived exactly as in Chapter 3 (using the transformed variables). However, in practice, we rarely (if ever) know ρ. Hence, we must replace ρ with an estimate $\widehat{\rho}$. There are several ways of getting a $\widehat{\rho}$, and we now turn to one, called the *Cochrane–Orcutt procedure*.

The Cochrane–Orcutt procedure

The Cochrane–Orcutt procedure begins by using OLS (which is still unbiased) to estimate the original regression and then uses the OLS residuals to estimate ρ. It goes through the following steps:

1. Run a regression of Y_t on an intercept, $X_1, \ldots, X_k$ using OLS and produce the residuals $\widehat{\varepsilon}_t$.
2. Run a regression of $\widehat{\varepsilon}_t$ on $\widehat{\varepsilon}_{t-1}$ using OLS and use the estimated coefficient as $\widehat{\rho}$.
3. Quasi-difference all variables to produce

$$Y_t^* = Y_t - \widehat{\rho} Y_{t-1},$$
$$X_{1t}^* = (X_{1t} - \widehat{\rho} X_{1t-1}),$$

etc.

4. Run a regression of Y_t^* on an intercept, $X_1^*, \ldots, X_k^*$ using OLS, thus producing GLS estimates of the coefficients.

The motivation for this procedure follows from the idea that

$$\varepsilon_t = \rho\varepsilon_{t-1} + u_t$$

looks like a regression model, but with dependent variable being ε_t and explanatory variable being ε_{t-1}. ε_t and ε_{t-1} are not observed, but we can replace these errors with the residuals $\widehat{\varepsilon}_t$ and $\widehat{\varepsilon}_{t-1}$ in order to obtain a regression that can be estimated in practice.

The Cochrane–Orcutt procedure is often generalized to produce the *iterated Cochrane–Orcutt Procedure*. The motivation for this estimator arises from the fact that the Cochrane–Orcutt procedure is using the inefficient OLS estimator (on the original data) to produce the residuals that are used to estimate ρ. But the Cochrane–Orcutt procedure itself can be used to produce residuals. Why not use these residuals to produce a better estimate of ρ, which can be used to quasi-difference the data to provide a new GLS estimator? This is indeed a sensible thing to do. And it can be done repeatedly or *iterated*. Formally, the iterated Cochrane–Orcutt procedure goes through the following steps:

1. Run an OLS regression of Y_t on an intercept, $X_1, \ldots, X_k$ and produce the OLS residuals $\widehat{\varepsilon}_t$.
2. Run an OLS regression of $\widehat{\varepsilon}_t$ on $\widehat{\varepsilon}_{t-1}$ which will provide a $\widehat{\rho}$.
3. Quasi-difference all variables to produce

$$Y_t^* = Y_t - \widehat{\rho}Y_{t-1},$$
$$X_1^* = (X_1 - \widehat{\rho}X_{1t-1}),$$

etc.

4. Run an OLS regression of Y_t^* on an intercept, $X_1^*, \ldots, X_k^*$, thus producing GLS estimates of the coefficients $\widehat{\alpha}, \widehat{\beta}_1, \ldots, \widehat{\beta}_k$.
5. Create new residuals using the GLS estimates of step 4, $\widehat{\varepsilon}_t = Y_t - \widehat{\alpha} - \widehat{\beta}_1 X_{1t} - \ldots - \widehat{\beta}_k X_{kt}$.
6. Now return to step 2 and repeat the process (over and over again until the estimates $\widehat{\rho}$ stop changing).

Most econometrics software packages allow you to do Cochrane–Orcutt estimation automatically. There are other popular estimation methods, including maximum likelihood. Maximum likelihood estimation will involve using non-linear maximization methods, something we do not discuss in this book. Nevertheless, it is worth noting that it can be done automatically in many econometrics packages.

Finally, another common estimation approach should be mentioned. With heteroskedasticity, we said that OLS could be used (since it was unbiased), but that we could not use the standard (from Chapter 3) formulae for confidence intervals and hypothesis testing procedures since $var(\widehat{\beta})$ (which appears in the formulae) was affected by the heteroskedasticity. However, using the correct expression for $var(\widehat{\beta})$ would allow for correct use of OLS methods. The estimator that did this correction was referred to as a heteroskedasticity consistent estimator (HCE). It was less efficient than GLS but at least was a correct second-best solution for the case where GLS was difficult to implement. Similar considerations hold for the regression model with autocorrelated errors. There exist *autocorrelation consistent estimators* which allow for the correct use of OLS methods when you have autocorrelated errors. We will not explain these in detail but note that many popular econometrics software packages include them. The most popular is the *Newey–West estimator*.

5.4.3 Testing for autocorrelated errors

If $\rho = 0$, then the errors are not autocorrelated and using standard OLS methods is fine. OLS is BLUE and standard results for confidence intervals and hypothesis testing procedures apply. However, if $\rho \neq 0$, then a GLS estimator such as the Cochrane–Orcutt estimator is better. This motivates testing the null hypothesis $H_0: \rho = 0$ against the alternative hypothesis $H_1: \rho \neq 0$. There are several such tests, and here we describe some of the most popular. These are also the ones that are often produced by computer software packages.

Likelihood-based testing

In Chapter 4, we saw how the likelihood ratio can be used in any case where we have restricted and unrestricted models that we want to compare. A likelihood ratio test of $H_0: \rho = 0$ against the alternative hypothesis $H_1: \rho \neq 0$ fits into this framework and is conceptually attractive. However, the likelihood ratio test requires maximum likelihood estimation of both the restricted and unrestricted models. Maximum likelihood estimation of the regression model with autocorrelated errors is not that difficult (and is included in many software packages), but is slightly complicated, involving non-linear optimization methods. For this reason, the likelihood ratio test for the presence of autocorrelated errors is not that common.

An alternative, closely related approach to testing (see the appendix to Chapter 4) is the Lagrange multiplier approach. This requires estimation only of the restricted model. Since, in this case, the restricted model is the familiar multiple regression model under the classical assumptions, the Lagrange multiplier test can be done quite simply. In this section, we have focused on the regression model with AR(1) errors, but the Lagrange multiplier test can easily handle the more general AR(p) case where the errors follow the process

$$\varepsilon_t = \rho_1 \varepsilon_{t-1} + \rho_2 \varepsilon_{t-2} + \ldots + \rho_p \varepsilon_{t-p} + u_t.$$

Hence, we show how the joint test of $H_0: \rho_1 = 0, \rho_2 = 0, \ldots, \rho_p = 0$ proceeds in the case of the multiple regression model. The Lagrange multiplier test of H_0 involves the following steps:

1. Run a regression of Y_t on an intercept $X_1, \ldots, X_k$ using OLS and produce the residuals $\widehat{\varepsilon}_t$.
2. Run a second regression of $\widehat{\varepsilon}_t$ on an intercept $X_1, \ldots, X_k, \widehat{\varepsilon}_{t-1}, \ldots, \widehat{\varepsilon}_{t-p}$ using OLS and produce the R^2.

3. Calculate the Lagrange multiplier test statistic

$$LM = TR^2.$$

Although we will not offer a proof, it turns out that, if H_0 is true, then LM has an (approximate) $\chi^2(p)$ distribution. Thus, the critical value for this test must be taken from statistical tables for the chi-square distribution. This test is often referred to as the *Breusch–Godfrey test*.

The Box–Pierce and Ljung tests

There are two popular, and closely related, tests that are based on the idea that, if the errors are not autocorrelated, then the correlations between different errors should be zero. Of course, errors are unobservable, but can be estimated by residuals. Thus, if $\widehat{\varepsilon}_t$ for $t = 1, \ldots, T$ are residuals from an OLS regression of Y on an intercept $X_1, \ldots, X_k$, then we can estimate the correlations (see Chapter 1 for a discussion of correlation) between ε_t and ε_{t-s} by[5]

$$r_s = \frac{\sum_{t=s+1}^{T} \widehat{\varepsilon}_t \widehat{\varepsilon}_{t-s}}{\sum_{t=s+1}^{T} \widehat{\varepsilon}_t^2}.$$

The *Box–Pierce test statistic* (often called the *Q-test statistic*) is

$$Q = T \sum_{j=1}^{p} r_j^2,$$

where the choice of p means that $AR(p)$ errors are being tested for. The *Ljung test statistic* is

$$Q^* = T(T+2) \sum_{j=1}^{p} \frac{r_j^2}{T-j}.$$

Both of these test statistics, which are included in many econometrics software packages, have (approximately) a $\chi^2(p)$ distribution if $H_0: \rho_1 = 0, \rho_2 = 0, \ldots, \rho_p = 0$ is true. Thus, the critical value for this test must be taken from statistical tables for the chi-square distribution.

A warning about these tests is in order. In some cases, one of the explanatory variables will be the dependent variable from a previous period. We will discuss such *lagged dependent variables* in Chapters 6 and 7 on time series. However, here we note that the Box–Pierce and Ljung tests are not appropriate if one of the explanatory variables is a lagged dependent variable. The Lagrange multiplier test, however, is still appropriate.

The Durbin–Watson statistic

Another popular test for the presence of $AR(1)$ errors uses the *Durbin–Watson statistic*. Like the previous tests, it begins by running an OLS regression of Y on an intercept,

$X_1, \ldots, X_k$, and then using the OLS residuals $\widehat{\varepsilon}_t$. The test statistic is

$$DW = \frac{\sum_{t=2}^{T} (\widehat{\varepsilon}_t - \widehat{\varepsilon}_{t-1})^2}{\sum_{t=1}^{T} \widehat{\varepsilon}_t^2}.$$

It can be shown that $0 \leq DW \leq 4$. To provide some intuition, note that, if there is positive correlation in errors, $\widehat{\varepsilon}_t$ and $\widehat{\varepsilon}_{t-1}$ will tend to be close to one another (and thus $(\widehat{\varepsilon}_t - \widehat{\varepsilon}_{t-1})^2$ will be small) and DW will be near 0. At the other extreme, if there is negative correlation in errors, then $\widehat{\varepsilon}_t$ and $\widehat{\varepsilon}_{t-1}$ will tend to be very different from one another and DW will be large (near 4). No autocorrelation is associated with intermediate values of DW (around 2). Another way of motivating these results is through the relationship (which we do not prove) that DW is approximately equal to $2(1 - \widehat{\rho})$, where $\widehat{\rho}$ is an estimate of ρ (see the discussion of the Cochrane–Orcutt procedure).

The Durbin–Watson statistic can be used informally (e.g. if it is near zero, then positive correlation in the errors is indicated), but it can also be used in a formal hypothesis test. Unfortunately, the distribution of DW (which is required to obtain a critical value for the test) is not a standard one (e.g. chi-square, Student t, etc.). Many econometrics software packages will present the P-value for the DW test. Remember that, for any test, if the P-value is less than 0.05 then you can reject H_0. Here, this means concluding that the errors are autocorrelated.

If your computer package does not produce P-values for the Durbin–Watson test, then you must use appropriate statistical tables. These are available in many econometrics textbooks or on the web.[6] From these tables you can obtain a lower (d_{L}) and upper bound (d_{U}). These depend on T and k and, thus, will be different for different applications. Given the value obtained for DW, you can use d_{L} and d_{U} as outlined in the following table:

Value of DW	What you conclude
$4 - d_{\mathrm{L}} < DW < 4$	Reject H_0; conclude $\rho < 0$
$4 - d_{\mathrm{U}} < DW < 4 - d_{\mathrm{L}}$	Result indeterminate
$2 < DW < 4 - d_{\mathrm{U}}$	Accept H_0; conclude $\rho = 0$
$d_{\mathrm{U}} < DW < 2$	Accept H_0; conclude $\rho = 0$
$d_{\mathrm{L}} < DW < d_{\mathrm{U}}$	Result indeterminate
$0 < DW < d_{\mathrm{L}}$	Reject H_0; conclude $\rho > 0$

Note that there are some values of DW where the result is indeterminate. The statistical table cannot clearly accept or reject H_0: $\rho = 0$. For this reason, the Durbin–Watson test is less popular than the previous tests. Furthermore, the Durbin–Watson test (like the Box–Pierce and Ljung tests) is not appropriate when one of the explanatory variables is a lagged dependent variable.

Durbin's h-statistic

The final test for autocorrelated errors that we will discuss is *Durbin's h-test*. This is a test developed by Durbin for the case where an explanatory variable is the lag of a dependent variable. As we will see in Chapters 6 and 7, using lags of the dependent variable as explanatory variables is common. An example of such a model is

$$Y_t = \alpha + \beta Y_{t-1} + \gamma X_t + \varepsilon_t.$$

Note that we are using β to indicate the coefficient on the lagged dependent variable. Durbin's *h*-test involves first running an OLS regression of Y on an intercept, the lagged dependent variable, and X (and any other explanatory variables in the regression) and obtaining the DW statistic and the OLS estimate of the variance of β (i.e. $var(\widehat{\beta})$). Next, the test statistic is calculated:

$$h = \left(1 - \frac{DW}{2}\right)\sqrt{\frac{T}{1 - Tvar(\widehat{\beta})}}$$

Critical values for this test can be obtained from normal statistical tables since (approximately)

$$h \text{ is } N(0,1).$$

Note that this test does not work if $Tvar(\widehat{\beta}) > 1$, since then you end up trying to take the square root of a negative number.

Example: Effect of computer purchases on sales

Dealing with autocorrelated errors is straightforward since, unlike with heteroskedasticity, extensive experimentation is not required to find a suitable GLS transformation. You simply use one or more tests for autocorrelated errors and, if the test finds autocorrelation to be present, you then use a GLS method such as the Cochrane–Orcutt procedure. To illustrate the tests, we use data collected by a company for 98 months to investigate whether investing in computers has made their workers more productive and, thus, improved sales. In particular, the dependent and explanatory variables are:

- $Y =$ the percentage change in sales relative to the previous month;
- $X =$ the percentage change in computer purchases relative to the previous month.

Using OLS methods, we find the fitted regression line to be

$$Y = \underset{(1.55)}{0.28} + \underset{(5.59)}{0.95} X,$$

where the number in parentheses below each coefficient is the *t*-statistic for testing whether the coefficient equals zero. Since the *t*-statistic for the slope coefficient is 5.59 and the 5 % critical value taken from the Student *t* statistical tables is 1.98, it seems the effect of computer investment on the change in sales is strongly significant. However, if the errors are autocorrelated, then this conclusion could be incorrect.

Accordingly, we carried out several tests for AR(p) errors. Since this example is intended only as an illustration, we set $p = 1$, but in practice you would typically try a few different values for p. The *LM* statistic we find to be 67.10, the Box–Pierce statistic 65.01, and the Ljung statistic 67.02. The 5 % critical value for all of these tests should be taken from the $\chi^2(1)$ distribution and is 3.84. Since all of these test statistics are much greater than the critical value, all tests reject the null hypothesis of no autocorrelation. Thus, we have strong evidence that the errors are autocorrelated.

As a final check, we have calculated the Durbin–Watson statistic to be 0.35. Looking at the Durbin–Watson statistical tables (using the 5 % level of significance), for the simple regression model with $T = 98$, we find $d_L = 1.65$ and $d_U = 1.69$. Since $0 < DW < d_L$, we can conclude that the errors are positively autocorrelated.

Since the tests indicate the errors are autocorrelated, the OLS results presented above are unreliable, we now use the Cochrane–Orcutt estimator. Using this estimator, we obtain a fitted regression line of

$$Y = \underset{(0.62)}{0.05} + \underset{(9.59)}{0.55} X,$$

where the number in parentheses below each coefficient is the *t*-statistic. These are the results you would include in a report. The marginal effect of computer investment on sales is a bit different from that in the original OLS regression, but it can be confirmed that it is still strongly significant. Note that we do not discuss the intercept since it has a different interpretation in the original and Cochrane–Orcutt regressions.

5.5   The instrumental variables estimator

The final assumption that will be relaxed in this chapter is the assumption that the explanatory variables are fixed (i.e. not random variables). This may be a realistic assumption in the experimental sciences where the experimenter selects values for the explanatory variables (e.g. the amount of a drug to be given in a medical experiment) and then observes the random outcome of the experiment (e.g. the heath status of the volunteers in the medical experiment). In this case, since the experimenter chooses the values for the explanatory variable, it is not a random variable. However, economics is rarely an experimental science, and thus the assumption that explanatory variables are fixed may not be realistic. As this section will demonstrate, allowing for the explanatory variables to be random does not cause any problems, unless the explanatory variables are correlated with the error. That is, if the explanatory variables are random but independent of the regression error, then OLS is still a good estimator and the formulae derived in Chapter 3 for confidence intervals and hypothesis tests can still be used. However, if any explanatory variable is correlated with the regression error, then OLS should not be used. In this case, OLS is typically biased and this motivates the need for another estimator. The estimator used in this case is called the *instrumental variables* (IV) estimator.

Unfortunately, when the explanatory variables are allowed to be random, many of the derivations done in previous chapters involving the expected value and variance operators (e.g. calculating the expected value and variance of the OLS estimator) become much more difficult (or impossible without making additional assumptions). For this reason, most relevant results are asymptotic. That is, they are derived assuming the sample size is infinite, the idea being that results that hold for infinite sample size can be used as approximations for finite sample sizes. The body of this textbook is written without using asymptotic theory, and hence the discussion of instrumental variable methods in this section will be informal. Formal, asymptotic proofs are given in the appendix to this chapter. Nevertheless, we will have to use one asymptotic concept in this section: that of a *consistent estimator*. This is defined in Appendix C. However, having the intuition that consistency is similar to unbiasedness is enough for you to understand the concepts of this section. The opposite of consistency is inconsistency (which is intuitively similar to biasedness).

For simplicity, derivations and proofs (including those in the appendix) will be done for the simple regression model, but results generalize to the case of multiple regression. Thus, we will work with the regression model (and return to the notation $i = 1, \ldots, N$ to denote observations)

$$Y_i = \beta X_i + \varepsilon_i,$$

but make one change to the classical assumptions. In this section, the assumptions will be as follows:

1. $E(\varepsilon_i) = 0$. Mean zero errors.
2. $var(\varepsilon_i) = \sigma^2$. Constant variance errors (homoskedasticity).
3. $cov(\varepsilon_i, \varepsilon_j) = 0$ for $i \neq j$. ε_i and ε_j are independent of one another.
4. ε_i is normally distributed.
5. X_i is a random variable.

Just saying 'the explanatory variables are random variables' is insufficient. Just as we had to make assumptions about the errors (e.g. that they were normally distributed, or uncorrelated with one another), we have to make assumptions about the random variable X_i in order to figure out properties of various estimators. We will distinguish between two cases. One where the explanatory variable is independent of the regression error and one where it is not.

5.5.1   Case 1: The explanatory variable is random but independent of the error

As X_i is now a random variable, we have to make some assumptions about its distribution and, in particular, what its mean and variance are. Here we will assume that X_i for

$i = 1, \ldots, N$ are i.i.d. random variables with

$$E(X_i) = \mu_X,$$
$$var(X_i) = \sigma_X^2.$$

Furthermore, most crucially for our derivations, we will assume the explanatory variable and regression errors are independent of one another. Appendix B, Definition B.4 provides a formal definition of independence. Note that independence is similar to uncorrelatedness but is a slightly stronger assumption. For our purposes, the most important implication of the independence assumption is that ε_i is uncorrelated with any function of X_i.

In Chapter 3, when working with the simple regression model under the classical assumptions, we worked out that the OLS estimator had the following distribution:

$$\widehat{\beta} \text{ is } N\left(\beta, \frac{\sigma^2}{\sum X_i^2}\right).$$

Using asymptotic theory (see the appendix to this chapter), it can be shown that this result still holds approximately in case 1. However, it is difficult to prove that it holds exactly. The fact that $E(\widehat{\beta}) = \beta$ means that OLS is unbiased. We can prove this result under the case 1 assumptions, using the independence of X_i and ε_i. That is, the OLS estimator is

$$\widehat{\beta} = \frac{\sum_{i=1}^{N} X_i Y_i}{\sum_{i=1}^{N} X_i^2}$$

and we can derive (as in Chapter 3)

$$\widehat{\beta} = \beta + \frac{\sum X_i \varepsilon_i}{\sum X_i^2}.$$

In order to prove that OLS is unbiased, we must take the expected value of both sides of this equation:

$$E(\widehat{\beta}) = \beta + E\left(\frac{\sum X_i \varepsilon_i}{\sum X_i^2}\right)$$

$$= \beta + E\left(\sum \left[\frac{X_i}{\sum X_i^2}\right] \varepsilon_i\right)$$

$$= \beta + \sum E\left(\frac{X_i}{\sum X_i^2}\right) E(\varepsilon_i)$$

$$= \beta,$$

since $E(\varepsilon_i) = 0$. In the proof, the crucial step arises since the explanatory variables and errors are independent and, thus, any function of the explanatory variables and the errors are uncorrelated. If this is confusing to you, remember that a general rule for two random variables, A and B, is $E(AB) \neq E(A)E(B)$. However, if A and B are uncorrelated, then $E(AB) = E(A)E(B)$. We have used this fact (with A being a function of the explanatory variables $\frac{X_i}{\sum X_i^2}$ and B being the error) to separate out the term $E(\varepsilon_i)$ and used the fact that it equals zero to prove unbiasedness. In case 2 (to be discussed shortly), this step of the proof will not work.

We do not derive the other aspects involved in the statement that $\widehat{\beta}$ is $N(\beta, \frac{\sigma^2}{\sum X_i^2})$. The interested reader is referred to the appendix to this chapter, where this result is proved to hold approximately. However, for empirical practice, the important point to remember is that, if we relax the classical assumption that the explanatory variables are fixed, we get exactly the same results as for OLS under the classical assumptions (but here they hold approximately), provided all the explanatory variables are uncorrelated with the error term.

5.5.2   Case 2: The explanatory variable is correlated with the error term

Now let us maintain all the case 1 assumptions, except in case 2 we will assume the explanatory variable and regression error are correlated with one another and thus

$$cov(X_i, \varepsilon_i) \neq 0.$$

In this case it turns out that OLS is biased and a new estimator is called for. That estimator is the instrumental variables (IV) estimator.

The appendix to this chapter offers asymptotic derivations for this case, showing, for instance, that OLS is inconsistent (an asymptotic concept similar to biased). The proof that OLS is biased begins in the same manner as the case 1 proof done previously. We can get up to the following stage in the proof:

$$E(\widehat{\beta}) = \beta + E\left(\frac{\sum X_i \varepsilon_i}{\sum X_i^2}\right),$$

but at this stage we can go no further than to note that there is no reason to think that, in case 2, $E\left(\frac{\sum X_i \varepsilon_i}{\sum X_i^2}\right) = 0$, and in fact it does not. If we ignore the $\sum X_i^2$ in the denominator, we could write the numerator as $E(\sum X_i \varepsilon_i) = \sum E(X_i \varepsilon_i) = \sum cov(X_i, \varepsilon_i) \neq 0$. Perhaps this will suffice to provide some intuition as to why $cov(X_i, \varepsilon_i) \neq 0$ implies OLS is biased. The important point to understand that, if the error and explanatory variable are correlated, then OLS is biased and should be avoided.

We will offer some explanation shortly as to why the error and explanatory variable might be correlated, but first we introduce a new estimator that should be used in this case.

The instrumental variables estimator

An *instrumental variable (or instrument)*, Z, is a random variable that is uncorrelated with the regression error but is correlated with the explanatory variable. The IV estimator is given by

$$\widehat{\beta}_{IV} = \frac{\sum_{i=1}^{N} Z_i Y_i}{\sum_{i=1}^{N} X_i Z_i}.$$

We will not give any justification for this formula. It can easily be calculated (and is in most econometrics software packages), so it is easy to use in practice. Most of the derivations and results relating to the IV estimator are asymptotic (see the appendix to this chapter). Suffice it to note here that this estimator has attractive properties. It is consistent and its variance can be estimated and used to construct confidence intervals and hypothesis testing procedures along the same lines as was done for the OLS estimator in Chapter 3.

To provide a bit more detail on the IV estimator, we define the following notation. The instrumental variable is a random variable and we will denote its mean and variance by

$$E(Z_i) = \mu_Z,$$
$$var(Z_i) = \sigma_Z^2.$$

The first key property of an instrumental variable is that it is uncorrelated with the regression error, and hence

$$cov(Z_i, \varepsilon_i) = 0.$$

The second is that it is correlated with the explanatory variable, and hence

$$cov(X_i, Z_i) = E(X_i Z_i) - \mu_Z \mu_X = \sigma_{XZ} \neq 0.$$

The asymptotic derivations in the appendix imply that the following can be treated as an approximate result:

$$\widehat{\beta}_{IV} \text{ is } N\left(\beta, \frac{(\sigma_Z^2 + \mu_Z^2)\sigma^2}{N(\sigma_{XZ} + \mu_X \mu_Z)^2}\right).$$

This result is comparable with the case 1 result that the OLS estimator, $\widehat{\beta}$, is approximately $N\left(\beta, \frac{\sigma^2}{\sum X_i^2}\right)$ but has a messier formula. In practice, the unknown means and variances can be replaced by their sample counterparts. Thus, μ_X can be replaced by $\overline{X}$, σ_Z^2 by the sample variance of $\frac{(Z_i - \overline{Z})^2}{N-1}$, etc. We will not provide additional details of how this is done, but note that econometrics software packages do allow for IV estimation and these will correctly calculate this formula when providing confidence intervals and hypothesis testing procedures.

As of right now, you probably will have little idea of how to obtain an instrumental variable (or instrumental variables) in practice. Do not worry about this at this stage. We will discuss this point shortly.

Using the instrumental variable estimator in practice

In practice, there are two questions that are not addressed by our discussion of IV estimation of the simple regression model above. The first is 'What if you have a multiple regression model involving more than one explanatory variable?', and the seconds 'What if you have more instrumental variables than you need?'. The answer to the first question is simple: you need at least one instrumental variable for each explanatory variable that is correlated with the error. So, for instance, if you have a multiple regression model with three explanatory variables and two of them are correlated with the error, then you need two instrumental variables. For such a case the formula for the IV estimator becomes a bit more complicated (and is not presented here), but econometrics software packages will easily calculate the IV estimator for you. It is worth stressing that, even if only one of the explanatory variables in a multiple regression model is correlated with the errors, then OLS estimation should be avoided as it will lead to biased estimates of all coefficients.

To illustrate how to proceed if you have more instrumental variables than you need, let us return to the simple regression model with one explanatory variable, X. X is correlated with the error, so an IV estimator is called for. Two instrumental variables exist: Z_1 and Z_2. You could choose one or the other of these, but a more sensible way of proceeding is to use the *generalized instrumental variables estimator* (GIVE). This involves running an initial regression of the explanatory variable on the instruments:

$$X_i = \gamma_0 + \gamma_1 Z_{1i} + \gamma_2 Z_{2i} + u_i,$$

where we are using the notation γ_0, γ_1 and γ_2 for the regression coefficients and u_i for the errors to make explicit that this is a different regression from the one involving β. OLS estimation of this initial regression provides you with fitted values: $\widehat{X}_i = \widehat{\gamma}_0 + \widehat{\gamma}_1 Z_{1i} + \widehat{\gamma}_2 Z_{2i}$. It can be shown that $\widehat{X}$ is uncorrelated with the errors in the original regression, and hence that it is a suitable instrument. This is what GIVE uses as an instrument. Thus, the GIVE is given by

$$\widehat{\beta}_{\text{GIVE}} = \frac{\sum_{i=1}^{N} \widehat{X}_i Y_i}{\sum_{i=1}^{N} X_i \widehat{X}_i}.$$

This estimator is consistent and uses the information in the two instruments in the most efficient manner. Most popular econometrics software packages will calculate GIVEs for you.

The Hausman test

If one or more explanatory variables in a multiple regression model are correlated with the error, then OLS is biased and you should use an IV estimator. However, if none of the explanatory variables is correlated with the error, then (under the classical assumptions) OLS is BLUE and hence is more efficient than IV. In this latter case, you would not want to use an IV estimator. This suggests that it is important to test whether the explanatory variable is correlated with the error. This is exactly what the *Hausman test* does. The formal derivation of this test requires econometric theory beyond that used in this textbook. Furthermore, most econometric software packages will calculate it for you automatically. For these reasons, we will not derive it nor offer a detailed discussion. However, an informal discussion of the Hausman test will provide some useful intuition.

Let H_0 be the hypothesis that the explanatory variables in a multiple regression model are uncorrelated with the error. The basic idea underlying the Hausman test is that, if H_0 is true, then both OLS and IV are consistent and should give roughly the same result. However, if H_0 is false, then OLS will be inconsistent whereas IV will be consistent, and hence they can be quite different. The Hausman test is based on this idea, using a test statistic that measures the difference between $\widehat{\beta}$ and $\widehat{\beta}_{IV}$.

Although many econometrics software packages allow you to calculate the Hausman test automatically, it is useful to note that it can be done using simple OLS methods. We will first illustrate how the Hausman test can be done in the case of simple regression with one instrument. Thus, the regression model of interest is

$$Y_i = \alpha + \beta X_i + \varepsilon_i.$$

The Hausman test, however, is not based on this regression but instead on one where the instrumental variable, Z, is included:

$$Y_i = \alpha + \beta X_i + \gamma Z_i + \varepsilon_i.$$

It turns out that the Hausman test is equivalent to the standard t-test of $H_0: \gamma = 0$. Thus, if you estimate the regression of Y on X and Z (using OLS methods) and find the coefficient on Z to be significant, then you can reject the hypothesis of no correlation between explanatory variable and error (i.e. if you reject H_0, you conclude that the IV estimator should be used). We will not explain why this is equivalent to the Hausman test, but note that it is a simple test to do.

We will illustrate how the Hausman test works in a multiple regression model using a GIVE in the case where we have three explanatory variables ($X_1, X_2,$ and X_3), two of which are potentially correlated with the error (X_2 and X_3). For X_2 we have two instrumental variables (Z_1 and Z_2), while for X_3 we have three instrumental variables ($Z_3, Z_4,$ and Z_5). In this case, the Hausman test proceeds by running initial regressions (see the discussion of the GIVE) to get fitted values, $\widehat{X}_2$ and $\widehat{X}_3$, and then augmenting the original regressions with these variables. To be precise, the Hausman test involves the following steps:

1. Run an OLS regression of X_2 on an intercept, Z_1 and Z_2. Obtain the fitted values, $\widehat{X}_2$.
2. Run an OLS regression of X_3 on an intercept, $Z_3, Z_4,$ and Z_5. Obtain the fitted values, $\widehat{X}_3$.

3. Run an OLS regression of Y on an intercept, $X_1, X_2, X_3, \widehat{X}_2$, and $\widehat{X}_3$.
4. Do an F-test of the hypothesis that the coefficients on $\widehat{X}_2$ and $\widehat{X}_3$ are jointly equal to zero.
5. If the F-test rejects, then proceed with generalized instrumental variables estimation. If not, use OLS on the original regression.

Thus, the Hausman test can be done using standard OLS techniques. We have illustrated the Hausman test in a particular context, but this should be enough to see how it works in general. Briefly, for every explanatory variable that is potentially correlated with the error you should either find an instrument or, if more than one instrument exists, obtain a fitted value from a regression of the explanatory variable on its instruments. Finally, you should run a regression involving the original explanatory variables, but also with the instruments or fitted values added. If these instruments and/or fitted values are significant (using t- or F-tests), then this suggests that an instrumental variables estimator should be used.

The Sargan test

Note that, in the previous material, we have described a coherent strategy for seeing whether it is necessary to do instrumental variables estimation, *if we have valid instrumental variables such as* Z. But how do we know that Z truly is a valid instrument? Remember that, to be a valid instrument, Z must be correlated with X (this is easy to check by running a regression of X on Z and looking at the t-statistic) but uncorrelated with the regression error. The latter is not easy to check, since regression error is not observed. The issue of testing whether instruments truly are valid ones is a complicated and difficult one. In fact, in the case where you have only one potential instrument for every explanatory variable, there is no way of testing whether the instrument is a valid one. To provide some intuition for this, let us return to the simple regression model

$$Y_i = \beta X_i + \varepsilon_i$$

and assume there is one potential instrument, Z. For this to be a valid instrument, it must be uncorrelated with the error, and thus $cov(Z_i, \varepsilon_i) = 0$. Since the error is unobserved, you might be tempted to replace it with a residual and create a test statistic based on $cov(Z_i, \widehat{\varepsilon}_i)$. But which residuals should you use? The IV residuals (i.e. $\widehat{\varepsilon}_i^{IV} = Y_i - \widehat{\beta}_{IV} X_i$) sound plausible, but these are inappropriate since they might be inconsistent. That is, it is possible Z is not a valid instrument (this is, after all, what we are trying to test) and hence $\widehat{\beta}_{IV}$ is inconsistent. The OLS residuals are inappropriate since they could very well be inconsistent (and there is no way you can use a Hausman test to check this, since you are not sure that Z is a valid instrument). In fact, there is no way of testing whether the instruments are valid in such a case. This is a serious worry with instrumental variable methods. As we shall see below, in some cases economic theory or common sense can suggest good instrumental variables. However, in an ideal world, there would be a statistical test we could use to confirm they are good instruments. In the case where you have only one potential instrument for every explanatory variable, there is simply no way of achieving this ideal.

If, as with the generalized instrumental variables estimator, we have more instruments than explanatory variables that are correlated with the error, then there are tests for whether the instruments are valid. To derive these tests would require econometric theory beyond the level of this textbook, but many econometrics software packages allow you to do them in practice. A popular one is known as the *Sargan test* and (even though we cannot derive it), it is simple to describe how it is done in practice. Consider the multiple regression model with k explanatory variables that all are potentially correlated with the error. In total, you have r instrumental variables, where $r > k$. The Sargan test involves the following steps:

1. Run a regression of Y on an intercept, $X_1, \ldots, X_k$ using the generalized instrumental variables estimator and obtain the IV residuals $\widehat{\varepsilon}_i^{IV}$.
2. Run an OLS regression of the IV residuals $\widehat{\varepsilon}_i^{IV}$ on an intercept and all the instruments $Z_1, \ldots, Z_r$ and obtain the R^2 from this regression.
3. The Sargan test statistic is NR^2, and critical values for this test can be obtained from the $\chi^2(r - k)$ distribution.

Note that this test statistic is of the form 'sample size times the R^2 from a certain regression'. We have seen this form before (e.g. in a test for autocorrelated errors). This form is characteristic of Lagrange multiplier tests and it is the case that the Sargan test is such a test. We have not been able to offer proofs of many instrumental variable results. However, to give you a hint of one of them, note that the critical values for the Sargan test involve the $\chi^2(r - k)$ distribution. If $r = k$, it does not work since there is no such thing as the $\chi^2(0)$ distribution. But if $r = k$, then there are exactly the same number of instruments as explanatory variables. This is the case warned about at the beginning of this section. If $r = k$ there is simply no way of testing whether the instruments are valid ones.

5.5.3 Why might the explanatory variable be correlated with error?

Thus far we have explained the consequences of an explanatory variable being correlated with an error, advised a course to take (i.e. use an IV estimator), and shown how to test whether an explanatory variable is correlated with an error (i.e. use a Hausman test). However, we have not said anything about *why* an explanatory variable might be correlated with the error. There are many reasons why this might occur. In this section, we give a few examples that show how such correlation can arise. This also allows us to offer some advice on the important issue of how you should select instrumental variables. That is, it is easy to say 'you should look for an instrumental variable that is correlated with the explanatory variable but not correlated with the regression error', but it can be hard to find such a variable in practice. In a time series context, it is common to use observations from previous periods (e.g. X_{t-1}) as instruments. Since time series variables are often autocorrelated, this means the instrument will be correlated with the explanatory variable.

Provided the regression error is not autocorrelated as well (something that should be tested for), the instrument would be uncorrelated with it. But in other contexts, the selection of instruments can be a difficult issue.

Measurement error in the explanatory variables
Suppose you want to run the regression

$$Y_i = \beta X_i + \varepsilon_i$$

and this regression satisfies the classical assumptions. However, you cannot run this regression since you do not observe X_i but instead observe

$$X_i^* = X_i + v_i,$$

where v_i is i.i.d. with mean zero and variance σ_v^2 and is independent of ε_i. In other words, X is observed with error. This, of course, can arise with many datasets. For instance, economists often work with survey data that are dependent on individuals filling out survey forms correctly. However, individuals often make errors in filling out surveys, and hence measurement errors creep into the data.

Usually, measurement error in the dependent variable is not a problem (see exercise 5 at the end of this chapter). However, measurement error in the explanatory variables can lead to a regression where explanatory variables are correlated with the error. To see why this is so, replace X_i in the original regression with $X_i^* - v_i$ to obtain a new regression model:

$$
\begin{aligned}
Y_i &= \beta(X_i^* - v_i) + \varepsilon_i \\
&= \beta X_i^* + \varepsilon_i^*,
\end{aligned}
$$

where $\varepsilon_i^* = \varepsilon_i - \beta v_i$. This new regression model is one that you could run since you have data on X_i^*. But what is the correlation between the explanatory variable, X_i^*, and the error, ε_i^*, in this new regression? We can use the definition of covariance and the properties of the expected value operator to work out

$$
\begin{aligned}
cov(X_i^*, \varepsilon_i^*) &= E(X_i^* \varepsilon_i^*) \\
&= E[(X_i + v_i)(\varepsilon_i - \beta v_i)] \\
&= -\beta \sigma_v^2.
\end{aligned}
$$

This covariance is not equal to zero, unless $\beta = 0$ (in which case the explanatory variable does not appear in the regression) or $\sigma_v^2 = 0$ (in which case the measurement error problem does not exist since $\sigma_v^2 = 0$ implies $v_i = 0$ for $i = 1, \ldots, N$). Hence, measurement error in the explanatory variables (but not the dependent variable) causes them to be correlated with the regression error. The OLS estimator will be biased, and ideally an IV estimator should be used.

The simultaneous equations model

Instrumental variable methods are often used with so-called *simultaneous equations models*. To understand the issues that arise in such models, we must introduce a few concepts with which you may be familiar from previous economic training. A variable is *endogenous* if it is determined within the model under study. It is *exogenous* if it is not. These concepts are closely related to the causality issues raised in Chapter 2. Recall that we stressed that regression is most easily interpreted if the explanatory variable causes the dependent variable (and not the opposite). In other words, the regression model assumes Y is determined by what happens to X. We did not specify how X was generated. In this case, Y, the dependent variable, is endogenous, and X, the explanatory variable, was assumed to be exogenous. Intuitively speaking, as long as your explanatory variables are exogenous, the use of OLS estimation is fine. However, if some of your explanatory variables are endogenous, then it is possible that they are correlated with the error and IV estimation is required.

The classic illustration of these points is through the model of supply and demand. Suppose the demand curve for some product is given by

$$Q_D = \beta_D P + \varepsilon_D$$

where Q_D is the quantity demanded which depends on price, P. We have added a regression error to this model and, throughout, are using 'D' subscripts to indicate the demand equation. Suppose the supply curve is given by

$$Q_S = \beta_S P + \varepsilon_S$$

where Q_S is the quantity supplied which depends on price, P. We are using 'S' subscripts to indicate the supply equation. In equilibrium, $Q_D = Q_S$, and this condition is used to solve for equilibrium price and quantity. Note that price and quantity are determined within the model so they are both endogenous variables. These two equations are referred to as a simultaneous equations model.

The previous discussion relates to the economics of the problem, but how about the econometrics? The econometrician would be interested in using data to obtain estimates of the slope of the supply and demand curves. What would happen if price and quantity data were obtained and a regression of quantity on price run? We would obtain OLS estimates of a slope coefficient. But would it be an estimate of β_D or β_S? There is no way of knowing. In practice, OLS will probably neither estimate the supply curve nor estimate the demand curve.

To illustrate in a more formal fashion the problems that arise in simultaneous equations models (and see how they relate to instrumental variables issues), let us augment one of the equations with an exogenous variable. Suppose, in particular, that the quantity demanded of the good depends also on the income, I:

$$Q_D = \beta_D P + \gamma I + \varepsilon_D$$

This is sensible in that purchases by individuals depend not only on the price of the goods they purchase but also on their income. Supply is decided by the companies making the product and, thus, is unlikely to depend on the income of the people buying the product. Thus, the supply equation does not depend on income. Note that income is an exogenous variable, it is not determined within the supply–demand model.

We will assume the errors in the supply and demand equations satisfy the classical assumptions (except for the assumption that the explanatory variables are uncorrelated with the errors), but use 'D' and 'S' subscripts to denote which equation they come from. So, for instance, the assumption that the demand equation has homoskedastic errors implies

$$var(\varepsilon_D) = \sigma_D^2.$$

In practice, of course, the econometrician will have data on $i = 1, \ldots, N$ (or $t = 1, \ldots, T$) observations, but we will not explicitly denote this in order to keep the notation from getting too cluttered.

The two equations of the original supply and demand model are referred to as the *structural form*. These are based on the economic theory (or economic structure) of the problem at hand and are characterized by having endogenous variables on both sides of the equation (i.e. having endogenous explanatory variables). Using some basic mathematics, we can also rearrange these equations so that there are only exogenous variables on the right-hand side and we have one equation for each endogenous variable. The result is a so-called *reduced form*. For the supply–demand model, we set the right-hand sides of the demand and supply equations equal to each other, and rearrange the result to isolate P on the left hand side:

$$P = \frac{-\gamma}{\beta_D - \beta_S} I + \frac{\varepsilon_S - \varepsilon_D}{\beta_D - \beta_S}$$
$$= \pi_1 I + \varepsilon_1,$$

where the last equation is intended simply to provide a compact notation (e.g. rather than writing out $\frac{-\gamma}{\beta_D - \beta_S}$, we simply call this coefficient in this reduced form equation π_1).

Now, if we label equilibrium output as Q (i.e. $Q_S = Q_D \equiv Q$) and substitute the expression for P just obtained into the supply equation, we can obtain the second reduced-form equation:

$$Q = \beta_S(\pi_1 I + \varepsilon_1) + \varepsilon_S$$
$$= \beta_S \pi_1 I + \beta_S \varepsilon_1 + \varepsilon_S$$
$$= \pi_2 I + \varepsilon_2.$$

We emphasize that these reduced-form equations are different from the original structural equations. The reduced form involves one equation for each endogenous variable and the explanatory variable in each is I which is exogenous.

Several important issues can be illustrated using these four equations (i.e. two for the reduced form and two for the structural form) based on the supply–demand model. Firstly, a naive researcher may look at the first structural-form equation (i.e. the one relating to the demand curve) and run an OLS regression of Q on P and I in order to estimate the demand curve. The reduced-form equation for P makes clear that this strategy will yield to biased estimates. That is, we can show that an explanatory variable, P, and the regression error, ε_D, in the naive researcher's regression are correlated with one another:

$$
\begin{aligned}
cov(P, \varepsilon_D) &= E(P\varepsilon_D) \\
&= E[(\pi_1 I + \varepsilon_1)\varepsilon_D] \\
&= E\left[\left(\frac{\varepsilon_S - \varepsilon_D}{\beta_D - \beta_S}\right)\varepsilon_D\right] \\
&= \frac{-\sigma_D^2}{\beta_D - \beta_S} \\
&\neq 0,
\end{aligned}
$$

where we have used the fact that I is exogenous (and thus can be assumed to be not a random variable) and various properties of the expected value operator in the previous derivations. Since an explanatory variable, P, is correlated with the regression error, we have established that direct OLS estimation of the demand equation (i.e. estimation of a structural equation where one of the explanatory variables is endogenous) leads to biased, inconsistent results. A similar derivation can be done to establish that direct OLS estimation of the supply equation will also lead to biased, inconsistent results.

Next, consider OLS estimation of the reduced-form equations. It can be shown (see exercise 6) that the reduced-form errors do satisfy the classical assumptions. And, since the only explanatory variable is exogenous (and thus can be assumed to be non-random), OLS is the best linear unbiased estimator for the reduced-form equation. Thus, the OLS estimates of the reduced-form coefficients, $\widehat{\pi}_1$ and $\widehat{\pi}_2$, are good ones and can easily be calculated. But what are these estimates of? The economist would typically be interested in the structural-form coefficients since these have an important interpretation (i.e. as the slope of the demand and supply curves). The reduced-form coefficients do not directly provide us with estimates of the slope of the supply or demand curves.

However, it is often the case that estimates of the reduced-form coefficients can be used to produce estimates of the structural-form coefficients. In our example we have

$$\pi_2 = \beta_S \pi_1.$$

Thus, we can use our unbiased estimates from the reduced form, $\widehat{\pi}_1$ and $\widehat{\pi}_2$, to provide us with an estimate of the slope of the supply curve:

$$\widehat{\beta}_S = \frac{\widehat{\pi}_2}{\widehat{\pi}_1}.$$

Such a strategy is called *indirect least squares*.

How does all this relate to the topic of instrumental variables? It turns out that indirect least squares is equivalent to instrumental variable estimation of the supply curve using I as an instrument (see exercise 7). In this textbook, we will not discuss simultaneous equations in detail, but there are several related estimation strategies that can be carried out. All of these are IV estimators. A popular one of these is called two-stage least squares.

In order to use these IV estimators in practice, it is necessary to come up with instruments. Our example sheds some light on how this might be done in a simultaneous equations model. Note that the indirect least-squares estimator given above provides us with an estimate of the slope of the supply curve. You can confirm that there is no way of obtaining an indirect least-squares estimator of β_D, the slope of the demand curve. Why is this? It turns out that the crucial issue is that income does not appear in the supply curve. A general rule is that, if you have an exogenous variable that is excluded from an equation, then it can be used as an instrumental variable for that equation. In our example there is no exogenous variable excluded from the demand equation, so it is impossible to find an IV estimator to allow us to estimate the slope of the demand curve. However, if the supply equation included an exogenous explanatory variable that was excluded from the demand equation (i.e. if the product was agricultural, then a variable reflecting the weather would be exogenous and influence supply of the product, but not demand for it), then IV estimation of the demand equation would be feasible.

The previous material should allow you to use econometric software (and interpret sensibly the results) for simultaneous equations models. However, simultaneous equations are a big topic, and there are several issues we have not discussed. For instance, we have not discussed what happens when an endogenous variable appears in one equation but not another (e.g. price appears in the demand equation but not in the supply equation). It turns out this can help with estimation. In the extreme case where there is an equation that has no endogenous explanatory variables, OLS estimation of that equation yields consistent estimates. This fact, along with the rule that, if you have an exogenous variable that is excluded from an equation, then it can be used as an instrumental variable for that equation, should allow you to do sensible empirical work in many contexts. However, if you are doing extensive work with simultaneous equations, it would be advisable to read more about this topic in an advanced econometrics textbook.

An Example where the explanatory variable could be correlated with the error

Economic theory (or common sense) can also suggest that an explanatory variable is correlated with an error and, if you are lucky, suggest a plausible instrumental variable. In this section, we provide an example that illustrates how this might occur.

Suppose we are interested in estimating the returns to schooling and have data from a survey of many individuals on the dependent variable Y = income, an explanatory variable X = years of schooling, and other explanatory variables such as experience, age, occupation, etc., which we will ignore here to simplify the exposition. The coefficient on X is the main focus of interest, being a measure of the returns to schooling. In such a regression it probably is the case that X is correlated with the error, and thus OLS will be inconsistent. To understand why, first think of how errors are interpreted in this regression. Individuals with a positive error are earning an unusually high level of income. That is, their income is more than their education would suggest. Individuals with a negative error are earning an unusually low level of income. That is, their income is less than their education would suggest. What might be correlated with this error? Perhaps each individual has some underlying quality (e.g. intelligence, ambition, drive, talent, luck – or even family encouragement). For simplicity, let us just call this quality 'talent'. This quality would likely be associated with the error (e.g. individuals with more talent tend to achieve unusually high incomes). But this quality could also affect the schooling choice of the individual. For instance, more talented individuals may be more likely to go to university (and, hence, achieve more years of schooling). Thus, we would likely face a state of affairs where talented individuals would tend both to have more schooling and to have an unusually high income (i.e. positive errors). So both the error and the explanatory variable would be influenced by talent. In this case, the error and the explanatory variable years of schooling would be correlated with one another.

The previous reasoning suggests that the regression of Y on X (and other explanatory variables) should not be estimated using OLS since the explanatory variable is correlated with the error. Researchers seeking to estimate returns to schooling have adopted two main approaches to this state of affairs. Some have sought to find another explanatory variable that would proxy the missing quality, talent, discussed in the previous paragraph (e.g. the score on an intelligence test could be used as another explanatory variable). Alternatively, many researchers have used instrumental variable methods. In our example, we want a variable that is correlated with the schooling decision but is unrelated to the error (i.e. unrelated to factors that might explain why individuals have unusually high/low incomes). An alternative way of saying this is that we want to find a variable that affects schooling choice but has no direct effect on income.

Some researchers have used characteristics of parents or older siblings as instruments. The justification for this is that, if either of your parents had a university degree, then you probably come from a family where education is valued. This will increase the chances of you going to university. However, your employer will not care that your parents went to university, so it will have no direct effect on your income. Hence, your parents' education affects your schooling decision but does not directly affect your income. The conclusion is that variables reflecting parents' education might be good instruments. Other researchers (usually in the USA) have used geographical location variables as instruments. The justification is that, if you live in a community where a university or college exists, you are more likely to go to university. However, your employer will not care where you live, so the location variable will have no direct effect on your income. Hence, the geographical location variable affects the schooling decision but does not directly affect income.

This example is intended to show how the nature of the economic problem under study can warn you if your explanatory variables are likely correlated with the errors and suggest possible instruments.

5.6   Chapter summary

In this chapter, we have discussed several violations of the classical assumptions and shown how (through hypothesis testing) one can check whether they are violated and how (through new estimators) one should proceed if they are violated. The chapter breaks logically into two parts. In the first part, we discussed assumptions 2 and 3. If these are violated, then OLS is unbiased. A naive use of OLS methods, however, will lead you astray since the resulting confidence intervals and hypothesis testing procedures will be incorrect. Nevertheless, there are estimators (e.g. heteroskedasticity or autocorrelation consistent estimators) that do allow for correct use of OLS methods. Even if this is possible, it is the case that OLS is not efficient. Accordingly, this chapter introduced the new generalized least-squares, (GLS) estimator, which is the best linear unbiased estimator. We showed how GLS can be interpreted as OLS on a suitably transformed model.

The second part of the chapter relates to assumption 5. We showed that, if the explanatory variable is correlated with the error, then the OLS estimator is biased and inconsistent and should be avoided. We developed a new estimator, the instrumental variables (IV) estimator, which should be used.

Within this general breakdown into GLS and IV sections, the following are the main points made:

1. If the regression errors either have different variances (heteroskedasticity) or are correlated with one another (autocorrelated errors), then OLS is unbiased but is no longer the best estimator. The best estimator is GLS.

2. If heteroskedasticity is present, then the GLS estimator can be calculated using OLS on a transformed model. The required transformation involves weighting each observation and hence is sometimes called weighted least squares. If a suitable transformation cannot be found, then a heteroskedasticity consistent estimator should be used.

3. There are many tests for heteroskedasticity, including the Goldfeld–Quandt test, the Breusch–Pagan test, and the White test.

4. With time series data it is common for the regression errors to be correlated with one another. A common way of modeling this is through autoregressive errors. The GLS estimator can be calculated using OLS on a transformed model. The required transformation involves quasi-differencing each variable. The Cochrane–Orcutt procedure is a popular way of implementing the GLS estimator.

5. There are many tests for autocorrelated errors, including an LM test, the Box–Pierce test, the Ljung test, the Durbin–Watson test, and Durbin's h-test.

6. In many applications it is implausible to treat the explanatory variables as fixed. Hence, it is important to allow for them to be random variables.

7. If the explanatory variables are random and all of them are uncorrelated with the regression error, then standard methods associated with OLS (as developed in Chapters 2, 3, and 4) still work.

8. If the explanatory variables are random and some of them are correlated with the regression error, then OLS is inconsistent. The IV estimator is consistent.

9. In multiple regression, at least one instrument is required for every explanatory variable that is correlated with the error.

10. If you have valid instruments, then the Hausman test can be used to test if the explanatory variables are correlated with the error.

11. In general, it is difficult to test whether an instrumental variable is a valid one. However, if you have more instruments than the minimum required, the Sargan test can be used to test if an instrument is valid.

12. An important case where the explanatory variables can be correlated with the error occurs when the explanatory variables are measured with error.

13. The simultaneous equations model is another important case where explanatory variables are correlated with the error.

Exercises

The data for these questions are provided on the website associated with this book.

1. Consider the simple regression model without an intercept. Assume the classical assumptions hold, except that heteroskedasticity is present: $var(\varepsilon_i) = \sigma^2 \omega_i^2$ and ω_i^2 is known.

   (a) Use the results in this chapter for the OLS estimator to derive a formula for a 95 % confidence interval for β.

   (b) Use the results in this chapter for the GLS estimator to derive a formula for a 95 % confidence interval for β.

   (c) Why do the confidence intervals in parts (a) and (b) differ? Which one is wider?

2. In previous chapters, we worked with a dataset for 70 tropical countries with the dependent variable being the deforestation rate and explanatory variables being population density and the changes in cropland and pasture land (this dataset is labeled FOREST.XLS). Population density is measured as the number of people per thousand hectares, while the other variables are all annual percentage changes averaged over the years 1981–1990.

   (a) Using Goldfeld–Quandt tests, investigate whether this regression suffers from heteroskedasticity.

   (b) If you find heteroskedasticity, investigate whether you can successfully transform the model to eliminate it.

   (c) Based on your findings in parts (a) and (b), select a set of final regression results that you think are the best. Justify why you think this regression the best and explain how it corrects the heteroskedasticity problem (if one exists).

Provide an interpretation of your empirical results as you would in a project or research paper.

3. In Chapter 2, we discussed an example involving costs of production in the electric utility industry for 123 electric utility companies in the USA in 1970 (dataset ELECTRIC.XLS). The dataset contains the following variables:

- Y = costs of production (measured in millions of dollars per year);
- X_1 = output (measured in thousands of kWh per year);
- X_2 = price of labour (measured in dollars per worker per year);
- X_3 = price of capital (measured in dollars per unit of capital per year);
- X_4 = price of fuel (measured in dollars per million BTUs).

  (a) Using the Breusch–Pagan and White tests, investigate whether this regression suffers from heteroskedasticity.
  (b) If you find heteroskedasticity, investigate whether you can successfully transform the model to eliminate it. If you log all of the variables, do your conclusions about heteroskedasticity change?
  (c) Based on your findings in parts (a) and (b), select a set of final regression results that you think are the best. Justify why you think this regression the best and explain how it corrects the heteroskedasticity problem (if one exists). Provide an interpretation of your empirical results as you would in a project or research paper.

4. In the section on autocorrelated errors, an example was provided using a dataset with $T = 98$ monthly observations on a company's computer purchases and sales. In particular, the dependent and explanatory variables were:

- Y = the percentage change in sales relative to the previous month;
- X = the percentage change in computer purchases relative to the previous month.

The file COMPUTE1.XLS contains data in the same format but for a different company. Repeat the example in the chapter using this dataset. That is, test for autocorrelated errors and, depending on the results of your tests, use a GLS or OLS estimator and present your preferred regression results.

5. (Measurement error in the dependent variable). Consider the regression model

$$Y_i = \beta X_i + \varepsilon_i.$$

This regression satisfies the classical assumptions. However, you cannot run this regression since you do not observe Y_i but instead observe

$$Y_i^* = Y_i + v_i,$$

where v_i is i.i.d. with mean zero and variance σ_v^2 and is independent of ε_i. Show that OLS is BLUE in the regression of Y^* on X.

6. In our discussion of the simultaneous equations model, an example involving a supply-demand model was given. For this model, show that the errors in the reduced-form equations satisfy the classical assumptions.

7. In our discussion of the simultaneous equations model, an example involving a supply–demand model was given and an indirect least-squares estimator, $\widehat{\beta}_S = \frac{\widehat{\pi_2}}{\widehat{\pi_1}}$, was given. Show that this indirect least-squares estimator is equivalent to the IV estimator of the supply equation, using income as an instrument.

8. Suppose you have a supply–demand model with the supply equation given by

$$Q_S = \beta_S P + \alpha R + \varepsilon_S$$

and

$$Q_D = \beta_D P + \gamma I + \varepsilon_D,$$

where all definitions and assumptions are the same as given in the supply–demand example in the body of the text and, in addition, R is a measure of rainfall (an exogenous variable).

(a) Derive the reduced form for this model.
(b) Derive indirect least-squares estimators of β_S and β_D.

9. Dataset RTS.XLS contains the following variables:

- EARNINGS = average hourly earnings (measured in dollars per hour);
- S = years of schooling;
- SM = years of schooling of mother;
- SF = years of schooling of father;
- MALE = dummy variable equaling 1 if the individual is male ($= 0$ if female);
- ETHBLACK = dummy variable equalling 1 if the individual is black ($= 0$ otherwise);
- ETHHISP = dummy variable equalling 1 if the individual is Hispanic ($= 0$ otherwise);
- TEST = result of an intelligence test score;
- SIBLINGS = number of siblings.

(a) Run an OLS regression of LGEARN (the log of the EARNINGS variable) on S, TEST, MALE, ETHBLACK, and ETHHISP.
(b) The TEST variable is a test score, but it is possible that this test score is a poor measure of the kind of ability relevant for earnings. Accordingly, rerun the previous regression using IV methods where SM is used as an instrument for TEST. Do OLS results differ from IV results?
(c) Repeat the exercise using SM, SF, and SIBLINGS jointly as instruments.
(d) Does the Hausman test indicate IV methods should be used?
(e) Where possible, do Sargan tests to investigate which instruments are valid.

(f) Select (and justify) a final set of results and interpret the coefficient estimates.

Discuss the statistical results (i.e. t-tests and confidence intervals).

Appendix: Asymptotic results for the OLS and instrumental variables estimators

Asymptotic properties in case 1

We begin this appendix with a discussion of the properties of the OLS estimator under
the case 1 assumptions. Remember that these were the same as the classical assumptions,
except that the explanatory variable is now random. In particular, X_i for $i = 1, \ldots, N$
are i.i.d. random variables with

$$E(X_i) = \mu_{X,}$$
$$var(X_i) = \sigma_X^2.$$

Furthermore, it was assumed that

$$cov(X_i, \varepsilon_i) = E(X_i \varepsilon_i) = 0.$$

Asymptotic results for this case were derived in Appendix 2 of Chapter 3. We will not
repeat these derivations here. However, it is worthwhile reminding you that $\widehat{\beta}$ is a consistent estimator of β and that the OLS estimator is asymptotically normal. In particular,
as $N \to \infty$ we have

$$\sqrt{N}(\widehat{\beta} - \beta) \text{ is } N\left(0, \frac{\sigma^2}{\sigma_X^2 + \mu_X^2}\right).$$

When using this result in practice, $(\sigma_X^2 + \mu_X^2)$ can be replaced with $\frac{1}{N}\sum X_i^2$ (since the
latter is a consistent estimator of $\sigma_X^2 + \mu_X^2$). Plugging in this estimator and rearranging,
we obtain the approximate result

$$\widehat{\beta} \text{ is } N\left(\beta, \frac{\sigma^2}{\sum X_i^2}\right).$$

But this was the starting point for many important calculations in Chapter 3 (e.g. confidence intervals and t-tests). Thus, if the case 1 assumptions hold, all our familiar OLS
results can still be used.

Asymptotic properties in case 2

Next we derive the asymptotic properties of the OLS and IV estimators under the case 2 assumptions. Remember that the case 2 assumptions are the same as case 1 except that we now assume $cov(X_i, \varepsilon_i) \neq 0$.

Property 1: $\widehat{\beta}$ is an inconsistent estimator of β.

Proof:

$$\text{plim}\left(\widehat{\beta}\right) = \text{plim}\left(\beta + \frac{\sum X_i \varepsilon_i}{\sum X_i^2}\right)$$

$$= \beta + \text{plim}\left(\frac{\sum X_i \varepsilon_i}{\sum X_i^2}\right) \text{ by Slutsky's theorem}$$

$$= \beta + \text{plim}\left(\frac{\frac{1}{N}\sum X_i \varepsilon_i}{\frac{1}{N}\sum X_i^2}\right)$$

$$= \beta + \frac{\text{plim}\left(\frac{1}{N}\sum X_i \varepsilon_i\right)}{\text{plim}\left(\frac{1}{N}\sum X_i^2\right)} \text{ by Slutsky's theorem.}$$

We can now use the law of large numbers (LLN) to say $\text{plim}\left(\frac{1}{N}\sum X_i^2\right) = E(X_i^2) = \sigma_X^2 + \mu_X^2$. The last equality is established by rearranging the formula for variance: $var(X_i) = E(X_i^2) - [E(X_i)]^2$.

Hence,

$$\text{plim}\left(\widehat{\beta}\right) = \beta + \frac{\text{plim}\left(\frac{1}{N}\sum X_i \varepsilon_i\right)}{\sigma_X^2 + \mu_X^2}.$$

Now we can use the LLN to figure out $\text{plim}\left(\frac{1}{N}\sum X_i \varepsilon_i\right)$:

$$\text{plim}\left(\frac{1}{N}\sum X_i \varepsilon_i\right) = E(X_i \varepsilon_i) = cov(X_i, \varepsilon_i) \neq 0.$$

Hence,

$$\text{plim}\left(\widehat{\beta}\right) = \beta + \frac{cov(X_i, \varepsilon_i)}{\sigma_X^2 + \mu_X^2} \neq \beta$$

and OLS is inconsistent.

Property 2: $\widehat{\beta}_{\text{IV}}$ is a consistent estimator of β.

Proof: Firstly we replace Y_i with $\beta X_i + \varepsilon_i$ and rearrange to write $\widehat{\beta}_{\text{IV}}$ as

$$\widehat{\beta}_{\text{IV}} = \beta + \frac{\sum Z_i \varepsilon_i}{\sum X_i Z_i}.$$

Taking the plim of this equation, we obtain

$$\text{plim}\left(\widehat{\beta}_{\text{IV}}\right) = \text{plim}\left(\beta + \frac{\sum Z_i \varepsilon_i}{\sum X_i Z_i}\right)$$

$$= \beta + \text{plim}\left(\frac{\sum Z_i \varepsilon_i}{\sum X_i Z_i}\right) \text{ by Slutsky's theorem}$$

$$= \beta + \text{plim}\left(\frac{\frac{1}{N}\sum Z_i \varepsilon_i}{\frac{1}{N}\sum X_i Z_i}\right)$$

$$= \beta + \frac{\text{plim}\left(\frac{1}{N}\sum Z_i \varepsilon_i\right)}{\text{plim}\left(\frac{1}{N}\sum X_i Z_i\right)} \text{ by Slutsky's theorem.}$$

But the LLN can be used to figure out $\text{plim}\left(\frac{1}{N}\sum Z_i \varepsilon_i\right)$. In particular, it says that

$$\text{plim}\left(\frac{1}{N}\sum Z_i \varepsilon_i\right) = E(Z_i \varepsilon_i) = 0.$$

We can also use the LLN to say $\text{plim}\left(\frac{1}{N}\sum X_i Z_i\right) = E(X_i Z_i) = \sigma_{XZ} + \mu_X \mu_Z$, where the formula for covariance is used to show the last equality. Hence,

$$\text{plim}(\widehat{\beta}_{\text{IV}}) = \beta + \frac{0}{\sigma_{XZ} + \mu_X \mu_Z} = \beta.$$

and consistency is proved.

Property 3: The IV estimator is asymptotically normal
As $N \to \infty$ we have

$$\sqrt{N}(\widehat{\beta} - \beta) \text{ is } N\left(0, \frac{(\sigma_Z^2 + \mu_Z^2)\sigma^2}{(\sigma_{XZ} + \mu_X \mu_Z)^2}\right).$$

Proof: The equation derived above

$$\widehat{\beta}_{\text{IV}} = \beta + \frac{\sum Z_i \varepsilon_i}{\sum X_i Z_i}.$$

can be written as

$$\sqrt{N}(\widehat{\beta}_{\text{IV}} - \beta) = \sqrt{N}\frac{\sum Z_i \varepsilon_i}{\sum X_i Z_i}$$

$$= \sqrt{N}\frac{\frac{1}{N}\sum Z_i \varepsilon_i}{\frac{1}{N}\sum X_i Z_i}.$$

But we can use the CLT on the numerator to say that, as $N \to \infty$,

$$\sqrt{N}\frac{1}{N}\sum Z_i\varepsilon_i \text{ is } N(0, var(Z_i\varepsilon_i)).$$

Using properties of expected values and variances (remember we have assumed Z_i and ε_i to be uncorrelated with one another and hence $cov(Z_i, \varepsilon_i) = 0$, we find

$$var(Z_i\varepsilon_i) = (\sigma_Z^2 + \mu_Z^2)\sigma^2.$$

In our proof of property 2 we have already shown that

$$\text{plim}\left(\frac{1}{N}\sum X_iZ_i\right) = \sigma_{XZ} + \mu_X\mu_Z.$$

Using Cramer's theorem we can say

$$\sqrt{N}(\widehat{\beta}_{IV} - \beta) \text{ converges to } N\left(0, \frac{(\sigma_Z^2 + \mu_Z^2)\sigma^2}{(\sigma_{XZ} + \mu_X\mu_Z)^2}\right).$$

Endnotes

1. Note that some textbooks get rid of the σ^2 altogether and simply write $var(\varepsilon_i) = \omega_i^2$. This will lead to results exactly the same as those in this textbook. The σ^2 is a factor common to all the error variances and it does not matter if it is bundled into a single expression for the error variance or left in front (as is done in this book).
2. *RSS* is defined in Chapter 2 in the discussion of R^2.
3. The clever reader will have noticed that we did not have to recalculate the *GQ* statistic for the second test since it is simply the inverse of the first *GQ* statistic we calculated.
4. In practice, it would be wise to do a Breusch–Pagan or White test on this transformed regression as a final check to be absolutely sure the heteroskedasticity problem is corrected.
5. The summations begin at $s + 1$ since $\widehat{\varepsilon}_{s-1}, \ldots, \widehat{\varepsilon}_0$ are not observed. This is equivalent to the common practice of setting initial conditions for errors to zero.
6. A web search using Google (or any popular search engine) turns up dozens of sites where you can find these tables.

CHAPTER 6

Univariate Time Series Analysis

6.1 Introduction

Many applications in economics, especially in the fields of macroeconomics and finance, are concerned with the analysis of time series data. However, most of the examples in previous chapters use cross-sectional data. This allowed us to build up the basic ideas underlying regression, including statistical concepts such as hypothesis testing and confidence intervals, in a simple manner. When working with time series variables, knowledge of such ideas is essential. However, some additional issues arise when working with time series data. This chapter and the following one describe these additional issues. In the present chapter, we focus on *univariate time series analysis* which involves a single variable. The end goal of most empirical studies is to work with a regression model or something similar. That is, to work with a model where there are several variables (i.e. a dependent variable and one or more explanatory variables). Thus, univariate time series analysis is not our end goal (our end goal, regression modelling with time series variables, is discussed in the following chapter). In light of this, you may be wondering why we devote an entire chapter to univariate time series analysis. There are two reasons for this. Firstly, by working with a single variable, we can introduce the basic ideas and notation relating to time series variables in the simplest case. Secondly, as you will see, when working with time series variables it is important to understand the properties of each individual variable before proceeding to a regression model involving many variables. The present chapter on univariate time series analysis develops the tools necessary to obtain this understanding.

To provide some more intuition for how econometric methods with time series variables differ from those using cross-sectional variables, remember that the goal is to develop a regression relating a dependent variable to some explanatory variables.

However, the analyst using time series data will face two problems that the analyst using cross-sectional data will not encounter:

1. One time series variable can influence another with a time lag.
2. If the variables are *non-stationary*, a problem known as *spurious regression* may arise.

The first problem can be understood intuitively with some simple examples. When we estimate a regression model we are interested in measuring the effect of one or more explanatory variables on the dependent variable. In the case of time series data we have to be very careful in our choice of explanatory variables since their effect on the dependent variable may take time to become manifest. For instance, if a central bank is worried that inflation is rising, it will likely raise interest rates. The impact of this interest rate change will doubtless take more than a year to feed through the economy and to affect inflation and other important variables (e.g. the unemployment rate). In general, all of the basic tools of monetary and fiscal policy the government has as its disposal will have impacts that will be felt only in some future period. This problem is most common in macroeconomics, but can also occur in microeconomics. To give an example: a firm's decision to carry out a new investment (e.g. purchase new computers) will not immediately affect production. It takes time to purchase the computers, install them, and train workers in their use. Investment will only influence production some time in the future. To put this concept in the language of regression, this means that the value of the dependent variable at a given point in time can depend not only on the value of the explanatory variable at that time period but also on values of the explanatory variable in the past.

At this stage, you will not understand the second problem listed above. The terms non-stationary, stationary and spurious regression will be discussed in detail below. But keep in mind a general rule that we will develop later: if you have non-stationary time series variables, then you should not simply include them in a regression model. The appropriate route is to transform the variables in order to make them stationary before running a regression. There is one exception to this general rule, which we will discuss in the next chapter. This exception occurs where the variables in a regression model are *cointegrated*. We will elaborate on what we mean by these terms later. If you find it confusing for them to be introduced now without definitions, just think in the following terms: some problems arise with time series data that do not arise with cross-sectional data. These problems make it risky naively to use multiple regression in the manner of the previous chapters. The purpose of this and the following chapter is to show you how to modify regression techniques with time series data correctly.

In this chapter, we focus on the so-called *autoregressive model*. This applies the ideas we developed for autocorrelated errors in Chapter 5, Section 5.4, to a time series variable. The autoregressive model is the most popular univariate time series model since it can be written as a regression model. Thus all of the discussion of regression in previous chapters is relevant here. The autoregressive model also allows for a simple discussion of the important issue of non-stationarity. In particular, we will motivate and define the concept of a *unit root*. If a time series variable has a unit root, then it is non-stationary. There are many tests for a unit root, the most popular of which is the *Dickey–Fuller test* which we will cover in this chapter. There are many other univariate time series models. In the appendix to this chapter, we will discuss one of them, called the *moving average model*. This chapter also discusses volatility, a topic of particular importance for financial economics.

6.2 Time series notation

In Section 5.4 of Chapter 5, we introduced the regression model with autocorrelated errors. Since autocorrelated errors almost invariably arise with time series data, that section offered some discussion of relevance for time series topics. You may wish to refresh your memory of the concepts of that section, since the present chapter deals with similar issues. Remember that, when working with time series variables, we will use our time series notation of $t = 1, \ldots, T$ to denote observations (rather than $i = 1, \ldots, N$). This chapter is about univariate time series methods, and we will denote our single variable as Y_t.

The concept of a lagged variable is fundamental to time series data, so we will describe in some detail what it means and how to construct and work with lagged variables on a computer. We do this mostly because it really helps to understand what lagged variables are by seeing how they are constructed. We have time series data for $t = 1, \ldots, T$ periods on our variable Y. Consider creating a new variable W which has observations $W_t = Y_t$ for $t = 2, \ldots, T$ and a new variable Z which has observations $Z_t = Y_{t-1}$ for $t = 2, \ldots, T$. Why do we write $t = 2, \ldots, T$ instead of $t = 1, \ldots, T$? If we had written $t = 1, \ldots, T$ then the first observation of the variable Z, Z_1, would be set equal to Y_0. But we do not know what Y_0 is since variable Y is observed only from $t = 1, \ldots, T$. In other words, W and Z have only $T - 1$ observations. Note also that, had we created another new variable $X_t = Y_{t-2}$, then this variable X would have observations from $t = 3, \ldots, T$ and contain only $T - 2$ observations.

The new variables W and Z both have $T - 1$ observations. If we imagine W and Z as two columns containing $T - 1$ numbers each (as in a spreadsheet), we can see that the first element of W will be Y_2 and the first element of Z will be Y_1. The second element of W and Z will be Y_3 and Y_2, etc. In other words, we say that Z contains Y one period ago or *lagged one period*. In general, we can create variables 'Y lagged one period' (or 'lagged Y' for short), 'Y lagged two periods', or, in general, 'Y lagged j periods'. You can think of 'Y', 'Y lagged one period', 'Y lagged two periods', etc., as different variables in the same way as (in the house price example used in previous chapters) you can think of 'house price', 'lot size', or 'number of bedrooms' as different variables. Much of univariate time series analysis can be thought of as creating a regression model using Y as the dependent variable and lags of Y as the explanatory variables.

Note, however, that, if you want to include several explanatory variables in a multiple regression model, all variables must have the same number of observations. Let us consider the implication of this statement in the present context. Since lagged variables contain fewer observations than the original variable, any regression you build with lagged variables must incorporate this fact. For instance, if Y is the dependent variable and the explanatory variables are 'Y lagged one period' and 'Y lagged two periods', then this last

Table 6.1 Creating lagged variables.

Row number	Y	Lagged Y	Y lagged two periods	Y lagged three periods
1	Y_4	Y_3	Y_2	Y_1
2	Y_5	Y_4	Y_3	Y_2
3	Y_6	Y_5	Y_4	Y_3
4	Y_7	Y_6	Y_5	Y_4
5	Y_8	Y_7	Y_6	Y_5
6	Y_9	Y_8	Y_7	Y_6
7	Y_{10}	Y_9	Y_8	Y_7

explanatory variable will contain only $T - 2$ observations. You must make sure that all variables have this number of observations by cutting off initial observations. The example below illustrates how this is done. In general, each variable in a time series regression must contain the number of observations equal to T minus the maximum number of lags that any variable has. The issues discussed in this paragraph are often referred to as relating to *initial conditions*. In this textbook, we will treat initial conditions as described in this paragraph, but note that there are more sophisticated methods for treating initial discussion that do not involve working with cutting off initial observations.

As an example, suppose we have ten observations on variable Y (i.e. $Y_1, Y_2, \ldots, Y_{10}$) and we wish to run a regression model that includes Y, lagged Y, Y lagged two periods and Y lagged three periods. Table 6.1 shows what the variables would look like when used in a regression.

Note that each of the variables contains seven observations, which is T minus the maximum number of lags (i.e. $10 - 3 = 7$). Looking across any row (e.g. row 4), you can see: (a) that Y contains data at a particular point in time (e.g. row 4 contains Y at period $t = 7$); (b) lagged Y will contain the observation from one period previously (e.g. row 4 will contain Y at period $t = 6$); (c) Y lagged two periods will contain the observation from two periods previously (e.g. row 4 will contain Y at period $t = 5$); and (d) Y lagged three periods will contain the observation from three periods previously (e.g. row 4 will contain Y at period $t = 4$). Most econometrics software packages (e.g. E-views, Stata, or MicroFit) will create lagged variables automatically with a simple command, but not most spreadsheet packages such as Excel. If you are using a spreadsheet, you will have to create a table like Table 6.1. This is a key reason why, when working with time series data, you might want to learn an econometrics software package and not work with a spreadsheet such as Excel.

It is also important to make sure that one more notational convention is clear. Note that, as with any variable, the subscript denotes which observation is referred to (e.g. Y_{10} is the tenth observation for the variable Y). So Y_{t-1} is the $(t - 1)$th observation of Y. However, we will also sometimes use Y_{t-1} to denote the entire variable 'Y lagged one period' (or Y_{t-j} to denote the entire variable 'Y lagged j periods'). Thus, our subscript notation, in terms of distinguishing between a variable and a particular observation of a variable, will be a little loose. This is okay (and common in textbooks), since the meaning will be fairly obvious from the context and the alternative is to clutter up equations with numerous subscripts.

6.3 Trends in time series variables

At the beginning of this chapter, we said that an important motivation for univariate time series analysis is that it is necessary to understand the properties of individual time series variables before proceeding to build a regression model. We said (without explanation) that, if the variables are non-stationary, then a problem known as spurious regression may arise. In practice, the issue of whether a variable is stationary or non-stationary is closely related to the concept of a trend. In this section, we define and discuss the concept of a trend as the first step in providing an intuitive understanding of the crucial issue of non-stationarity.

We will illustrate some of the relevant issues using an important macroeconomic variable: personal income. Figure 6.1 is a time series plot of the logarithm of personal income in the USA from the first quarter of 1954 through to the last quarter of 1994. In other words, Y_t is the log of personal income for $t = 1954Q1, \ldots, 1994Q4$. The original personal income variable is measured in millions of dollars.

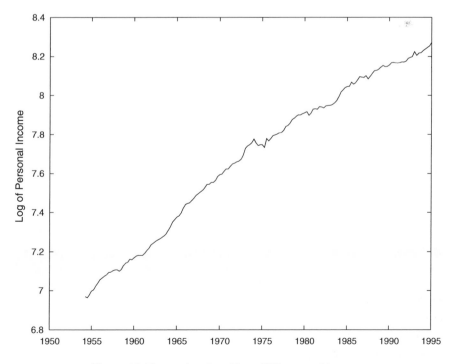

Figure 6.1 Time series plot of log of US personal income.

Note that the log of personal income seems to be increasing over time at a roughly constant rate. You can see some variation (e.g. the brief falls in personal income corresponding to the recessions of the mid-1970s and early 1980s), but overall the time series plot is roughly a straight line with a positive slope. This sustained (in this case upward) movement is referred to as a *trend*. Many macroeconomic and financial variables (e.g. GDP, the price level, industrial production, consumption, government spending, stock market indices, etc.) exhibit trends of this sort.

It is convenient at this point to introduce the concept of *differencing*. Formally, if Y_t is a time series variable, then $\Delta Y_t = Y_t - Y_{t-1}$ is the first difference of Y_t. ΔY_t measures the change or growth in a variable over time. If Y_t is a variable that has been logged, then the properties of the log operator imply that $100 \times \Delta Y_t$ measures the percentage change in the original variable between time $t - 1$ and t. This convenient result is another justification for working with logs of variables.[1] ΔY_t is often called 'delta Y' or 'the change in Y'.

Figure 6.2 plots the change in the log of personal income using the data in Figure 6.1. The values on the Y axis can be interpreted as percentages in the sense that 0.02 corresponds to 2 %, etc. Note that Figure 6.2 looks very different from Figure 6.1. The trend behavior noted in Figure 6.1 has disappeared completely (we will return to this point later as it is an important one). The figure indicates that personal income tends to be growing around 1 % per quarter, although there is considerable variability to this growth rate

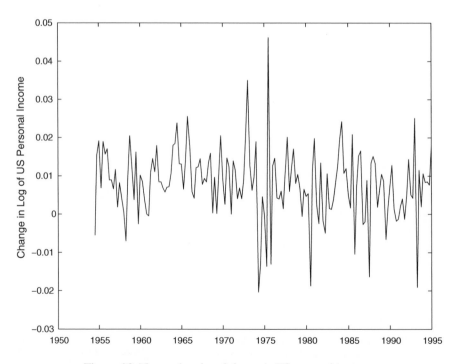

Figure 6.2 Time series plot of change in US personal income.

over time. In some recessionary periods personal income is falling, while in some expansionary periods it is growing by as much as 3 or 4 % per quarter.

Another property of time series data, not usually present in cross-sectional data, is the existence of correlation across observations. Personal income today, for example, is highly correlated with personal income last quarter. In fact, if we calculate the correlation between personal income and lagged personal income we obtain a value of 0.999716 which is very close to 1 (the value that indicates perfect correlation). Yet, if we calculate the correlation between the change in personal income and the change in personal income lagged once, we obtain -0.00235 (a value close to zero which indicates a complete lack of correlation). These findings make intuitive sense. Macroeconomic time series such as income, GDP, consumption, etc., change only slowly over time; even in deep recessions they rarely fall by more than 1 or 2 % per quarter. Consequently, this quarter's income tends to be quite similar to last quarter's, and thus they are highly correlated with one another. In contrast, the change or growth of macroeconomic time series is more erratic. This quarter's and last quarter's change in personal income can be quite different, as reflected in the near-zero correlation between them.

Figures 6.1 and 6.2 and the correlation results discussed in the previous paragraph were calculated using US personal income. But other macroeconomic time series in many other countries exhibit very similar types of behavior. Y, in other words, tends to exhibit trend behavior and to be highly correlated over time, but ΔY tends to the opposite, i.e. exhibits no trend behavior and is not highly correlated over time. These properties are quite important to regression modeling with time series variables as they relate closely to the issue of non-stationarity. Accordingly, we will spend the rest of this chapter developing formal tools and models for dealing with them.

6.4   The autocorrelation function

The correlations discussed above are simple examples of *autocorrelations* (i.e. correlations involving a variable and a lag of itself). The *autocorrelation function* is a common tool used by researchers to understand the properties of a time series variable. In general, we may be interested in the correlation between Y and Y lagged p periods. For instance, our personal income data are observed quarterly, so the correlation between Y and Y lagged $p = 4$ periods is the correlation between income now and income a year ago (i.e. a year is four quarters). We will denote such correlations by r_p so that

$$r_p = corr(Y_t, Y_{t-p}).$$

The autocorrelation function treats r_p as a function of p (i.e. it calculates r_p for $p = 1, \ldots, P$). P is the maximum lag length considered and is typically chosen to be quite large (e.g. $P = 12$ for monthly data).

As a practical aside, note that r_p is the correlation between a variable (say, Y) and Y lagged p periods. Remember that Y lagged p periods contains $T - p$ observations. So

Table 6.2   Autocorrelation functions.

Lag length, p	Personal income, Y	Change in personal income, ΔY
1	0.9997	−0.0100
2	0.9993	0.0121
3	0.9990	0.1341
4	0.9986	0.0082
5	0.9983	−0.1562
6	0.9980	0.0611
7	0.9978	−0.0350
8	0.9975	−0.0655
9	0.9974	0.0745
10	0.9972	0.1488
11	0.9969	0.0330
12	0.9966	0.0363

when we calculate r_p we are implicitly 'throwing away' the first p observations. If we considered extremely long lags, we would be calculating autocorrelations with very few observations. In the extreme case, if we set $p = T$ we have no observations left to use. This is a justification for not letting p get too big. Note also that the autocorrelation function involves using different lagged variables. In theory, we can use data from $t = 2, \ldots, T$ to calculate r_1, data from $t = 3, \ldots, T$ to calculate r_2, etc., ending with data from $t = P + 1, \ldots, T$ to calculate r_P. However, this means that each autocorrelation is calculated with a different number of data points, and hence they are not directly comparable. For this reason, it is standard practice to select a maximum lag, P, and use data from $t = P + 1, \ldots, T$ for calculating all of the autocorrelations.

Table 6.2 presents the autocorrelation functions for $Y = $ US personal income and $\Delta Y = $ the change in personal income using a maximum lag of 12 (i.e. $P = 12$). A striking feature of the table is that autocorrelations tend to be virtually 1 for personal income even in the case of high lag lengths. In contrast, the autocorrelations for the change in personal income are very small and exhibit a pattern that looks more or less random; the autocorrelations, in other words, are essentially zero. This pattern is common to many or most macroeconomic time series: the time series itself has autocorrelations near 1, but the change in the series has autocorrelations that are much smaller (often near zero).

Below are a few ways of thinking about these autocorrelations:

- Y is highly correlated over time. Even personal income 3 years ago (i.e. $p = 12$) is highly correlated with income today. ΔY does not exhibit this property. The growth in personal income this quarter is essentially uncorrelated with the growth in previous quarters.
- If you knew past values of personal income, you could make a very good estimate of what personal income was this quarter. However, knowing past values of the change in personal income will not help you predict the change in personal income this quarter.

- Informally speaking, Y 'remembers the past' (i.e. it is highly correlated with past values of itself). This is an example of *long memory* behavior. ΔY does not have this property.
- Y is a non-stationary series while ΔY is stationary. We have not formally defined the words 'non-stationary' and 'stationary', but they are quite important in time series econometrics. We will have more to say about them later, but note for now that the properties of the autocorrelation function for Y are characteristic of non-stationary series.

6.5 The autoregressive model

The autocorrelation function is a useful tool for summarizing the properties of a time series variable.[2] However, as we have argued previously, correlations have their limitations and in most cases regression is a preferable tool. The same reasoning holds here. Autocorrelations, in other words, are just correlations, and for this reason it may be desirable to develop more sophisticated models to analyze the relationships between a variable and lags of itself. Many such models have been developed in the statistical literature on univariate time series analysis, but the most common model, which can also be interpreted as a regression model, is the so-called *autoregressive* model. As the name suggests, it is a regression model where the explanatory variables are lags of the dependent variable (i.e. 'auto' means 'self' and hence an autoregression is a regression of a variable on lags of itself). The word 'autoregressive' is usually shortened to 'AR'. We have briefly discussed some aspects of the AR model in Chapter 5. In that chapter, we assumed that the errors in a regression had an AR structure. In this chapter, we use the AR structure for the variable itself.

6.5.1 The AR(1) model

We begin by discussing the autoregressive model with the explanatory variable being the dependent variable lagged one period. This is called the AR(1) model:

$$Y_t = \alpha + \rho Y_{t-1} + \varepsilon_t$$

for $t = 2, \ldots, T$. It looks exactly like the simple regression model discussed in previous chapters, except that the explanatory variable is Y_{t-1}. The value of ρ in the AR(1) model is closely related to the behavior of the autocorrelation function and to the concept of non-stationarity. To introduce some other jargon relating to the AR(1) model, note that, when Y_t has an AR model, we sometimes say it is an *autoregressive process*.

In the Chapter 5 discussion of autocorrelated errors, we used the notation ρ to indicate the coefficient on the lagged error in the AR model for the regression errors. The ρ in the present chapter is not exactly the same, but does play a very similar role. You may wish to look back at Chapter 5, Section 5.4.1 on 'Properties of Autocorrelated Errors' to see the role that ρ plays in determining the properties of the errors. We could do virtually identical derivations in this chapter in order to discover the properties of a time series

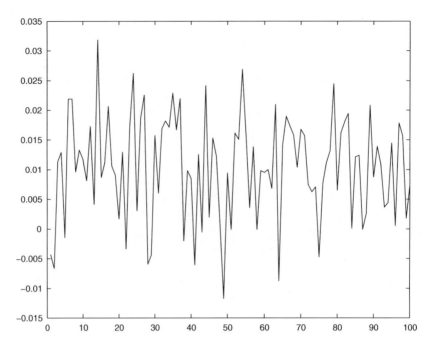

Figure 6.3 AR(1) time series with $\rho = 0$.

variable when it follows an AR(1) model. We do not provide these derivations here since they are so similar (see also exercise 2), but instead provide some practical illustrations of the properties of the AR(1) model.

In order to understand the types of behavior characteristic of an AR(1) process, let us artificially simulate three different time series using three different choices for $\rho : \rho = 0$, $\rho = 0.8$ and $\rho = 1$. All three series have the same values for α (i.e. $\alpha = 0.01$) and the same errors. Figures 6.3, 6.4, and 6.5 provide time series plots of the three datasets.

Note that Figure 6.3 (with $\rho = 0$) exhibits random-type fluctuations around an average of about 0.01 (the value of α). In fact, it is very similar to Figure 6.2, which contains a time series plot of the change in personal income. Figure 6.5 (with $\rho = 1$) exhibits trend behavior and looks very similar to Figure 6.1, which plots personal income. Figure 6.4 ($\rho = 0.8$) exhibits behavior that is somewhere in between the random fluctuations of Figure 6.3 and the strong trend of Figure 6.5.

Figures 6.3 to 6.5 illustrate the types of behavior that AR(1) models can capture and show why they are commonly used in macroeconomics and finance. For different values of ρ, these models can allow for the randomly fluctuating behavior typical of growth rates of many macroeconomic and financial time series, for the trend behavior typical of the macroeconomic and financial time series themselves, or for intermediate cases between these extremes.

Note also that $\rho = 1$ implies the type of trend behavior we have referred to as non-stationary above, while the other values of ρ imply stationary behavior. This allows us

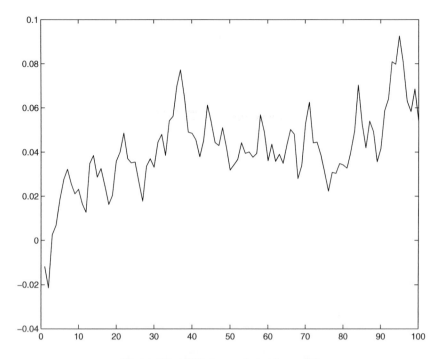

Figure 6.4 AR(1) time series with $\rho = 0.8$.

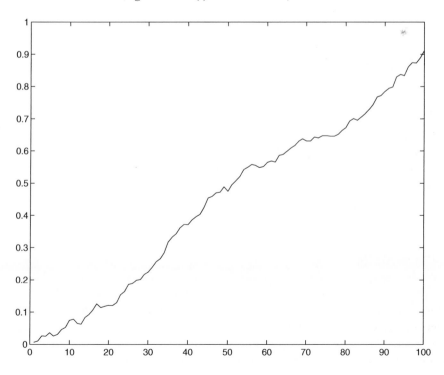

Figure 6.5 AR(1) time series with $\rho = 1$.

to provide a formal definition of the concepts of stationarity and non-stationarity, at least for the AR(1) model: for the AR(1) model, we can say that Y is stationary if $|\rho| < 1$ and is non- stationary if $\rho = 1$. The other possibility, $|\rho| > 1$, is rarely considered in economics. The latter possibility implies that the time series is exhibiting explosive behavior over time. Since such explosive behavior is only observed in unusual cases (e.g. hyperinflation), it is of little empirical relevance and we will not discuss it here.

Thus far, we have introduced the terms 'non-stationary' and 'stationary' without providing any formal definition (except for the AR(1) model). As we will see, the distinction between stationary and non-stationary time series is an extremely important one. We will formally define these concepts shortly. Before we do this, we provide some general intuition for these concepts.

Formally, 'non-stationary' merely means 'anything that is not stationary'. Economists usually focus on the one particular type of non-stationarity that seems to be present in many macroeconomic time series: unit root non-stationarity. We will generalize this concept later, but at this stage it is useful to think of a *unit root* as implying $\rho = 1$ in the AR(1) model. Different ways of thinking about whether a time series variable, Y, is stationary or has a unit root are as follows:

- In the AR(1) model , if $\rho = 1$, then Y has a unit root. If $|\rho| < 1$, then Y is stationary.
- If Y has a unit root, then its autocorrelations will be near 1 and will not drop much as lag length increases.
- If Y has a unit root, then it will have a long memory. Stationary time series do not have a long memory.
- If Y has a unit root, then the series will exhibit trend behavior (especially if α is non-zero).
- If Y has a unit root, then ΔY will be stationary. For this reason, series with unit roots are often referred to as *difference stationary* series.

The final point can be seen most clearly by subtracting Y_{t-1} from both sides of the equation in the AR(1) model, yielding

$$Y_t - Y_{t-1} = \alpha + \rho Y_{t-1} - Y_{t-1} + \varepsilon_t$$

or

$$\Delta Y_t = \alpha + \phi Y_{t-1} + \varepsilon_t,$$

where $\phi = \rho - 1$. Note that, if $\rho = 1$, then $\phi = 0$ and the previous equation implies that ΔY_t fluctuates randomly around α. For future reference, note that we can test for $\phi = 0$ to see if a series has a unit root. Furthermore, we have said that a time series will be stationary if $-1 < \rho < 1$ which is equivalent to $-2 < \phi < 0$. We will refer to this as the *stationarity condition*.

By way of providing more intuition (and jargon) for the AR(1) model, let us consider the case where $\rho = 1$ (or, equivalently, $\phi = 0$). In this case we can write the AR(1) model as

$$Y_t = \alpha + Y_{t-1} + \varepsilon_t.$$

This is referred to as a *random walk* model. More precisely, the random walk model has no intercept (i.e. $\alpha = 0$), while the preceding equation is referred to as a *random walk with drift*. The presence of the intercept allows for the growth rate of the time series to be, on average, non-zero. Since $\rho = 1$, Y has a unit root and is non-stationary. The pure random walk model is commonly thought to hold for phenomena such as stock prices. The price of a stock today is the price of a stock yesterday plus an (unpredictable) error term. The random walk with drift model is more appropriate for macroeconomic variables such as GDP which are, on average, growing over time. This line of argument provides additional force to the idea that non- stationarity exists in many time series in macroeconomics and finance.

The AR(1) model is a regression model. Accordingly, we can use OLS to regress the variable Y on an intercept and lagged Y. If we do this for the US personal income data used to create Figure 6.1, we find $\widehat{\alpha} = 0.039$ and $\widehat{\rho} = 0.996$. Since the OLS estimate, $\widehat{\rho}$, and the true value of the AR(1) coefficient, ρ, will rarely if ever be identical, it is quite possible that $\rho = 1$ since the OLS estimate is very close to 1. Note that, if we regress ΔY_t on Y_{t-1}, we obtain an OLS estimate of $\widehat{\phi} = -0.004$ which is $1 - \widehat{\rho}$ as we would expect.

6.5.2   Extensions of the AR(1) model

We have argued above that the AR(1) model can be interpreted as a simple regression model where Y is the dependent variable and lagged Y is the explanatory variable. However, it is possible that more lags of Y should be included as explanatory variables. This can be done by extending the AR(1) model to the autoregressive of order p, AR(p), model:

$$Y_t = \alpha + \rho_1 Y_{t-1} + \cdots + \rho_p Y_{t-p} + \varepsilon_t$$

for $t = p + 1, \ldots, T$. We will not discuss the properties of this model, other than to note that they are similar to the AR(1) model but are more general in nature (see exercise 2). That is, this model can generate the trend behavior typical of macroeconomic time series and the randomly fluctuating behavior typical of their growth rates, as well as intermediate cases.

As with the AR(1) model, when discussing unit root behavior it is convenient to subtract Y_{t-1} from both sides of the equation and rearrange the AR(p) model. If we do this, it can be shown (see exercise 3) that we can write the AR(p) model as

$$\Delta Y_t = \alpha + \phi Y_{t-1} + \gamma_1 \Delta Y_{t-1} + \cdots + \gamma_{p-1} \Delta Y_{t-p+1} + \varepsilon_t,$$

where the slope coefficients in this regression, $\phi, \gamma_1, \ldots, \gamma_{p-1}$, are simple functions of $\rho_1, \ldots, \rho_p$ from the original AR(p) model. For instance, $\phi = \rho_1 + \cdots + \rho_p - 1$. We stress that this is identical to the original AR(p) model, but is just written differently. Hence we refer to both previous equations as AR(p) models. In case you are wondering where the Y_{t-p} term from the first equation went to in the second, note that it appears in the second equation in the ΔY_{t-p+1} term (i.e. $\Delta Y_{t-p+1} = Y_{t-p+1} - Y_{t-p}$). Note also that both variants have the same number of coefficients, $p + 1$ (i.e. the first variant has $\alpha, \rho_1, \ldots, \rho_p$ while the second variant has $\alpha, \phi, \gamma_1, \ldots, \gamma_{p-1}$).

The key points to note here are as follows: the above equation is still in the form of a regression model; $\phi = 0$ implies that the AR(p) time series Y contains a unit root; if $-2 < \phi < 0$, then the series is stationary. Looking at the previous equation with $\phi = 0$ clarifies an important way of thinking about unit root series which we have highlighted previously: if a time series contains a unit root, then a regression model involving only ΔY and its lags is appropriate (i.e. if $\phi = 0$, then the term Y_{t-1} will drop out of the equation and only terms involving ΔY or its lags appear in the regression). It is common jargon to say that 'if a unit root is present, then the series can be differenced to induce stationarity'.

As we will discuss in the next chapter, with the exception of a case called cointegration, we do not want to include unit root variables in regression models. This motivates why it is important to know whether Y has a unit root. In the past, we have emphasized that unit root series exhibit trend behavior. Does this mean that we can simply examine time series plots of Y for such trending to determine if it indeed has a unit root? The answer is no. To explain why, let us introduce another model.

We showed previously that many macroeconomic time series contain trends and that AR models with unit roots imply trend behavior. However, there are other models that also imply trend behavior. Imagine that Figure 6.1 (or Figure 6.5) is an XY plot where the X axis is labeled time, and that we want to build a regression model using these data. You might be tempted to fit the following regression line:

$$Y_t = \alpha + \delta t + \varepsilon_t,$$

where the explanatory variable is simply time (and we have used δ to denote the coefficient on this explanatory variable). Note that you can interpret the previous regression as involving the variable Y and another variable with observations $1, 2, 3, 4, \ldots, T$. This is another regression model that yields trend behavior. To introduce some jargon, the term δt is referred to as a *deterministic trend* since it is an exact (i.e. deterministic) function of time. In contrast, unit root series contain a so-called *stochastic trend*.

We can even combine this model with the AR(1) model to obtain

$$Y_t = \alpha + \rho Y_{t-1} + \delta t + \varepsilon_t.$$

To illustrate the kind of properties such a model has, consider Figure 6.6 which is a time series plot of artificial data generated from the previous model with $\alpha = 0$, $\rho = 0.2$,

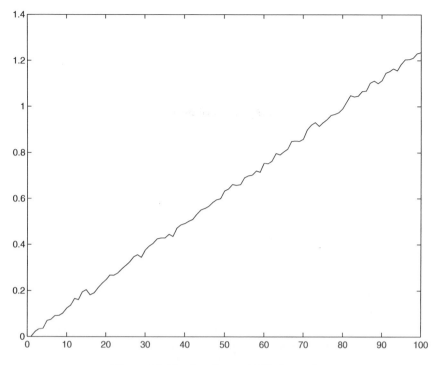

Figure 6.6 Trend stationary AR(1) time series.

and $\delta = 0.01$. Note that this series is stationary since $|\rho| < 1$. Yet Figure 6.6 looks much like Figure 6.5 (or Figure 6.1). Stationary models with a deterministic trend can yield time series plots that closely resemble those from non-stationary models having a stochastic trend. Thus, you should remember that looking at time series plots alone is not enough to tell whether a series has a unit root.

The discussion in the previous paragraph motivates jargon that we will use and introduce in the context of the following summary:

- The non-stationary time series variables on which we focus are those containing a unit root. These series contain a stochastic trend. But if we difference these time series, the resulting time series will be stationary. For this reason, they are often called *difference stationary*.
- The stationary time series on which we focus have $-2 < \phi < 0$ in the AR(p) model. However, these series can exhibit trend behavior through the incorporation of a deterministic trend. In this case, they are referred to as *trend stationary*.

If we add a deterministic trend to the AR(p) model, we obtain a very general model that is commonly used in univariate time series analysis:

$$\Delta Y_t = \alpha + \phi Y_{t-1} + \gamma_1 \Delta Y_{t-1} + \cdots + \gamma_{p-1} \Delta Y_{t-p+1} + \delta t + \varepsilon_t.$$

The above equation is referred to as the $AR(p)$ *with deterministic trend model.* You may wonder why we don't just use the original $AR(p)$ specification introduced at the beginning of this section (i.e. the one where the explanatory variables are $Y_{t-1}, \ldots, Y_{t-p}$). There are two reasons. Firstly, we are soon going to test for a unit root. With the present specification, this is simply a test of $\phi = 0$. Testing for whether regression coefficients are zero is a topic that we have learned previously (refer to the discussion of t-statistics in Chapters 2 and 3). With the original $AR(p)$ model, testing for a unit root is more complicated. Secondly, $Y_{t-1}, \ldots, Y_{t-p}$ are often highly correlated with each other (see the autocorrelation function in Table 6.2). If we were to use them as explanatory variables in our regression, we would often run into multicollinearity problems (see Chapters 2 and 4). However, in the present model we use $Y_{t-1}, \Delta Y_{t-1}, \ldots, \Delta Y_{t-p+1}$ as explanatory variables, which tend not to be highly correlated, thereby avoiding the problem.

Thus far our discussion of univariate time series has mostly focused on models (i.e. autoregressive models) as opposed to methods (i.e. estimators or test statistics). We will discuss hypothesis testing shortly. With regards to estimation, there are many ways of estimating AR models, and most relevant computer software packages will allow you to choose from several possible estimation methods such as maximum likelihood. However, the OLS estimator is very commonly used.[3] It can be shown (see exercise 4) to be the maximum likelihood estimator if we treat the initial p observations as fixed (as we are doing in this textbook to avoid problems caused by the fact that $Y_0, \ldots, Y_{1-p}$ are not observed).

Example: US personal income

Table 6.3 contains output from an OLS regression of ΔY_t on an intercept, $Y_{t-1}, \Delta Y_{t-1}, \Delta Y_{t-2}, \Delta Y_{t-3}$, and a deterministic time trend, created using the US personal income data. In other words, it provides regression output for the AR(4) with deterministic trend model. We suspect this personal income series may contain a unit root, a supposition supported somewhat by the table. In particular, a unit root is present if ϕ (the coefficient on Y_{t-1}) is zero. As we can see, the estimate of ϕ is indeed very small (i.e. $\widehat{\phi} = -0.018$).

Table 6.3   AR(4) with deterministic trend model.

Variable	OLS estimate	t-statistic	P-value
Intercept	0.138	1.279	0.203
Y_{t-1}	−0.018	−1.190	0.236
ΔY_{t-1}	−0.017	−0.217	0.829
ΔY_{t-2}	0.014	0.172	0.863
ΔY_{t-3}	0.130	1.627	0.106
t	0.0001	0.955	0.341

6.5.3 Testing in the AR(p) with deterministic trend model

In Chapters 2, 3, and 4, we described various hypothesis testing procedures in the regression model. In particular, we described how to test whether regression coefficients were equal to zero using the t-statistic and how tests of hypotheses involving several restrictions can be done using the F-statistic. These techniques can be used in the AR(p) with deterministic trend model (i.e. you may wish to omit explanatory variables whose coefficients are not significantly different from zero). In particular, testing is usually done to help choose lag length, p, and to decide whether the series has a unit root. In fact, it is common firstly to test to select lag length, and then to test for a unit root.

However, there is one important complication that occurs in the AR(p) model that was not present in earlier chapters. To understand it, let us divide the coefficients in the model into two groups: (1) $\alpha, \gamma_1, \ldots, \gamma_{p-1}, \delta$, and (2) ϕ. In other words, we consider hypothesis tests involving ϕ independently of those involving the other coefficients.

Testing involving $\alpha, \gamma_1, \ldots, \gamma_{p-1}$ and δ

Many sophisticated statistical criteria and testing methods exist to determine the appropriate lag length in an AR(p) model. Below we will discuss the use of so-called *information criteria* which can be used to select lag length. However, simply looking at t-statistics or F-statistics can be quite informative. For instance, an examination of Table 6.3 reveals that the P-values associated with the coefficients on the lagged ΔY terms are insignificant, and this suggests that they may be deleted from the regression (i.e. their P-values are greater than 0.05). Alternatively, a more common route is to choose a maximum lag length, *pmax*, and then sequentially drop lags if the relevant coefficients are insignificant.

In the AR(p) with deterministic trend model we also have to worry about testing whether $\delta = 0$. This can be accomplished in the standard way by checking whether its P-value is less than the level of significance (e.g. 0.05). This test can be done at any stage, but it is common to carry it out after following the sequential procedure for choosing p.

This testing strategy can be summarized as follows:

- *Step 1.* Choose the maximum lag length, *pmax*, that seems reasonable.
- *Step 2.* Estimate using OLS the AR(*pmax*) with deterministic trend model. If the P-value for testing $\gamma_{pmax-1} = 0$ is less than the significance level you choose (e.g. 0.05), then go to step 5, using *pmax* as lag length.[4] Otherwise go on to the next step.
- *Step 3.* Estimate the AR(*pmax* − 1) model. If the P-value for testing $\gamma_{pmax-2} = 0$ is less than the significance level you choose, then go to step 5, using *pmax* − 1 as lag length. Otherwise go on to the next step.
- *Step 4.* Repeatedly estimate lower-order AR models until you find an AR(p) model where $\gamma_{p-1} = 0$ is statistically significant (or you run out of lags).
- *Step 5.* Now test for whether the deterministic trend should be omitted; that is, if the P-value for testing $\delta = 0$ is greater than the significance level you choose, then drop the deterministic trend variable.

Example: US personal income (continued)

If we carry out the preceding strategy on the personal income data, beginning with *pmax* = 4, the model reduces to

$$\Delta Y_t = \alpha + \phi Y_{t-1} + \varepsilon_t.$$

That is, we first estimated an AR(4) with deterministic trend (see Table 6.3) and found the coefficient on ΔY_{t-3} to be insignificant. Accordingly, we estimated an AR(3) with deterministic trend and found the coefficient on ΔY_{t-2} to be insignificant. We then dropped the latter variable and ran an AR(2), etc. Eventually, after finding the deterministic trend to be insignificant, we settled on the AR(1) model. OLS estimation results for this model are given in Table 6.4.

Table 6.4   AR(1) model.

Variable	OLS estimate	t-statistic	P-value
Intercept	0.039	2.682	0.008
Y_{t-1}	−0.004	−2.130	0.035

Model selection versus model averaging

As a digression, it is worth noting that the strategy outlined above is a good example of a *sequential testing procedure*. That is, a sequence of hypothesis tests are carried out with the goal of selecting a single best model. Most econometricians use this strategy of *model selection*. For instance, in our example, we estimated five models: the AR(4) with deterministic trend, the AR(3) with deterministic trend, the AR(2) with deterministic trend, the AR(1) with deterministic trend, and the AR(1) model.

Sequential testing procedures have been criticised by many. We do not provide formal proofs of the basic results that underlie these criticisms. However, it is worthwhile intuitively motivating their nature. Firstly, each time a hypothesis test is carried out, the possibility always exists that a mistake will be made (i.e. the researcher will reject the 'better model' for a 'not so good' one). The possibility of making a mistake quickly multiplies as sequences of hypothesis tests are carried out. So, for instance, a claim that a P-value of 0.05 on a regression coefficient (e.g. β_j) means that $H_0: \beta_j = 0$ is rejected at the 5 % level of significance is potentially misleading if the regression is selected on the basis of previous hypothesis tests. Secondly, even if a sequential hypothesis testing procedure does lead to the selection of the 'best' model, common sense suggests that it is rarely desirable simply to present results for this model and ignore all evidence from the 'not quite so good' models. Generally speaking, these worries about model selection are reflected in the common empirical wisdom that, if you mine the data long enough, you are bound to find something – but you should not put too much trust in your finding.

For these reasons, the strategy of selecting a single model has been criticised by some (particularly Bayesian econometricians, see Chapter 10). Bayesians (and some non-Bayesians) tend to prefer a strategy of *model averaging*. That is, instead of selecting a single model, empirical results would be presented in a research paper that are a weighted average of those in all of the models used. Of course, not all models are equal. Some fit the data better than others. The weights in the weighted average are geared to give the better models more weight. This short description will not be enough for you to do model averaging in practice.[5] However, we provide this brief discussion so that you can at least have an intuitive grasp of this important issue.

Using information criteria to select a model

An alternative approach to model selection is to use an *information criterion*. Intuitively, this is a measure of how good the model is. To use an information criterion, you simply calculate it for every model and select the model that yields the highest information criterion. Most econometric software packages calculate information criteria automatically, so they are easy to use in practice. Information criteria can be used with any type of model. For instance, if you have two regression models with the same dependent variable but different explanatory variables, an information criterion can be used to choose between them. In fact, the familiar $\bar{R}^2$ discussed in Chapter 4 can be interpreted in a similar manner to an information criterion. Nevertheless, information criteria are most commonly used with time series models (e.g. for lag length selection), so this is a convenient place to discuss them.

Formal derivation and motivation of any of the various information criteria used by econometricians would involve technical details beyond the scope of this textbook. Hence, we just provide some general intuition and then define a few popular choices. We have used different notation in the various regression models used in this book. For instance, in the simple regression model we used β to denote the regression coefficient, in the AR(1) model we used ρ as the coefficient on the lagged dependent variable, and in a variant on the AR(1) model we used ϕ. Since information criteria can be used with all these models, we will use a general notation, θ, to denote 'all the coefficients in the model'. The likelihood function is thus $L(\theta)$. The likelihood function can loosely be interpreted as a measure of how well the model is fitting the data. It is sensible that this should enter information criteria, and indeed it does. Information criteria typically have the form

$$IC(\theta) = 2\ln[L(\theta)] - g(p),$$

where p is the number of coefficients in the model and $g(p)$ is an increasing function of p. The traditional use of information criteria involves evaluating $IC(\theta)$ at a particular point (e.g. the OLS or maximum likelihood estimates for θ) for every model under consideration and choosing the model with the highest information criteria. Information criteria differ in the functional form used for $g(p)$. This is a function that rewards parsimony. That it, it penalizes models with excessive numbers of coefficients.

In our discussion of R^2 and $\bar{R}^2$ in Chapter 4, we noted that R^2 should not be used to select models since adding new explanatory variables (even if they are not significant) will always increase it. By adding a new explanatory variable, there is no way the fit can be made worse. After all, the regression could always set the coefficient on the new variable to zero and achieve exactly the same fit as before. In general, the fit gets better by adding a new explanatory variable. The same kind of thing happens with likelihood functions: by adding a new explanatory variable, the likelihood function (evaluated at the maximum likelihood estimator) will always get larger, even if the new explanatory variable is insignificant. This motivates why we add the $g(p)$ term in $IC(\theta)$ which ensures that adding extra explanatory variables is penalized. So, for instance, an information criterion will only suggest adding an extra lag into an $AR(p)$ model if the benefit of adding it (in terms of an increase in the likelihood function) is worth the cost (in terms of the penalty function, $g(p)$).

Probably the most common information criterion is the *Bayesian information criterion* (or BIC):

$$BIC(\theta) = 2\ln[L(\theta)] - p\ln(T).$$

This is sometimes referred to as the *Schwarz criterion*. Two other popular information criteria are the *Akaike information criterion* (or AIC), given by

$$AIC(\theta) = 2\ln[L(\theta)] - 2p,$$

and the *Hannan–Quinn criterion* (or HQ), given by

$$HQ(\theta) = 2\ln[L(\theta)] - pc_{HQ}\ln[\ln(N)],$$

where c_{HQ} is a constant and various choices for this constant have been recommended. HQ is a consistent model selection criterion[6] if $c_{HQ} > 2$.

Testing involving ϕ: unit root testing

To complete our discussion of hypothesis testing in the $AR(p)$ with deterministic trend model, we need to address one more, extremely important, testing question: does Y contain a unit root? Remember that, if $\phi = 0$, then Y contains a unit root. In this case, the series must be differenced in the regression model (i.e. the series is difference stationary). You may think that you can simply test $\phi = 0$ in the same manner as you tested the significance of the other coefficients. For instance, in Table 6.4 the t-statistic for the coefficient ϕ is -2.13. If you look in the Student t statistical tables (for the appropriate sample size), you find a 5 % critical value of approximately 1.97. Since the absolute value of the test statistic is greater than the critical value, you may be tempted to conclude that ϕ is not zero, and, therefore, that Y does not have a unit root. THIS IS INCORRECT! In hypothesis testing, ϕ is different from other coefficients and we must treat it differently.

To understand fully why you cannot carry out a unit root test of $\phi = 0$ in the same manner as you would test other coefficients requires that you have knowledge of statistics beyond that covered in this book. Suffice it to note here that, if you just select the OLS option in econometric software packages, they implicitly assume that all of the variables in the model are stationary when they calculate *P*-values. If the explanatory variable Y_{t-1} is non-stationary, its *P*-value will be incorrect.

An alternative way of making this point is to note that, in Chapter 3, we showed how the *t*-statistic had a Student *t*-distribution. Thus, the critical value for the *t*-test must be taken from statistical tables for the Student *t*-distribution. When testing whether $\phi = 0$, we can calculate a *t*-statistic. But it no longer has a Student *t*-distribution. To show why this is so would involve some more difficult mathematics, but a little bit of intuition is provided in the following paragraph.

In Chapter 3, when we were working with the simple regression model under the classical assumptions, we derived

$$\widehat{\beta} \text{ is } N\left(\beta, \frac{\sigma^2}{\sum X_i^2}\right)$$

and then used it to work out the distribution of the *t*-statistic. With the autoregressive model, the classical assumptions do not hold. In particular, we cannot assume that the explanatory variables are fixed (i.e. not random variables). After all, the explanatory variables are lags of the dependent variable. If the dependent variable is random, then so should be the explanatory variables. In the simple regression model, with a random explanatory variable, the preceding equation is replaced by

$$\widehat{\beta} \text{ is } N\left(\beta, \frac{\sigma^2}{TE(X^2)}\right).$$

In the AR(1) model (with ϕ being the coefficient on the lagged dependent variable), you would think this should become

$$\widehat{\phi} \text{ is } N\left(\phi, \frac{\sigma^2}{TE(Y_{t-1}^2)}\right).$$

Note, however, that $E(Y_{t-1}^2) = var(Y_{t-1}) + [E(Y_{t-1})]^2$ in the previous expression and remember that Y (and, hence, lagged Y) has a unit root if the hypothesis $\phi = 0$ is true. The variance of a unit root variable is infinite (see Section 5.4 of Chapter 5 or exercise 2), and thus $E(Y_{t-1}^2)$ is infinite. Hence, the type of derivations we did in Chapter 3 will not work here. To work out the correct distribution of $\widehat{\phi}$ is more complicated, requiring tools not covered in this textbook. This paragraph is meant only to provide some intuition for why the standard derivations we have done for the simple regression model do not work in the case of ϕ.

Table 6.5 Critical values for the Dickey–Fuller test.

	$T = 25$	$T = 50$	$T = 100$	$T = \infty$
	AR model does not have deterministic trend			
1 % critical value	−3.75	−3.59	−3.50	−3.42
5 % critical value	−2.99	−2.93	−2.90	−2.80
	AR model does have deterministic trend			
1 % critical value	−4.38	−4.15	−4.04	−3.96
5 % critical value	−3.60	−3.50	−3.45	−3.41

A correct way of testing for a unit root has been developed by two statisticians named Dickey and Fuller and is known as the *Dickey–Fuller test*. As a test statistic, they still use the familiar *t*-statistic for testing $\phi = 0$. However, they show that, if the null hypothesis is true, then the distribution of this test statistic is not Student *t*, but rather a different distribution often called the *Dickey–Fuller distribution*. To complicate matters more, the distribution of the test statistic differs between the cases where the AR model does or does not include a deterministic trend. We will not explain why this is so, but instead just provide (in Table 6.5) the critical values you will need to use the Dickey–Fuller test in practice. Finally, to introduce some terminology, some authors use the term 'Dickey–Fuller test' for testing for $\phi = 0$ in the AR(1) model and use the term 'augmented Dickey–Fuller test' for testing in the AR(p) model (i.e. the basic unit root test is 'augmented' with extra lags). Since these are basically the same test, involving the same statistical tables, we will simply use the term 'Dickey–Fuller test' for both.

To do unit root testing in practice, you should first estimate the AR(p) model with deterministic trend

$$\Delta Y_t = \alpha + \phi Y_{t-1} + \gamma_1 \Delta Y_{t-1} + \cdots + \gamma_{p-1} \Delta Y_{t-p+1} + \delta t + \varepsilon_t$$

and use the hypothesis testing procedures described above or information criteria to select a lag length and decide whether the deterministic trend should be included. Once you have selected a preferred specification, you should record the *t*-statistic corresponding to the coefficient ϕ and then compare it with the appropriate Dickey–Fuller critical value from Table 6.5.

Table 6.5 provides the 1 % and 5 % critical values for the Dickey–Fuller test. Remember that $\phi = 0$ implies that the AR(p) time series Y contains a unit root; if $-2 < \phi < 0$, then the series is stationary. So stationarity is consistent with $\hat{\phi}$, and therefore its *t*-statistic being negative. Thus, the unit root hypothesis is only rejected in favor of stationarity if the *t*- statistic is negative (and more negative than the critical value taken from Table 6.5). If $\hat{\phi}$ is positive, it suggests that Y is exhibiting explosive behavior (a highly non-stationary case). Remember that the *t*-statistic for ϕ has a distribution that depends on sample size and whether the model does or does not contain a deterministic trend. Table 6.5 presents critical values for a range of sample sizes. Intermediate sample sizes will yield critical values between the nearest values in the table. For instance, if you have $T = 78$ and are working with an AR model without deterministic trend, you can use Table 6.5 to tell you that the 5 % critical value lies between -2.93 and -2.90 (the values for $T = 50$ and $T = 100$). For most applications, this will be enough information to allow you to do the Dickey–Fuller test.[7]

The Dickey–Fuller test is the most popular unit root test, but there are many others. We will not describe these tests, but note that many econometrics software packages allow you to do them automatically.

Some words of warning about unit root testing. The Dickey–Fuller test exhibits what statisticians refer to as 'low power'. In other words, the test can make the mistake of finding a unit root even when none exists. Intuitively, trend stationary series can look a lot like unit root series (compare Figures 6.5 and 6.6), and it can be quite hard to tell them apart. Furthermore, other kinds of time series model can also appear to exhibit unit root behavior, when in actuality they do not have unit roots. A prime example is the time series model characterized by abrupt changes or breaks. These structural breaks can occur in macroeconomic time series models and can be precipitated by events such as wars or crises in supply (e.g. the OPEC oil embargo). Stock prices can exhibit structural breaks due to market crashes, and commodity prices structural breaks due to droughts and other natural disasters. All in all, structural breaks are potentially a worry for many types of time series data, and some caution needs to be taken when interpreting the results of Dickey–Fuller tests.

Example: US personal income (continued)

In the previous example using the personal income data, we selected an AR(1) model that did not include a deterministic trend. We have $T = 163$.[8] Table 6.5 tells us that the 5 % critical value is between -2.90 and -2.80. From Table 6.4 we can see that the t- statistic for ϕ is -2.13, which is not more negative than the critical value. Hence, we can accept the hypothesis that personal income contains a unit root at the 5 % level of significance.

6.6 Defining stationarity

So far we have motivated the concepts of stationarity and non-stationarity as being related to the absence or presence of a trend. Furthermore, in the context of a particular class of models (the AR(p)), we have defined a particular sort of non-stationarity: unit root non-stationarity. However, we have not provided a formal definition of the concepts. For empirical practice, this is probably not of great importance since autoregressive models (and the extensions of these to be discussed in the next chapter) dominate empirical work and unit root non- stationarity has the most important implications for empirical practice. Nevertheless, for completeness, we offer a formal definition of a stationarity:

A time series variable, Y_t, is stationary[9] if:

1. $E(Y_t)$ is the same for all values of t.
2. $var(Y_t)$ is finite and the same for all values of t.
3. $cov(Y_t, Y_{t-s})$ depends only on s, but not on t.

Intuitively, these concepts capture the ideas that the basic statistical properties of the model (i.e. means, variances, and covariances) do not change over time. As we have seen, non– stationarity simply means 'anything that is not stationary'.

For the AR(1) model

$$Y_t = \alpha + \rho Y_{t-1} + \varepsilon_t,$$

where the errors satisfy the classical assumptions, you can confirm that stationarity occurs if $|\rho| < 1$, but that any other value for ρ does not result in stationarity. That is, if $|\rho| < 1$, you can work out that[10]

$$E(Y_t) = \frac{\alpha}{1 - \rho},$$

$$var(Y_t) = \frac{\sigma^2}{1 - \rho^2},$$

and

$$cov(Y_t, Y_{t-s}) = \frac{\rho^s \sigma^2}{1 - \rho^2},$$

where $\sigma^2 = var(\varepsilon_t)$. Thus, the mean and variance are constant over time, and the covariance between variables s periods apart depends only on s (i.e. not on t). The conditions for stationarity are satisfied if $|\rho| < 1$. These conditions are not satisfied if a unit root is present and $|\rho| = 1$.

For a model with a deterministic trend such as

$$Y_t = \alpha + \delta t + \varepsilon_t,$$

you can confirm that

$$E(Y_t) = \alpha + \delta t,$$
$$var(Y_t) = \sigma^2,$$

and

$$cov(Y_t, Y_{t-s}) = 0.$$

Since $E(Y_t)$ depends on t, this model is non-stationary. However, it would be stationary if we removed the deterministic trend. This helps motivate the terminology introduced before for such models: trend stationary.

6.7 Modeling volatility

Previously, we developed methods for use with time series variables. Throughout, we were always interested in the variables themselves. For instance, we might be interested in explaining the behavior of GDP growth, stock or bond returns, exchange rates and yield spreads. However, there are many cases where we are not interested in the variables themselves, but in their *volatility*. For instance, a popular model in finance is the capital asset pricing model (CAPM). We will not provide details here other than to note that an issue arising in it is that risk is important for investment decisions. The risk of investing in the stock of a particular company can be related to the volatility of its share price (and other factors).

Another very important field of research relates to the pricing of financial derivatives (e.g. options and other securities whose payoff is derived from the price of an underlying asset). If you have studied the theory of finance, you may be aware of the Black–Scholes option price formula and other similar derivative pricing methods. In these formulae, the volatility of the price of the underlying asset plays a crucial role. The methods introduced in this section are commonly used to provide estimates of this volatility.

Issues relating to volatility arise most often in financial economics, and hence we will focus on financial examples in this section (although there is a growing interest in modeling changing volatility in some macroeconomic applications) and talk about the pricing of assets such as stocks and bonds. We begin our discussion of volatility in asset prices informally, staying with familiar regression methods. We then discuss a very popular method for estimating financial volatility called *autoregressive conditional heteroskedasticity* (ARCH). The ARCH model shares a great deal of intuition with the regression model (including the AR model), but is not exactly the same as a regression model. Accordingly, estimation of ARCH models is slightly complicated. However, most econometrics software packages allow you to estimate ARCH models using maximum likelihood (or other methods) at the click of a button. So the fact that the theory underlying the estimation of ARCH models is a bit more difficult than standard regression theory need not preclude your using them in practice. Some extensions of ARCH models (discussed below) can also be estimated in most econometrics software packages.

6.7.1 Volatility in asset prices: introduction

To provide some intuition, recall the random walk (with drift) model

$$Y_t = \alpha + Y_{t-1} + \varepsilon_t$$

or

$$\Delta Y_t = \alpha + \varepsilon_t.$$

There are good reasons for believing that such a model might be appropriate for financial assets such as stock prices or exchange rates. For instance, it implies that stock prices, on average, increase by α per period, but are otherwise unpredictable. Equivalently, stock returns (exclusive of dividends) are on average α but are otherwise unpredictable.[11]

In this section, we will assume that the random walk model for an asset price is the correct one. To eliminate worrying about the drift, we will let Δy_t indicate the variable with deviations from the mean taken (i.e. $\Delta y_t = \Delta Y_t - \overline{\Delta Y}$ where $\overline{\Delta Y} = \frac{\Sigma \Delta Y_t}{T}$). Note that taking deviations from the mean implies that there is no intercept in the model. Thus, even if the asset price is drifting upwards over time, we can ignore the drift term and simply work with the pure random walk model

$$\Delta y_t = \varepsilon_t.$$

Although the ARCH model (to be defined shortly) provides a better definition for volatility, it is possible simply to use Δy_t^2 as an estimate of volatility at time t. To motivate this choice, note that high volatility is associated with big changes, either in a positive or in a negative direction. Since any number squared becomes positive, large rises or large falls in the price of an asset will imply Δy_t^2 is positive and large. In contrast, in stable times the asset price will not be changing much and Δy_t^2 will be small. Hence, our measure of volatility will be small in stable times and large in chaotic times.

Alternatively, you can use the formula for estimating the variance (see Chapter 1) to see that Δy_t^2 could be considered as an estimate of the variance of ΔY_t using only one observation. A point we should stress here is that, in many financial applications, we want to allow the volatility of an asset to change over time. The volatility at time t might be different from that at time $t - 1$ or $t + 1$.

You can calculate the Δy_t^2 measure of volatility of an asset price quite easily in any spreadsheet or computer package simply by differencing the stock price data, taking deviations from the mean and then squaring them. Once this is done, you will have a new time series variable – volatility – which you can then analyze using the tools introduced elsewhere in this book. For instance, autoregressive models are commonly used to model *clustering in volatility*, which is often present in financial time series data. Consider an AR(1) model that uses volatility as the time series variable of interest:

$$\Delta y_t^2 = \alpha + \rho \Delta y_{t-1}^2 + \varepsilon_t.$$

This model has volatility in a period depending on volatility in the previous period. If $\rho > 0$ (as it often is in financial applications), then if volatility was unusually high last period (e.g. Δy_{t-1}^2 was very large) it will also tend to be unusually high this period. Alternatively, if volatility was unusually low last period (e.g. Δy_{t-1}^2 was near zero), then this period's volatility will also tend to be low. In other words, if the volatility is low it will tend to stay low, if it is high it will tend to stay high. Of course, the presence of the error, ε_t, means that there can be exceptions to this pattern. However, in general this model implies that we will tend to observe intervals (or clusters in time) where volatility is low and intervals where it is high. In empirical studies of asset prices, such a pattern is very common. As an example, recall that in Chapter 1 we plotted the £/$ exchange rate (see Figure 1.1). If you look back at this figure, you can see long spells when the exchange rate changed very little (e.g. 1949–1967 and 1993–1996) and other, longer spells (e.g. 1985–1992) where it was more volatile.

The previous discussion refers to the AR(1) model, but it can be extended to the AR(p) model. All of the intuition given previously in this chapter is relevant here. The only difference is that the interpretation relates to the volatility of the series rather than to the series itself. Furthermore, all of the econometric techniques we described in the chapter are relevant here. Provided the series is stationary (e.g. $|\rho| < 1$ in the AR(1) case), then OLS estimates, t-statistics, and P-values can be interpreted in the standard way. Testing for a unit root can be conducted using a Dickey–Fuller test. In short, there is nothing statistically new here.

Example: Volatility in stock prices

Figure 6.7 contains a time series plot of weekly observations of the (logged) stock price of a certain company. You can see that the price of this stock has tended to increase over time, although there are several periods when it also fell. The price of the stock was $24.53 per share in the first month, increasing to $30.14 in the 208th month.[12]

Figure 6.8 plots ΔY, the percentage change in Y.[13] An examination of this figure indicates that the change in stock price in any given week was usually positive, but that there were some weeks when the price fell. In the middle of the period of study (i.e. roughly weeks 90–110) there were many large changes (both in a positive and a negative direction). For instance, in weeks 94 and 96 the stock price increased by over 1.5 %. This is a huge increase in one week. If increases of this magnitude were to keep on occurring for a year, the price of the stock would more than double (i.e. a weekly return of 1.5 % becomes an annualized return of over 100 %). However, in weeks 92, 93, and 95, stock prices fell by almost as much. All in all, the stock price in this middle period was much more volatile than in others.

In order to investigate the volatility properties of the stock price in more depth we take deviations from the mean for the observations of the differenced data used to create Figure 6.8 and then square them. That is, we (i) calculate the average change in stock price, (ii) subtract this average from every stock price change, and (iii) square the result. Figure 6.9 plots the resulting series which is our measure of volatility. Note that volatility is the square of the stock price and hence cannot be negative. The pattern most evident in Figure 6.9 is the large increase in volatility in weeks 90–97 and, to a lesser extent, in weeks 4–8 and 101–107. This provides visual evidence that the volatility of this stock does indeed seem to vary over time.

More formal evidence on the pattern of volatility can be found by building an AR(p) model using the techniques described earlier in this chapter and volatility as the variable of interest. The sequential testing procedure yields the AR(1) model for Δy_t^2 given in Table 6.6.

It can be seen that last week's volatility has strong explanatory power for this week's volatility, since its coefficient is strongly statistically significant. Furthermore, $R^2 = 0.54$, indicating that 54 % of the variation in volatility can be explained by

Table 6.6   AR(1) model for Δy_t^2.

Variable	OLS estimate	*t*-statistic	*P*-value
Intercept	0.024	1.624	0.106
Δy_{t-1}^2	0.737	15.552	0.000

last period's volatility. Consequently, it does seem as if volatility clusters are present. If volatility is high one period, it will also tend to be high the next period.

This information might be of great interest to investors wishing to purchase this stock. Suppose investors have just observed that $\Delta y_{t-1} = 0$ and therefore that $\Delta y_{t-1}^2 = 0$. In other words, the stock price changed by its average amount in period $t - 1$. The investors are interested in predicting volatility in period t in order to judge the likely risk involved in purchasing the stock. Since the error is unpredictable, the investors ignore it (i.e. it is just as likely to be positive as negative) and use the fitted regression line in Table 6.6 to predict volatility in period t. Since $\Delta y_{t-1}^2 = 0$, the investors predict volatility in period t to be 0.024. However, had they observed $\Delta y_{t-1}^2 = 1$, they would have predicted volatility in period t to be 0.761 (i.e. $0.024 + 0.737$). This kind of information can be incorporated into financial models of investor behavior.

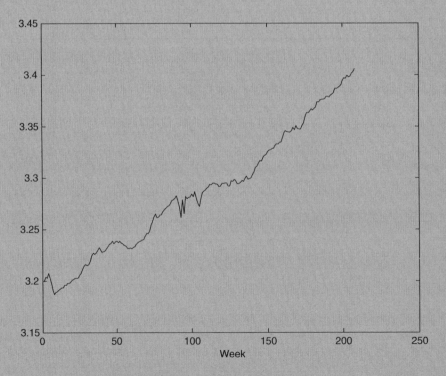

Figure 6.7 Time series plot of log of stock price.

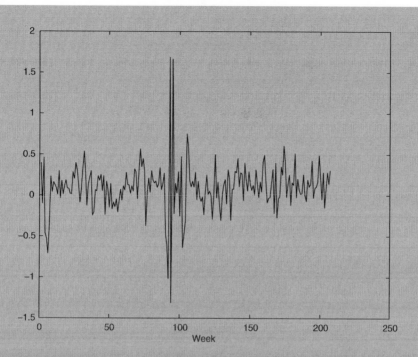

Figure 6.8 Time series plot of change in stock price.

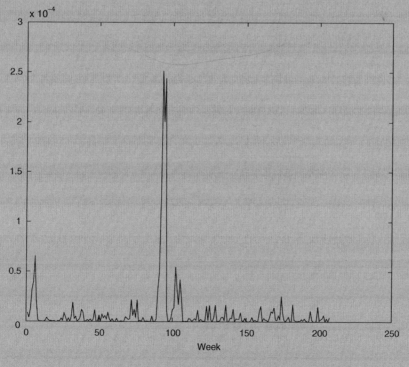

Figure 6.9 Time series plot of volatility.

6.7.2   Autoregressive conditional heteroskedasticity (ARCH)

The class of ARCH models (including extensions) is probably the most popular one for working with financial volatility. To allow for a great deal of generality, we will explain it in the context of the familiar regression model

$$Y_t = \alpha + \beta_1 X_{1t} + \cdots + \beta_k X_{kt} + \varepsilon_t.$$

Note that this general model contains many of the other models we have been working with. For instance, if $X_{1t} = Y_{t-j}$ (i.e. the explanatory variables are lags of the dependent variable), then this is an AR model. Another interesting case we will focus on below occurs if there are no explanatory variables at all (i.e. $\alpha = \beta_1 = \cdots = \beta_k = 0$), in which case the ARCH model we will describe shortly simply relates to the dependent variable itself, Y. If we set this dependent variable to be the de-meaned stock return (i.e. Δy_t), then we will be working with a model of financial volatility analogous to that used in the preceding section.

The ARCH model relates to the variance (or volatility) of the error, ε_t. To simplify notation (and adopt a very common notation in financial econometrics), we will let

$$\sigma_t^2 = var(\varepsilon_t).$$

In other words, σ_t^2 will be our notation for volatility at time t. It is this that is crucial in many financial applications. Remember that we are allowing volatility to vary over time – which is quite important in light of our previous discussion of clustering of volatility. Since the error variances are not constant, this model has heteroskedasticity which accounts for the 'H' in ARCH.

The ARCH model with p lags (denoted by ARCH(p)) assumes that today's volatility is an average of past errors squared:

$$\sigma_t^2 = \gamma_0 + \gamma_1 \varepsilon_{t-1}^2 + \cdots + \gamma_p \varepsilon_{t-p}^2,$$

where $\gamma_0, \gamma_1, \ldots, \gamma_p$ are coefficients that can be estimated (e.g. by maximum likelihood) in many econometrics software packages. In the case where we have no explanatory variables and the dependent variable is the de-meaned stock return, Δy_t, we have

$$\sigma_t^2 = \gamma_0 + \gamma_1 \Delta y_{t-1}^2 + \cdots + \gamma_p \Delta y_{t-p}^2$$

and the ARCH volatility depends on recent values of Δy_t^2 – the metric for volatility we were using in the preceding section. The ARCH model is closely related to the autoregressive model (which accounts for the 'AR' part of the name ARCH), and ARCH models have similar properties to AR models – except that these properties relate to the volatility of the series.

There are many ways of estimating ARCH models, including maximum likelihood and least squares. However, since they involve non-linear optimization we will not explain them here in detail. We stress, though, that most econometrics software packages allow for estimation of ARCH models.

Example: Volatility in stock prices (continued)

With ARCH models we do not need to worry about subtracting the mean from stock returns as we did in the preceding section (i.e. by simply including an intercept in the regression model we are allowing for a random walk with drift). Accordingly, we use the logged stock price data and simply take the first difference to create the variable ΔY. If we estimate an ARCH(1) model with ΔY as the dependent variable and an intercept in the regression equation, our econometrics software package produces a table similar to Table 6.7.

The upper part of Table 6.7 refers to the coefficients in the regression equation. In this case, we have only included an intercept. The lower part of the table refers to the ARCH equation. Since we are working with an ARCH(1) model, the equation includes an intercept (with the coefficient labeled γ_0 in the ARCH equation) and one lag of the errors squared (labeled γ_1 in the ARCH equation). The numbers in the table can be read in the same manner as the tables of regression outputs we have reported previously. That is, the numbers in the column labeled 'Coefficient estimate' are estimates of the coefficients (although, in this case, they are not OLS estimates but rather maximum likelihood estimates). The numbers in the columns labeled 'P-value' are P-values for testing the hypothesis that the corresponding coefficient equals zero. In this case, since the P-values are all less than 0.05, we can conclude all the coefficients (in the regression equation and the ARCH equation) are statistically significant at the 5 % level. The final column contains a 95 % confidence interval.

The estimate of γ_1 (i.e. the coefficient on the lagged errors squared in the ARCH equation) is 0.660, indicating that volatility this week depends strongly on the errors squared last week. This shows that there is persistence in volatility of a similar degree to that found using the simpler methods in the preceding section. Remember that we previously found that the AR(1) coefficient for the variable Δy_t^2 was estimated to be 0.737.

Table 6.7 ARCH(1) model using stock return data.

Variable	Coefficient estimate	P-value	95% confidence interval
Regression equation with ΔY as dependent variable			
Intercept	0.105	0.000	[0.081, 0.129]
ARCH equation			
Intercept	0.024	0.000	[0.016, 0.032]
$\Delta \varepsilon_{t-1}^2$	0.660	0.000	[0.302, 1.018]

Table 6.8   ARCH(2) model using stock return data.

Variable	Coefficient estimate	P-value	95% confidence interval
Regression equation with ΔY as dependent variable			
Intercept	0.109	0.000	[0.087, 0.131]
ARCH equation			
Intercept	0.025	0.000	[0.016, 0.033]
$\Delta\varepsilon_{t-1}^2$	0.717	0.000	[0.328, 1.107]
$\Delta\varepsilon_{t-2}^2$	−0.043	0.487	[−0.165, 0.079]

Lag length selection in ARCH models can be done in the same manner as with any time series model. That is, you can use an information criterion to select a model, or simply look at *P*-values for whether coefficients equal zero (and, if they do seem to be zero, the accompanying variables can be dropped). For instance, if we estimate an ARCH(2) model using the stock return data, we obtain Table 6.8.

The coefficient estimates in this table are very similar to those for the ARCH(1) model. However, the coefficient on $\Delta\varepsilon_{t-2}^2$ (i.e. γ_2) is not significant, since its *P*-value is greater than 0.05. Thus, we have evidence that an ARCH(1) model is adequate and the second lag added by the ARCH(2) model does not add significant explanatory power to the model. For many purposes (e.g. pricing financial derivatives), an estimate of σ_t^2 is required for every time period. This will be provided by any relevant econometric software package.

Extensions of ARCH models

There are many extensions of the ARCH model that are used by financial econometricians. For instance, Stata lists seven different variants of the ARCH model with acronyms like GARCH, SAARCH, TARCH, AARCH, NARCH, and NARCHK. Another popular alternative model that is not in the ARCH class is called *stochastic volatility*. If you are doing a great deal of work on financial volatility, you should do further study to learn more about these models. Here we will only introduce the most popular of these extensions: *generalized ARCH* or *GARCH*. This takes the ARCH model and adds on lags of the volatility measure itself (instead of just adding lags of squared errors). Thus, a GARCH model with (p, q) lags is denoted by GARCH(p, q) and has the volatility equation

$$\sigma_t^2 = \gamma_0 + \gamma_1\varepsilon_{t-1}^2 + \cdots + \gamma_p\varepsilon_{t-p}^2 + \lambda_1\sigma_{t-1}^2 + \cdots + \lambda_p\sigma_{t-p}^2.$$

The properties of the GARCH model are similar to those of the ARCH model. For instance, the coefficients can be interpreted in a similar fashion to AR coefficients and related to the degree of persistence in volatility. However, it can be shown that the

GARCH model is much more flexible, much more capable of matching a wide variety of patterns of financial volatility.

Example: Volatility in stock prices (continued)

If we estimate a GARCH(1, 1) model with our stock return data, we obtain the results in Table 6.9.

Table 6.9 GARCH(1,1) model using stock return data.

Variable	Coefficient estimate	P-value	95% confidence interval
	Regression equation with ΔY as dependent variable		
Intercept	0.109	0.000	[0.087, 0.131]
	ARCH equation		
Intercept	0.026	0.000	[0.015, 0.038]
$\Delta \varepsilon_{t-1}^2$	0.714	0.000	[0.327, 1.101]
σ_{t-1}^2	−0.063	0.457	[−0.231, 0.104]

The numbers in this table can be interpreted in the same manner as for the ARCH tables. Here, however, we have an extra row labeled 'σ_{t-1}^2' that contains results for λ_1 (i.e. the lagged volatility). It can be seen that this coefficient is insignificant, since its P-value is greater than 0.05. Thus, for this dataset, the extension to a GARCH(1,1) model does not seem necessary. The ARCH(% 1) model does perfectly well.

6.8 Chapter summary

In this chapter, we have introduced the basic concepts of univariate time series analysis, with a particular focus on the most popular univariate time series model: the autoregressive model. This model is popular since it can be written as a regression model, and thus the regression methods discussed in earlier chapters are relevant. Univariate time series methods are useful for understanding the properties of a single time series variable. Of particular importance are the trending properties of a series and the issue of whether a series contains a unit root. The Dickey–Fuller test is the most popular unit root test. The chapter ends with a discussion of models of volatility, with an emphasis on the ARCH model.

The main points covered in this chapter are as follows:

1. Regressions with time series variables involve two issues we have not dealt with in the past. Firstly, one variable can influence another with a time lag. Secondly, if the variables are non-stationary, the spurious regression problem can result. The latter issue will be dealt with in the next chapter.

2. Many time series exhibit trend behavior, while their differences do not exhibit such behavior.

3. The autocorrelation function is a common tool for summarizing the relationship between a variable and lags of itself.

4. Autoregressive models are regression models used for working with time series variables. Such models can be written in two ways: one with Y_t as the dependent variable, the other with ΔY_t as the dependent variable.

5. The distinction between stationary and non-stationary series is a crucial one.

6. Series with unit roots are the most common type of non-stationary series considered in economics.

7. If Y_t has a unit root, then the AR(p) model with ΔY_t as the dependent variable can be estimated using OLS. Standard statistical results hold for all coefficients except the coefficient on Y_{t-1}.

8. In the AR(p) model with deterministic trend, sequential hypothesis testing procedures can be used to select lag length and decide whether a deterministic trend should be included. Alternatively, information criteria can be used to make these choices.

9. The Dickey–Fuller test is a test for the presence of a unit root. It involves testing whether the coefficient on Y_{t-1} is equal to zero using the t-statistic. In this case, the t-statistic does not have a Student t-distribution, and critical values must be taken from the Dickey–Fuller statistical tables.

10. A formal definition of stationarity was provided.

11. This chapter has an appendix that defines and discusses another popular univariate time series model called the moving average model.

12. Many time series variables, particularly asset prices, seem to exhibit random walk behavior. For this reason, it is hard to predict how they will change in the future. However, such variables often do exhibit predictable patterns of volatility.

13. The square of the change in an asset price is a measure of its volatility.

14. Standard time series methods can be used to model the patterns of volatility in asset prices. The only difference is that volatility of the asset price is used as the dependent variable.

15. ARCH models are a more formal way of measuring volatility. They contain two equations. One is a standard regression equation. The second is a volatility equation, where volatility is defined as being the (time-varying) variance of the regression error.

16. ARCH models share similarities with AR models, except that the 'AR' part relates to the volatility equation.

17. There are many extensions of ARCH, of which GARCH is the most popular.

18. ARCH and GARCH models can be estimated using many common econometrics software packages.

Exercises

The data for some of these questions are provided on the website associated with this book.

1. The file INCOME.XLS contains data on (the logs of) personal income and consumption in the USA from 1954Q1 to 1994Q4.

    (a) For each of these two series, individually create an XY plot between the variable and the variable lagged one period.
    (b) Calculate the autocorrelation function for each time series using a maximum lag of 4.
    (c) Difference each of these variables and repeat (a) and (b). How would you interpret the autocorrelations and XY plots?
    (d) For each of these variables, select and estimate an AR(p) with deterministic trend model using a maximum lag of 4. That is, use the sequential testing procedure described in this chapter to choose lag length and decide whether a deterministic trend should be included.
    (e) Test for a unit root in each of these variables.
    (f) Test for a unit root in the difference of each of these variables.

2. (a) Calculate the autocorrelation function for Y, assuming that it follows the AR(1) model

$$Y_t = \alpha + \rho Y_{t-1} + \varepsilon_t,$$

   and assuming that $|\rho| < 1$. How would your answer change if $|\rho| = 1$?

    (b) Under the assumptions of part (a), calculate the autocorrelation function of ΔY. How would your answer change if $|\rho| = 1$?
    (c) Now assume that Y follows an AR(2) model which can be written as

$$\Delta Y_t = \alpha + \phi Y_{t-1} + \gamma_2 \Delta Y_{t-1} + \varepsilon_t.$$

   Calculate the autocorrelation function for Y assuming $-2 < \phi < 0$. How would your answer change if $|\phi| = 0$?
    (d) Under the assumptions of part (c), calculate the autocorrelation function of ΔY. How would your answer change if $|\phi| = 0$?

3. Consider the AR(p) with deterministic trend model

$$Y_t = \alpha + \rho_1 Y_{t-1} + \cdots + \rho_p Y_{t-p} + \delta t + \varepsilon_t.$$

    (a) Show that this model can be written as

$$\Delta Y_t = \alpha + \phi Y_{t-1} + \gamma_1 \Delta Y_{t-1} + \cdots + \gamma_{p-1} \Delta Y_{t-p+1} + \delta t + \varepsilon_t.$$

(b) What are the relationships between the coefficients in these two specifications?

4. Consider the AR(1) model (without intercept)

$$Y_t = \rho Y_{t-1} + \varepsilon_t,$$

with ε_t being i.i.d. $N(0, \sigma^2)$ for $t = 1, \ldots, T$.

(a) Derive the likelihood function for this model. Note that, as we have done in this chapter, you may condition on the initial observation and, hence, derive the likelihood function using data from $t = 2, \ldots, T$. Hint: the likelihood function is the joint probability density function for the data, $p(Y_2, Y_3, \ldots, Y_T)$. With cross-sectional data, the observations are independent of one another, and hence $p(Y_2, Y_3, \ldots, Y_T) = \prod_{t=2}^{T} p(Y_2) \ldots p(Y_T)$. With the AR(1) model, the observations are not independent of one another, but we can use the rules of conditional probability to write:

$$p(Y_2, Y_3, \ldots, Y_T) = \prod_{t=2}^{T} p(Y_t | Y_{t-1}).$$

(b) Show how your result from part (a) implies that the maximum likelihood estimator of ρ is equivalent to the OLS estimator. Note that, since we are using data from $t = 2, \ldots, T$ and treating Y_1 as a fixed initial condition, this estimator is referred to as the *conditional maximum likelihood estimator*.

5. This exercise could be interpreted as an empirical project and could be short or long, depending on what you are interested in achieving. The book *Nonlinear Time Series Models in Empirical Finance* by Philip Hans Franses and Dick van Dijk (Cambridge University Press) is one you may use in your future studies. It has a website containing a rich collection of datasets from several countries on stock prices and exchange rates which you can download (see http://www.few.eur.nl/few/people/djvandijk/nltsmef/nltsmef.htm). In particular, stock price indices from Amsterdam (EOE), Frankfurt (DAX), Hong Kong (Hang Seng), London (FTSE100), New York (S&P 500), Paris (CAC40), Singapore (Singapore All Shares), and Tokyo (Nikkei) are provided. The exchange rates are the Australian dollar, British pound, Canadian dollar, German Deutschmark, Dutch guilder, French franc, Japanese yen, and the Swiss franc, all expressed as number of units of the foreign currency per US dollar. The sample period for the stock indices runs from 6 January 1986 until 31 December 1997, whereas for the exchange rates the sample covers the period from 2 January 1980 until 31 December 1997.

(a) Investigate the random walk hypothesis using these data. Do stock prices appear to follow a random walk in every country? Do exchange rates?

(b) Note that these data are available at a daily frequency. You may want to work with the data at this frequency or at a weekly frequency (e.g. by just using data every Wednesday) or monthly frequency (e.g. by just using data from the last day of each month). Do your results for the unit root tests depend on whether you use daily, weekly, or monthly data?

6. NYSE.XLS contains data on $\Delta Y =$ the percentage change in stock prices each month from 1952 to 1995 on the New York Stock Exchange (NYSE). For those interested in precise details, the data are value-weighted stock returns exclusive of dividends deflated using the consumer price index. Note that these data are already in differenced form, but deviations from the mean have not been taken.

(a) Make a time series plot of these data and comment on any patterns you observe.

(b) Using the techniques discussed in the chapter, comment on the univariate time series properties of ΔY. What does its autocorrelation function look like? If you build an AR(p) model using these data, what is p? Is ΔY stationary? Are stock returns on the NYSE predictable (i.e. can past stock returns help you to predict current values)?

(c) Assume that the original series, Y, follows a random walk (possibly with an intercept). Calculate and plot the volatility of this variable as measured by Δy_t^2. Does it appear that volatility clustering is present?

(d) Construct an AR(p) model for Δy_t^2 and discuss its properties. Can past values of volatility on the stock market help you to predict current volatility?

(e) Estimate ARCH(p) models for ΔY_t for various values of p. Is there volatility clustering in these data (i.e. does an ARCH model beat a simpler model where there is constant volatility which means $\gamma_1 = \cdots = \gamma_p = 0$)? Which value of p is preferable?

(f) For your preferred choice of p, make a time series plot of volatility (i.e. plot a graph of σ_t^2) and compare it with the plot you constructed in part (c).

(g) Repeat parts (e) and (f) using a GARCH(p, q) model. Does your graph of volatility look the same with ARCH and GARCH models?

7. This exercise is a substantive empirical project and uses the stock return and exchange rate data from the book *Nonlinear Time Series Models in Empirical Finance* by Philip Hans Franses and Dick van Dijk (Cambridge University Press). The data are available at http://www.few.eur.nl/few/people/djvandijk/nltsmef/ nltsmef.htm. This dataset was used in exercise 5 and more details are provided there.

(a) Investigate financial volatility using these data with ARCH and GARCH models. Do stock returns appear to exhibit volatility? Do exchange rates?

(b) An issue much studied by financial researchers is whether volatility in financial markets differs depending on the frequency a financial market is observed. For instance, stock markets might be more volatile when observed every day than when observed monthly. Investigate this issue using this dataset. Note that it is available at a daily frequency. When you work with weekly data you can use data every Wednesday. For monthly frequency use the last day of each month.

Appendix: MA and ARMA models

In the body of the chapter, we have focused on autoregressive models. However, there are other popular univariate time series models. Perhaps the most popular of these is the class of *moving average* or MA models. The moving average of order 1 or MA(1) model is defined as

$$Y_t = \varepsilon_t - \theta \varepsilon_{t-1},$$

where the ε_ts are assumed to be uncorrelated random variables with mean zero and variance σ^2. In time series econometrics it is common to refer to these errors as *innovations*, and the assumptions made about them imply they are *white noise*. In contrast to the AR model, the MA model focuses on the innovations.

Straightforward manipulations with the expected value and variance operator can be done to show that

$$E(Y_t) = 0,$$
$$var(Y_t) = \sigma^2(1 + \theta^2)$$

and

$$cov(Y_t, Y_{t-1}) = -\theta,$$
$$cov(Y_t, Y_{t-s}) = 0 \quad \text{if} \quad s \geq 2.$$

These facts imply that an MA(1) series is stationary, regardless of the value of θ, and hence MA models cannot be directly used to address unit root issues. Furthermore, the autocorrelation function has different properties to the AR(1) autocorrelation function. Remember that, for the AR(1) model the autocorrelation function is ρ^s, and hence the autocorrelation function dies out gradually as s gets larger. With the MA(1) model the autocorrelation function cuts off abruptly to zero for $s \geq 2$. Of course, the choice between AR and MA models depends on your dataset. For some datasets the AR model might be appropriate, for others the MA might be better.

The MA(1) model can be extended to the MA(q) model as

$$Y_t = \varepsilon_t - \theta_1 \varepsilon_{t-1} - \cdots - \theta_q \varepsilon_{t-q}.$$

This has properties similar to the MA(1) model, but more general. For instance, with the MA(q) model the autocorrelation function cuts off abruptly to zero for $s \geq q + 1$.

There is a close relationship between AR and MA models in that you can always write one in the form of the other. Consider, for instance, the following manipulations with the stationary AR(1) model:

$$
\begin{aligned}
Y_t &= \rho Y_{t-1} + \varepsilon_t \\
&= \rho(\rho Y_{t-2} + \varepsilon_{t-1}) + \varepsilon_t \\
&= \rho^2 Y_{t-2} + \rho \varepsilon_{t-1} + \varepsilon_t \\
&= \rho^3 Y_{t-3} + \rho^2 \varepsilon_{t-2} + \rho \varepsilon_{t-1} + \varepsilon_t \\
&= \cdots \\
&= \varepsilon_t + \rho \varepsilon_{t-1} + \rho^2 \varepsilon_{t-2} + \rho^3 \varepsilon_{t-3} + \cdots \\
&= \sum_{i=0}^{\infty} \rho^i \varepsilon_{t-i}.
\end{aligned}
$$

Note that we have written the AR(1) model with $|\rho| < 1$ in terms of its innovations. That is, we have written it as an MA(∞) model. This illustrates a general rule that any stationary autoregressive model can be written as a moving average model.

We can also reverse the process and write the MA(1) model as an AR(1) model, provided $|\theta| < 1$. The latter is referred to as the *invertibility condition*. In general, any invertible MA process can be written as a stationary AR process.

We can combine the autoregressive and moving average models to produce the *autoregressive moving average* (ARMA) model. If there are p autoregressive lags and q moving average lags, we have the ARMA(p, q) model

$$
Y_t = \alpha + \rho_1 Y_{t-1} + \cdots + \rho_p Y_{t-p} + \varepsilon_t - \theta_1 \varepsilon_{t-1} - \cdots - \theta_q \varepsilon_{t-q}.
$$

This model combines the properties of the autoregressive and moving average models and thus is very flexible. We can also add a deterministic trend to this model.

Finally, if Y_t contains a unit root, then we may wish to work with ΔY_t. If this is done with an ARMA model, then the result is an *autoregressive integrated moving average model* or ARIMA model:

$$
\Delta Y_t = \alpha + \rho_1 \Delta Y_{t-1} + \cdots + \rho_p \Delta Y_{t-p} + \varepsilon_t - \theta_1 \varepsilon_{t-1} - \cdots - \theta_q \varepsilon_{t-q}.
$$

A large advantage of the autoregressive model is that the OLS estimator, involving a closed-form formula, can be evaluated. With MA or ARMA models, one can use a least-squares estimator, but it does not have a closed-form formula and numerical optimization methods are required. Maximum likelihood estimation is also popular, but it, too, requires numerical optimization methods. Nevertheless, most econometrics software packages allow for the estimation of MA and ARMA models.

Endnotes

1. In fact it is so common to work with logs of macroeconomic variables that it is common to drop the phrase for the sake of brevity and refer to 'personal income' instead of 'the logarithm of personal income'.
2. Note that the phrase 'Y is a time series variable' is often shortened to 'Y is a time series' or simply 'Y is a series'.
3. Small statistical problems arise with OLS estimation of this model, particularly if the model is non-stationary or nearly so (i.e. ϕ is close to zero). In particular, if sample size is small, OLS can be biased downwards.
4. Remember that the AR(p) with deterministic trend model has γ_{p-1} as the coefficient on the longest lag.
5. The interested reader is referred to Chapter 11 of Koop (2003).
6. A consistent model selection criterion is one that chooses the correct model with probability 1 as sample size goes to infinity.
7. More complete statistical tables containing critical values for the Dickey–Fuller distribution can be found in many places on the web (e.g. do a Google search on the phrase 'Dickey–Fuller test critical values').
8. Note that the original data series has $T = 164$, but including one lag in the AR(1) reduces sample size by one.
9. Formally, what is provided here is the definition of weak (or covariance) stationarity. Strong stationarity has the additional implication that all the Y_ts have the same distribution.
10. We do not do these derivations here since they are very similar to those done in Section 5.4 of Chapter 5. See also exercise 2.
11. If excess stock returns were predictable, then investors would instantly buy up the stocks expected to rise and sell the stocks expected to fall. The price of the former would instantly rise and the latter would instantly fall to the points where returns were no longer predictable. This is an example of a market efficiency argument: that efficient stock markets should not allow for abnormal profits and should instantly adjust to all available news or information relevant for stock prices.
12. This follows from the fact that the data are logged and ln(24.53) is 3.200 and ln(30.14) is 3.406.
13. We have multiplied the first difference of the data used to create Figure 6.7 by 100 to make it into a percentage.

CHAPTER 7

Regression with Time Series Variables

7.1 Introduction

In regression analysis, researchers are typically interested in measuring the effect of an explanatory variable or variables on a dependent variable. As mentioned in Chapter 6, this goal is complicated when the researcher uses time series data since an explanatory variable may influence a dependent variable with a time lag. This often necessitates the inclusion of lags of the explanatory variable in the regression. Models with lags of the explanatory variable are referred to as *distributed lag models*. Furthermore, the dependent variable may be correlated with lags of itself, suggesting that lags of the dependent variable should also be included in the regression (as in the autoregressive model).

These considerations motivate the commonly used *autoregressive distributed lag*[1] (or ADL) model:

$$Y_t = \alpha + \delta t + \rho_1 Y_{t-1} + \cdots + \rho_p Y_{t-p} + \beta_0 X_t + \beta_1 X_{t-1} + \cdots + \beta_q X_{t-q} + \varepsilon_t.$$

In this model, the dependent variable, Y, depends on p lags of itself, the current value of an explanatory variable, X, as well as q lags of X. The model also allows for a deterministic trend t. Since the model contains p lags of Y and q lags of X, we denote it by $\text{ADL}(p, q)$. To make the notation simple, we focus on the case where there is only one explanatory variable, X. Note, however, that in practice you will often have several explanatory variables and, hence, will want to include them (and their lags). The same basic ideas apply in this case.

Estimation and interpretation of the ADL(p, q) model depend on whether the series X and Y are stationary or not. We consider these two cases separately here. Note, though, that we assume throughout that X and Y have the same stationarity properties; that is, they either must both be stationary or both have a unit root.[2] Intuitively, regression analysis involves using X to explain Y. If X's properties differ from Y's, it becomes difficult for X to explain Y. For instance, it is hard for a stationary series to explain the stochastic trend variation in a unit root series. In practice this means that, before running any time series regression, you should examine the univariate properties of the variables you plan to use. In particular, you should carry out unit root tests along the lines described in Chapter 6 for every variable in your analysis.

In this chapter, we discuss the ADL model as well as an important extension of it called the *error correction model* (ECM). The latter relates to a concept called *cointegration* which is discussed in detail in this chapter. The latter half of this chapter shows how all these concepts are used in practice by researchers. Topics discussed include *Granger causality*, *vector autoregressive* (VAR) models, and forecasting. Forecasting is a huge topic, so we only briefly introduce it in this chapter. An appendix provides an introduction to the econometric theory underlying forecasting.

7.2 Time series regression when *X* and *Y* are stationary

When X and Y are stationary, OLS estimation of the ADL(p, q) regression model can be carried out in the standard way described in earlier chapters in this book. Hypothesis testing can be done using t-statistics or F-statistics in the standard fashion. Such tests can in turn be used to select p and q, the number of lags of the dependent and explanatory variables respectively. Alternatively, information criteria (see Chapter 6, Section 6.4) can be used to select preferred lag lengths and decide whether a deterministic trend should be included. You should note, however, that the interpretation of results is somewhat different from the standard case, as elaborated below.

In the case of the AR(p) model in Chapter 6, it proved convenient, both for OLS estimation and interpretation of results, for us to rewrite the model with ΔY as the dependent variable. Similar considerations hold for the ADL(p, q), which can be rewritten as

$$\Delta Y_t = \alpha + \delta t + \phi Y_{t-1} + \gamma_1 \Delta Y_{t-1} + \cdots + \gamma_{p-1} \Delta Y_{t-p+1} + \theta X_t + \omega_1 \Delta X_{t-1}$$
$$+ \cdots + \omega_{q-1} \Delta X_{t-q+1} + \varepsilon_t.$$

It should be emphasised that this model is the same as that in the original form of the ADL(p, q); it has merely undergone a few algebraic manipulations. Just as we had two different variants of the AR(p) model in Chapter 6, we now have two variants of the ADL(p, q) model. As before, we use new Greek letters for the coefficients in the regression to distinguish them from those in the original variant of the ADL(p, q) model. This model may look complicated, but it is still nevertheless just a regression model.

As discussed in Chapter 6, macroeconomic time series variables are often highly correlated with their lags. This implies that the original form of the ADL model frequently runs into multicollinearity problems. With the rewritten form we will typically not encounter such problems. Most importantly, as we will see, it has a further benefit, one that lies in the interpretation of the coefficients. For these reasons we will work mainly with this second variant of the ADL(p, q) model.

In Chapter 2, we discussed how to interpret regression coefficients, placing special emphasis on *ceteris paribus* conditions. Recall that we made statements of the form: 'The coefficient measures the influence of an explanatory variable on the dependent variable, *holding all other explanatory variables constant*'. In the ADL(p, q) model, such an interpretation can still be made, but there are other ways of interpreting coefficients. One common way is through the concept of a multiplier. You are probably familiar with this idea since it is very common in the social sciences; economists, for instance, use a multiplier when they measure the effect of a change in government spending on national income. In the present context, this concept is a little more complicated since we have to specify a timing for the effect.

It is common to focus on the *long-run* or *total multiplier*, which is what we will do here. To motivate this measure, suppose that X and Y are in an equilibrium or steady state, i.e. are not changing over time. All of a sudden, X changes by one unit, affecting Y, which starts to change, eventually settling down in the long-run to a new equilibrium value. The difference between the old and new equilibrium values for Y can be interpreted as the long-run effect of X on Y and is the long-run multiplier. This multiplier is often of great interest for policymakers who want to know the eventual effects of their policy changes in various areas.

It is worth stressing that the long-run multiplier measures the effect of a permanent change in X. That is, the story in the previous paragraph had X being at some value, and then X changed permanently to a new level one unit higher than the original value. The long-run multiplier measures the effect of this sort of change. In some cases, you might be interested in the effect of a temporary change in X (i.e. X starts at some original level, then increases by one unit for one period before going back to the original level the next). The long-run multiplier does not measure the effect of this type of change. We can use the traditional 'marginal effect' interpretation of regression coefficients for such temporary changes.

It can be shown (see exercise 1) that the long-run multiplier for the ADL(p, q) model is

$$-\frac{\theta}{\phi}.$$

In other words, only the coefficients on X_t and Y_{t-1} in the rewritten ADL model matter for long-run behavior. This means that we can easily obtain an estimate of the long-run multiplier.

It is worth stressing that we are assuming X and Y are stationary. In Chapter 6, we discussed how $\phi = 0$ in the AR(p) model implied the existence of a unit root. The ADL model is not the same as the AR model, but, to provide some intuition, note that, if

$\phi = 0$, then the long-run multiplier is infinite. In fact, it can be shown that, for the model to be stable, we must have $\phi < 0$. In practice, if X and Y are stationary, this condition will be satisfied.

Example: The effect of computer purchases on sales

In recent years, companies have been purchasing more computers on the assumption that this will improve workforce productivity. The purpose of this example is to investigate this assumption empirically. We have data collected by a company for 98 months on their computer purchases and a variable reflecting the productivity of their sales force. In particular, the dependent and explanatory variables are:

- Y = the percentage change in sales relative to the previous month;
- X = the percentage change in computer purchases relative to the previous month.

The means of these two variables are 0.30 and 0.01 % per month, indicating that this company has not increased spending on computers by much on average. Note, however, that this average hides wide variation. In some months computer spending increased considerably, while in other months it decreased. Assuming that both variables are stationary, we can estimate an ADL(2, 2) model using OLS. Remember that, if the variables in a model are stationary, then the standard regression quantities (e.g. OLS estimates, P-values, confidence intervals) can be calculated in the same way as in Chapters 1 to 4. Table 7.1 contains the results of this procedure.

Using the formula for the long-run multiplier, we can see that its OLS estimate is

$$-\left(\frac{0.125}{-0.120}\right) = 1.042.$$

The following are a few different ways of expressing this information (remember that the dependent and explanatory variables are percentage changes):

Table 7.1   ADL(2, 2) with deterministic trend model.

Variable	OLS estimate	t-statistic	P-value
Intercept	−0.028	−0.685	0.495
Y_{t-1}	−0.120	−9.460	0.000
ΔY_{t-1}	0.794	25.628	0.000
X_t	0.125	2.605	0.011
ΔX_t	0.838	19.111	0.000
ΔX_{t-1}	0.002	0.103	0.918
t	0.0001	0.984	0.328

- An examination of the original data tells us, on average, computer purchases in this company have been increasing by 0.01 % per month and sales by 0.30 % per month. If the company decides that its computer budget should increase by 1.01 % in each month (i.e. increase by one unit from 0.01 to 1.01), then in the long run sales should start increasing by 1.342 % per month (i.e. the initial 0.30 plus the long-run multiplier of 1.042).
- The long-run multiplier effect of computer purchases on sales is 1.042 %.
- If X permanently increases by 1 %, the equilibrium value of Y will increase by 1.042 %.

The statistical information, though, indicates that this might not be a good model, since some of the explanatory variables are not significant (e.g. the P-values for the coefficients on ΔX_{t-1} and the time trend both imply insignificance at the 5 % level). This raises the issue of lag length selection in the ADL(p, q) model. Remember that the strategies for selecting p in the AR(p) model (see Chapter 6) can be used here. If you do a sequential hypothesis testing procedure, there is no general convention about whether you should first select p, then q, then decide whether the deterministic trend should be included, or make another ordering (e.g. select q, then p, then trend or select q, then trend, then p, etc.).

7.3 Time series regression when Y and X have unit roots

In this section, we will assume that Y and X have unit roots. In practice, of course, you would have to test whether this is the case using the Dickey–Fuller test of the previous chapter. We begin by focusing on the case of regression models without lags, then proceed to models similar to the ADL(p, q) model.

7.3.1 Spurious regression

Suppose we are interested in estimating the following regression:

$$Y_t = \alpha + \beta X_t + \varepsilon_t.$$

It is extremely important to know that, if Y and X contain unit roots, then OLS estimation of this regression can yield results that are completely wrong. For instance, even if the true value of β is 0, OLS can yield an estimate, $\hat{\beta}$, that is very different from zero. Statistical tests (using the t-statistic or P-value) may indicate that β is not zero. Furthermore, if $\beta = 0$, then the R^2 should be zero. In fact, the R^2 will often be quite large.

To put it another way: if Y and X have unit roots, then all the usual regression results might be misleading and incorrect. This is the so-called *spurious regression problem*. We do not have the statistical tools to prove why this problem occurs, but it is important to stress its practical implication. With the one exception of cointegration that we discuss below, *you should never run a regression of Y on X if the variables have unit roots*.

7.3.2   Cointegration

The one time where you do not have to worry about the spurious regression problem occurs when Y and X are cointegrated. This case not only surmounts the spurious regression problem but also provides some nice economic intuition. Cointegration has received a great deal of attention recently in the economics literature, so it is worthwhile discussing the topic in detail here.

Some intuition for cointegration can be obtained by considering the errors in the above regression model:

$$\varepsilon_t = Y_t - \alpha - \beta X_t.$$

Written in this way, it is clear that the errors are just a linear combination of Y and X. Since X and Y both exhibit non-stationary unit root behavior, you would expect the error also to exhibit non-stationary behavior. After all, if you add two things with a certain property together, the result generally tends to have that property. The error does indeed usually have a unit root. Statistically, it is this unit root in the error term that causes the spurious regression problem. However, it is possible that the unit roots in Y and X 'cancel each other out' and that the resulting error is stationary. In this special case, called *cointegration*, the spurious regression problem vanishes and it is valid to run a regression of Y on X. To summarize: if Y and X have unit roots, but some linear combination of them is stationary, then Y and X are cointegrated.

The intuition behind cointegration is clearest for the case where $\alpha = 0$ and $\beta = 1$ (although, of course, in practice α and β can take on any values). Keep this in mind when you read the following statements. Remember also that variables with unit roots tend to exhibit trend behavior (e.g. they can be increasing steadily over time and therefore can become very large).

- If X and Y have unit roots, then they have stochastic trends. However, if they are cointegrated, the error does not have such a trend. In this case, the error will not get too large and Y and X will not diverge from one another; Y and X, in other words, will trend together. This fact motivates other jargon used to refer to cointegrated time series. You may hear them referred to as either having *common trends* or *co-trending*.
- If we are talking about an economic model involving an equilibrium concept, ε is the equilibrium error. If Y and X are cointegrated, then the equilibrium error stays small. However, if Y and X are not cointegrated, then the equilibrium error will have a trend and departures from equilibrium become increasingly large over time. If such departures from equilibrium occur, then many would hesitate to say that the equilibrium is a meaningful one.
- If Y and X are cointegrated, then there is an equilibrium relationship between them. If they are not, then no equilibrium relationship exists. (This is essentially just a restatement of the previous point.)
- In the real world, it is unlikely that an economic system will ever be in precise equilibrium since shocks and unexpected changes to it will always occur. However,

departures from equilibrium should not be too large, and there should always be a tendency to return to equilibrium after a shock occurs. Hence, if an economic model that implies an equilibrium relationship exists between Y and X is correct, then we should observe Y and X as being cointegrated.

- If Y and X are cointegrated then their trends will cancel each other out.

To summarize: if cointegration is present, then not only do we avoid the spurious regression problem, but we also have important economic information (e.g. that an equilibrium relationship exists or that two series are trending together).

Example: Cointegration between the prices of two goods

Economic theory suggests that similar goods should be close substitutes for each other, and therefore their prices should be cointegrated. As an example, we have time series data for 181 months on the prices of regular oranges and organic oranges in a certain market. These are two closely related products, but many consumers are willing to pay somewhat more for organic oranges. We might expect the prices of these two goods to be cointegrated, since the difference in prices between the two cannot increase too much. That is, many people are willing to pay slightly more for organic products, but if the premium gets too large they will switch to regular oranges. For instance, many consumers may be willing to pay an extra 20 cents per pound to receive the supposed health and environmental benefits of organic oranges, but not 40 cents per pound. Thus, if the price gap between organic and regular products becomes too large, many people will stop buying organic products and their price will fall. On the other hand, if the price of organic oranges falls to roughly the same price as regular oranges, more people will go organic and fewer will eat regular oranges. In this case, the price of regular oranges will drop.

In short, although the prices of these two products will fluctuate owing to the vagaries of supply and demand, market forces will always keep the price difference between the two goods roughly constant. This is the intuition behind cointegration.

Figure 7.1 plots these two series and provides strong visual evidence that the prices of these two types of orange are indeed cointegrated. That is, even though the prices of organic oranges are higher than regular ones, the general trend behavior in the two variables looks quite similar.

There are many other examples of cointegration, especially in macroeconomics and finance. Short-term and long-term interest rates, for example, may not move precisely together in the short run, but it is unlikely that they will deviate too much in the long run. If long-term interest rates are significantly higher than short-term rates, then traders will buy long term and sell short term, forcing the former down and the latter up. This example implies cointegration. Two prominent economic theories that imply the presence

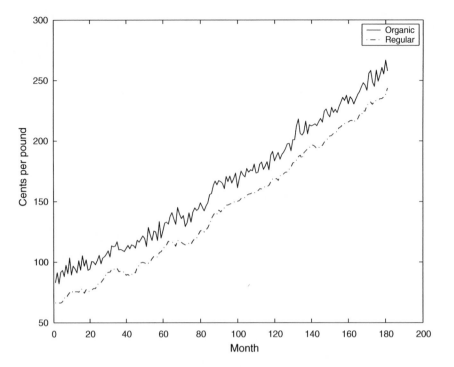

Figure 7.1 The prices of regular and organic oranges.

of cointegration between macroeconomic variables are the theory of purchasing power parity and the permanent income hypothesis. Even theories of money demand have been used to justify cointegration findings. All in all, cointegration is an important concept for macroeconomists and financial economists.

7.3.3   Estimation and testing with cointegrated variables

As mentioned above, if Y and X are cointegrated, then the spurious regression problem does not apply. Consequently, we can run an OLS regression of Y on X and obtain valid results. Furthermore, the coefficient from this regression is the long-run multiplier. Thus, in so far as interest centers on the long-run multiplier, estimation with cointegrated variables is very easy. We will not prove why this is so. But the intuition underlying the proofs is that, if cointegration occurs, then the errors are stationary. Loosely speaking, they can be assumed to obey the classical assumptions (or similar assumptions). The proofs we did, e.g. in Chapter 3, relied to a large extent on the properties of the errors and, in particular, the classical assumptions. Hence, similar proofs can be done if cointegration occurs.

Before using results from the regression of Y on X (the so-called *cointegrating regression*), it is important to verify that Y and X are in fact cointegrated. Remember that, if they are not cointegrated, then the spurious regression problem holds and the results you obtain can be completely meaningless. An examination of time series plots such as Figure 7.1 can be quite informative, but remember that visual examinations of graphs should not be considered substitutes for a statistical test.

Many tests for cointegration exist. The statistical methods underlying these tests are typically quite difficult, using statistical derivations beyond the scope of this textbook. Nevertheless, some computer software packages allow you to perform very sophisticated procedures at a touch of a button. Later on, once we have introduced the concept of a vector autoregressive model, we will discuss one of these tests called the *Johansen test*. Here we describe a simpler test that can be motivated using regressions.

The test for cointegration described here is referred to as the *Engle–Granger* test, after the two econometricians who developed it. It is based on the regression of Y on X. Remember that, if cointegration occurs, then the errors from this regression will be stationary. Conversely, if cointegration does not occur, then the errors will have a unit root. Given the close relationship between the errors and the residuals, it is reasonable to examine the properties of the residuals in order to investigate the presence of cointegration. In Chapter 6 we discussed testing for a unit root in a time series variable. Here, we test for a unit root in the residuals using the same techniques. In particular, the test for cointegration involves the following steps:

1. Run the regression of Y on an intercept and X and save the residuals.
2. Carry out a unit root test on the residuals (without including a deterministic trend).
3. If the unit root hypothesis is rejected, then conclude that Y and X are cointegrated. However, if the unit root is accepted, then conclude cointegration does not occur.

It is worthwhile stressing that the Engle–Granger test is based on a unit root test, so that the problems described in Chapter 6 will arise. Although the cointegration test is based on the *t*-statistic from a regression (in this case, one involving the residuals from a preliminary regression), you do not use the Student *t* distribution to obtain the critical value. The correct critical values are published in many places (and are slightly different from the critical values for the Dickey–Fuller test). Table 7.2 contains critical values for the most common case where we do not include a deterministic trend nor an intercept.[3] If such a trend were included, it could mean the errors could be growing steadily over time. This would violate the idea of cointegration (e.g. the idea that the system always returns to equilibrium and, hence, that errors never grow too big). Furthermore, since the residuals are estimates of errors, they should have mean zero, and hence often

Table 7.2 Critical values for the Engle–Granger test.

	$T = 25$	$T = 50$	$T = 100$	$T = \infty$
1 % critical value	−4.37	−4.12	−4.01	−3.90
5 % critical value	−3.59	−3.46	−3.39	−3.33

an intercept is not included. That is, the regression in step 2 above, involving the residuals from step 1, $\widehat{\varepsilon}_t$, is usually

$$\Delta\widehat{\varepsilon}_t = \phi\widehat{\varepsilon}_{t-1} + \gamma_1\Delta\widehat{\varepsilon}_{t-1} + \cdots + \gamma_{p-1}\Delta\widehat{\varepsilon}_{t-p+1} + u_t.$$

Table 7.2 provides critical values for this case.

Note also that, in the Dickey–Fuller test, we test the hypothesis that $\phi = 0$ (i.e. the null hypothesis is the unit root). In the cointegration test, we use the Dickey–Fuller methodology, but cointegration is found if we reject the unit root hypothesis for the residuals. This implies that the null hypothesis in the Engle–Granger test is 'no cointegration', and we conclude 'cointegration is present' only if we reject this hypothesis.

Example: Cointegration between the prices of two goods (continued)

Dickey–Fuller tests indicate that each of the two orange price series plotted in Figure 7.1 has a unit root. If we run a regression of $Y =$ the price of organic oranges on $X =$ the price of regular oranges, we obtain the following fitted regression model:

$$\widehat{Y}_i = 20.686 + 0.996 X_i.$$

The cointegration testing strategy above suggests that we should next carry out a unit root test on the residuals, $\widehat{\varepsilon}_t$, from this regression. The first step in doing the unit root test is to select the lag length correctly. If we use the sequential strategy outlined in Chapter 6, we can conclude that an AR(1) specification for the residuals is appropriate. With this choice made, the Dickey–Fuller strategy suggests we should regress $\Delta\widehat{\varepsilon}_t$ on $\widehat{\varepsilon}_{t-1}$. The t-statistic on $\widehat{\varepsilon}_{t-1}$ in the resulting regression is -14.54. Given that the sample size is 180, Table 7.2 says that the 5 % critical value is between -3.39 and -3.33. Since the test statistic is more negative than the critical we reject the unit root hypothesis and conclude that the residuals do not have a unit root. In other words, we conclude that two price series are indeed cointegrated.

Since we have found cointegration, we do not need to worry about the spurious regression problem. Hence, we can proceed to an interpretation of our coefficients without worrying that the OLS estimates are meaningless. The fact that $\widehat{\alpha} = 20.69$ in the original regression of Y on X reflects the premium of roughly 20 cents per pound that consumers are willing to pay for organic over regular oranges. Furthermore, the long-run multiplier is 0.996. This indicates that, in the long run, an increase in the price of regular oranges by 1 cent would cause an increase in the price of organic oranges of 0.996 of a cent.

In our discussion of cointegration, we have focused on the case where there are two variables, Y and X. In practice, you may have many more variables. Most of what we have discussed above can be extended in a simple fashion to allow for more explanatory variables. For example, the cointegrating regression above was a simple regression. If you have many explanatory variables, the cointegrating regression becomes a multiple regression. The Engle–Granger test statistic can still be calculated in the same manner, using residuals from this multiple regression. However, when you have three or more variables, then a new issue arises: it is possible that there may be more than one cointegrating relationship. To illustrate this point, consider the three variables: income Y, consumption C, and investment I. Although all of these variables fluctuate over time, some macroeconomists claim that the ratios $\frac{C}{Y}$ and $\frac{I}{Y}$ are roughly stable in the long run. That is, consumption's share of income and investment's share of income may vary in the short run, but are stable in the long run. Remember that it is common to take logs of macroeconomic variables, and if we do this we obtain

$$\ln(C) - \ln(Y) \approx \text{constant}$$

and

$$\ln(I) - \ln(Y) \approx \text{constant}.$$

Given that macroeconomic variables often contain unit roots, it is plausible that $\ln(C), \ln(Y)$, and $\ln(I)$ all contain unit roots. However, the line of reasoning above suggests that two linear combinations of these variables might be stationary. Thus, there could be two cointegrating relationships. If two cointegrating relationships exist and you used the Engle–Granger test (based on a cointegrating regression involving all three variables), it should find cointegration. But it will not tell you whether there are one or two cointegrating relationships. What should you do in this case? The best option is to use the Johansen test (to be described shortly). However, it is worth noting that you can also do multiple Engle–Granger tests using different combinations of your variables. For instance, in the example above, you could do an Engle–Granger test with all three variables, $\ln(C), \ln(Y)$, and $\ln(I)$. If you find cointegration, then you know at least one cointegrating relationship exists. Then you could do three more Engle–Granger tests: using $\ln(C)$ and $\ln(Y)$, using $\ln(I)$ and $\ln(Y)$, and using $\ln(C)$ and $\ln(I)$. If two cointegrating relationships exist, then these latter tests will indicate it. Note that, if you have K variables, then there are at most $K - 1$ cointegrating relationships.

This example can also serve to illustrate another empirically important point with cointegrating testing. Often the researcher has a suspicion as to what the cointegrating relationship should be. For instance, if consumption's share in income is stable, and thus represents a cointegrating relationship, then the regression

$$\ln(C) = \alpha + \beta \ln(Y) + \varepsilon$$

should have coefficient $\beta = 1$. Step 1 of the Engle–Granger test uses OLS to estimate β. However, you could simply set $\beta = 1$ if you wanted to test whether $\ln(C)$ and $\ln(Y)$ are cointegrated with a cointegrating coefficient of $\beta = 1$. You could do this test by constructing a new variable, Z, where

$$Z = \ln(C) - \ln(Y),$$

and then test whether Z has a unit root using a Dickey–Fuller test. If Z is found to be stationary, then you know $\ln(C) - \ln(Y)$ is stationary and you know this is a cointegrating relationship. Thus, if you want to test whether particular coefficient values are cointegrating relationships, then you can dispense with step 1 of the Engle–Granger test and simply use Dickey–Fuller tests on suitably transformed variables.

It is also worth reminding you that, before you do any cointegration tests, you should do Dickey–Fuller tests on each variable individually. Only if the unit root hypothesis is accepted for all your variables should you proceed with a cointegration test.

7.3.4   Time series regression when Y and X are cointegrated: the error correction model

In empirical applications it is often vital to establish that Y and X are cointegrated. As emphasised above, cointegration can be related to the idea of Y and X trending together or bearing an equilibrium relationship to each other. A second important task is to esti-mate the long-run multiplier or the long-run influence of X on Y. Both cointegration testing and estimation of the long-run multiplier can be done using the regression of Y on X. Accordingly, in many empirical projects you may never need to move beyond this regression. However, in some cases you may be interested in understanding short-run behavior in a manner that is not possible using only the regression of Y on X. In such cases, we can estimate an *error correction model* (or ECM for short).

An important theorem, known as the *Granger representation theorem*, says that, if Y and X are cointegrated, then the relationship between them can be expressed as an ECM. In this section we will assume that Y and X are cointegrated. Error correction models have a long tradition in time series econometrics, and the Granger representation theorem motivates their popularity. In order to understand the properties of ECMs, let us begin with the following simple version:

$$\Delta Y_t = \varphi + \lambda \varepsilon_{t-1} + \omega_0 \Delta X_t + e_t,$$

where ε_{t-1} is the error obtained from the cointegrating regression (i.e. $\varepsilon_{t-1} = Y_{t-1} - \alpha - \beta X_{t-1}$) and e_t is the error in the ECM. Note that, if we knew ε_{t-1}, then the ECM would be just a regression model (although we have introduced some new Greek letters to make sure that the coefficients and error in this model do not get confused with those in other regression models). That is, in this ECM, ΔY_t is the dependent variable and ε_{t-1} and ΔX_t are explanatory variables. In this model, we assume that $\lambda < 0$ (you will see why shortly).

To aid in interpreting the ECM, remember that ΔY is its dependent variable and any regression model attempts to use explanatory variables to explain the dependent variable. With this in mind, note that the ECM says that ΔY depends on ΔX – an intuitively sen-sible point (i.e. changes in X cause Y to change). In addition, ΔY_t depends on ε_{t-1}. This latter aspect is unique to the ECM and gives it its name.

Remember that ε can be thought of as an equilibrium error. If it is non-zero, then the model is out of equilibrium. Let us assume that $\Delta X_t = 0$ and $e_t = 0$ so that we can focus on the role that ε_{t-1} plays in the ECM. Consider what happens when ε_{t-1} is positive. The latter implies that Y_{t-1} is too high to be in equilibrium (i.e. Y_{t-1} is above its equilibrium level of $\alpha + \beta X_{t-1}$). Since $\lambda < 0$, the term $\lambda \varepsilon_{t-1}$ will be negative and so

ΔY_t will be negative. In other words, if Y_{t-1} is above its equilibrium level, then it will start falling in the next period and the equilibrium error will be 'corrected' in the model; hence the term 'error correction model'. In the case where $\varepsilon_{t-1} < 0$ the opposite will hold (i.e. Y_{t-1} is below its equilibrium level and $\lambda \varepsilon_{t-1} > 0$ which causes ΔY_t to be positive, triggering Y to rise in period t).

These examples show why we must have $\lambda < 0$. If $\lambda > 0$, equilibrium errors will be magnified instead of corrected. Such behavior is inconsistent with cointegration.

In sum, the ECM has both long-run and short-run properties built into it. The former properties are embedded in the ε_{t-1} term (remember β is still the long-run multiplier and ε_t is the error from the cointegrating regression). The short-run behavior is partially captured by the equilibrium error term, which says that, if Y is out of equilibrium, it will be pulled towards it in the next period. Further aspects of short-run behavior are captured by the inclusion of ΔX_t as an explanatory variable. This term implies that, if X changes, the equilibrium value of Y will also change, and Y will also change accordingly. All in all, the ECM has some very sensible properties that are closely related to economic equilibrium concepts.

The ECM also has some nice statistical properties which means that we do not have to worry about the spurious regression problem. Y and X both have unit roots; hence ΔY and ΔX are stationary. Furthermore, since Y and X are cointegrated, the equilibrium error is stationary. Hence, the dependent variable and all explanatory variables in the ECM are stationary. This property means that we can use OLS estimation and carry out testing using t-statistics and P-values in the standard way.

The only new statistical issue in the ECM arises owing to the inclusion of ε_{t-1} as an explanatory variable. Of course, the errors in a model are not directly observed. This raises the issue of how they can be used as an explanatory variable in a regression. Some sophisticated econometric techniques have been developed to estimate the ECM. For instance, many econometrics software packages will allow you to carry out maximum likelihood estimation. However, the simplest thing to do is merely to replace the unknown errors with the residuals from the cointegrating regression (i.e. replace ε_{t-1} with $\widehat{\varepsilon}_{t-1}$ in the ECM). That is, a simple technique based on two OLS regressions proceeds as follows:

1. Run a regression of Y on X and save the residuals.
2. Run a regression of ΔY on an intercept, ΔX and the residuals from step 1 lagged one period.

It should be emphasised that, before carrying out this two-step estimation procedure for the ECM, you must verify that Y and X have unit roots and are cointegrated.

So far we have discussed the simplest error correction model. In practice, just as the ADL(p, q) model has lags of the dependent and explanatory variables, the ECM may also have lags. It may also have a deterministic trend. Incorporating these features into the ECM yields[4]

$$\Delta Y_t = \varphi + \delta t + \lambda \varepsilon_{t-1} + \gamma_1 \Delta Y_{t-1} + \cdots + \gamma_p \Delta Y_{t-p} + \omega_0 \Delta X_t + \cdots + \omega_q \Delta X_{t-q} + e_t.$$

This expression is still in the form of a regression model and can be estimated using the two-step procedure described above. The adjustment to equilibrium intuition also holds for this model. The decisions on whether to include a deterministic trend and on which precise values for p and q are appropriate can be made in the same manner as for the ADL model (i.e. using information criteria or sequential testing procedures). In fact, the ECM is closely related to the ADL model in that it is a restricted version of it.

Example: Cointegration between the prices of two goods (continued)

In the previous part of this example we found that the variables Y = price of organic oranges and X = the price of regular oranges were cointegrated. This suggests that we can estimate an error correction model. To do so, we begin by running a regression of Y on an intercept and X and saving the residuals (which was done in the previous part of the example). The residuals, $\widehat{\varepsilon}_t$, can then be included (in lagged form) in the following ECM:

$$\Delta Y_t = \varphi + \lambda \varepsilon_{t-1} + \omega_0 \Delta X_t + e_t.$$

Table 7.3 gives results from OLS estimation of this model.

The information in Table 7.3 can be interpreted in the standard way. We can say that (with the exception of the intercept) all the coefficients are strongly statistically significant (since their P-values are much less than 0.05).

We noted before that $\widehat{\beta} = 0.996$, and this is the estimate of the long-run multiplier. The point estimates in the table of λ and ω_0 summarize the short-run properties. To aid in interpretation, note that all variables in the model are measured in cents. The coefficient on $\widehat{\varepsilon}_{t-1}$ of -1.085 measures how much Y responds to equilibrium errors. Since this coefficient is negative, positive errors tend to cause ΔY to be negative and, hence, Y to fall. In particular, an equilibrium error of 1 cent tends to cause Y to fall by 1.085 cents in the next period, *ceteris paribus*. This is a very quick adjustment to an equilibrium error! The coefficient on ΔX_t is estimated to be 1.044. Imagine, in other words, what would happen if X were to remain unchanged for some time ($\Delta X = 0$), but then suddenly were to change by 1 cent. The ECM implies that Y would instantly change by 1.044 cents. In other words, the price of organic oranges responds very quickly to price changes in regular oranges. Perhaps since oranges are perishable, grocers will almost immediately react to price changes in regular oranges in order to make sure that their organic oranges do not remain unsold.

Table 7.3 Two-step estimation of the simple error correction model.

Variable	OLS estimate	t-statistic	P-value
Intercept	−0.023	−0.068	0.946
$\widehat{\varepsilon}_{t-1}$	−1.085	−14.458	0.000
ΔX_t	1.044	5.737	0.000

7.4 Time series regression when Y and X have unit roots but are NOT cointegrated

You may encounter instances where unit root tests indicate that your time series have unit roots, but cointegration tests indicate that the series are not cointegrated. That is, the series may not be trending together and may not have an equilibrium relationship. In these cases, you should not run a regression of Y on X owing to the spurious regression problem. The presence of such characteristics suggests that you should rethink your basic model and include other explanatory variables. Instead of working with Y and X themselves, for example, you could difference them. (Remember that if Y and X have unit roots, then ΔY and ΔX should be stationary.) In this case, you could work with the changes in your time series and estimate the ADL model using the techniques described at the beginning of this chapter. In other words, you may wish to estimate the original ADL model, but with changes in the variables:

$$\Delta Y_t = \alpha + \delta t + \gamma_1 \Delta Y_{t-1} + \cdots + \gamma_{p-1} \Delta Y_{t-p+1} + \omega_0 \Delta X_t + \omega_1 \Delta X_{t-1}$$
$$+ \cdots + \omega_{q-1} \Delta X_{t-q+1} + \varepsilon_t.$$

If Y and X have unit roots, then all the variables in the regression above will be stationary and OLS methods for estimation and testing can be used.

However, it is important to emphasise that the interpretation of regression results will likewise change. To illustrate this point, let us suppose $Y =$ an exchange rate and $X =$ an interest rate. If Y and X are cointegrated, or if both are stationary, we can obtain an estimate of the long-run effect of a small change in interest rates on exchange rates. If Y and X have unit roots but are not cointegrated and we estimate the preceding equation, we can obtain an estimate of the long-run effect of a small change in the change of interest rates on the change in exchange rates. This may or may not be a sensible thing to measure, depending on the particular empirical exercise.

As another example, suppose $Y =$ the log of wages and $X =$ the log of prices and that both have unit roots but are not cointegrated. In this case, you would want to work with ΔY and ΔX. But these variables have a nice interpretation as being wage inflation and price inflation respectively. Estimating the preceding equation using these variables would yield estimates that have a sensible interpretation.

Note that earlier in this chapter we provided an example of the effect of computer purchases on sales. In this example, the variables were already measured as percentage changes. If we had begun with $Y =$ sales and $X =$ computer purchases, we would have found they had unit roots but were not cointegrated. Hence, we would have run into the spurious regression problem. This was why we worked with percentage changes.

7.5 Granger causality

In the first part of this chapter, we discussed the building of time series regression models for the three main cases: when all variables are stationary, when all variables have unit roots and are cointegrated, and when all variables have unit roots but are not cointegrated. In each of these cases we have shown how estimation and testing can be done. However, we have not extensively discussed what these models can be used for in practice. Of course, as with any regression model, ADLs and ECMs can be used to measure the marginal effect of explanatory variables on a dependent variable. Furthermore, we have shown how the long-run multiplier can be estimated in each model. Time series regression models are also used for forecasting (something we will discuss shortly). However, there are many other things time series regression models are used for. In this section, partly to give an example of these other things and partly since the topic is important in its own right, we will discuss *Granger causality*.

In Chapters 1 and 2 of this book we referred to causality quite a bit; however, mostly through warnings about interpreting correlation and regression results as reflecting causality. For instance, in Chapter 1 we discussed an example where alcohol drinking and lung cancer rates were correlated with one another, even though alcohol drinking does not cause lung cancer. Here correlation did not imply causality. In fact, it was cigarette smoking that caused lung cancer, but a correlation between cigarette smoking and alcohol drinking produced an apparent relationship between alcohol and lung cancer.

In our discussion of regression, we were on a little firmer ground, since we attempted to use economic reasoning and common sense in labeling one variable the dependent variable and the others the explanatory variables. In many cases, because the latter 'explained' the former, it was reasonable to talk about X 'causing' Y. For instance, in our house price example used in several chapters, the price of the house could be said to be 'caused' by the characteristics of the house (e.g. number of bedrooms, number of bathrooms, etc.). However, in our discussion of omitted variables bias in Chapter 2, it became clear that multiple regressions could provide a misleading interpretation of the degree of causality present if important explanatory variables were omitted. Furthermore, there are many regressions in which it is not obvious which variable causes which. For instance, in the preceding section we mentioned a regression of Y = wage inflation on X = price inflation. It is possible that price inflation causes wage inflation (i.e. X causes Y), since workers will demand higher wage settlements if prices are rising rapidly. However, one could also argue that Y causes X, since wage increases will eat into profits, causing companies to raise prices. So wage inflation could cause price inflation. In other words, the causality could run in either direction – or both! Hence, when using the word 'cause' with regression or correlation, a great deal of caution has to be taken and common sense has to be used.

However, with time series data we can make slightly stronger statements about causality simply by exploiting the fact that time does not run backwards. That is, if event A happens before event B, then it is possible that A is causing B. However, it is not possible that B is causing A. In other words, events in the past can cause events to happen today. Future events cannot.

These intuitive ideas can be investigated through regression models incorporating the notion of Granger causality. The basic idea is that a variable X Granger causes Y if past values of X can help explain Y. Of course, if Granger causality holds, this does not guarantee that X causes Y. This is why we say 'Granger causality' rather than just 'causality'. Nevertheless, if past values of X have explanatory power for current values of Y, it at least suggests that X might be causing Y.

Granger causality is only relevant with time series variables. To illustrate the basic concepts, we will consider Granger causality between two variables (X and Y) that are both stationary. A non-stationary case, where X and Y have unit roots but are cointegrated, will be mentioned below.

7.5.1 Granger causality in the ADL model

Let us begin by assuming that X and Y are stationary and, thus, that an ADL model is appropriate. Suppose that the following ADL model holds:

$$Y_t = \alpha + \rho Y_{t-1} + \beta X_{t-1} + \varepsilon_t.$$

This model implies that last period's value of X has explanatory power for the current value of Y. The coefficient β is a measure of the influence of X_{t-1} on Y_t. If $\beta = 0$, then past values of X have no effect on Y and there is no way that X could Granger cause Y. In other words, if $\beta = 0$, then X does not Granger cause Y. An alternative way of expressing this concept is to say that 'if $\beta = 0$, then past values of X have no explanatory power for Y beyond that provided by past values for Y'. Since, as we have seen, OLS methods can be used to estimate the ADL and carry out hypothesis tests, it is simple to test for Granger causality. That is, we can use a t-test of the hypothesis that $\beta = 0$. If β is statistically significant, then we conclude that X Granger causes Y. Note that the null hypothesis being tested here is H_0: $\beta = 0$ which is the hypothesis that Granger causality does not occur. So we should formally refer the test of $\beta = 0$ as a test of Granger non-causality, but we will adopt the more common informal terminology and just refer to this procedure as a Granger causality test.

Of course, the above ADL model is quite restrictive in that it incorporates only one lag of X and Y. In general, we would want to select lag lengths using the methods described previously and work with an ADL(p, q) model:

$$Y_t = \alpha + \delta t + \rho_1 Y_{t-1} + \cdots + \rho_p Y_{t-p} + \beta_1 X_{t-1} + \cdots + \beta_q X_{t-q} + \varepsilon_t.$$

You can also use the alternative form for the ADL model introduced previously.

As a digression, note that (unlike the ADLs discussed previously), we have not included the current value of X as an explanatory variable. If current values of X were included, then we would allow for *contemporaneous causality*. This raises different issues from Granger causality which focuses on whether past values of X cause Y. Nevertheless, you can include X_t in the previous regression if you wish to investigate contemporaneous causality.

In the previous regressions, X Granger causes Y if any or all of $\beta_1, \ldots, \beta_q$ are statistically significant. In other words, if X at any time in the past has explanatory power for the current value of Y, then we say that X Granger causes Y. Since we are assuming X and Y do not contain unit roots, OLS regression analysis can be used to estimate this model. Hence, we can use an F-test of the joint hypothesis $H_0: \beta_1 = 0, \ldots, \beta_q = 0$ as a Granger causality test.

Example: Does wage inflation Granger cause price inflation?

We have annual data from 1855 to 1987 on UK prices and wages. Dickey–Fuller tests indicate that both the log of wages and the log of prices have unit roots, but the Engle–Granger test indicates they are not cointegrated. However, the differences of these series are stationary and can be interpreted as inflation rates (i.e. wage and price inflation). We will use this dataset to investigate whether past wage inflation causes price inflation. There is good reason to think that this may indeed be the case. After all, if wages are increasing, companies will have an incentive to increase prices to stop their profit margins from falling.

Table 7.4 contains results from OLS estimation of the regression of ΔP = price inflation on four lags of itself, four lags of ΔW = wage inflation, and a deterministic trend.

An examination of the P-values in this table indicates that only the deterministic trend and last period's price inflation have significant explanatory power for present inflation. All of the coefficients on the lags of wage inflation are insignificant. This suggests that, contrary to our expectations, wage inflation does not seem to Granger cause price inflation. However, we have to do an F-test to do a formal test of Granger causality since a joint test of $H_0: \beta_1 = 0, \ldots, \beta_q = 0$ is not the same as q individual t-tests of $H_0: \beta_j = 0$ for $j = 1, \ldots, q$.

Many econometrics software packages will provide you with a P-value for the test of $H_0: \beta_1 = 0, \ldots, \beta_q = 0$ automatically. However, as a useful review, we provide the details of how the F-test is done in the case of Granger causality. Remember

Table 7.4   ADL with price inflation as dependent variable.

Variable	OLS estimate	t-statistic	P-value
Intercept	−0.751	−1.058	0.292
ΔP_{t-1}	0.822	4.850	0.000
ΔP_{t-2}	−0.041	−0.222	0.825
ΔP_{t-3}	0.142	0.762	0.448
ΔP_{t-4}	−0.181	−1.035	0.303
ΔW_{t-1}	−0.016	−0.114	0.909
ΔW_{t-2}	−0.118	−0.823	0.412
ΔW_{t-3}	−0.042	−0.292	0.771
ΔW_{t-4}	0.038	0.266	0.791
t	0.030	2.669	0.009

(see Chapter 4) that the F-statistic is

$$F = \frac{(R^2_{UR} - R^2_R)/r}{(1 - R^2_{UR})/(T - k - 1)},$$

where the subscripts UR and R distinguish between the R^2s from the unrestricted and restricted regression models. The number of restrictions being tested is r, and k is the number of explanatory variables in the unrestricted regression. In this example, we have $T = 128$ and $k = 9$ (i.e. $p = q = 4$ plus we have the deterministic trend in the model). The hypothesis that Granger causality does not occur involves four restrictions ($\beta_1 = 0, \beta_2 = 0, \beta_3 = 0$, and $\beta_4 = 0$), and hence $r = 4$. The restricted regression model is

$$Y_t = \alpha + \delta t + \rho_1 Y_{t-1} + \cdots + \rho_p Y_{t-p} + \varepsilon_t.$$

OLS estimation of the unrestricted and restricted models yields $R^2_{UR} = 0.616$ and $R^2_R = 0.613$. Plugging these values into the formula for the F-statistic yields $F = 0.145$. The critical value for this test is taken from the $F_{r, T-k-1} = F_{4,118}$ distribution. The 5 % critical value is approximately 2.37. Since $0.145 < 2.37$, we cannot reject the hypothesis that $\beta_1 = 0, \ldots, \beta_4 = 0$ at the 5 % level of significance. Accordingly, we accept the hypothesis that wage inflation does not Granger cause price inflation.

Causality in both directions

In many cases it is not obvious which way causality should run. For instance, should past wage inflation cause price inflation or should the reverse hold? In such cases, when causality may be in either direction, it is important that you check for it. If Y and X are the two variables under study, in addition to running a regression of Y on lags of itself and lags of X (as above), you should also run a regression of X on lags of itself and lags of Y.

Note that it is possible to find that Y Granger causes X and that X Granger causes Y. In the case of complicated economic models, such bidirectional causality is quite common and even reasonable. Think, for instance, of the relationship between interest rates and exchange rates. It is not unreasonable from a macroeconomic perspective to say that interest rate policy may affect future exchange rates. However, it is also equally reasonable to think that exchange rates may also affect future interest rate policy (e.g. if the exchange rate is perceived to be too high now, the central bank may be led to decrease interest rates in the next period).

Example: Does price inflation Granger cause wage inflation?

In the previous example we investigated whether wage inflation Granger caused price inflation. We found that it did not. However, it is possible that causality runs

Table 7.5 ADL with wage inflation as dependent variable.

Variable	OLS estimate	t-statistic	P-value
Intercept	−0.609	−0.730	0.467
ΔW_{t-1}	0.053	0.312	0.755
ΔW_{t-2}	−0.040	−0.235	0.814
ΔW_{t-3}	−0.058	−0.348	0.728
ΔW_{t-4}	0.036	0.215	0.830
ΔP_{t-1}	0.854	4.280	0.000
ΔP_{t-2}	−0.217	−0.993	0.323
ΔP_{t-3}	0.234	1.067	0.288
ΔP_{t-4}	−0.272	−1.323	0.188
t	0.046	3.514	0.001

in the opposite direction; that is, that price inflation may actually cause wage inflation. After all, workers and unions often look at inflation when deciding on their wage demands.

Table 7.5 contains results from OLS estimation of the regression of $\Delta W =$ wage inflation on four lags of itself, four lags of $\Delta P =$ price inflation, and a deterministic trend. Here we do find evidence that price inflation Granger causes wage inflation. In particular, the coefficient on ΔP_{t-1} is highly significant, indicating that last year's price inflation rate has strong explanatory power for wage inflation. This is confirmed by the F-test for Granger causality.

In particular, calculating the F-statistic as described above yields $F = 33.412$. As in the previous example, the 5 % critical value for this test is approximately 2.37. Since $33.412 > 2.37$, we reject the hypothesis that $\beta_1 = 0, \ldots, \beta_q = 0$ at the 5 % level of significance. Accordingly, we accept the hypothesis that price inflation does Granger cause wage inflation.

Our discussion of Granger causality has focused on two variables, X and Y. However, there is no reason why these basic techniques cannot be extended to the case of many variables. For instance, if we had three variables, X, Y, and Z, and were interested in investigating whether X or Z Granger cause Y, we would simply regress Y on lags of Y, lags of X, and lags of Z. If, for example, the lags of Z were found to be significant (using an F-test) and the lags of X not, then we could say that Z Granger causes Y, but X does not.

7.5.2   Granger causality with cointegrated variables

Testing for Granger causality among cointegrated variables is very similar to the method outlined above for stationary variables. It is common to work with a variant of the ECM:

$$\Delta Y_t = \varphi + \delta t + \lambda \varepsilon_{t-1} + \gamma_1 \Delta Y_{t-1} + \cdots + \gamma_p \Delta Y_{t-p} + \omega_1 \Delta X_{t-1} + \cdots + \omega_q \Delta X_{t-q} + e_t.$$

Note that, as with our discussion of Granger causality in the ADL model, we are omitting the contemporaneous value for X in order to avoid issues raised by contemporaneous causality. Remember that this is an ADL model (using differenced data) except for the presence of the term $\lambda \varepsilon_{t-1}$. Remember that $\varepsilon_{t-1} = Y_{t-1} - \alpha - \beta X_{t-1}$, an estimate of which can be obtained by running a regression of Y on an intercept and X and using the residuals as estimates of the errors. Intuitively, X Granger causes Y if past values of X have explanatory power for current values of Y. Applying this intuition to the ECM, we can see that past values of X appear in the terms $\Delta X_{t-1}, \ldots, \Delta X_{t-q}$ and ε_{t-1}. This implies that X does not Granger cause Y if $\lambda = 0, \omega_1 = 0, \ldots, \omega_q = 0$. This hypothesis can be tested using an F-test or a likelihood ratio test.

In the previous paragraph we described how to test whether X Granger causes Y. Testing whether Y Granger causes X is achieved by reversing the roles that X and Y play in the ECM. One interesting consequence of the Granger representation theorem is worth noting here (without the proof). If X and Y are cointegrated, then some form of Granger causality must occur. That is, either X must Granger cause Y or Y must Granger cause X (or both).

7.6　Vector autoregressions

Our discussion of Granger causality naturally leads us to the topic of *vector autoregressions* or VARs. Before discussing their popularity and estimation, we will first define what a VAR is. Initially, we will assume that all variables are stationary. If the original variables have unit roots, then we assume that differences have been taken such that the model includes the changes in the original variables (which do not have unit roots). Subsequently, we will consider the extension of this case to that of cointegration.

When we investigated Granger causality between X and Y, we began with an ADL(p, q) model with Y as the dependent variable. We used it to investigate if X Granger caused Y. We then went on to consider causality in the other direction, which involved switching the roles of X and Y in the ADL; in particular, X became the dependent variable. We can write the two equations as follows:

$$Y_t = \alpha_1 + \delta_1 t + \rho_{11} Y_{t-1} + \cdots, + \rho_{1p} Y_{t-p} + \beta_{11} X_{t-1} + \cdots, + \beta_{1q} X_{t-q} + \varepsilon_{1t},$$
$$X_t = \alpha_2 + \delta_2 t + \rho_{21} Y_{t-1} + \cdots, + \rho_{2p} Y_{t-p} + \beta_{21} X_{t-1} + \cdots, + \beta_{2q} X_{t-q} + \varepsilon_{2t}$$

The first of these equations can be used to test whether X Granger causes Y, and the second to test whether Y Granger causes X. Note that now the coefficients have subscripts indicating which equation they are in. For instance, α_1 is the intercept in the first equation, and α_2 the intercept in the second. Furthermore, the errors now have subscripts to denote the fact that they will be different in the two equations.

These two equations comprise a VAR. A VAR is the extension of the autoregressive (AR) model to the case in which there is more than one variable under study. Remember that the AR model introduced in Chapter 6 involved one dependent variable, Y_t, which depended only on lags of itself (and possibly a deterministic trend). A VAR has more than one dependent variable (e.g. Y and X) and thus has more than one equation (e.g. one where Y_t is the dependent variable and one where X_t is). Each equation uses as its explanatory variables lags of all the variables under study (and possibly a deterministic trend).

The two equations above constitute a VAR with two variables. For instance, you can see that, in the first equation, Y depends on p lags of itself and on q lags of X. The lag lengths, p and q, can be selected using information criteria or sequential testing methods. However, especially if the VAR has more than two variables, many different lag lengths need to be selected (i.e. one for each variable in each equation). In light of this, it is common to set $p = q$ and use the same lag length for every variable in every equation. The resulting model is known as a VAR(p) model. The following VAR(p) has three variables, Y, X, and Z:

$$Y_t = \alpha_1 + \delta_1 t + \rho_{11} Y_{t-1} + \cdots + \rho_{1p} Y_{t-p} + \beta_{11} X_{t-1} + \cdots + \beta_{1p} X_{t-p}$$
$$+ \kappa_{11} Z_{t-1} + \cdots + \kappa_{1p} Z_{t-p} + \varepsilon_{1t},$$
$$X_t = \alpha_2 + \delta_2 t + \rho_{21} Y_{t-1} + \cdots + \rho_{2p} Y_{t-p} + \beta_{21} X_{t-1} + \cdots + \beta_{2p} X_{t-p}$$
$$+ \kappa_{21} Z_{t-1} + \cdots + \kappa_{2p} Z_{t-p} + \varepsilon_{2t},$$
$$Z_t = \alpha_3 + \delta_3 t + \rho_{31} Y_{t-1} + \cdots + \rho_{3p} Y_{t-p} + \beta_{31} X_{t-1} + \cdots + \beta_{3p} X_{t-p}$$
$$+ \kappa_{31} Z_{t-1} + \cdots + \kappa_{3p} Z_{t-p} + \varepsilon_{3t}.$$

Note that, in addition to an intercept and deterministic trend, each equation contains p lags of all variables under study. VAR(p) models with more than three variables can be obtained in an analogous manner.

Since we assume that all the variables in the VAR(p) are stationary, estimation and testing can be carried out in the standard way. That is, you can obtain estimates of coefficients in each equation using OLS. P-values or t-statistics will then allow you to ascertain whether individual coefficients are significant. We should note, however, that other estimators exist for the VAR (and many econometrics software packages will let you choose from a menu of different estimation options). In the unrestricted VAR written above, doing OLS estimation one equation at a time yields efficient estimates (if the errors satisfy the classical assumptions). However, in a restricted VAR (i.e. one where some of the coefficients are restricted, such as $\beta_{31} = \beta_{32} = 0$), other more efficient estimators exist. Still, OLS methods are popular and commonly used with VARs.

VARs are, then, easy to use. However, you may be wondering why we would want to work with such models. One reason is Granger causality testing. That is, VARs provide a framework for testing for Granger causality between each set of variables. However, there are deeper reasons for why we would want to use them that we try to motivate in the following paragraphs.

Throughout this book, we have stressed the need for care when interpreting correlation or regression results as reflecting causality or influence. Economic theory or common sense can be a big help to you in many cases. In previous chapters, we worked through many examples in which we could comfortably say that the regressions reflected causality. For instance, X (population density) caused Y (deforestation) or X (lot size) influenced Y (house price). In both cases it is not plausible for us to say that Y influenced or caused X.

However, there are many instances when neither economic theory nor common sense can provide you with a regression model that can be interpreted as reflecting causality. For instance, does Y (wage inflation) cause X (price inflation)? Or does the opposite happen? Economic theory and common sense tell us that either can happen, and that Granger causality tests can shed light on these questions. The field of macroeconomics, in particular, is filled with such examples. Should interest rates cause exchange rates to change, or vice versa? Both? Should GDP growth cause interest rates to change? The opposite? Both? The answers are unclear, and it is hard to know how to interpret coefficients in a regression of Y_t on X_t.

In our discussion of VARs, we have so far ignored the issues of cointegration and the long-run multiplier. However, even if cointegration is present, we have to be careful when interpreting regression results as reflecting causality. For instance, in a previous example we found the prices of Y (price of organic oranges) and of X (regular oranges) to be cointegrated and the long-run multiplier effect of X on Y to be 0.996. These results probably indicate that X influenced Y (i.e. if the price of regular oranges went up by 1 cent, the price of organic oranges would rise by 0.996 of a cent in the long run). However, it is unlikely that the price of organic oranges would influence regular oranges since the former are such a small part of the market. Hence, X influences Y, but Y does not influence X. If we had reversed things and the price of regular oranges was our dependent variable and the price of organic oranges the explanatory variable, we would still have found cointegration and calculated a long-run multiplier. But we would be wrong in using it as a measure of the influence of organic orange prices on regular orange prices.

The issues raised in the previous paragraphs either do not arise at all or arise to a far less extent in VAR models. That is, all of the variables we are using to explain the current value of the dependent variable occurred in the past (e.g. in the first equation the explanatory variables are all dated $t - 1$ or earlier, whereas the dependent variable is Y_t). It is possible that the past might influence the present, but it is not possible for the present to influence the past. Hence, in the VAR model, the explanatory variables might influence the dependent variable, but there is no possibility that the dependent variable influences the explanatory variable. Problems of interpretation that arise with the regression of Y_t on X_t do not arise in the VAR case.

One of the controversial things about VARs is that they are *atheoretical*; that is, do not draw heavily on economic theory. Theory is limited to selecting the variables in the VAR. Consider, for instance, the relationship between interest rates, the price level, money supply, and real GDP. Macroeconomic theorists have created many sophisticated models of this relationship. The IS-LM model extended for inflation is perhaps the best known, but many others do exist. Whereas the macroeconomic theorist would like this theory to influence empirical work, the VAR practitioner does not draw on it at all. A VAR model states: 'Interest rates, price level, money supply, and real GDP are related. We model this relationship as implying only that each variable depends on lags of itself and all other variables'. There is no real link between the empirical VAR and a theoretical macro-economic model (e.g. IS-LM).

The VAR user would defend the VAR by noting its excellent forecasting performance. We will discuss this trait in greater detail below, but you should merely note now that this constitutes a strong reason for using them. In many cases, VARs have been shown to have better forecasting ability than sophisticated macroeconomic models. The fact that simple regression-based methods can often outperform complicated macroeconomic models that are created and maintained by specialists in government or the private sector is a strong motivation for using VARs.

Example:　A VAR(1) with RMPY variables

Economists often use such important macroeconomic variables as R = the interest rate, M = the money supply, P = the price level, and Y = real GDP. Owing to the symbols used, models using these variables are sometimes informally referred to as RMPY models. In this example we use quarterly data on these variables for the USA from 1947Q1 to 1992Q4. To be precise:

- R is the 3 month Treasury bill rate;
- M is the money supply (M2) measured in billions of dollars;
- P is the price level measured by the GDP deflator (a price index with 1987 = 1.00);
- Y is real GDP measured in billions of 1987 dollars.

Before carrying out an analysis using time series data, you must conduct unit root tests. Remember that, if unit roots are present but cointegration does not occur, then the spurious regression problem exists. In this case you should work with dif-ferenced data. Alternatively, if unit roots exist and cointegration does occur, then you will have important economic information that the series are trending together.

In the present case, tests indicate that we cannot reject the hypothesis that unit roots exist in all variables and that cointegration does not occur. In order to avoid the spurious regression problem, we work with differenced data. In particular, we take logs of each series, then take differences of these logged series, then multiply them by 100. This implies that we are working with percentage changes in each vari-able (e.g. a value of 1 implies a 1 % change). Thus:

- ΔR is the percentage change in the interest rate;
- ΔM is the percentage change in the money supply;
- ΔP is the percentage change in the price level (i.e. inflation);
- ΔY is the percentage change in GDP (i.e. GDP growth).

Table 7.6 presents results from OLS estimation of a VAR(1). Note that this table is in a slightly different format from previous ones. Since there are four variables in our VAR

Table 7.6 The RMPY VAR(1) using ΔR, ΔM, ΔP, and ΔY as dependent variables.

Explanatory variable	Dependent variable ΔR		Dependent variable ΔM		Dependent variable ΔP		Dependent variable ΔY	
	Coeff.	*P*-value	Coeff.	*P*-value	Coeff.	*P*-value	Coeff.	*P*-value
Intercept	−3.631	0.162	0.335	0.001	0.161	0.138	0.495	0.005
ΔR_{t-1}	0.222	0.003	−0.013	0.000	0.010	0.002	0.000	0.940
ΔM_{t-1}	3.391	0.007	0.749	0.000	0.121	0.021	0.283	0.001
ΔP_{t-1}	1.779	0.228	0.061	0.303	0.519	0.000	−0.117	0.242
ΔY_{t-1}	3.224	0.004	−0.032	0.480	−0.039	0.407	0.309	0.000
t	−0.056	0.011	0.000	0.695	0.002	0.048	−0.003	0.035

(i.e. ΔR, ΔM, ΔP, and ΔY), there are four equations to estimate. We have put results for all equations in one table. Each equation regresses a dependent variable on one lag of all the variables in the VAR. To save space, we have included only the OLS estimate (labelled 'Coeff.') and the *P*-value for testing the significance of each coefficient.

If we examine the significant coefficients (i.e. those with a *P*-value less than 0.05), some interesting patterns emerge. Firstly, in every equation the lag of the dependent variable is significant. That is, in the equation with ΔR_t as the dependent variable, ΔR_{t-1} provides significant explanatory power. In the equation with ΔM_t as the dependent variable, ΔM_{t-1} provides significant explanatory power, etc.

Secondly, the results for the four equations demonstrate some interesting patterns of Granger causality. In the equation with ΔR as the dependent variable, we can see that both GDP growth and money growth Granger cause interest rate changes. In other words, past values of GDP growth and money growth have explanatory power for current interest rate changes. In the case of the $\Delta R/\Delta M$ (interest rate/money supply) relationship, the equation with ΔM as the dependent variable shows that the causality flows in both directions since interest rate changes also Granger cause money growth. However, interest rate changes do not Granger cause GDP growth. The Granger causality results with respect to inflation are particularly interesting since it can be seen that inflation does not Granger cause any other variable, but that both ΔR and ΔM Granger cause inflation.

A macroeconomist could use these results to address theoretical questions of interest (e.g. Is inflation purely a monetary phenomenon? Are monetarist views of the economy supported? Are Keynesian views of the economy supported? Is the real economy affected by inflation?, etc.), but it is beyond the scope of this book to discuss them in detail.

The results in the previous example are based on a VAR(1). That is, we set $p = 1$ and used one lag of each variable to explain the dependent variable. In general, of course, we might want to set p to values other than 1. As with all the models discussed in this chapter, information criteria, *F*-statistics, and *t*-statistics all provide useful information on lag length. This is illustrated in the following example.

Example: A VAR(2) with RMPY variables

In the previous example, we used data on ΔR, ΔM, ΔP, and ΔY to estimate a VAR(1). The following table repeats the analysis using a VAR(2).

Table 7.7 shows that several of the coefficients on variables two periods ago are significant. For instance, ΔR_{t-2} is significant in the equation with ΔR_t as the dependent variable. In a serious piece of empirical research, you should use information criteria or other hypothesis testing procedures to help decide lag length. But an examination of the t-statistics does indicate that the VAR(1) used in the previous example was not appropriate.

To give you an idea of the costs of using an incorrect model, take a careful look at the equation with ΔY as the dependent variable. Recall that in the VAR(1) model we concluded that inflation did not Granger cause GDP growth. However, the VAR(2) indicates that inflation does Granger cause GDP growth since ΔP_{t-2} is significant. Since the relationship between GDP growth and the inflation rate is the source of much controversy in modern macroeconomics, the cost of incorrectly using a VAR(1) is quite large.

7.6.1 Forecasting with VARs

We have said very little in the book so far about forecasting, in spite of the fact that this is an important activity of economists. There are two main reasons for this lack of emphasis. Firstly, the field of forecasting is enormous. Given the huge volume of research and issues to consider, it is impossible to do justice to the field in a short section of a book like this. Secondly, basic forecasting using the computer is either very easy or very hard,

Table 7.7 The RMPY VAR(2) using ΔR, ΔM, ΔP, and ΔY as dependent variables.

Explanatory variable	Dependent variable ΔR		Dependent variable ΔM		Dependent variable ΔP		Dependent variable ΔY	
	Coeff.	P-value	Coeff.	P-value	Coeff.	P-value	Coeff.	P-value
Intercept	-4.000	0.103	0.261	0.017	0.113	0.311	0.513	0.006
ΔR_{t-1}	0.315	0.000	-0.017	0.000	0.009	0.004	0.002	0.670
ΔM_{t-1}	2.824	0.106	0.655	0.000	0.086	0.280	0.310	0.019
ΔP_{t-1}	3.049	0.061	-0.020	0.785	0.366	0.000	0.074	0.545
ΔY_{t-1}	3.696	0.000	-0.051	0.270	-0.010	0.835	0.270	0.001
ΔR_{t-2}	-0.346	0.000	0.003	0.298	-0.001	0.795	-0.010	0.085
ΔM_{t-2}	-2.201	0.213	0.157	0.045	0.025	0.755	-0.094	0.480
ΔP_{t-2}	1.164	0.457	0.095	0.170	0.282	0.000	-0.233	0.049
ΔY_{t-2}	1.085	0.303	0.036	0.445	-0.046	0.334	0.153	0.054
t	-0.045	0.029	0.000	0.798	0.001	0.209	-0.003	0.104

depending on the exact model you are using and what computer software you have. To be precise, many econometrics computer packages have forecasting facilities that are simple to use. Once you have estimated a model (e.g. a VAR or an AR), you can forecast simply by clicking on an appropriate option. In other words, many computer packages can allow you to undertake basic forecasting without a deep knowledge of the topic. However, for sophisticated models, forecasting can become quite difficult.

In light of these issues, we will offer only a brief introduction to some of the practical issues and intuitive ideas relating to forecasting. In this section, our discussion will relate to forecasting with VARs, but it is worth noting that the ideas also relate to forecasting with univariate time series models. After all, an AR model is just a VAR with only one equation. In the appendix to this chapter, we offer some discussion of the econometric theory underlying forecasting, illustrating the basic ideas using an AR model.

Forecasting is usually done using time series variables. The idea is that you use your observed data to predict what you expect to happen in the future. In more technical terms, you use data for periods $t = 1, \ldots, T$ to forecast periods $T + 1, T + 2$, etc.

To provide some intuition for how forecasting is done, consider a VAR(1) involving two variables, Y and X:

$$Y_t = \alpha_1 + \delta_1 t + \rho_{11} Y_{t-1} + \beta_{11} X_{t-1} + \varepsilon_{1t},$$
$$X_t = \alpha_2 + \delta_2 t + \rho_{21} Y_{t-1} + \beta_{21} X_{t-1} + \varepsilon_{2t}.$$

You cannot observe Y_{T+1} but you want to make a guess at what it is likely to be (i.e. you want an estimate of it). Using the first equation of the VAR and setting $t = T + 1$, we obtain an expression for Y_{T+1}:

$$Y_{T+1} = \alpha_1 + \delta_1(T + 1) + \rho_{11} Y_T + \beta_{11} X_T + \varepsilon_{1,T+1}.$$

This equation cannot be directly used to obtain Y_{T+1} since we don't know what $\varepsilon_{1,T+1}$ is. In words, we don't know what unpredictable shock or surprise will hit the economy next period. Furthermore, we don't know what the coefficients are. However, if we ignore the error term (which cannot be forecast) and replace it with its expected value (i.e. $E(\varepsilon_{t,T+1}) = 0$) and replace the coefficients with OLS estimates, we obtain a forecast that we denote as

$$\widehat{Y}_{T+1} = \widehat{\alpha}_1 + \widehat{\delta}_1(T + 1) + \widehat{\rho}_{11} Y_T + \widehat{\beta}_{11} X_T.$$

If you are using a good econometrics software package, you will never have to evaluate an expression such as this. But it is worth noting that everything in the formula can be taken from either the original data or from the output from the regression command. It is conceptually easy just to plug all the individual numbers (i.e. the OLS estimates of the coefficients and $T + 1$, Y_T, and X_T) into a formula to calculate $\widehat{Y}_{T+1}$. A similar strategy can be used to obtain $\widehat{X}_{T+1}$.

The previous paragraph described how to forecast one period into the future. We can use the same strategy for two periods, provided that we make one extension. In the one-period case we used X_T and Y_T to create $\widehat{Y}_{T+1}$ and $\widehat{X}_{T+1}$. In the two-period case, $\widehat{Y}_{T+2}$ and $\widehat{X}_{T+2}$ depend on X_{T+1} and Y_{T+1}. But since our data only run until period T, we do not know what X_{T+1} and Y_{T+1} are. However, we can replace X_{T+1} and Y_{T+1} with $\widehat{Y}_{T+1}$ and $\widehat{X}_{T+1}$. In general, we can use the relevant equation from the VAR, replace the error with its expected value of zero, replace the coefficients with their OLS estimates, and replace past values of the variables that we do not observe with their forecasts. Such a strategy can be written in a formula as

$$\widehat{Y}_{T+2} = \widehat{\alpha}_1 + \widehat{\delta}_1(T+2) + \widehat{\rho}_{11}\widehat{Y}_{T+1} + \widehat{\beta}_{11}\widehat{X}_{T+1},$$

and, similarly, for $\widehat{X}_{T+2}$, we have

$$\widehat{X}_{T+2} = \widehat{\alpha}_2 + \widehat{\delta}_2(T+2) + \widehat{\rho}_{21}\widehat{Y}_{T+1} + \widehat{\beta}_{21}\widehat{X}_{T+1}.$$

Above we have focused on the VAR(1) and forecasting one or two periods in the future. We can use the general strategy of ignoring the error, replacing coefficients with OLS estimates, and replacing lagged values of variables that are unobserved with forecasts to obtain forecasts for any number of periods in the future for any VAR(p).

The previous discussion demonstrated how to calculate point estimates of forecasts. Of course, in reality, what actually happens is rarely identical to your forecast. When developing estimators for coefficients, we discussed a similar issue. There we pointed out that OLS only provides estimates of coefficients, and that these will not be precisely correct. For this reason, in addition to OLS estimates, we also recommended that you present confidence intervals. These reflect the level of uncertainty about the coefficient estimate. When forecasting, confidence intervals can also be calculated, and these can be quite informative. It is increasingly common for government agencies, for instance, to present confidence intervals for their forecasts. For instance, central banks often make statements of the form: 'Our forecast of inflation next year is 1.8 %. We are 95 % confident that it will be between 1.45 % and 2.15 %'. Many computer packages automatically provide confidence intervals for forecasts, and thus you may not need to know their precise formula when forecasting. We do not derive the relevant formulae here, but an appendix to this chapter offers some related derivations.

In practice, two types of forecasting are popular. The first is simply to try to forecast the future. For instance, at the time of writing, data for many macroeconomic variables are available up to 2006. We can use these data, along with a VAR, to forecast what will happen in 2007, 2008, 2009, etc. This is referred to as *out-of-sample* forecasting. However, particularly when choosing a model, you might be interested in seeing how your model would have forecast in the past. So, if annual data are available from 1950 to 2006, you could estimate a VAR using data up to 2005 and then forecast 2006 values for your variables. The actual value for 2006 would be compared with the forecast you just made. In general, if you have data for $t = 1, \ldots, T$, you could estimate a VAR using data from

Table 7.8 Forecasts of inflation and GDP growth.

	ΔP		ΔY	
	Forecast	Actual	Forecast	Actual
1992Q1	0.626	0.929	−0.019	0.865
1992Q2	0.731	0.689	0.220	0.698
1992Q3	0.862	0.289	0.275	0.838
1992Q4	0.940	0.813	0.271	1.393

$t = 1, \ldots, \tau$ (where $\tau < T$) and then forecast. If you tried many different values for τ, you would have a series of forecasts. Such forecasts can be compared with the actual observations and the forecasting performance of your VAR assessed. This sort of exercise is referred to as *recursive* forecasting.

Example: A VAR(2) with RMPY variables (continued)

In this example, we consider forecasting using the data on ΔR, ΔM, ΔP, and ΔY. As above, we use a VAR(2), recalling that we have data on these variables from 1947Q2 to 1992Q4. Here we use data from 1947Q2 to 1991Q4 to estimate the VAR(2). We forecast from 1992Q1 to 1992Q4, and then compare our forecasts for the year 1992 with what actually happened in 1992. Doing so will give us some idea of the forecast performance of our model. Table 7.8 contains the forecasts and actual observations for 1992 for two of the most important variables: inflation and GDP growth.

To aid in interpretation, note that all figures are percentage changes over the quarter. For example, the forecast for quarterly inflation for 1992Q2 of 0.731 translates into a 2.96 % annual inflation rate. The table indicates that the VAR(2) did reasonably well at forecasting inflation, except for 1992Q3, when actual inflation was unusually low. The forecasting performance for GDP growth is not quite as good, with our VAR consistently predicting slower growth than had actually occurred.

7.6.2 Vector Autoregressions with cointegrated variables

In the preceding discussion of VARs, we assumed that all variables were stationary. If some of the original variables have unit roots and are not cointegrated, then the ones with unit roots should be differenced and the resulting stationary variables should be used in the VAR. This covers every case except the one where the variables have unit roots and are cointegrated. This case is covered in this section.

Recall that, in this case in our discussion of Granger causality, we recommended that you work with an ECM. The same strategy can be employed here. In particular, instead of working with a vector autoregression (VAR), you should work with a *vector error correction model* (VECM). Like the VAR, the VECM will have one equation for each variable in the model. In the case of two variables, Y and X, the VECM is[5]

$$\Delta Y_t = \varphi_1 + \delta_1 t + \lambda_1 \varepsilon_{t-1} + \gamma_{11} \Delta Y_{t-1} + \cdots + \gamma_{1p} \Delta Y_{t-p} + \omega_{11} \Delta X_{t-1}$$
$$+ \cdots + \omega_{1q} \Delta X_{t-q} + e_{1t}$$

and

$$\Delta X_t = \varphi_2 + \delta_2 t + \lambda_2 \varepsilon_{t-1} + \gamma_{21} \Delta Y_{t-1} + \cdots + \gamma_{2p} \Delta Y_{t-p} + \omega_{21} \Delta X_{t-1}$$
$$+ \cdots + \omega_{2q} \Delta X_{t-q} + e_{2t}.$$

As before, $\varepsilon_{t-1} = Y_{t-1} - \alpha - \beta X_{t-1}$. Furthermore, in the same manner as with the VAR, the VECM can be extended to the case of many variables. But remember that, when you have more than two variables, it is possible that there is more than one cointegrating relationship. If this occurs, then there will be more than one error correction term to be included in each equation (e.g. instead of a single ε_{t-1} there will be $\varepsilon_{1,t-1}$ and $\varepsilon_{2,t-1}$ in the case of two cointegrating relationships).

Most relevant econometrics software packages will allow you to carry out maximum likelihood estimation of this model. Alternatively, the two-step procedure for estimating the ECM described previously can be done for each equation of the VECM. That is, the VECM is the same as a VAR with differenced variables, except for the term ε_{t-1}. An estimate of this error correction variable can be obtained by running an OLS regression of Y on X and saving the residuals. We can then use OLS to estimate ECMs, and P-values and confidence intervals can be obtained. Lag length selection and forecasting can be done in a similar fashion to the VAR, with the slight added complication that forecasts of the error correction term, ε_t, must be calculated. However, this is simple using OLS estimates of α and β and replacing the error, ε_t, with the residual $\widehat{\varepsilon}_t$.

Of course, as with any of the models used in this chapter, you should always do unit root tests to see if your variables are stationary or not. If your variables have unit roots, then it is additionally necessary to test for cointegration. Above, we introduced the Engle–Granger test for cointegration. This was based on checking whether there is a unit root in the residuals from the cointegrating regression. However, there is a more popular cointegration test called the *Johansen test*. This is a likelihood ratio test for cointegration. To explain this test in detail would require a discussion of concepts beyond the scope of this book. However, many econometrics software packages do the Johansen test, and hence it is simple to use in practice. Accordingly, we offer a brief intuitive description of this test.

If you are working with M time series variables, then it is possible to have up to $M - 1$ cointegrating relationships (and, thus, up to $M - 1$ lagged cointegrating residuals included in the VECM). The Johansen test can be used to test for the number of cointegrating relationships using VECMs. For reasons we will not explain, the 'number of cointegrating relationships' is referred to as the 'cointegrating rank'. The details of the Johansen test statistic are quite complicated. However, like any hypothesis test, you can compare the test statistic with a critical value and, if the test statistic is greater than the critical value, you reject the hypothesis being tested. Fortunately, many software packages will calculate all these numbers for you. We will see how this works in the following example.

Before working through this example, note that, when you do the Johansen test, you have to specify the lag length and the deterministic trend term. The former we have discussed before. That is, lag length can be selected using information criteria as described above. With VECMs it is possible simply to put an intercept and/or deterministic trend in the model (as we have done in the equations above – see the terms in the VECM with coefficients φ_j and δ_j for $j = 1, 2$ on them). However, it is also possible to put an intercept and/or deterministic trend actually in the cointegrating residual (e.g. if you say $Y_t - \alpha - \beta X_t$ is the cointegrating residual, you are putting an intercept into it). The Johansen test varies slightly depending on the exact configuration of deterministic terms you use, so you will be asked to specify these before doing the Johansen test.

Example: Consumption, aggregate wealth and expected stock returns

In an influential paper in the *Journal of Finance* in 2001, 'Consumption, aggregate wealth and expected stock returns,' Lettau and Ludvigson present financial theory arguing that the so-called cay variables should be cointegrated and the cointegrating residual should be able to predict excess stock returns. The cay variables are consumption (c), assets (a), and income (y). They present empirical evidence in favor of their theory. In a subsequent paper,[6] using the cay data, they build on this argument using VECMs and present variance decompositions that shed light on their theory (we will discuss variance decompositions below).

We will not repeat the theory (nor will we consider the forecasting aspect of their paper). However, their work uses all the tools we have been developing in this chapter: testing for cointegration, estimation of a VECM, and variance decompositions. We will investigate the presence of cointegration here using US data from 1951Q4 to 2003Q1 on:

- c which is the log of real per capita expenditures on non-durables and services excluding shoes and clothing;
- a which is the log of a measure of real per capita household net worth including all financial and household wealth as well as consumer durables;
- y which is the log of after-tax labour income.

Unit root tests indicate that all of these variables have unit roots. If we do the Johansen test using a lag length of 1 and restricting the deterministic term to allow

Table 7.9   Johansen test for cointegration using CAY data.

Rank	Trace statistic	5 % critical value
0	37.27	29.68
1	6.93	15.41
2	0.95	3.76

for intercepts only (i.e. no deterministic trends such as those with coefficients δ_1 and δ_2 in the previous equations are allowed for), we get the results in Table 7.9.

How should you interpret this table? Note firstly that 'trace statistic' is the name of the test statistic used in the Johansen test, and 'rank' indicates the number of cointegrating relationships, with Rank $= 0$ indicating cointegration is not present. With the Johansen test, the hypothesis being tested is always a certain cointegrating rank, with the alternative hypothesis being that cointegrating rank is greater than the rank in the hypothesis being tested.

If we compare the trace statistic with its critical value, we can see, for Rank $= 0$, that the test statistic is greater than the 5 % critical value. This means we can reject the hypotheses that Rank $= 0$ at the 5 % level of significance (in favour of the hypothesis that Rank $= 1$). Thus, the Johansen test indicates that cointegration is present. However, if we look at the row with Rank $= 1$, we see that the test statistic is less than the critical value. Thus, we can accept that hypothesis that Rank $= 1$ (and are not finding evidence in favour of Rank $= 2$). Overall, we are finding evidence that Rank $= 1$. As expected by Lettau and Ludvigson, we are finding evidence that one cointegrating relationship exists in this dataset.

Armed with the information that one cointegrating relationship seems to exist, you can then (following Lettau and Ludvigson) calculate the residual from the cointegrating regression and investigate whether this has predictive power for expected stock returns. Alternatively, you could use this information to specify a VECM with one cointegrating relationship (and, thus, one error correction term). Following Lettau and Ludvigson, you could then do a variance decomposition to investigate further issues in financial economics.

7.6.3   Using VARs: impulse response functions and variance decompositions

After a VAR (or a VECM) has been estimated, macroeconomists and financial economists often calculate so-called *variance decompositions* and *impulse response functions*. To explain fully what these are would be too big a digression, involving complicated derivations. Nevertheless, since many research papers discuss them and some econometrics software packages calculate them, it is worthwhile providing a brief intuitive discussion of what they are.

As the cay example shows, variance decompositions are popular in finance and macroeconomics. Another financial example can be found in an influential paper in the *Journal of Finance* in 1993 ('What moves the stock and bond markets? A variance decomposition for long-term asset returns' by Campbell and Ammer). This paper investigates the factors that influence the stock and bond markets in the long run. Without going into the theoretical derivations, suffice it to note here that the authors develop a model where, at a given point in time, unexpected movements in excess stock returns should depend on changes in expectations (i.e. news) about future dividend flows, future excess stock returns, and future real interest rates. Similarly, current unexpected movements in excess bond returns should depend on news of relevance for future inflation, future interest rates, and future excess bond returns. The question of interest is which of these various factors is most important in driving the stock and bond markets. The authors' model is much more sophisticated, but a simplified version could be written as

$$uer = newsd + newser,$$

where *uer* is the component capturing unexpected movements in expected returns, *newsd* is the component reflecting news about future dividends, and *newser* is the component reflecting news about future expected returns. Do not worry where these components come from, other than to note that they can be calculated using the data and the coefficients from a VAR.

Financial researchers are interested in the relative roles played by *newsd* and *newser* in explaining *uer.* One way of measuring this is through variances. That is, we can measure the proportion of the variability of *uer* that comes from *newsd* (or *newser*) and use this as a measure of the role played by *newsd* (or *newser*) in explaining *uer.* This is a simple example of a variance decomposition.

Formally, if *newsd* and *newser* are independent of one another, we have

$$var\left(uer\right) = var\left(newsd\right) + var\left(newser\right).$$

If we divide both sides of this equation by $var\left(uer\right)$, then we get

$$1 = \frac{var\left(newsd\right)}{var\left(uer\right)} + \frac{var\left(newser\right)}{var\left(uer\right)}.$$

The two terms on the right-hand side of this equation can be interpreted as measures of the relative roles of news about dividends and news about excess returns. For instance, the first of them can be used to say: 'The proportion of the variability in unexpected excess returns that can be explained by news about future dividends is $\frac{var\left(newsd\right)}{var\left(uer\right)}$', and it can be calculated using the VAR.

The Lettau and Ludgvigson example using the cay data allows us to describe another common sort of variance decomposition. The empirical puzzle this paper is investigating is why the huge swings in stock markets over the last decade (e.g. the DotCom boom

followed by the bust) did not have larger effects on consumption. The VECM they estimate, along with a variance decomposition, indicates a sensible story: that many fluctuations in the stock market were treated by households as being transitory, and these did
not have large effects on their consumption. Only permanent changes in wealth affected
consumption. This kind of variance decomposition is a so-called 'permanent–transitory
decomposition'.

Remember (see Chapter 6) that unit root variables have a long memory property. Errors
in unit root variables tend to have permanent effects. However, the cointegrating error
is, by definition, stationary. This can be interpreted as implying the cointegrating error
will have only a transitory effect on any of the variables. In a VECM, our variables have
unit roots in them, but the cointegrating error is stationary. Thus, it has some errors
that have permanent effects and others that have transitory effects. Using the VECM,
you can figure out these permanent and transitory components and do a variance decomposition in the same way as described above.

That is, a simplified version of such a model would imply

$$a = permanent + transitory,$$

where *permanent* and *transitory* are the permanent and transitory components of assets
(denoted by *a*). As before, we can take variances of both sides of the equation and divide
by the variance of assets to obtain

$$1 = \frac{var(permanent)}{var(a)} + \frac{var(transitory)}{var(a)},$$

and then use the first term on the right-hand side of the equation as a measure of the role
of permanent shocks in driving fluctuations in assets.

These two examples are meant only to give you some intuition about what variance
decompositions are all about and how they are used in practice. Additional reading (e.g.
of a time series econometrics textbook) would be necessary fully to understand how variance decompositions are calculated.

Impulse responses are another popular way of summarizing the information in a time
series model. Intuitively, an impulse response function measures the effect of an unexpected shock on current and future values of a time series variable. For instance, if the
central bank unexpectedly raises interest rates or changes the money supply, then this
will have an effect on key macroeconomic variables (e.g. inflation or GDP growth), and
it is important to know the magnitude of such effects (both immediately and in the
near future). In the context of time series models such as VARs, an 'unexpected shock' is
the error. With univariate time series models, the definition of an impulse response function is straightforward. Consider, for instance, the AR(1) model

$$Y_t = \rho Y_{t-1} + \varepsilon_t.$$

As shown in our discussion of AR models in Chapter 6 (see also Chapter 5, Section 5.4), we can write this model as

$$Y_t = \sum_{i=0}^{\infty} \rho^i \varepsilon_{t-i}.$$

With this expression, the impulse response function can immediately be deduced. That is, suppose an unexpected shock of size 1 occurs two periods ago. That is, suppose $\varepsilon_{t-2} = 1$. You can see that the coefficient on ε_{t-2} is ρ^2. Thus, a shock of size 1 two periods ago will have an effect of ρ^2 on Y_t.[7] This is an example of an impulse response. We obtain an impulse response function by calculating the impulse response for every lag $s = 0, 1, \ldots$. For the AR(1) model the effect of a shock s periods ago is ρ^s. This is the impulse response function.

For VARs, impulse response functions can be calculated in the same manner. However, a problem of interpretation arises since there are several different shocks. For instance, the two-variable VAR has errors ε_{1t} and ε_{2t}. We could calculate four different impulse response functions: one that measures the effect of $\varepsilon_{1,t-s}$ on Y_t, one that measures the effect of $\varepsilon_{1,t-s}$ on X_t, one that measures the effect of $\varepsilon_{2,t-s}$ on Y_t, and one that measures the effect of $\varepsilon_{2,t-s}$ on X_t. Hence, with VARs the number of impulse response functions can be very large. More worryingly, they can be hard to interpret. In macroeconomics we might want to measure 'the effect of a shock to the money supply on output'. To measure this, you might think, in a RMPY VAR, that you could just look at the error in the equation with M (or ΔM) as the dependent variable, and calculate the impulse response of this error on Y (or ΔY). But this will not necessarily work. The errors in the different equations will typically be correlated with one another. If this happens, it is not necessarily sensible to interpret the error in the money equation as 'a shock to the money supply'. In practice, what researchers often do is work with variants of VARs called *structural VARs*. We will not explain what these are. The intention of this paragraph is only to give you some ideas of what an impulse response function is and what problems in interpretation arise when you are calculating them in VARs, and to whet your appetite for further reading about impulse response analysis in a time series econometrics textbook.

7.7 Chapter summary

1. If all variables are stationary, then an ADL(p, q) model can be estimated using OLS. Econometric techniques are all standard.
2. A variant of the ADL model is often used to avoid potential multicollinearity problems. It provides a straightforward estimate of the long-run multiplier.
3. If all variables are non-stationary, great care must be taken in the analysis owing to the spurious regression problem.

4. If all variables are non-stationary but the regression error is stationary, then cointegration occurs.
5. If cointegration is present, the spurious regression problem does not occur.
6. Cointegration is an attractive concept for economists since it implies that an equilibrium relationship exists.
7. Cointegration can be tested using the Engle–Granger test. This test is a Dickey–Fuller test on the residuals from the cointegrating regression.
8. If the variables are cointegrated, then an error correction model (ECM) can be used. This model captures short-run behavior in a way that the cointegrating regression cannot.
9. If the variables have unit roots but are not cointegrated, you should not work with them directly. Rather, you should difference them and estimate an ADL model using the differenced variables.
10. ADLs and ECMs are commonly used to investigate Granger causality. X Granger causes Y if past values of X have explanatory power for Y.
11. If X and Y are stationary, standard statistical methods based on an ADL model can be used to test for Granger causality.
12. If X and Y have unit roots and are cointegrated, statistical methods based on an ECM can be used to test for Granger causality.
13. Vector autoregressions, or VARs, have one equation for each variable being studied. Each equation chooses one variable as the dependent variable. The explanatory variables are lags of all the variables under study.
14. Vector error correction models, or VECMs, are used instead of VARs when the variables are cointegrated.
15. The Johansen test is a popular test for cointegration that is based on a VECM.
16. VARs and VECMs are commonly used for investigating Granger causality, forecasting, calculating impulse response functions, and calculating variance decompositions.

Exercises

The data for these questions are provided on the website associated with this book.

1. Consider the ADL(p, q) model given by

$$\Delta Y_t = \alpha + \delta t + \phi Y_{t-1} + \gamma_1 \Delta Y_{t-1} + \cdots + \gamma_{p-1} \Delta Y_{t-p+1} + \theta X_t + \omega_1 \Delta X_{t-1}$$
$$+ \cdots + \omega_{q-1} \Delta X_{t-q+1} + \varepsilon_t.$$

Derive the long-run multiplier.

2. Use the variables Y = percentage change in sales and X = percentage change in computer purchases in dataset COMPUTER.XLS to decide whether the model estimated in Table 7.1 is a good one. In particular:

(a) Establish whether Y and X really do not have unit roots as was assumed in the example.

(b) Beginning with an ADL(3, 3) model with deterministic trend, perform statistical tests to choose suitable lag lengths. Were good choices for p and q made in the example? Should we have included a deterministic trend?

(c) If you found the variables do not have unit roots and made different choices for p and q from the ones in the example, calculate the long-run multiplier and compare with the result in the example.

3. Dataset COMPUTE1.XLS contains variables of the same form as COMPUTER.XLS, but for a company in a different industry.

(a) Repeat the analysis of exercise 2 using the data in COMPUTE1.XLS. That is, verify that Y and X are stationary and then test to find a suitable ADL(p, q) specification.

(b) Calculate the long-run multiplier for the model estimated in (a).

4. Use the data in ORANGE.XLS used to create Figure 7.1.

(a) Do a Dickey–Fuller test to verify that both orange price series have unit roots.

(b) Use a sequential testing procedure to check if the Engle–Granger test done in the example in this chapter is correct. That is, is an AR(1) model for the cointegrating residuals appropriate?

5. LONGGDP.XLS contains annual data on real GDP per capita for four of the largest English-speaking countries (USA, UK, Canada, and Australia) for the years 1870–1993.[8] Investigate whether there are common movements or trends between GDP in these different countries. In particular, you should go through the following steps to answer this question.

(a) Plot all the data in one time series graph and discuss your results (e.g.: Does GDP seem to be trending in all countries? Do there appear to be common trend patterns across countries?).

(b) Carry out unit root tests on the time series. Discuss your findings.

(c) For the time series that have unit roots, carry out cointegration tests. Begin by carrying out cointegration tests between different combinations of two countries (e.g. first do USA and UK, then USA and Canada, etc.). Does GDP seem to be cointegrated between any pair of countries?

(d) In this chapter, we have focused mainly on the case considered in part (c), namely where there are only two variables. Using $Y = $ USA and all the other countries as explanatory variables, test for cointegration among all the time series. Discuss your results.

(e) Depending on your answer to part (d), estimate either a VAR or a VECM using these data and investigate Granger causality issues (e.g. does GDP growth in the USA Granger cause GDP growth in any other country?).

6. Use the data on Y = personal income and X = personal consumption in INCOME.XLS.

   (a) Use Dickey–Fuller tests to verify that Y and X have unit roots.
   (b) Run a regression of Y on X and save the residuals.
   (c) Carry out a unit root test on the residuals using an AR(1) model.
   (d) Carry out a unit root test on the residuals using an AR(2) model.
   (e) Carry out a unit root test on the residuals using an AR(3) model.
   (f) What can you conclude about the presence of cointegration between Y and X?[9]
   (g) Assume (perhaps incorrectly) that Y and X are cointegrated. Estimate an error correction model. Begin with a model containing a deterministic trend and $p = q = 4$ and then carry out statistical tests to find an appropriate ECM. Test whether Y Granger causes X. Test whether X Granger causes Y. Discuss your results. Pay particular attention to your estimate of λ and discuss what it tells you about the speed of adjustment to equilibrium.

7. WP.XLS contains annual data for the years 1857–1987 on X = wages and Y = the consumer price index in the UK. It is commonly thought that wage pressures are a prime cause of inflation. You wish to investigate this claim by carrying out a time series analysis on the data. In particular:

   (a) Construct a time series plot of wages and prices. Do they both seem to be trending? Do they seem to be trending together?
   (b) Carry out unit root tests on X and Y. You should find evidence that they both have unit roots.
   (c) Carry out a cointegration test on X and Y. You should find evidence that they are not cointegrated.
   (d) Difference the data to obtain ΔX and ΔY. Repeat parts (a) and (b) with these new variables. You should find that they do not have unit roots.
   (e) Specify and estimate an ADL(p, q) model using the new variables ΔX and ΔY. Discuss your results. Note that the change in the log of a price level is inflation. That is, ΔX and ΔY can be interpreted as wage and price inflation respectively.

8. Use the data on R, M, P, and Y in RMPY.XLS. These data are described in the section on VARs.

   (a) Test for unit roots in each of the variables.
   (b) Test for cointegration among the variables.
       Use the data on ΔR, ΔM, ΔP, and ΔY for the rest of this question.
   (c) Test for a unit root in each of the variables.
   (d) Beginning with a maximum lag length of 5, select an appropriate lag length for a VAR.

(e) Using your results from (d), discuss Granger causality among the variables ΔR, ΔM, ΔP, and ΔY.

9. Use the data from CAY.XLS which contains the variables $c =$ consumption, $a =$ assets, and $y =$ income. All variables are logged and the data run from 1951Q4 to 2003Q1.

(a) Test for unit roots in all the variables in this dataset.
(b) Test for cointegration in these variables using the Engle–Granger and Johansen tests. Do these tests yield the same findings?
(c) Are the results of the Johansen test sensitive to the choice of lag length?
(d) Discuss the issue of lag length selection in this dataset using information criteria.
(e) Depending on your results for the previous parts, estimate either a VAR or VECM for these data and carry out a forecasting exercise. Begin by using data from 1951Q4 to 2002Q4 and forecast for 2003Q1. Then experiment with different base dates for your forecast (e.g. instead of using data to 2002Q4 to forecast 2003Q1, use data to 2002Q1 to forecast 2002Q2, etc.).
(f) Now try forecasting for longer and longer periods. For instance, in (e) you forecasted for one quarter. Now try two quarters, three quarters, etc. Discuss your results.

Appendix: The theory of forecasting

We will begin by illustrating some theoretical concepts in forecasting using the simple regression model (without intercept)

$$Y_i = \beta X_i + \varepsilon_i.$$

under the classical assumptions (i.e. X_i is not random and ε_i for $i = 1, \ldots, N$ are i.i.d. $N(0, \sigma^2)$). You have $i = 1, \ldots, N$ data points. Interest centres on forecasting Y_{N+1} for a value of explanatory variable X_{N+1}. As an example, consider our house price dataset which contains the price for each of $N = 546$ houses as well as their characteristics (e.g. the lot size of each house). Now suppose a new house, the $(N + 1)$th house, is put on the market and you are interested in what it will sell for. You know what its characteristics are (i.e. you know X_{N+1}), but you do not know what it will sell for (i.e. you do not know Y_{N+1} and are interested in predicting it).

You can use the $N = 546$ data points in the manner described in Chapter 3 to carry out so called *in-sample* estimation and testing. In particular, you can produce the OLS estimates of β and σ^2: $\hat{\beta}$ and s^2. However, you are interested in *out-of-sample* forecasting. In order to produce forecasts you must begin by assuming that the regression model out-of-sample[10] is the same as that in-sample, and thus

$$Y_{N+1} = \beta X_{N+1} + \varepsilon_{N+1}.$$

With this assumption, we can use the properties of the expected value to derive

$$
\begin{aligned}
E(Y_{N+1}) &= E(\beta X_{N+1} + \varepsilon_{N+1}) \\
&= \beta X_{N+1} + E(\varepsilon_{N+1}) \\
&= \beta X_{N+1}.
\end{aligned}
$$

Since β is unobserved, let us replace it with its unbiased estimator, $\widehat{\beta}$.

Let $\widehat{Y}_{N+1}$ denote the forecast of Y_{N+1}. The previous paragraph implies that an unbiased forecast for Y_{N+1} is

$$\widehat{Y}_{N+1} = \widehat{\beta} X_{N+1}.$$

A forecast is only an estimate of Y_{N+1}. As with any estimator, it is desirable to calculate its variance in order to capture the uncertainty inherent in the forecast (or as a step in formally deriving a confidence interval). We can use the properties of the variance operator to derive

$$
\begin{aligned}
var(\widehat{Y}_{N+1}) &= var(\widehat{\beta} X_{N+1}) \\
&= X_{N+1}^2 var(\widehat{\beta}) \\
&= \frac{X_{N+1}^2 \sigma^2}{\sum X_i^2},
\end{aligned}
$$

where the last line uses the formula for $var(\widehat{\beta})$ from Chapter 3. The derivations in Chapter 3 also tell us that $\widehat{\beta}$ is normal and, thus, $\widehat{Y}_{N+1}$ is normal. Putting all these facts together, we have

$$\widehat{Y}_{N+1} \sim N\left(Y_{N+1}, \frac{X_{N+1}^2 \sigma^2}{\sum X_i^2}\right).$$

This result can be used to derive a confidence interval for our forecast. That is, a derivation virtually the same as the confidence interval derivation of Chapter 3 can be used to establish that

$$\widehat{Y}_{N+1} - 1.96\sqrt{\frac{X_{N+1}^2 \sigma^2}{\sum X_i^2}} \le Y_{N+1} \le \widehat{Y}_{N+1} + 1.96\sqrt{\frac{X_{N+1}^2 \sigma^2}{\sum X_i^2}}$$

is a 95 % confidence interval Y_{N+1}. In practice, σ^2 is usually unknown and must be replaced by its estimator, s^2. As discussed in Chapter 3, when σ^2 is replaced by s^2, $\widehat{Y}_{N+1}$ is no longer normal, but instead has a Student t distribution. Thus, the 1.96 in the confidence interval formula must be replaced by an appropriate value from the t_{N-1} statistical tables. When we have a multiple regression with an intercept and k explanatory variables, the formula becomes slightly different (e.g. the t_{N-k} is used), but the basic ideas are unaffected.

Forecasting is mostly done with time series data, so it is important to discuss how the previous derivations are altered in this case. Since the time series models we have been working with are basically regression models, the formulae above go through basically unchanged. Suppose, for instance, you have data from $t = 1, \ldots, T$, are interested in forecasting Y_{T+1}, and are working with an AR(1) model

$$Y_t = \rho Y_{t-1} + \varepsilon_t.$$

Then the previous derivations can be repeated to obtain $\widehat{Y}_{T+1} = \widehat{\rho} Y_T$ as an unbiased forecast. If $|\rho| < 1$, then

$$\widehat{Y}_{T+1} \sim N\left(Y_{T+1}, \frac{Y_T^2 \sigma^2}{\sum Y_{t-1}^2}\right),$$

which can be used to derive a confidence interval for the forecast. However, if a unit root is present, a different formula applies. Furthermore, the previous discussion relates to forecasting one period in the future (i.e. interest centred on Y_{T+1}). What if we want to forecast Y_{T+2}? The previous derivations still hold and we can say $\widehat{Y}_{T+2} = \widehat{\rho} Y_{T+1}$ is an unbiased forecast. However, this unbiased forecast depends on Y_{T+1} which is unobserved. Hence, this is not a forecast that can be used in practice. To create a forecast that can be used in practice, we have to replace Y_{T+1} with its forecast. Thus, the forecast for period $T + 2$ is

$$\widehat{Y}_{T+2} = \widehat{\rho}^2 Y_T.$$

In general, if we are interested in forecasting h periods in the future, we have

$$\widehat{Y}_{T+h} = \widehat{\rho}^h Y_T.$$

These are good point forecasts, but the derivation of their distribution becomes quite complicated owing to the $\widehat{\rho}^h$ term. Thus, deriving forecast confidence intervals is difficult and will not be done here. However, we stress that many econometrics software packages will calculate confidence intervals or something similar (e.g. standard deviations of the forecast) for you. The same basic ideas and similar formulae hold for ADLs, VARs, and VECMs.

Endnotes

1. In this book, we will not explicitly discuss distributed lag models. But they can be interpreted as a special case of the ADL model with $\rho_1 = \cdots = \rho_p = 0$.

2. This is a useful rule of thumb, but there are some rare cases where you can violate it in the case where you have more than two variables. In this case, if some of the variables are cointegrated (a concept to be defined below) and the rest are stationary, it is acceptable to have them all together in a regression.

3. Note also the critical values for the Engle–Granger test depend on the number of explanatory variables in the original regression. Table 7.2 is for the simple regression case with one explanatory variable.

4. Note that we do not include more lags of ε_t as explanatory variables owing to an implication of the Granger representation theorem which we will not discuss here.

5. Note that in VARs we only include lagged values of each variable on the right-hand side of each equation. For the same reasons, in the VECM we have only included lagged variables. In our previous discussion of error correction models, we included the term $\omega_0 \Delta X_t$.

6. This paper is 'Understanding trend and cycle in asset values: Reevaluating the wealth effect on consumption' in the *American Economic Review* in 2004.

7. Another way of making this point is through some basic calculus. It can be seen that $\frac{\partial Y_t}{\partial \varepsilon_{t-2}} = \rho^2$.

8. Note that each of these time series is an index (with $1913 = 100$). If you look at the data, you will see that the value of the data for the UK is 64.85 in 1870. The fact that the variables are indices means that we cannot interpret the value of each observation as saying, for instance, that GDP per capita in the UK was 64.85 in 1870. We can, however, interpret changes in the series as GDP growth rates. More importantly for cointegration analysis, the trend in the index for each country accurately reflects trend behavior in GDP per capita.

9. You might find that cointegration seems to be present for some lag lengths but not for others. This is a common occurrence in practical applications, so do not be dismayed by it. Economic theory and time series plots of the data definitely indicate that cointegration should occur between Y and X. But the Engle–Granger test does not consistently indicate cointegration.

10. An important current research issue is whether such an assumption is reasonable in some time series empirical applications. Sometimes time series models produce poor forecasts, and one reason this may be happening is that the past (i.e. the in-sample data used for estimation) may be a poor guide to the future (i.e. the out-of-sample data used for forecasting).

CHAPTER 8

Models for Panel Data

8.1 Introduction

As discussed in Chapter 1, many economic applications involve panel data. These are data that have both cross-sectional and time series aspects. For instance, the labour economist might work with a survey of 1000 workers where the survey is given every year for 10 years. The macroeconomist has access to many variables (e.g. GDP, prices, etc.) that are available for many countries for many years. The financial economist might observe the return from holding the shares of many companies for many years. All of these are examples of panel data. When working with panel data, some specialized tools are required that we have not covered in previous chapters. These will be discussed in the present chapter. However, in spite of some differences, there are great similarities between the tools used with panel data and the multiple regression methods covered in Chapters 1 to 5. For instance, all of our models will relate a dependent variable to explanatory variables and the coefficients can be interpreted as marginal effects. The basic ideas (e.g. that t-statistics can be used for testing whether a coefficient is significant, etc.) are all regression ideas covered before. Furthermore, two of the main models for panel data are the *random effects* and *fixed effects* models. The first of these can be interpreted as a regression model where generalized least-squares (GLS) methods are required, and the second as a regression model that contains many dummy variables. Since GLS was discussed in Chapter 5 and dummy variables in Chapter 2, the present chapter will build on familiar material.

Before beginning, we must establish notational conventions. We will do all derivations and discuss many issues in panel data modeling using only a single explanatory variable. Just as in previous chapters, all ideas from the simple regression model extend to the case of many explanatory variables (except the notation gets a bit messier). Depending on the precise empirical application, the cross-sectional aspect of panel data can relate different workers, companies, countries, etc. In this chapter, we will simply refer to the 'individual', and thus Y_{it} is the observation of the dependent variable for individual i at time t. X_{it} is the observation of the explanatory variable for individual i at time t. The subscript i goes from $1, \ldots, N$ and t goes from $1, \ldots, T$.

8.2 The pooled model

We begin by briefly discussing the *pooled model* which treats all observations as though they came from the same regression model. Thus, the pooled model is

$$Y_{it} = \alpha + \beta X_{it} + \varepsilon_{it}.$$

This is just a standard regression model. If we assume ε_{it} satisfies the classical assumptions, then all the results we derived under the classical assumptions in Chapter 3 will hold. For instance, OLS will be the best linear unbiased estimator. The formulae we derived in Chapter 3 for confidence intervals, hypothesis tests, etc., will still hold. The extension to the case of multiple regression can be handled exactly as in Chapter 4 (or Chapter 2). On the other hand, if ε_{it} satisfies the classical assumptions except that heteroskedasticity is present, then the GLS methods of Chapter 5 are relevant. In short, nothing is new with the pooled model. It is just a regression model of the kind discussed previously. Why, then, do we need a separate chapter to deal with panel data? The answer is that it turns out that with most panel datasets the pooled model is inappropriate. To explain why this is so, we introduce a new class of models that are commonly used with panel data.

8.3 Individual effects models

There are two main individual effects models, called *the fixed effects model* and *the random effects model*. Before discussing estimation and hypothesis testing in these models, it is important to explain the basic ideas behind individual effects models and motivate why they are so often used with panel data instead of the pooled model. We will do so with an example from labour economics. Consider the regression of $Y =$ income on $X =$ years of education. In practice, you would likely include many other explanatory variables in such a regression, but here we omit such variables in order to motivate things in the simple regression model.[1]

Suppose we have survey data from many years, and thus panel data on the dependent and explanatory variables are available. A pooled regression of the form

$$Y_{it} = \alpha + \beta X_{it} + \varepsilon_{it}$$

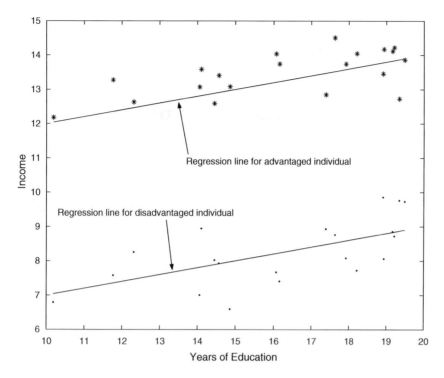

Figure 8.1 Relationship between education and income for two individuals.

assumes all individuals have the same relationship between education and income. Remember that the intercept, α, can be interpreted as the predicted or fitted income when $X_{it} = 0$. That is, it predicts the income for an individual with no schooling. Intuitively, the intercept is the starting point, the benchmark from which an individual's earnings develop. This will usually be different for different people. For instance, even ignoring education, individuals from advantaged backgrounds probably do better than those without advantages. Someone with an advantaged background probably earns a higher wage than a disadvantaged person with the same education level. These considerations suggest intercepts should vary across individuals. In empirical practice, it often does seem that this should be the case.

These points are illustrated in Figure 8.1 which contains 20 years of data for each of two hypothetical individuals (one an 'advantaged' individual and one a 'disadvantaged' one) on their education and income. Each of the regression lines in Figure 8.1 plots the predicted income corresponding to different levels of schooling. It can be seen that the regression line for the advantaged individual at every point lies above the regression line for the disadvantaged individual. So, for instance, even if the two individuals both complete a university degree, the advantaged individual will make a higher income than the disadvantaged one. There are many reasons why this might occur. For instance, the advantaged individual might be more intelligent, or have had the opportunity to go to a better university, or had better family connections making it possible to get a better job upon graduation. The point to note here is that this kind of pattern appears to exist in many datasets. An examination of Figure 8.1 suggests that the appropriate econometric model will estimate a different regression line for each individual. This is what individual effects models allow for.

As with any regression model, it is unlikely that the actual data points will lie precisely on the regression lines in Figure 8.1. We have illustrated this by having the data points for the advantaged individual (labelled with * symbols) lie near the regression line for the advantaged individual and the data points for the disadvantaged individual lie near the disadvantaged regression line.[2] We have also scattered these points widely, with values of the explanatory variable between 10 and 20. Furthermore, in Figure 8.1 we have plotted two regression lines that have the same slope (although the two lines have different intercepts). With such a configuration, OLS estimation using the pooled model might provide a reasonable estimate of the slope coefficient (but not the intercept). However, Figure 8.2 illustrates how OLS estimation of the pooled model can yield seriously misleading estimates of the slope coefficient.

Figure 8.2 has the same basic set-up as Figure 8.1. There are two different regression lines, one for the advantaged individual, one for the disadvantaged. Both of these regression lines are upward sloping, indicating that there are positive returns to schooling for

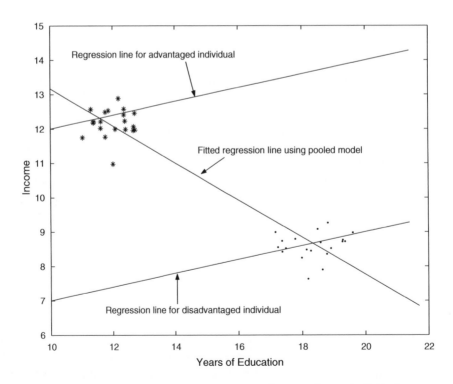

Figure 8.2 Relationship between education and income for two individuals.

both individuals. However, in Figure 8.2 all the actual data points for the advantaged individual correspond to values of the explanatory variable being roughly 12 (e.g. the advantaged individual stopped schooling after secondary school and then took a job). In contrast, the actual data for the disadvantaged individual correspond to values of the explanatory variable being closer to 20 (e.g. the disadvantaged individual stopped schooling after extensive university study and then took a job). The naive researcher, ignoring the fact that the individuals have different regression lines, would use the pooled model and estimate it using OLS and produce a single best-fitting regression line. This fitted regression line is plotted in Figure 8.2. Note that it does pass near the data points, suggesting it is fitting the data well. However, it is completely wrong! It is downward sloping, indicating that the returns to schooling are negative. The naive researcher using the pooled model would make the wrong conclusion.

We could present more graphs here, showing how far wrong the pooled model can go for different configurations of data. However, Figure 8.2 makes the basic point: if different individuals have different regression lines and you ignore this fact, you can be seriously misled. Such a consideration suggests that we should work with an individual effects model which does allow for different individuals to have different regression lines.

For the case of simple regression (with multiple regression being a straightforward extension), the individual effects model is written as

$$Y_{it} = \alpha_i + \beta X_{it} + \varepsilon_{it}.$$

This is almost the same as the pooled model, but, crucially, α_i varies across individuals. Each individual's intercept, α_i, is referred to as an 'individual effect'. The incorporation of such individual effects allows for each individual to have a different regression line. Although note that the regression lines all have the same slope. Later on in this chapter, we will discuss the relaxation of this assumption.

Thus far, we have motivated why an individual effects specification might be desirable. Basically, in many panel data situations involving people, countries, or companies, the assumption that they all have exactly the same regression model is a poor one. Individuals are heterogeneous (i.e. different from one another). With cross-sectional data it is hard to deal with such heterogeneity other than to hope it is picked up by the explanatory variables and errors. With panel data we have richer datasets and this allows for us to deal with heterogeneity through individual effects models. We now turn to a discussion of how to work with such models in practice.

8.3.1 The fixed effects model

The fixed effects model uses dummy variables to model the individual effect. Dummy variables were discussed in Chapter 2, and you may wish to read over the material in that chapter again if you have forgotten what dummy variables are and how coefficients are interpreted when dummies are used as explanatory variables. A dummy variable is either 0 or 1. A common example is the dummy variable for gender. This can be constructed so as to equal 1 for individuals who are female and 0 for individuals who are male.

For the fixed effects model, N different dummy variables must be constructed, which we will call $D^{(j)}$ for $j = 1, \ldots, N$. The dummies are defined so that $D_{it}^{(j)} = 1$ for the jth individual and equals zero for all other individuals. To make explicitly clear how these variables are interpreted, consider $D^{(3)}$ which is the dummy for the third individual. When working with an econometrics software package (or a spreadsheet), a variable is a long column of data with one value for each observation. In this case, $D^{(3)}$ will be a column of length TN. It will be made up of zeros, except for the observations for the third individual. If $N = 4$ and $T = 2$, the first two values will be for the first individual, the next two for the second individual, etc., and we will have

$$
D^{(3)} = \begin{bmatrix} 0 \\ 0 \\ 0 \\ 0 \\ 1 \\ 1 \\ 0 \\ 0 \end{bmatrix}.
$$

The fixed effects approach involves running the following regression:

$$
Y_{it} = \alpha_1 D_{it}^{(1)} + \alpha_2 D_{it}^{(2)} + \cdots + \alpha_N D_{Nt}^{(N)} + \beta X_{it} + \varepsilon_{it}.
$$

This regression has lots of explanatory variables (N dummy variables plus the regular explanatory variable – or variables in the case of multiple regression), but it is simply a regression model. Hence, everything we have derived and discussed before for the linear regression model holds here. For instance, if the errors, ε_{it}, satisfy the classical assumptions, then OLS is BLUE, confidence intervals and hypothesis tests can be done in standard way (see Chapter 3), etc.

Interpretation of results with the fixed effects model is just the same as in any regression model with dummy variables. For instance, the second individual has $D^{(2)} = 1$ (and all other dummy variables equalling zero). Formally, this means $D_{2t}^{(2)} = 1$ (i.e. we are replacing the i subscript with 2 to denote the second individual) and $D_{2t}^{(1)} = D_{2t}^{(3)} = \cdots = D_{2t}^{(N)} = 0$. Plugging these values into the regression equation, we have

$$
Y_{2t} = \alpha_2 + \beta X_{2t} + \varepsilon_{2t}.
$$

We emphasize that, since we have put $i = 2$ in the subscripts on all the variables, this regression equation is referring to the second individual. Thus, we have a regression model for the second individual that is characterized by having an intercept that is different from that of every other individual. In general, the *i*th individual has the regression line

$$Y_{it} = \alpha_i + \beta X_{it} + \varepsilon_{it},$$

which is exactly the individual effects specification.

A problem with the fixed effects specification is that it will often lead to a regression with a huge number of explanatory variables. For instance, labour economists often work with panel datasets where thousands of individuals are surveyed for a small number of years (e.g. $N = 5\,000$ and $T = 5$ might be the size of a typical dataset). In a multiple regression model with k regular explanatory variables, this means the fixed effects model will have $N + k$ coefficients to estimate. In general, you can think of a regression model as seeking to estimate coefficients using information in the data. The dataset only provides you with a certain amount of information. Given the information in the data, the more coefficients you try to estimate, the harder it is to obtain precise estimates. For instance, in a multiple regression model with cross-sectional data, it is usually possible to obtain very precise estimates with $N = 100$ and $k = 2$. But if you only have a very small dataset, e.g. $N = 10$, then it is very hard to obtain precise estimates of $k = 2$ coefficients. In extreme cases, where $k \geq N$ it is simply impossible to estimate the coefficients using data information alone. In the fixed effects model, unless T is large, similar considerations apply. It can be very hard to obtain precise estimates of all of the coefficients if N is too large.

Another problem with the fixed effects estimator is that it can be hard to compute because so many coefficients are being estimated. This leads to a trick used in some econometrics software packages. If we difference the fixed effects model (or any individual effects model), then the individual effect disappears (see exercise 2). That is, if we take first differences (e.g. $\Delta Y_{it} = Y_{it} - Y_{i,t-1}$), we end up with a regression model of the form

$$\Delta Y_{it} = \beta \Delta X_{it} + \Delta \varepsilon_{it}.$$

This only has one coefficient (or k coefficients in the case of multiple regression) to estimate. Depending on the structure of the errors, a suitable estimator for β can be found. For instance, if $\Delta \varepsilon_{it}$ satisfies the classical assumptions, then OLS can be used (i.e. OLS is BLUE). However, if the original errors, ε_{it}, satisfy the classical assumptions, then $\Delta \varepsilon_{it}$ will not. In particular, they will violate assumption 3 since $cov(\Delta \varepsilon_{it}, \Delta \varepsilon_{i,t-1}) \neq 0$. In this case (or if you simply do not know that much about the error), then you could use an autocorrelation consistent estimator such as the Newey–West estimator (see Chapter 5, Section 5.4).

In the time series chapters, we saw how differencing meant that an initial observation was lost (i.e. $\Delta Y_{i1} = Y_{i1} - Y_{i0}$ and, since we do not know Y_{i0}, we cannot use this observation and have to start with ΔY_{i2}). In many cases, this is only a minor drawback and estimating the fixed effects model using differenced data is a popular strategy. However, there is one more problem that arises in some empirical cases with this estimator. In some panel datasets there are important explanatory variables that do not vary over time. In our returns to schooling example, the dependent variable was income which varied over time, and many explanatory variables (e.g. years of work experience, years of schooling) would also vary over time. However, some might not vary over time (e.g. years of schooling of your parents, or individual characteristics such as race or gender). Suppose Z_i is such a time-invariant explanatory variable and you want to estimate the fixed effects model

$$Y_{it} = \alpha_i + \beta_1 Z_i + \beta_2 X_{it} + \varepsilon_{it}.$$

With this model, if you do the trick of differencing the model, you end up with (see exercise 2)

$$\Delta Y_{it} = \beta_2 \Delta X_{it} + \Delta \varepsilon_{it}.$$

That is, differencing eliminates not only the individual effect but also every time-invariant explanatory variable. There is no way to estimate β_1 when you difference. For this reason, it is not common to do fixed effects estimation when some of the explanatory variables are constant over time. This problem does not arise with the random effects model which we will describe shortly.

Hypothesis testing in the fixed effects model

Since the fixed effects model is simply a regression model, any hypothesis test can be conducted in the same manner as discussed in previous chapters. For instance, if the errors obey the classical assumptions, then t-statistics can be used to test the hypothesis that an individual coefficient equals zero, and F-statistics can be used to test joint hypotheses involving several coefficients. A hypothesis of particular interest is whether the pooled model is acceptable. That is, it is desirable to test whether including all the fixed effects dummy variables (resulting in less precise estimation of the coefficients) is really necessary. The hypothesis to be tested is

$$H_0: \alpha_1 = \cdots = \alpha_N.$$

This is an example of a joint hypothesis involving many restrictions. As discussed in Chapter 4, an F-test can be used to test this hypothesis. Looking at the formula from that chapter, and noting that with panel data the same size is TN and the fixed effects model has $N + k$ explanatory variables (in the multiple regression case) whereas the pooled model only has $k + 1$, we obtain the following test statistic:

$$F = \frac{(R_{UR}^2 - R_R^2)/(N - 1)}{(1 - R_{UR}^2)/(TN - N - k)},$$

where the subscripts UR and R distinguish between the R^2s from the unrestricted and restricted regression models. In this case, the unrestricted model is the fixed effects model whereas the restricted model is the pooled model.[3] The critical value for this test statistic should be taken from the $F_{N-1, TN-N-K}$ distribution.

8.3.2 The random effects model

The random effects model does not use dummy variables but assumes that the individual effect is a random variable. The random effects model is written as an individual effects model:

$$Y_{it} = \alpha_i + \beta X_{it} + u_{it}$$

where

$$\alpha_i = \alpha + v_i$$

and v_i is a random variable. This last fact means that the individual effect, α_i, is a random variable that motivates the terminology *random effects* model.

Note that we have labeled the error in the regression u_{it}. An alternative way of writing the two previous equations is

$$Y_{it} = \alpha + \beta X_{it} + \varepsilon_{it}$$

where

$$\varepsilon_{it} = v_i + u_{it}.$$

Thus, the random effects model can be written as a regression model, but the error in the regression has a new form. Note that the random effects model only has an intercept and a single explanatory variable (or k explanatory variables in the case of multiple regression). It does not require N dummy explanatory variables like the fixed effects model. Thus it does not run into the previously discussed problems with the fixed effects model owing to the need to estimate so many coefficients.

As we have seen in previous chapters, knowledge of the properties of the errors is crucial to deriving a good estimator and working out appropriate hypothesis testing procedures. With the random effects model, it is common to assume that u_{it} satisfies the classical assumptions. In other words, we assume that u_{it} are independent random variables each with a $N(0, \sigma_u^2)$ distribution. Note that we are introducing the notation $var(u_{it}) = \sigma_u^2$ to make clear this is the variance of u and not of any of the other errors in this model. We also assume that v_i satisfies the classical assumptions and use the notation $var(v_i) = \sigma_v^2$, and thus we have v_i being independent random variables each with a $N(0, \sigma_v^2)$ distribution. Finally, we assume that u_{it} and v_i are uncorrelated with one another.

We can use the properties of the errors u_{it} and v_i to work out the properties of ε_{it}. You are asked to do this in exercise 1. Using the properties of the expected value and variance operators, it can be shown that

$$\begin{aligned} E(\varepsilon_{it}) &= 0, \\ var(\varepsilon_{it}) &= \sigma_u^2 + \sigma_v^2, \\ cov(\varepsilon_{it}, \varepsilon_{jt}) &= 0 \quad \text{for } i \neq j, \\ cov(\varepsilon_{it}, \varepsilon_{js}) &= 0 \quad \text{for } i \neq j \text{ and } s \neq t, \\ cov(\varepsilon_{it}, \varepsilon_{is}) &= \sigma_v^2 \quad \text{for } s \neq t. \end{aligned}$$

The key aspect of this derivation is that the errors for the same individual in different time periods are correlated with one another (i.e. $cov(\varepsilon_{it}, \varepsilon_{is}) \neq 0$). Thus, the regression errors ε_{it} do not satisfy the classical assumptions. In particular, they violate assumption 3 which says errors should be uncorrelated with one another. But now we can draw on the theory outlined in Chapters 3 and 5 which says that when the classical assumptions are violated OLS is no longer BLUE. If assumption 3 is the only assumption being violated (as it is with the random effects model under the given assumptions), then OLS will still be unbiased but will have a larger variance than the GLS estimator. Furthermore, if we run the regression of Y on X and an intercept using a standard OLS command in an econometrics software package, then it will use the incorrect formula for $var(\widehat{\beta})$, and everything that depends on this (e.g. confidence intervals and t-tests) will be incorrect.

In light of these considerations, you should use the GLS estimator for the random effects model. If this is unavailable, then OLS estimation can be done provided the correct formula for $var(\widehat{\beta})$ is used. We will not provide details of this GLS estimator, nor the correct formula for $var(\widehat{\beta})$. Suffice it to note that the more sophisticated computer packages such as Stata or PC Give will calculate it for you (but not Excel). For instance, Stata has several GLS estimators (depending on whether u_{it} satisfies the classical assumptions or is heteroskedastic or is autocorrelated). Stata also allows for OLS estimation with what it calls *panel-corrected standard errors*. These are the panel data analogue of the heteroskedasticity consistent and autocorrelation consistent estimators which were discussed in Chapter 5.[4]

In summary, the random effects model falls into the same general category as the regression models discussed in Chapter 5. These are all models where the classical assumptions about the errors are violated. Thus, you should use either GLS estimation or OLS estimation with an appropriate adjustment to obtain the correct standard errors (and, thus, correct confidence intervals and hypothesis testing procedures). In this section we have assumed that u_{it} satisfies the classical assumptions. But, in an application, it might be heteroskedastic or autocorrelated. GLS estimators that combine the appropriate ideas from Chapter 5 with those outlined here can be developed (e.g. see exercise 4). Alternatively, as mentioned above, the better econometrics software packages will allow you to do OLS with panel-corrected standard errors.

Hypothesis testing in the random effects model
Testing of hypotheses involving the regression coefficients can be done in the same manner as for any multiple regression model. For instance, if OLS estimation is done using an econometrics software package that calculates panel-corrected standard errors, then the software package will also use these when calculating t-statistics. These can be used in the standard fashion to test for the significance of coefficients. Software packages with panel-corrected standard errors also allow you to calculate correct F-statistics for any joint hypothesis. Similarly, if the econometrics package uses GLS, then it will do hypothesis tests (e.g. t- and F-tests) in the standard way using the appropriate estimate of the variance of the GLS estimator. In short, a good econometrics software package will allow you to do random effects estimation and carry out hypothesis testing procedures in the standard manner.

Another hypothesis that the researcher may wish to test is whether the pooled model is adequate or whether estimation of the random effects model is required. If you remember that variance is a measure of dispersion and, hence, that a variance of zero means that there is no dispersion, you can see that, if $\sigma_u^2 = 0$, then the individual effects in the random effects model exhibit no dispersion (i.e. they are all the same). Thus, a test of the null hypothesis $H_0: \sigma_u^2 = 0$ is a test of whether the pooled model is acceptable. A likelihood ratio test can be obtained through maximum likelihood estimation of the pooled model and maximum likelihood estimation of the random effects model. However, it is more common to do a Lagrange multiplier test. The appendix to Chapter 4 discussed Lagrange multiplier tests in detail. Suffice it to note here that they are closely related to likelihood ratio tests (and are asymptotically equivalent to them), but involve estimation only of the model implied by H_0. In this case, this means only estimation of the pooled model is required. We will not formally derive the test statistic and figure out its distribution. Suffice it to note here that many econometrics software packages will calculate the test statistic for you. Alternatively, if you are working with an econometrics software package that does not, then you can calculate the test statistic using only results produced by OLS estimation of the pooled model. The test statistic is

$$ LM = \frac{TN}{2(T-1)} \left[\frac{\sum_{i=1}^{N} \left[\sum_{t=1}^{T} \widehat{\varepsilon}_{it} \right]^2}{\sum_{i=1}^{N} \sum_{t=1}^{T} \widehat{\varepsilon}_{it}^2} - 1 \right]^2, $$

where $\widehat{\varepsilon}_{it}$ for $i = 1, \ldots, N$ and $t = 1, \ldots, T$ are the OLS residuals from the pooled model. Remember that, for any test, you can just look at the P-value if this is provided by your econometrics software. If the P-value is less than 0.05, then you can reject H_0 at the 5 % level of significance (else you accept H_0). Alternatively, if your software package does not provide a P-value, then you must evaluate the test statistic and then compare it with a critical value. If the test statistic is greater than the critical value, then you reject H_0. In this case, the critical value should be taken from the χ_1^2 distribution since this is the (approximate) distribution of LM if H_0 is true.

If tests indicate that an individual effects specification is required, then the researcher must choose between the fixed and random effects specifications. The random effects specification has the large advantage that it has so many fewer parameters to estimate than the fixed effects model. However, it has one potential drawback in that it is possible that the error, ε_{it}, is correlated with the explanatory variables. As we have seen in Chapter 5, if the regression error is correlated with the explanatory variable, then OLS (and GLS) estimators are biased and instrumental variables estimation is called for.

To motivate why the explanatory variable and error might be correlated in the random effects model, let us return to our returns to schooling example and suppose we have panel data on a dependent variable $Y =$ income and an explanatory variable $X =$ years of schooling. In Chapter 5 we went through this example in a cross-sectional context to motivate the need for an instrumental variable estimator. Briefly, we suspect that there might be some unobservable quality (e.g. talent or intelligence) that would have a direct effect on both income and schooling. We argued that this could cause the regression error and X to be correlated with each other. In the panel data context, the individual effect, α_i, would pick up the effect of the unobservable quality on the income of individual i. This is a key advantage of panel data: it allows you to estimate aspects of individual heterogeneity in a way that cannot be done with cross-sectional data. However, with the random effects model the individual effect enters the regression error. If α_i is correlated with X_{it} (as it may be in many applications), in the random effects model this will automatically imply the regression error is correlated with the explanatory variable. This would mean that the random effects estimator is biased. In the next section, we will discuss instrumental variables estimation in the random effects model as a way of getting around this problem. However, note that it does not arise with the fixed effects model since it (through the use of dummy variables) models the individual effect through explanatory variables rather than incorporating it in the error term.

The discussion of the preceding two paragraphs suggests we should use the random effects model unless the individual effect is correlated with the explanatory variables. If the latter occurs, the fixed effects model should be used (or instrumental variable estimation of the random effects model can be done). The Hausman test can be used to choose between the fixed and random effects specifications. The Hausman test was explained in Chapter 5 in the section on instrumental variables estimation. The general idea underlying the Hausman test can be used in many contexts. One of the most common uses is with panel data to decide whether the random effects or fixed effects model is appropriate. We can slightly modify the intuition given in Chapter 5 for the Hausman test as follows. Let H_0 denote the hypothesis that the individual effect is uncorrelated with any of the explanatory variables. The basic idea underlying the Hausman test is that, if H_0 is true, then both random and fixed effects estimators are consistent[5] and should give roughly the same result. However, if H_0 is false, then random effects will be inconsistent whereas fixed effects will be consistent, and hence, they can be quite different. The exact formula for this version of the Hausman test is somewhat complicated, and hence we will not provide a precise formula. Nevertheless, some intuition is provided by noting that, if $\widehat{\beta}_{RE}$ and $\widehat{\beta}_{FE}$ are the random and fixed effects estimators, then the Hausman test is similar to $(\widehat{\beta}_{RE} - \widehat{\beta}_{FE})^2$. In practice, many popular econometrics software packages will calculate the Hausman test statistic automatically. As with any test statistic, we need to work out its distribution assuming H_0 is true. This distribution is then used to obtain a critical value for the test. It turns out that the Hausman test statistic has (approximately) a χ^2_{k-1} distribution, where k is the number of explanatory variables (not including the intercept nor the dummy variables in the fixed effects estimator).

Instrumental variables estimation in the random effects model

Given the advantage of the random effects model (i.e. in having many fewer coefficients to estimate than the fixed effects model), many researchers prefer to use it. When the individual effect is correlated with other explanatory variables, they use instrumental variables methods. The instrumental variables methods used with panel data are somewhat complicated, and hence, we do not provide precise details here. Two of the most popular are the *Hausman–Taylor estimator* and the *Arellano–Bond estimator.*[6] The purpose of this section is to provide some intuition and partial explanation of these estimators. Several econometrics packages (e.g. Stata) allow you to use these estimators. The hope is that, with some intuition, you can use them in practice, even if you do not know precise details. Furthermore, many research papers use these estimators. With the intuition below, you should at least be able to understand what such research papers are doing.

To motivate the Hausman–Taylor estimator, note that there are four types of explanatory variable that you might have in a random effects model: those that are time varying and not correlated with the individual effect (call these $X_{it}^{(1)}$); those that are time varying and correlated with the individual effect (call these $X_{it}^{(2)}$); those that are constant over time and not correlated with the individual effect (call these $Z_i^{(1)}$); and those that are constant over time and correlated with the individual effect (call these $Z_i^{(2)}$). Let K_1, K_2, L_1, and L_2, respectively, be the numbers of these four types of explanatory variable. Remember that you need at least one instrumental variable for each explanatory variable that is correlated with the error term. So, in general, we need $K_2 + L_2$ instrumental variables. However, to illustrate some points, we will begin by assuming there is one explanatory variable of each type (i.e. $K_1 = K_2 = L_1 = L_2 = 1$) and that the random effects model of interest is

$$Y_{it} = \alpha + \beta_1 X_{it}^{(1)} + \beta_2 X_{it}^{(2)} + \beta_3 Z_i^{(1)} + \beta_4 Z_i^{(2)} + \varepsilon_{it},$$

where

$$\varepsilon_{it} = v_i + u_{it}$$

and the assumptions about u_{it} and v_i are the standard random effects model assumptions given above.

Remember that, for the fixed effects model, we showed how differencing eliminated the individual effect. Here we will use a similar transformation. We will use a notation where bars over variables denote averages over time. For instance,

$$\overline{X}_i^{(1)} = \frac{\sum_{t=1}^{T} X_{it}^{(1)}}{T}.$$

If we average the random effects model over time and subtract it from the original random effects equation (i.e. take 'deviations from individual means'), we obtain the equation

$$\left(Y_{it} - \overline{Y}_i\right) = \beta_1 \left(X_{it}^{(1)} - \overline{X}_i^{(1)}\right) + \beta_2 \left(X_{it}^{(2)} - \overline{X}_i^{(2)}\right) + \varepsilon_{it} - \overline{\varepsilon}_i.$$

It turns out (see exercise 2) that the error in this regression is not correlated with the explanatory variables. That is, the transformation that takes deviations from individual means will eliminate the individual effect term from the error. Thus, this transformed equation can be estimated using OLS and consistent estimates of β_1 and β_2 can be obtained. The reason we have provided this transformation is to motivate that deviations from individual means can be used as instruments. For instance, $(X_{it}^{(2)} - \overline{X}_i^{(2)})$ can be used as an instrument for $X_{it}^{(2)}$, the variable that is correlated with the error.

The previous discussion is sufficient to cover the case where all explanatory variables vary over time. Instrumental variables can be constructed by taking deviations from means. But note that the 'deviations from means' operation removes the time-invariant explanatory variables $Z_i^{(1)}$ and $Z_i^{(2)}$. The Hausman–Taylor estimator (like any random effects estimator) allows us to estimate the coefficients on such time-invariant variables. In this case, we require an instrumental variable for $Z_i^{(2)}$ since it is assumed to be correlated with the individual effect. How can we obtain such an instrument? We will not explain why, but it turns out that $\overline{X}_i^{(1)}$ is a valid instrument for $Z_i^{(2)}$. Thus, we can obtain instruments for all of the explanatory variables that are correlated with the error. So far we have focused on the case where $K_1 = K_2 = L_1 = L_2 = 1$. What happens when this is not the case? Since we must have at least one instrumental variable for each explanatory variable that is correlated with the individual effect, it should not surprise you that it must be the case that $K_1 \geq L_2$ for the Hausman–Taylor estimator to work.

In summary, the Hausman–Taylor estimator is an instrumental variables estimator for the random effects model that uses deviations from individual means as well as the means themselves as instruments. We will not provide the formula for this estimator, but suffice it to note that many econometrics software packages will calculate it for you automatically. Remember that the Hausman test can always be used to see if instrumental variables estimation of the random effects model is required.

The Arellano–Bond estimator is another popular instrumental variables estimator for random effects models. We will not derive it nor discuss it in detail. Here we note only that, in addition to the instruments considered by Hausman and Taylor, we can get many more instruments by considering variables at different points in time. For instance, if $X_{it}^{(1)}$ is uncorrelated with ε_{it}, then so will $X_{i,t-1}^{(1)}$ or $X_{i,t+1}^{(1)}$ be, and these can be used as instruments. The Arellano–Bond estimator uses such additional instruments in an efficient fashion.

8.3.3   Extensions to individual effects models

Thus far we have worked with individual effects models of the form

$$Y_{it} = \alpha_i + \beta X_{it} + \varepsilon_{it},$$

with different assumptions about α_i. We have mentioned that the extension to multiple regression is a direct one, and also discussed what happens when some of the explanatory variables do not vary over time (e.g. gender or race in an application involving a survey of individuals are constant over time). Another popular extension is to allow for time effects. That is, comparable with the individual effect, we might want to add an effect that is distinct to each time period (e.g. to capture business cycle considerations). Such a model can be written as

$$Y_{it} = \alpha_i + \gamma_t + \beta X_{it} + u_{it}.$$

In a fixed effects model, the time effect can be modeled through inclusion of a dummy variable for each point in time. A random effects model would add to the assumptions made previously the additional assumption that

$$\gamma_t = \gamma + w_t.$$

The random effects model with both individual and time effects could be written as a regression model (with intercept being a combination of the α and γ):

$$Y_{it} = (\alpha + \gamma) + \beta X_{it} + \varepsilon_{it},$$

where

$$\varepsilon_{it} = v_i + w_t + u_{it}.$$

With this model the same pattern emerges as with our previous random effects model. The errors are correlated with one another, and hence a GLS estimator should be used (or OLS with panel-corrected standard errors). The GLS estimator for the random effects model with a time effect will be slightly different from the usual random effects GLS estimator, but the same basic ideas hold.

Panel data, of course, have a time series dimension. You may be wondering why we are not using the time series methods developed in Chapters 6 and 7 in this chapter (e.g. to develop panel unit root tests or panel cointegration tests). There are indeed many research papers that propose various methods for dealing with such issues. However, many of these issues are too advanced for coverage in this textbook. In our discussion of instrumental variables estimation with panel data, we wrote a random effects model as

$$Y_{it} = \alpha + \beta_1 X_{it}^{(1)} + \beta_2 X_{it}^{(2)} + \beta_3 Z_i^{(1)} + \beta_4 Z_i^{(2)} + \varepsilon_{it},$$

where the definitions of all variables and coefficients and the error are as above. A popular extension that incorporates some time series aspects is

$$Y_{it} = \alpha + \rho Y_{i,t-1} + \beta_1 X_{it}^{(1)} + \beta_2 X_{it}^{(2)} + \beta_3 Z_i^{(1)} + \beta_4 Z_i^{(2)} + \varepsilon_{it}.$$

With such a model, we have the worry that $Y_{i,t-1}$ is very likely to be correlated with the error since both of them include the individual effect (i.e. the v_i in the individual effect appears in both ε_{it} and $\varepsilon_{i,t-1}$ and the latter appears in the expression for $Y_{i,t-1}$). For this reason, instrumental variables estimation is commonly done with this model. Both the Arellano–Bond and the Hausman–Taylor estimators can be used to estimate this model.

A final important extension of the random effects model is the *random coefficients model* which, in the case of a single explanatory variable, extends the individual effects specification to

$$Y_{it} = \alpha_i + \beta_i X_{it} + \varepsilon_{it}.$$

Note that the random coefficient model puts an i subscript on the slope coefficient. Thus, the random coefficients model allows for each individual to have a different marginal effect of X on Y. Such models allow for a great deal of individual heterogeneity. Such specifications are popular in marketing, where consumers react to different sales promotions in different ways. For instance, there might be some consumers who are loyal to particular brands and, thus, do not respond to special offers on new products. Other consumers are more comfortable experimenting with new products, and thus a special offer on a new product could cause them to buy it. These two types of consumers would have different βs in a marketing application. In our returns to schooling example, it is possible that different individuals benefit from additional schooling to a different degree. In this case, too, a random coefficients model would be appropriate.

Note that the random coefficients model is saying that each individual can have a completely different regression line (i.e. one that is different in both intercept and slope coefficients). You may be wondering why, in this case, we do not simply run different regressions for each individual. This is indeed sometimes done. However, unless T is large, it can be hard to get precise estimates of regression coefficients by running N different regressions. After all, in the multiple regression case, you would be estimating $N(k+1)$ coefficients (where k is the number of explanatory variables). It can be very hard to obtain precise estimates of that many coefficients unless your dataset is huge. The random coefficients model is a nice compromise between this strategy (which allows each individual to have completely different slope coefficients) and the more restrictive choice of an individual effects model (which assumes the slope coefficients are the same for all individuals). The random coefficients model allows for slope coefficients to be different, but places some common structure across individuals, by assuming the β_is are all drawn from some common distribution. There are many possible distributions that could be used. For instance, the normal distribution is a popular one. But our marketing example, involving two types of consumer, suggests that a distribution involving two possible values for the slope coefficient would be a sensible one. We will not describe in detail how to estimate random coefficients models (some econometrics software packages will do this for you automatically). However, we note that there is currently a great deal of research involving random coefficients being done. This is an area where Bayesian methods (see Chapter 10) are popular and so-called *hierarchical* models are commonly used.

8.4 Chapter summary

This chapter describes models for use with panel data and associated estimation methods and hypothesis testing procedures. The following is a summary of the topics covered.

1. The pooled model involves simply taking all observations and treating them as though they came from the same regression model. If this is done, then the methods developed for multiple regression models in Chapters 2 to 5 can be used directly.

2. In many applications, the pooled model is not appropriate since it is often the case that different individuals have different regression lines. This helps motivate the use of individual effects models which allow different individuals to have regression lines with different intercepts but the same slope coefficients.

3. The fixed effects model is a popular individual effects model. It models the individual effect through including a dummy explanatory variable for each individual. It is thus a multiple regression model, and the methods developed for the multiple regression model in Chapters 2 to 5 can be used directly. However, the fixed effects model has $N + k$ coefficients, and it can be hard to estimate so many coefficients precisely.

4. The random effects model is a popular individual effects model. It assumes that the individual effect is a random variable. The random effects model can be written as a multiple regression model with only $k + 1$ coefficients, but with an error that violates the classical assumptions. Thus, estimation of the random effects model should either be done using GLS or using OLS with panel-corrected standard errors.

5. A Hausman test can be used to decide whether a fixed or random effects specification is appropriate.

6. The random effects model has many fewer coefficients to estimate than the fixed effects model and thus leads to more accurate estimation. However, the random effects model can often lead to regression errors being correlated with the explanatory variables. If the latter occurs, then the random effects model will yield biased estimates unless instrumental variables methods are used.

7. Popular instrumental variables estimators used with panel data include the Hausman–Taylor and the Arellano–Bond estimators.

8. Extensions of the random and fixed effects models discussed in this chapter include panel data models which allow for formal consideration of time series issues such as unit roots and cointegration. The random coefficients model is another popular extension that allows for the slope coefficient to differ across individuals. Some econometric software packages allow you to estimate such models.

Exercises

The data for these questions are provided on the website associated with this book. Several of the following questions use the same notation as in the body of this chapter. That is, Y_{it} and X_{it} are the values of the dependent and explanatory variables, respectively, for $i = 1, \ldots, N$ individuals for $t = 1, \ldots, T$ time periods.

1. Consider the random effects model

$$Y_{it} = \alpha_i + \beta X_{it} + u_{it},$$

where

$$\alpha_i = \alpha + v_i$$

and v_i is a random variable. The errors in this model are u_{it} and v_i. Assume these are both mean zero, i.i.d. random variables (uncorrelated with one another) with variances $var(u_{it}) = \sigma_u^2$ and $var(v_i) = \sigma_v^2$. Show how this model can be written as a regression model with a constant intercept and a new error term. What are the variances and covariances of this new error term?

2.

(a) Consider transforming the data in the individual effects model using the difference operator, Δ, defined as

$$\Delta Y_{it} = Y_{it} - Y_{i,t-1}.$$

Suppose the fixed effects model is the correct one, but you wished to use ΔY_{it} as the dependent variable. What regression model is implied by this choice? What are the properties of the errors in this new regression model? Can you use this new regression to estimate β? If yes, explain how. How would your answer change if you had a multiple regression model and one of the explanatory variables was time invariant?

(b) Consider transforming the data in the random effects model using deviations from individual means. The definitions and error assumptions relating to the random effects model are given in exercise 1. Remember that deviations from individual means are defined using the notational convention

$$\overline{Y}_i = \frac{\sum_{t=1}^{T} Y_{it}}{N},$$

deviations from individual means are

$$Y_{it} - \overline{Y}_i,$$

and deviations from individual means for the explanatory variable (or variables) are defined in a similar manner. Suppose you specify a random effects regression where the dependent and explanatory variables are in deviations from individual means form. What are the properties of the errors in this new regression model? Which estimator would you use in this new model? Why?

3. Consider the random effects model with both individual and time effects:

$$Y_{it} = \alpha_i + \gamma_t + \beta X_{it} + u_{it},$$

where

$$\alpha_i = \alpha + v_i$$

and

$$\gamma_t = \gamma + w_t.$$

The errors in this model are u_{it}, w_t, and v_i. Assume these are all mean zero, independent random variables (uncorrelated with one another) with variances $var(u_{it}) = \sigma_u^2$, $var(w_t) = \sigma_w^2$, and $var(v_i) = \sigma_v^2$. Show how this model can be written as a regression model with a constant intercept and a new error term. What are the variances and covariances of this new error term? How would you estimate this model?

4. Consider the random effects model:

$$Y_{it} = \alpha_i + \beta X_{it} + u_{it}$$

where

$$\alpha_i = \alpha + v_i.$$

The errors in this model are u_{it} and v_i. In contrast with the assumptions used in the body of the chapter, assume that u_{it} is autocorrelated. That is, as before, u_{it} and v_i are both mean zero random variables (uncorrelated with one another and $cov(v_i, v_j) = 0$ for $i \neq j$) with variances $var(u_{it}) = \sigma_u^2$, and $var(v_i) = \sigma_v^2$. But now assume

$$u_{it} = \rho u_{i,t-1} + e_{it},$$

where e_{it} is a mean zero random variable with $var(e_{it}) = \sigma_e^2$ (and all the e_{it}s are independent of one another). Show how this model can be written as a regression model with a constant intercept and a new error term. What are the variances and covariances of this new error term? How would you estimate this model?

5. The file HOSPITAL.XLS contains panel data relevant for estimating a hospital cost function. It contains data for $N = 382$ hospitals for $T = 5$ years. All variables except for the dummy variables have been logged. The variables are:

- $Y =$ log of hospital operating costs (in thousands of dollars);
- $BEDS =$ log of number of beds in hospital;
- $INPATIENT =$ log of number of inpatient visits;
- $OUTPATIENT =$ log of number of outpatient visits;
- $CASEMIX =$ log of a case mix index (do not worry about its exact definition, other than to note that higher values of it imply a hospital is handling more difficult cases);
- $K =$ log of capital stock (measured in thousands of dollars);
- $NONPROFIT = 1$ for non-profit hospitals ($= 0$ otherwise);
- $FORPROFIT = 1$ for for-profit hospitals ($= 0$ otherwise).[7]

(a) Estimate a pooled regression model using these data.
(b) Estimate a fixed effects model using these data.
(c) Estimate a random effects model using these data.
(d) Compare your results for parts (a) to (c). Which model do you prefer? Carry out appropriate hypothesis tests to justify your answer.

(e) For your preferred model, write up your results as you would in an empirical project. Pay particular attention to the question of whether organisational structure (i.e. whether a hospital is non-profit, for-profit, or government run) has an impact on how cost effective it is.

Endnotes

1. Furthermore, in returns to schooling regressions it is common to log the dependent variable, and, as we have seen in Chapter 5, such a regression might require the use of IV methods. We ignore such issues here.
2. But note that the way we have placed the data points in Figure 8.1 is slightly unreasonable. For each individual, we have labelled incomes corresponding to everything from 10 to 20 years of schooling. In practice, information of this sort is usually unavailable, since most individuals do not start working full time until after their schooling is complete. For instance, most people start school at age 5, and hence an individual who starts working after secondary school will have approximately 12 years of schooling. Unless the individual returns to school later in life, the data will always report $X = 12$ years of school each year on the survey. This is different from the scattering of different values of X shown in Figure 8.1.
3. Note that the pooled model has one intercept whereas the fixed effects model has N intercepts. This difference implies that the pooled model imposes $N-1$ restrictions on the fixed effects model.

4. If you are using Stata, it is useful to note that Stata uses the terminology 'cross-sectional time series' to refer to panel data.

5. Remember that consistency is an asymptotic concept that is similar to unbiasedness.

6. The Arellano–Bond estimator was derived as a generalized methods of moments estimator (a concept not explained in this textbook). However, it can be interpreted as an instrumental variables estimator.

7. If a hospital is neither for-profit nor non-profit, then it is government run.

CHAPTER 9

Qualitative Choice and Limited Dependent Variable Models

9.1 Introduction

Regression is a powerful tool for measuring the effect of explanatory variables on a dependent variable. In the previous chapters, we have considered a wide variety of models that can all be interpreted as regression models. However, although we did not stress it at the time, the dependent variables in all previous chapters were continuous random variables. That is, they could take on any value. But there are many cases where your dependent variable is restricted to take on a limited range of values. For instance, it could be a dummy variable that is restricted to take on the values 0 or 1. Or it could be a count and be restricted to take on values $0, 1, 2, \ldots$. In these cases, the regression methods described in the previous chapters are not appropriate. The question arises as to how you can build something similar to a regression model (i.e. where explanatory variables can affect a dependent variable) to handle these cases. The purpose of this chapter is to answer this question. In the first part of this chapter, we consider *qualitative choice models* where the dependent variable arises from a choice. In the latter part, we will consider *limited dependent variable models* which involve different limitations on the dependent variable. However, we stress that, although some of the terminology and methods in this chapter may sound new and unfamiliar, the same basic ideas hold as in previous chapters. That is, we are seeking to relate a dependent variable to explanatory variables.

In this chapter, we will begin with the case where the dependent variable is a dummy. Dummy explanatory variables were discussed in Chapter 2. However, in many cases it is the dependent variable that is a dummy. As an example, suppose the researcher are interested in investigating why some people choose to travel to work by car and others choose to travel by public transport. The data available to the researcher are based on a survey where commuters are asked whether they travelled by car or public transport and are asked to provide personal characteristics (e.g. distance to work, their salary, etc.). If the researcher tried to construct a regression model, the explanatory variables would be these personal characteristics. However, the dependent variable would be a dummy variable (i.e. with a value of 1 if the the commuter travelled by car and a value of 0 if the commuter travelled by public transport). In the previous chapters, we often worked with the classical assumptions, one of which was that the dependent variable was normally distributed. It would not make sense to assume that such a 0–1 dummy variable had a normal distribution. This is one reason why standard regression methods are inappropriate in this case. In light of this (and other reasons), new methods are necessary for dealing with this case, and accordingly we introduce two models referred to as *probit* and *logit*.

Probit and logit models are appropriate when a choice is being made between two things (e.g. car or public transport). For this reason, they are referred to as *binary choice* models. However, in many cases, the dependent variable is a choice between many alternatives. For instance, in our transportation example, it is possible that the researcher collects data on whether each individual commutes by car, by public transport, or by bicycle (i.e. three alternatives). The field of marketing has many similar examples. For instance, many marketing papers involve data where a consumer is observed choosing one brand from many possibilities (e.g. a choice of one brand of ketchup out of five possibilities available in a store). These are referred to as *multinomial choice models*. We describe how probit and logit models can be extended to deal with this case. The resulting models are referred to as *multinomial probit* and *multinomial logit*. We also introduce an important special case of multinomial logit referred to as *conditional logit*.

In the latter half of this chapter, models where the dependent variable is limited in some other way are discussed. Many models exist for use when the dependent variable is *censored* in some way. We discuss the *tobit model* as an example of a model that deals with censoring of a particular sort. Next we discuss *count data models* which are used when the dependent variable is a count (e.g. $0, 1, 2, \ldots$). Many other models exist for use when the dependent variable is restricted in other ways. We cannot discuss all of them in this chapter. However, the chapter ends with a brief summary of some other limited dependent variable models, so that you can at least know what models to investigate (e.g. in an advanced econometrics textbook) should you ever have a dataset that requires their use.

9.2   Qualitative choice models

9.2.1   Binary choice models

Before getting into details of the probit and logit models, it is worthwhile bringing in a little economics to help motivate how they arise. This will help us when it comes to interpretation.

Probit and logit models often (but not invariably) arise in cases where an individual is making a choice. Assume that an individual has to make a choice between two alternatives. An economist would formalize such a situation by specifying a utility function. Let U_{ji} be the utility that individual i (for $i = 1, \ldots, N$) gets if alternative j (for $j = 0, 1$) is chosen. The individual makes choice 1 if $U_{1i} \geq U_{0i}$ and makes choice 0 otherwise. Since $U_{1i} \geq U_{0i}$ is equivalent to $U_{1i} - U_{0i} \geq 0$, the choice can be seen to depend on the difference in utilities across the two alternatives and we define this difference as

$$Y_i^* = U_{1i} - U_{0i}.$$

In our transport example, this is simply saying that the individual's choice of whether to take the car or public transport depends on which yields him higher utility. The transport economist would say that Y_i^* should depend on an individual's characteristics (e.g. his salary, the time it takes him to drive to work, the time it takes him to take public transport to work, etc.). The econometrician would say that this sounds like a multiple regression model:

$$Y_i^* = \alpha + \beta_1 X_{1i} + \beta_2 X_{2i} + \cdots + \beta_k X_{ki} + \varepsilon_i,$$

where, as before, we are using i subscripts to denote individual observations, $i = 1, \ldots, N$ and $X_1, \ldots, X_k$ are explanatory variables that might affect the individual's utility. As we have often done before, to make the derivations easier, we will write some of the formulae below in terms of the simple regression model

$$Y_i^* = \beta X_i + \varepsilon_i.$$

The problem with this regression is that we do not observe individuals' utility and, thus, Y_i^* is unobservable. But it is still useful to write it out since the probit model can be interpreted as this regression, where the errors are assumed to satisfy the classical assumptions. Most importantly they are assumed to be normally distributed. The logit model can also be interpreted as this regression, where the errors are assumed to satisfy all the classical assumptions except one. The exception is that the errors are assumed to have a *logistic distribution*. Do not worry about exact definition of the latter distribution at this stage, we will shortly describe some of its key properties.

Y_i^* is unobservable, but we do observe the choice made by the individual which serves to shed some light on Y_i^*. In particular, we observe $Y_i = 1$ if individual i makes choice 1 and $Y_i = 0$ if choice 0 is made. The following equations summarize the relationship between Y_i and Y_i^*:

$$Y_i = 1 \quad \text{if} \quad Y_i^* \geq 0,$$
$$Y_i = 0 \quad \text{if} \quad Y_i^* < 0.$$

In words, the individual makes choice 1 if the utility associated with that alternative is highest (otherwise alternative 0 is chosen).

Given this set-up, involving a regression model for the unobservable Y_i^* and the equations linking Y_i and Y_i^*, how do we develop econometric methods for estimating regression coefficients and how do we interpret the results? For both purposes, it proves convenient to think in terms of the probability of making a choice. The following derivations relate to the probability of making choice 1. The probability of making choice 0 will be 1 minus this probability. Since the individual will choose alternative 1 if its utility is higher than alternative 0, the probability of making choice 1 is

$$\Pr(Y_i = 1) = \Pr(Y_i^* \geq 0) = \Pr(\beta X_i + \varepsilon_i \geq 0) = \Pr(\varepsilon_i \geq -\beta X_i).$$

Given an assumption about the error distribution, we can work out $\Pr(\varepsilon_i \geq -\beta X_i)$.

Remember that the probit model assumes the regression errors are normally distributed and the logit model assumes they are logistically distributed. The normal distribution is a familiar one and probabilities involving it can be calculated using normal statistical tables (or a computer software package). Appendix B, Definition B.7 introduces the notion of a distribution function (also called a cumulative distribution function) which, for any random variable Z and any point z, is

$$\Pr(Z \leq z).$$

If Z is a standard normal (i.e. $N(0,1)$), it is common to use the notation

$$\Phi(z)$$

for the distribution function. With this notation, we can now say that for the probit model

$$\Pr(Y_i = 1) = \Pr(\varepsilon_i \geq -\beta X_i) = 1 - \Phi(-\beta X_i) = \Phi(\beta X_i)$$

where the last of the equals signs arises since the standard normal distribution is symmetric about zero. Since $\Pr(Y_i = 0) = 1 - \Pr(Y_i = 1)$, we can also say $\Pr(Y_i = 0) = \Phi(-\beta X_i)$.

Although we will not prove it, it turns out that, with the logit model, where ε_i has a logistic distribution, we obtain

$$\Pr(Y_i = 1) = \frac{\exp(\beta X_i)}{1 + \exp(\beta X_i)}$$

and thus

$$\Pr(Y_i = 0) = \frac{1}{1 + \exp(\beta X_i)}.$$

These formulae can be used to interpret results in the probit and logit models. Remember that, with regression models, we interpret coefficients as measuring the marginal effect of an explanatory variable on a dependent variable. With probit and logit, it is not so straightforward to obtain a marginal effects interpretation. However, once we have $\widehat{\beta}$ (which is an estimate of β), we can work out the probability of making a choice for selected individuals. As an example, let us return to the transportation example where $Y = 1$ denotes the choice to commute by car and X is an explanatory variable that measures the time it takes to drive to work (measured in minutes). Once you have estimated a probit model, you can estimate, for example, the probability that individuals with 30, 60, and 120 minute drives to work will take the car as

$$\Pr(Y = 1|X = 30) = 1 - \Phi(-30\widehat{\beta}),$$
$$\Pr(Y = 1|X = 60) = 1 - \Phi(-60\widehat{\beta}),$$
$$\Pr(Y = 1|X = 120) = 1 - \Phi(-120\widehat{\beta}).$$

Often, policymakers are interested in this sort of information. For a logit model, you would plug the 30, 60, and 120 values into the formula above arising from the logistic distribution.

It is also possible to obtain something akin to a marginal effects interpretation, except in terms of the probability. That is, the conventional regression marginal effects interpretation in simple regression is: 'How much does Y change when you change X?', and β is the answer to this. With qualitative choice models, we alter this to: 'How much does *the probability of making choice* 1 change when you change X?', but it is not simply β that is the answer to this. Using calculus, you can derive the following marginal effects. For the probit model, the marginal effect of X on the probability of making choice 1 is

$$\phi(\beta X)\beta,$$

where $\phi(.)$ is the formula for the normal p.d.f. (see Appendix B, Definition B.10). For the logit model, the marginal effect of X on the probability of making choice 1 is

$$\frac{\exp(\beta X_i)}{1 + \exp(\beta X_i)} \frac{1}{1 + \exp(\beta X_i)} \beta.$$

These formulae for marginal effects may look complicated, but the key thing is that they can be calculated in any relevant computer software package. Note, though, that, unlike with simple regression, with probit and logit these marginal effects depend on X. So, for instance, a commuter with a $X = 30$ minute drive to work will have different marginal effect than a commuter with a $X = 60$ minute drive to work. In light of this, it is common for computer packages to evaluate marginal effects at the average value for the explanatory variables.

It is also common to present marginal effects relating to the *odds ratio*. The odds ratio is the ratio of the probabilities of making the two choices:

$$\frac{\Pr(Y_i = 1)}{\Pr(Y_i = 0)}.$$

For the logit model, this can be simplified as follows:

$$\frac{\Pr(Y_i = 1)}{\Pr(Y_i = 0)} = \frac{\dfrac{\exp(\beta X_i)}{1 + \exp(\beta X_i)}}{\dfrac{1}{1 + \exp(\beta X_i)}} = \exp(\beta X_i).$$

Note that the log of the odds ratio is simply βX_i. Hence, β can be interpreted (somewhat awkwardly) as a marginal effect in terms of the log odds ratio (i.e. if you increase X by one unit, the log of the odds ratio will change by β units).

In this section, we have been working with probit and logit models with one explanatory variable. The extension to many explanatory variables is straightforward. So far we have said nothing about estimating and testing in probit and logit models. For many purposes it suffices to note that many econometric software packages estimate such models and will provide the standard empirical quantities that we have discussed in the context of regression. For instance, in a probit or logit model involving many explanatory variables, estimates of $\alpha, \beta_1, \ldots, \beta_k$ will be provided along with P-values (to test whether individual coefficients are significant or not) and confidence intervals. As an example, LIMDEP is a popular computer package for use with limited dependent variables (and many other topics). LIMDEP's probit command will carry out maximum likelihood estimation of the probit model. It will present maximum likelihood estimates $\widehat{\alpha}, \widehat{\beta}_1, \ldots, \widehat{\beta}_k$ along with P-values for testing each of the hypotheses $H_0: \beta_j = 0$ (as well as many other things). These would allow you to present point estimates of all the coefficients and discuss their significance. It will also calculate the marginal effect of each explanatory variable on the probability of making choice 1 for an individual with explanatory variables set at their mean values. For instance, LIMDEP will calculate the marginal effect of explanatory variable j on the probability of choice 1 using the formula

$$\phi\left(\widehat{\alpha} + \widehat{\beta}_1 \overline{X}_1 + \cdots + \widehat{\beta}_k \overline{X}_k\right)\widehat{\beta}_j,$$

where $\overline{X}_j$ is the average of the jth explanatory variable (i.e. $\frac{\sum_{i=1}^{N} X_{ji}}{N}$). Alternatively, LIMDEP will let you specify other values for the explanatory variables calculation of marginal effects. LIMDEP also produces many other empirical results (e.g. the value of the log likelihood that would be useful for doing a likelihood ratio test). LIMDEP also handles other qualitative choice models such as logit. It is also worth noting that, as with any regression model, heteroskedasticity could be a problem in the probit model. LIMDEP has an estimation option that estimates the probit model when the errors are heteroskedastic (analogous to the heteroskedasticity consistent estimators discussed in Chapter 5).

The most popular way of estimating probit or logit models is by use of maximum likelihood methods. The general principles associated with maximum likelihood are described in Chapter 3. Remember that the likelihood function is the joint probability density function for $Y_1, \ldots, Y_N$, evaluated at the actual observations. If, as in this case, the observations are independent of one another, we can write the likelihood function as

$$L(\beta) = p(Y_1, \ldots, Y_N) = \prod_{i=1}^{N} p(Y_i).$$

The idea of maximum likelihood estimation is that it finds the value for β that maximizes this function. That is, $\widehat{\beta}$ will be the value that yields the specific p.d.f. that could most plausibly have generated $Y_1, \ldots, Y_N$.

Such likelihood-based procedures can be used with probit and logit. Our previous derivations show how this can be done. That is, our previous derivations provide us with $p(Y_i)$ and, thus, the likelihood function. For probit, $p(Y_i)$ is defined by noting that $\Pr(Y_i = 1) = \Phi(\beta X_i)$ and $\Pr(Y_i = 0) = \Phi(-\beta X_i)$. Thus, the likelihood function is

$$L(\beta) = \prod_{i=1}^{N} p(Y_i) = \prod_{i=1}^{N} \Phi(\beta X_i)^{Y_i} \Phi(-\beta X_i)^{1-Y_i}.$$

To aid in interpretation of this formula, note that, when we plug in the actual observations, we have either $Y_i = 1$ or $Y_i = 0$, and so for each individual we will either have a $\Phi(\beta X_i)$ or a $\Phi(-\beta X_i)$ in the formula for the likelihood function.

The likelihood function for the logit model involves the same sorts of derivation:

$$L(\beta) = \prod_{i=1}^{N} \left(\frac{\exp(\beta X_i)}{1 + \exp(\beta X_i)} \right)^{Y_i} \left(\frac{1}{1 + \exp(\beta X_i)} \right)^{1-Y_i}.$$

Remember that, for the simple regression model, the maximum likelihood estimator was the OLS estimator. Thus, there was a formula we could use (i.e. $\widehat{\beta} = \frac{\Sigma X_i Y_i}{\Sigma X_i^2}$) to calculate the maximum likelihood estimator. With probit and logit, no such formula exists. In practice, the key thing to know about these likelihood functions is that computer software packages will be able to maximize them.[1] And, as discussed before, any relevant computer package will also present something analogous to a t-test. That is, for each individual coefficient, a P-value will be provided to test whether it equals zero. These P-values can be used to see which explanatory variables are significant and which are not.

As we have seen with the regression model, associated with maximum likelihood are a series of hypothesis testing procedures: the likelihood ratio, Wald, and Lagrange multiplier tests. Any of these can be used to test any hypothesis of interest with probit or logit. For instance, in Chapter 4 we introduced the likelihood ratio test in the context of the multiple regression model. This could be used to test joint hypotheses (e.g. $H_0: \beta_1 + \beta_2 = 1, \beta_3 = 0$). To use this test in practice, we had to find the value of the likelihood function for the unrestricted model and the restricted one, where the restricted one imposed the hypothesis to be true (e.g. the restrictions $\beta_1 + \beta_2 = 1$ and $\beta_3 = 0$ are imposed on the model). The likelihood ratio statistic was a simple function of these two values. If you estimate the restricted and unrestricted variants of logit and probit models, computer packages will provide the likelihood for each. Thus, a likelihood ratio test can easily be done with probit and logit.

You may also be asking the question 'How do I know whether to use probit or logit?'. To be honest, in the majority of empirical applications, it does not matter too much. Probit and logit tend to yield very similar results. However, it is worth mentioning that various tests do exist and, with a little bit of additional reading in a more advanced textbook[2], it is not hard to figure out how to use them in practice. The question of whether to use extensions of probit or logit becomes more important when there are many choices, and we will provide more discussion on this point in the next section.

Example: Choosing to have an affair

The decision to have an extramarital affair is discussed in a popular paper.[3] This paper used surveys conducted by popular magazines to construct a dataset to shed light on this issue. In this example we use binomial choice methods with some of these data. In particular, we have $N = 601$ observations on the following variables:

- $AFFAIR = 1$ if individual has had an affair ($= 0$ otherwise);
- $MALE = 1$ if the individual is male ($= 0$ otherwise);
- $YEARS$ is the number of years the individual has been married;
- $KIDS = 1$ if the individual has children from the marriage ($= 0$ otherwise);
- $RELIG = 1$ if the individual classifies himself or herself as religious ($= 0$ otherwise);
- $EDUC$ is the years of schooling completed;
- $HAPPY = 1$ if the individual person views his or her marriage as happier than average ($= 0$ otherwise).

$AFFAIR$ is the dependent variable and the others are the explanatory variables. Table 9.1 presents logit estimates of all the coefficients (using maximum likelihood methods) as well as estimates of the marginal effects relating to the odds ratio (i.e. $\exp(\beta_j)$ which is the effect of a one-unit change in the jth explanatory variable on the odds ratio, holding the other explanatory variables constant). An examination of the P-values for testing the hypothesis that the individual coefficients are zero reveals that $YEARS$, $RELIG$, and $HAPPY$ are statistically significant. But, since

Table 9.1 Logit results for affair data.

Variable	Logit Coeff.	P-value for $\beta_j = 0$	95 % confidence interval	Odds ratio Coeff.	Logit (robust) Coeff.	P-value for $\beta_j = 0$
Intercept	−1.29	0.07	[−2.71,0.13]	—	−1.29	0.09
MALE	0.25	0.26	[−0.18,0.67]	1.28	0.25	0.27
YEARS	0.05	0.03	[0.01,0.09]	1.05	0.05	0.03
KIDS	0.44	0.12	[−0.12,1.00]	1.55	0.44	0.13
RELIG	−0.89	0.00	[−1.32,−0.47]	0.41	−0.89	0.00
EDUC	0.01	0.75	[−0.07,0.10]	1.01	0.01	0.75
HAPPY	−0.87	0.00	[−1.28,−0.46]	0.42	−0.87	0.09

logit coefficients do not directly measure marginal effects, it is hard to interpret them. We can, however, interpret the signs on the coefficients. For instance, the fact that the coefficients on *RELIG* and *HAPPY* are negative means that individuals who are either religious or happily married are less likely to have extramarital affairs. The fact that the coefficient on *YEARS* is positive means that individuals who have been married longer are more likely to have affairs. However, it is difficult to interpret the magnitude of the coefficients.

Table 9.1 also contains results (in the column labelled 'Odds ratio') for the marginal effects on the odds ratios. These are somewhat more easy to interpret. Consider, for instance, the coefficient estimate of this marginal effect for the variable *HAPPY*. This is 0.42. How do we interpret this number? *HAPPY* is a dummy variable change, so that a 'one-unit change' means a change from an unhappy marriage to a happy one. So we can say: 'If an individual's marriage switches from an unhappy one to a happy one (holding other explanatory variables constant), then the odds ratio in favor of having an affair will be 42 % of what it was before.' To make this concrete, suppose an individual initially had an odds ratio of 4. This means $\Pr(Y_i = 1) = \frac{4}{5}$ and $\Pr(Y_i = 0) = \frac{1}{5}$ and there is 80 % chance the individual will have an affair. If this individual's marriage becomes happy, the odds ratio becomes 42 % as high as before. This means it becomes $4 \times 0.42 = 1.68$. This number implies there is a 63 % chance the individual will have an affair.

The final two columns of Table 9.1 (labelled 'Logit (robust)') are included to illustrate some of the other things that computer software packages (in this case Stata) can do. In Chapter 5, we discussed heteroskedasticity and introduced the notion of a heteroskedasticity consistent estimator. This could be used to calculate the correct variances of the OLS estimator (which fed into the formulae for hypothesis testing procedures and confidence intervals) when heteroskedasticity existed. With logit (and probit), similar so-called *robust variance estimators* can be produced. Results using one of these are presented in Table 9.1. Note that the estimates of the coefficients (in the column labelled 'Coeff') for logit (robust) are the same as in the column for logit.

Table 9.2   Probit results for affair data.

Variable	Probit Coeff.	Probit P-value for $\beta_j = 0$	Probit 95% confidence interval	Marginal effects Coeff.	Probit (robust) Coeff.	Probit (robust) P-value for $\beta_j = 0$
Intercept	−0.74	0.08	[−1.56,0.09]	—	−0.74	0.11
MALE	0.15	0.23	[−0.10,0.40]	0.05	0.15	0.24
YEARS	0.03	0.03	[0.00,0.05]	0.01	0.03	0.02
KIDS	0.25	0.12	[−0.07,0.57]	0.07	0.25	0.13
RELIG	−0.51	0.00	[−0.75,−0.27]	−0.15	−0.51	0.00
EDUC	0.01	0.81	[−0.04,0.06]	0.00	0.01	0.81
HAPPY	−0.51	0.00	[−0.76,−0.27]	−0.17	−0.51	0.09

However, the *P*-values for testing $H_0: \beta_j = 0$ are slightly different. These *P*-values tend to be a little bit larger than with the standard logit model. This is consistent with the robust variance estimator being slightly larger than the standard result. Nevertheless, for this dataset it seems that heteroskedasticity is not a problem since the logit and logit (robust) results are virtually the same. Of course, just as with regular regression, there are tests for heteroskedasticity that can be used. We will not describe them here other than to note that they are included in many econometrics software packages.

Table 9.2 presents results similar to those in Table 9.1, except for the case of probit. The pattern of results is the same as for logit. For instance, being in a happy marriage or being religious will significantly reduce an individual's chance of having an affair. Similarly, the use of a robust variance estimator (see the columns labelled 'Probit (robust)') causes only very minor alterations to the basic probit results, indicating heteroskedasticity is not a problem in this dataset. However, just as with logit, it is hard to interpret coefficients directly. Accordingly, many econometrics packages calculate

$$\phi\left(\widehat{\alpha} + \widehat{\beta}_1 \overline{X}_1 + \cdots + \widehat{\beta}_k \overline{X}_k\right)\beta_j.$$

As discussed above, this is the marginal effect of explanatory variable *j* on the probability of choice 1 (holding all other explanatory variables constant). An examination of these (in the column labelled 'Marginal effects') shows, for instance, that the marginal effect associated with *KIDS* is 0.07. This number can be interpreted as saying: 'If the number of children increases by 1, the probability of having an affair increases by 0.07 (holding all other explanatory variables constant at their average values)'. Note, however, that the coefficient on *KIDS* is not statistically significant.

There are many other empirical features of interest you can present using probit or logit models. For instance, you can calculate the predicted probability of having an affair for hypothetical individuals (e.g. you can answer questions like: 'What is the probability that a religious man with 16 years of schooling, who has been married happily for 2 years and has children, will have an affair?'). Alternatively, you can calculate the predicted probability of having an affair for each of your $i = 1, \ldots, N$ individuals. These probabilities can be used informally to gauge how well the model is fitting the data. That is, if the predicted probabilities of having an affair are high for individuals who actually had an affair (and are low for those who did not have an affair), then the model is fitting well. There are more formal measures of fit (similar to the R^2 in the multiple regression model) that are based on these predicted probabilities. We will not discuss such formal measures of fit (see an advanced econometrics book for more information).

9.2.2   Multinomial choice models

Multinomial probit and multinomial logit

The previous discussion of probit and logit models can be extended to allow for a choice between several alternatives. To do this, we slightly modify the set-up of the earlier section by assuming that Y_i can take on values $0, 1, \ldots, J$ to indicate the different alternatives. That is, there are $J + 1$ alternatives and we will use subscripts $\{j = 0, \ldots, J\}$ to indicate them. The individual will make the choice that yields the highest utility. As before, let U_{ji} be the utility of individual i when he or she chooses alternative j (for $i = 1, \ldots, N$ and $j = 0, \ldots, J$). In the binomial choice model, we talked about the probability of making choice 1 (with the probability of choice 0 being 1 minus this). We talked about how choice 1 was made if $U_1 \geq U_0$ and said that this was equivalent to saying that choice 1 would be made if $U_1 - U_0 \geq 0$ (i.e. it was the difference in utility between choices 1 and 0 that mattered). In the case of multinomial choice models, we do something similar by selecting one alternative as the benchmark alternative. Every other alternative is compared with this benchmark in terms of its utility. In an empirical exercise, it will not matter which choice you make as the benchmark. For instance, in our multinomial transport example, each individual would choose between commuting to work by car, public transport, or bicycle. It does not matter which of car, public transport, or bicycle you choose as the benchmark alternative. In our discussion of multinomial choice models, we will refer to alternative 0 as the benchmark choice.

In the binomial choice models, we developed our models beginning with the utility difference between alternatives 1 and 0. With many alternatives, we will have many such differences in utility between making a choice and a benchmark choice. Thus, we will have

$$Y_{ji}^* = U_{ji} - U_{0i}$$

for $j = 1, \ldots, J$. Y_{ji}^* is unobservable, but we do observe the choice made by the individual. In particular, we observe $Y_i = j$ if individual i makes choice j. Formally, we have the following relationship between the unobserved utility difference and the actual choice made: if $Y_{ji}^* < 0$ for $j = 1, \ldots, J$, then individual i chooses the benchmark alternative and $Y_i = 0$. Otherwise, individual i chooses the alternative that yields the highest value for Y_{ji}^*.

Just as with the probit and logit models, these utility differences can depend on explanatory variables (e.g. the travel time of each alternative would help explain why you prefer taking public transport to taking your car). Thus, we use a regression model:

$$Y_{ji}^* = \alpha_j + \beta_{j1}X_{1i} + \beta_{j2}X_{2i} + \cdots + \beta_{jk}X_{ki} + \varepsilon_{ji}.$$

Look carefully at the extra subscripts we have put on variables and coefficients in this equation. Note now that, unlike with binomial choice, we do not have a single regression, but rather J different regressions (one for comparing each of alternatives $j = 1, \ldots, J$ with alternative 0). In each of the regressions, we have different coefficients (i.e. α_j is the intercept in regression involving the difference in utility between alternative j and alternative 0, β_{j1} is the coefficient on the first explanatory variable in this regression, etc.).

As a digression, note that we have not put j subscripts on the explanatory variables. Thus, although each of the regressions could have different explanatory variables (i.e. some of the coefficients could be zero in some equations, which would imply the associated explanatory variable is omitted), we are assuming the value of each explanatory variable is the same in each equation. This makes sense when the explanatory variables are characteristics of the individual. For instance, in our transport example, the commuting choice may depend on an individual's income. Thus, we might want to include $X_{1i} =$ income of individual i as an explanatory variable. The value for this explanatory variable will be the same in every regression equation. However, it is reasonable to expect the commuting choice to depend on the time it would take to travel to work by the various alternative modes of travel. This will vary across alternatives (i.e. commuting time will be different for car, public transport, and bicycle). Our specification above suggests that such explanatory variables are not allowed for. But this is not the case. We can handle explanatory variables whose values vary across alternatives if we use a clever trick. Instead of having one explanatory variable (i.e. one explanatory variable called 'commuting time'), we can make up $J + 1$ different explanatory variables (i.e. one explanatory variable that is commuting time if the car is taken, another that is commuting time if public transport is taken, and another that is commuting time if the bicycle is taken). Thus, the multinomial probit and logit frameworks that we will describe can handle explanatory variables whose values vary across individuals and/or alternatives. As we will see later (in our discussion of the conditional logit model), this distinction between types of explanatory variable can be important in some cases.

The multinomial probit and multinomial logit models are based on the previous set of J regressions but differ in the assumptions made about the errors. The multinomial probit model assumes the errors are normally distributed, whereas the multinomial logit makes another assumption about the distribution of the errors. Do not worry about the exact form of the latter distribution. The important thing to note is that, for the multinomial logit model, the probability of individual i making any choice (say the jth choice) has the form

$$\Pr\left(Y_i = j\right) = \frac{\exp(\beta_j X_i)}{1 + \sum_{s=1}^{J} \exp(\beta_s X_i)},$$

where we have now (to keep the formulae simple) returned to the simple regression case with a single explanatory variable.

For the multinomial probit model, we can work out $\Pr(Y_i = j)$ using the properties of the normal distribution. However, in this case we have to use the *multivariate* normal distribution. This is an extension of the normal distribution, but we will not formally define it in this textbook. Instead we will provide a bit of explanation and intuition. Remember that, with multinomial probit, we will have a different error in each of the regressions involving each utility difference (i.e. ε_{ji} for $j = 1, \ldots, J$). These errors could be correlated with one another. For instance, in the case of three alternatives (and, thus, two regressions involving the utility differences Y^*_{1i} and Y^*_{2i}), we could have $corr(\varepsilon_{1i}, \varepsilon_{2i}) \neq 0$. The multivariate normal distribution allows for this. It is an extension of the normal distribution which says that each of the errors (individually) is normal, but also allows for correlation between them. But note that the number of possible correlations between errors increases rapidly the more alternatives you have. For instance, when facing a choice between four alternatives you would have three different correlations $corr(\varepsilon_{1i}, \varepsilon_{2i})$, $corr(\varepsilon_{1i}, \varepsilon_{3i})$ and $corr(\varepsilon_{2i}, \varepsilon_{3i})$. In general, with $J + 1$ choices, we will have $\frac{J(J+1)}{2}$ correlations. We do not know what these correlations are and, thus, have to estimate them. The multinomial probit model already has many coefficients to estimate (i.e. you must estimate all the regression coefficients in each of J equations). But the multinomial probit model will also have to estimate all these correlations between errors. Unless you have a great deal of data or few alternatives to choose between, it is difficult to obtain precise estimation in the multinomial probit model. For this reason, multinomial probit is typically used only if the number of alternatives is relatively small.[4]

When the number of alternatives is large, the multinomial logit model is the more popular choice. This model assumes that the errors in the different equations are uncorrelated with one another. Thus, with multinomial logit, one does not have to worry about estimating all the correlations between errors that are present in the multinomial probit model (although you still must estimate regression coefficients in each of J equations). However, this aspect of the multinomial logit model does have one implication that, in some empirical applications, might be undesirable. This is that the choice probabilities implied by the multinomial logit model must satisfy an *independence of irrelevant alternatives* (or IIA) property.

To explain what IIA means, we will use our transport example. Suppose that, initially, a typical commuter has a choice between taking a car ($Y = 0$) or public transport ($Y = 1$). The IIA property relates to the odds ratio between two choices. This is the ratio of probabilities of these two choices (i.e. $\frac{\Pr(Y=0)}{\Pr(Y=1)}$). The IIA assumption says that this odds ratio will be the same, regardless of what the other alternatives are. Suppose, initially, that $\frac{\Pr(Y=0)}{\Pr(Y=1)} = 1$ so that the typical commuter is equally likely to take the car or public transport. Now suppose that a bicycle lane is constructed so that commuters can now cycle to work ($Y = 2$ is now an alternative). The IIA property says that the addition of this new alternative does not alter the fact that $\frac{\Pr(Y=0)}{\Pr(Y=1)} = 1$. In this example, it is possible that the IIA property is reasonable. Originally we have assumed $\Pr(Y = 0) = \Pr(Y = 1) = \frac{1}{2}$. Suppose that, once the bicycle lane is built, there is a 20 %

chance that the commuter will cycle to work. This is consistent with $\Pr(Y = 0) = \Pr(Y = 1) = 0.40$, which still implies $\frac{\Pr(y=0)}{\Pr(y=1)} = 1$.

However, to illustrate where the IIA property is unreasonable, econometricians tweak the previous example to create the so-called 'red bus–blue bus' problem. This assumes that the commuter originally has a choice between taking a car ($Y = 0$) or a red bus ($Y = 1$) to work. Now suppose the bus company paints half of their buses blue and you treat this as a new alternative ($Y = 2$). In this example it would probably not be reasonable to assume IIA holds and, hence, not be reasonable to work with a multinomial logit model. Suppose, for instance, that initially $\Pr(Y = 0) = \Pr(Y = 1) = \frac{1}{2}$ and, thus, $\frac{\Pr(Y=0)}{\Pr(Y=1)} = 1$. Since the blue bus is virtually identical to the red bus, the introduction of this alternative would probably leave the commuter just as likely to take the car to work, and thus $\Pr(Y = 0) = 0.50$ and $\Pr(Y = 1) = \Pr(Y = 2) = 0.25$. Hence, the introduction of the new alternative implies $\frac{\Pr(Y=0)}{\Pr(Y=1)} = 2$. Such changes are a violation of IIA and are not allowed for by the multinomial logit model. We stress that the question of whether IIA is reasonable or not depends on the dataset you are working with. Sometimes it is reasonable, but other times not.

Several variants of logit models have been developed to surmount the restrictive IIA property of the multinomial logit model. One popular variant is the *nested logit model* which assumes a nested structure for the decision-making process. For instance, in the red bus–blue bus example, the econometrician would first use a logit model for a commuter who makes a choice between car and public transportation. If the latter choice is made, then a second logit model is used for the commuter's choice between the red bus and the blue bus. Hence, one logit model is nested within another logit model. We will not discuss such models in this textbook, but note that relevant econometric software packages (e.g. LIMDEP and Stata) allow for their estimation.

We will not describe in detail estimation and testing with multinomial choice models. Suffice it to note that maximum likelihood methods are typically used with these models and they are an extension of those described above for probit and logit models. Any relevant computer package will provide point estimates of coefficients, P-values for telling whether coefficients are significant, and various predicted probabilities and marginal effects. Likelihood ratio tests can be used for testing other hypotheses. In the following example, we will illustrate how multinomial logit and multinomial probit empirical results are interpreted.

Before we move to an example, it is worthwhile summarizing some of the main features of multinomial logit and multinomial probit models. Both of them involve estimation of several equations, and the coefficients in each equation involve the utility difference between a particular alternative and the benchmark alternative. An implication of this is that both of these models can have many coefficients to estimate, particularly if there are many alternatives. With a small dataset it can be hard to estimate precisely so many coefficients. For the multinomial probit model, this problem becomes even worse since you must also estimate the correlations between errors. For these reasons, unless the number of alternatives is small, researchers tend to choose the multinomial logit model if at all possible. The main problem with the multinomial logit model is that it has an IIA assumption. This is an assumption that can be tested using a variant of a Hausman test. We will not describe this test, but note that it can be done in a straightforward fashion in relevant computer packages.

Example: Interpretation of empirical results in multinomial choice models

To illustrate the multinomial logit model, we use a dataset taken from a marketing application.[5] We use data from $N = 136$ households in Rome, Georgia. For each household, data are available on which of four brands of crackers, Sunshine, Keebler, Nabisco and Private label, was purchased. The data were taken from supermarket optical scanners. Thus, the dataset contains four alternatives. We select 'Private label' as the benchmark alternative. For every alternative, we use an intercept and the price of all four brands of crackers in the store at time of purchase as explanatory variables. Thus, our multinomial logit model will involve three different regressions: the first based on the utility difference between Sunshine and Private label crackers, the second based on the utility difference between Keebler and Private label crackers, and the third based on the utility difference between Nabisco and Private label crackers. Each of these regressions involves an intercept and four explanatory variables (i.e. the price of the four brands of crackers). Maximum likelihood estimation of the multinomial logit model yields the results in Table 9.3. Note that, just as

Table 9.3 Multinomial logit results for cracker data.

	Mean	*P*-value for $\beta_{ji} = 0$	95 % confidence interval
Sunshine			
α_1	−10.06	0.15	[−23.59,3.46]
β_{11}	−7.98	0.01	[−13.78,−2.20]
β_{12}	12.39	0.04	[0.77,24.02]
β_{13}	0.37	0.91	[−5.83,6.57]
β_{14}	4.83	0.36	[−5.54,15.20]
Keebler			
α_2	−2.53	0.73	[−16.90,11.85]
β_{21}	−3.10	0.30	[−9.01,2.81]
β_{22}	−0.60	0.92	[−12.99,2.81]
β_{23}	1.15	0.70	[−4.67,6.97]
β_{24}	5.33	0.25	[−3.66,14.32]
Nabisco			
α_3	−7.01	0.09	[−15.09,1.07]
β_{31}	−1.38	0.48	[−5.23,2.48]
β_{32}	5.57	0.12	[−1.37,12.50]
β_{33}	0.86	0.65	[−2.84,4.56]
β_{34}	4.72	0.06	[−0.23,9.67]

with probit and logit, we could have used a heteroskedasticity consistent estimator (also known as a robust variance estimator).

How do we interpret the coefficients in Table 9.3? Note first that there are three separate sets of regression results (in the panels of the table labeled Sunshine, Keebler, and Nabisco respectively). As with any regression coefficient in a qualitative choice model, the size of the coefficients can be hard to interpret. However, the sign of any coefficient can provide some information. Remember that these coefficients can be interpreted as marginal effects relating to the utility differences, Y_{ji}^*, and the utility difference is always relative to a benchmark alternative (here Private label crackers). However, if this utility difference increases, then an individual is more likely to choose alternative j relative to the benchmark choice. This line of argument allows us to interpret the sign of any coefficient. For instance, the estimate of β_{11} is negative. This coefficient is from the regression model for Sunshine crackers (i.e. where the utility difference between Sunshine and Private label crackers is the dependent variable) and appears on the explanatory variable 'price of Sunshine crackers'. The negativity of this coefficient gives us the following marginal effects interpretation: 'If the price of Sunshine crackers increases (holding the price of other crackers constant), then the probability of choosing Sunshine crackers over Private label crackers will fall'. This is a sensible result (i.e. if the price of a good increases, consumers are less likely to buy it).

The other coefficients in Table 9.3 can be interpreted in a similar fashion. Any relevant computer package will also print out the P-value for testing whether each individual coefficient is zero. In our case, this is in the column labeled 'P-value for $\beta_{ji} = 0$'. With very few exceptions, the explanatory variables look to be statistically insignificant. Perhaps this is due to small sample size. Perhaps, also, there are many omitted explanatory variables (e.g. individual characteristics such as income) that are important in explaining cracker choice.

As with logit or probit models, there are many ways of presenting information that can be more informative than simply looking at the regression coefficients in Table 9.3. For instance, in our discussion of the logit model we introduced the concept of an odds ratio. With multinomial logit, we can define odds ratios for each alternative relative to the benchmark alternative:

$$\frac{\Pr(Y_i = j)}{\Pr(Y_i = 0)},$$

for $j = 1, 2, 3$. The effect of a one unit change in the explanatory variable on each odds ratio is calculated in many econometrics software packages. Alternatively, you can calculate the predicted probability of choosing each alternative for an individual with a specified set of characteristics.

In Table 9.4, we illustrate another type of information that can be produced easily in any relevant computer package. The formula for calculating $\Pr(Y_i = j)$ was given

Table 9.4 Predicted probabilities for cracker data.

Probability of being chosen	Mean	Standard deviation	Minimum	Maximum
Sunshine	0.08	0.11	0.01	0.64
Keebler	0.07	0.03	0.02	0.16
Nabisco	0.60	0.10	0.31	0.80
Private label	0.25	0.11	0.02	0.49

in the previous section. In that section, the formula was given for simple regression, but the extension to multiple regression is immediate. The computer can calculate $Pr(Y_i = j)$ for $i = 1, \ldots, N$ and $j = 0, \ldots, J$. In words, the computer will estimate the probability of choosing every alternative for every individual. For our empirical example, we have $N = 136$ individuals and four alternatives, so the computer will produce 544 probabilities. This is too many to present in a report. However, in some cases you might be interested in particular individuals (e.g. if you are working for Nabisco and, for some reason, individual 60 is of interest, you can present the probability that individual 60 will choose Nabisco crackers). Or you can take the $N = 136$ probabilities for each of the four alternatives and calculate descriptive statistics. This is what is done in Table 9.4. As an example, consider the row for Nabisco. The computer has calculated the probability that each individual will choose Nabisco crackers. The average probability is 0.60, the minimum is 0.31, and the maximum is 0.80. The minimum tells us that every individual in the sample has at least a 31 % chance of choosing Nabisco. The maximum tells us there is at least one individual 80 % sure of choosing Nabisco. The fact that this number is not higher (e.g. there is no individual who is 99 % sure to choose Nabisco) reflects the fact that most of our explanatory variables are not significant (i.e. our model does not have many explanatory variables with strong explanatory power).

Results for the multinomial probit model are similar. However, we do not present them here. This is partly for the sake of brevity and partly due to the fact that many computer packages (e.g. Stata or LIMDEP 7.0) will only estimate the multinomial probit model for up to three alternatives (not the four alternatives that this example involves). However, it is worth noting that most computer packages will estimate something called *ordered probit* even if there are many alternatives. We will not explain the ordered probit model in this book, other than to note that it can be used when the alternatives follow a natural ordering. For instance, in a survey, if a consumer is asked if a product is excellent, good, fair, poor, or very poor, then she must choose between five alternatives but they fall in a natural order (i.e. poor is better than very poor, fair is better than poor, etc.). In our cracker example, no such natural ordering of alternatives exists, so the ordered probit model is not appropriate.

Conditional logit

The conditional logit model is another popular model when multiple alternatives exist. We will assume the same basic set-up and notation as for multinomial logit and probit. Remember that, for these models, we said there was one regression model comparing each alternative with a benchmark alternative. Thus, for $j = 1, \ldots, J$ we had

$$Y_{ji}^* = \alpha_j + \beta_{j1} X_{1i} + \beta_{j2} X_{2i} + \cdots + \beta_{jk} X_{ki} + \varepsilon_{ji}.$$

With the conditional logit model, these J regression models are replaced by a single regression model. Thus, conditional logit is more compact and involves estimating fewer coefficients. However, conditional logit is only appropriate with certain types of data.

To define exactly what the conditional logit model is, remember that for multinomial logit with one explanatory variable we had

$$\Pr(Y_i = j) = \frac{\exp(\beta_j X_i)}{1 + \sum_{s=1}^{J} \exp(\beta_s X_i)}$$

for $j = 1, \ldots, J$. For conditional logit, this is replaced by

$$\Pr(Y_i = j) = \frac{\exp(\beta X_{ji})}{\sum_{s=1}^{J} \exp(\beta X_{si})}.$$

If you examine the subscripts carefully, you can see how conditional logit differs from multinomial logit. With conditional logit, there is only a single β (this becomes $\alpha, \beta_1, \ldots, \beta_k$ when we generalize to many explanatory variables). For multinomial logit, the β has a j subscript, and thus there are J of them (this becomes $(k+1) \times J$ of them when we add an intercept and k explanatory variables). Furthermore, the multinomial logit explanatory variable has an i subscript (i.e. the explanatory variable is something like income which differs across individuals but is the same for every choice the individual might make), whereas the conditional logit model has an additional j subscript (i.e. the explanatory variable is something like commuting time which, for a given individual, varies over the alternatives).

Thus, the key difference between multinomial and conditional logit is that the former is suitable when explanatory variables vary across individuals, whereas the latter is suitable when explanatory variables vary across alternatives. With conditional logit, we cannot have explanatory variables that vary only across individuals. To see why this is so, let us suppose we have one explanatory variable that varies across choices (X_j) and a second one that varies across individuals (Z_i) and extend the conditional logit model as

$$\Pr(Y_i = j) = \frac{\exp(\beta_1 X_{ij} + \beta_2 Z_i)}{\sum_{s=1}^{J} \exp(\beta_1 X_{is} + \beta_2 Z_i)}.$$

The properties of the exponential operator can be used to show that you can never estimate β_2. That is,

$$
\begin{aligned}
\Pr(Y_i = j) &= \frac{\exp(\beta_1 X_{ij} + \beta_2 Z_i)}{\sum_{s=1}^{J} \exp(\beta_1 X_{is} + \beta_2 Z_i)} \\
&= \frac{\exp(\beta_1 X_{ij}) \exp(\beta_2 Z_i)}{\sum_{s=1}^{J} \exp(\beta_1 X_{is}) \exp(\beta_2 Z_i)} \\
&= \frac{\exp(\beta_1 X_{ij}) \exp(\beta_2 Z_i)}{\exp(\beta_2 Z_i) \sum_{s=1}^{J} \exp(\beta_1 X_{is})} \\
&= \frac{\exp(\beta_1 X_{ij})}{\sum_{s=1}^{J} \exp(\beta_1 X_{is})}.
\end{aligned}
$$

Thus, terms involving explanatory variables that only vary across individuals drop out of the conditional logit model.

As with all the qualitative choice models, it is hard directly to interpret conditional logit coefficients. However, as we have illustrated with the other qualitative choice models, you can estimate various predicted probabilities or various marginal effects with respect to the probabilities. For instance,

$$
\frac{\partial \Pr(Y_i = j)}{\partial X_{ji}}
$$

can be calculated (although, as with probit and logit, this marginal effect depends on X_j, not just on the regression coefficient).

We have said that conditional logit should be used when your explanatory variables vary across alternatives (but not across individuals). As a final empirical note, we should mention that the conditional logit model can be tricked into dealing with explanatory variables that vary over individuals by creating appropriate explanatory variables. To see how this is done, suppose we have an explanatory variable, Z_i, that does not vary across the alternatives. You can create dummy variables for alternatives $j = 1, \ldots, J$. Let us call these D_{ij} (e.g. $D_{i1} = 1$ denotes the first alternative, $D_{i2} = 1$ denotes the second, etc.). You can include these dummy variables in a conditional logit model (since they take on different values for the different alternatives). However, you can also interact them with explanatory variables such as Z_i (i.e. you can create $Z_i \times D_{ij}$ and use these as a new set of explanatory variables that do vary across alternatives). In this way, the conditional logit model can be estimated even if you have explanatory variables that do not vary over the alternatives. However, with this trick you are adding a great many explanatory variables to the model (i.e. J dummy variables will be created, and if you interact each of these with Z_i then you are adding J explanatory variables). In fact, you can show that, if you use this trick, the conditional logit model will end up being equivalent to the multinomial logit model. Hence, by appropriate definitions of coefficients and explanatory variables, the two models end up being the same. Thus, it was not strictly necessary to have separate sections of this textbook on multinomial and conditional logit. Nevertheless, since both terms are commonly used, it is useful to explain them fully.

Given the close relationship between conditional and multinomial logit models, we will not discuss estimation and testing in detail. Suffice it to note that relevant computer packages can do maximum likelihood estimation and likelihood-based hypothesis testing and implement various other estimators (e.g. heteroskedasticity consistent estimators).

9.3   Limited dependent variable models

In this section of the chapter, we will consider some regression-type models where the dependent variable is not continuous but rather is restricted in various ways. We begin with the *tobit* model, which is an example of a model where the dependent variable is censored. Following that, we discuss the case where the dependent variable is a count (i.e. the dependent variable can take on values $0, 1, 2, 3, \ldots$).

9.3.1   Tobit

In some cases, you will find that your data are censored in some manner. For instance, in a survey, individuals may be asked to report their income, but if it is above \$100 000, their income will be recorded as '\$100 000 or above'. In the example we used for the probit and logit models, we used data on whether an individual had an extramarital affair or not, which involved a 0–1 dummy dependent variable. However, the survey actually asked the number of affairs an individual had. Each individual could answer 0, 1, 2, etc. and the final category was 'ten or more'. So individuals who had 11, 12, etc. affairs all would answer 'ten or more'. These are examples of censoring. For individuals affected by the censoring, we do not know the true value of the dependent variable, but only know it is more or less than some amount.

There are many types of censoring that could occur, and many appropriate econometric models have been developed. In this section, we will discuss only one of them: the tobit model. Other models for censored data are similar and, if you understand the tobit model, you should have no problem figuring them out.

The tobit model has the dependent variable as being censored at zero. That is, we have the multiple regression model

$$Y_i^* = \alpha + \beta_1 X_{1i} + \beta_2 X_{2i} + \cdots + \beta_k X_{ki} + \varepsilon_i.$$

We do not observe the dependent variable Y_i^*. Instead we observe Y_i where

$$Y_i = Y_i^* \text{ if } Y_i^* > 0,$$
$$Y_i = 0 \text{ if } Y_i^* \leq 0.$$

As an example of how a tobit model might arise, consider an economic model that relates the desired investment level of a firm to its characteristics. The corresponding regression model would have desired investment being the dependent variable and firm characteristics being the explanatory variables. However, in practice, data on desired investment are rarely available. Instead, actual investment is observed. If negative investment is impossible, then actual investment is only equal to desired investment if the latter is positive. Negative values of desired investment become zero values of actual investment.

Before discussing the tobit model, we should explain why simply using OLS on the regression model using the observed data is not appropriate. That is, you may think you can just run the regression

$$Y_i = \alpha + \beta_1 X_{1i} + \beta_2 X_{2i} + \cdots + \beta_k X_{ki} + \varepsilon_i.$$

It turns out that, in this case, the OLS estimator is biased. We will not prove this, but rather illustrate the problems associated with the use of OLS methods in graphs. Figure 9.1 is an XY plot of a dataset that has been artificially simulated from the simple regression model

$$Y_i^* = \alpha + \beta X_i + \varepsilon_i.$$

Also drawn on Figure 9.1 is the true regression line used to construct the data.

Now suppose that the data in Figure 9.1 are censored. In particular, we construct $Y_i = Y_i^*$ for positive values of Y_i^*. Otherwise we set $Y_i = 0$. These data are plotted in Figure 9.2 (look at all those data points at $Y = 0$). Also on Figure 9.2 is the true regression line (the same as in Figure 9.1) along with a fitted regression line obtained by running a regression of Y on X. You can see that the OLS estimator regression line is far from the true one (i.e. OLS is biased). In order to fit the data as well as possible, the OLS

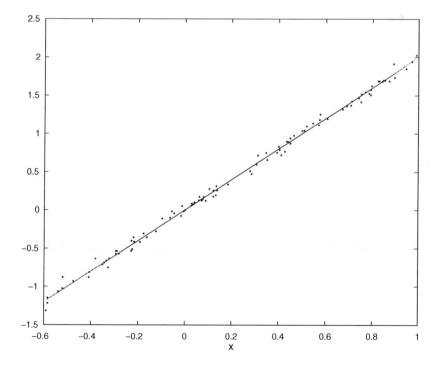

Figure 9.1 XY plot of original dataset and true regression line.

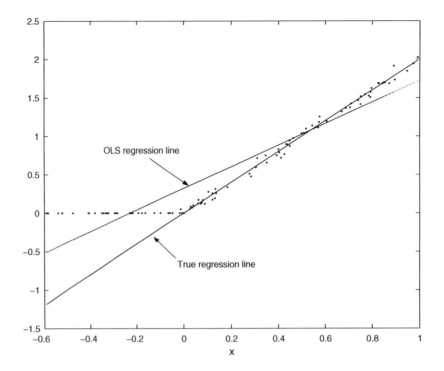

Figure 9.2 *XY* plot of censored dataset and true and OLS regression lines.

line gets pulled in the direction of all those censored observations. Figure 9.2 also suggests that, the more censored points you have, the worse the bias will be. This is indeed the case.

The previous figures and discussion make the point that, if you have censored observations, you should not simply use OLS. Instead you should use an appropriate estimator that recognises the censored nature of the dependent variable. This is the tobit estimator. We will not describe it in detail, other than to note that it is a maximum likelihood estimator that correctly takes into account the censoring. The tobit estimator is available in most econometrics software packages. So you can automatically produce tobit estimates of $\alpha, \beta_1, \ldots, \beta_k$ along with the usual statistical information (e.g. a P-value for the test of whether each coefficient equals zero, a confidence interval for each coefficient, etc.). Likelihood-based hypothesis testing procedures can also easily be carried out. As with any regression model, the errors could be heteroskedastic. Relevant computer packages will contain heteroskedasticity consistent estimators for the tobit model.

We will say little about the interpretation of tobit results, since they are the same as for any regression model. For instance, β_j will have the usual marginal effects interpretation, only with respect to Y^*. That is, β_j is the marginal effect of X_j on Y^*, holding all other explanatory variables constant. Thus, if you have a good econometrics software package, estimation and testing in the tobit model is straightforward and interpretation of results is simple.

9.3.2 Working with count data

There are some applications where the dependent variable can only take on whole-number values $(0, 1, 2, 3, \ldots)$. We refer to data that takes this form as *count data*. The empirical example we will present below is taken from the health economics literature. The dependent variable is the number of doctor visits in a given year. Health economists are interested in investigating whether this dependent variable can be explained by variables such as family income, whether the individual has private health insurance, and other individual characteristics. This suggests that a multiple regression model is appropriate:

$$Y_i = \alpha + \beta_1 X_{1i} + \beta_2 X_{2i} + \cdots + \beta_k X_{ki} + \varepsilon_i.$$

The only problem with simply running this regression using OLS techniques is that it is not reasonable to assume that the dependent variable and the errors have normal distributions. A normal distribution is only suitable for a continuous random variable (one that allows for any value of the dependent variable to occur). For count data, the normal distribution is not appropriate.

Remember that all our basic theoretical derivations for the regression model in Chapter 3 were made under the classical assumptions, one of which is that the dependent variable and errors are normally distributed. However, many of the Chapter 3 derivations did not use all of the assumptions. For instance, the proof that OLS was unbiased did not use the normality assumption. The derivation of the variance of the OLS operator did not involve the normality assumption. This suggests that, even if we have count data, OLS might be acceptable. In many instances this is indeed the case. However, there are better estimators that can be used when the dependent variable is a count. In the next section, we introduce the main one of these – the *Poisson regression model* – and offer some discussion of other estimators.

The Poisson regression model

The Poisson regression model is the same as the regression model under the classical assumptions with one exception. The exception is that the dependent variable is assumed to have a Poisson distribution. In this textbook, we will not formally define the Poisson distribution. The key point is that it is a commonly used distribution for random variables that can take on values $0, 1, 2, 3, \ldots$. Given the Poisson assumption, the likelihood function can be defined and a maximum likelihood estimator developed. This estimator is available in many econometrics software packages. So you can automatically obtain estimates of $\alpha, \beta_1, \ldots, \beta_k$ in the Poisson regression model along with the usual statistical information (e.g. a P-value for the test of whether each coefficient equals zero, a confidence interval for each coefficient, etc.). Likelihood-based hypothesis testing procedures can also easily be carried out. As with all the other models in this chapter, econometrics packages allow for robust estimation of the variance of coefficients (i.e. heteroskedasticity consistent estimation can be done).

Hence, estimation and testing in the Poisson regression model can easily be done if you have an appropriate econometrics computer package. We must now turn to interpretation. The Poisson distribution (like the normal and most other distributions) has a mean. This mean is commonly denoted by λ. So, if the dependent variable, Y_i, has a Poisson distribution, we say

$$E(Y_i) = \lambda_i.$$

Under the classical assumptions, remember, we had (in the case of simple regression) $E(Y_i) = \beta X_i$. The Poisson regression model could achieve this by setting

$$E(Y_i) = \lambda_i = \beta X_i.$$

In practice, since Y_i cannot be negative, it is more common to set

$$E(Y_i) = \lambda_i = \exp(\beta X_i),$$

and it is this latter choice that is included in most econometrics computer packages. We will assume this form for the Poisson regression model in the following material.

Coefficients in the Poisson regression model can be related to marginal effects by noting that

$$\frac{dE(Y_i)}{dX_i} = \beta \exp(\beta X_i).$$

The extension to multiple regression is straightforward. That is, if

$$E(Y_i) = \lambda_i = \exp(\alpha + \beta_1 X_{1i} + \beta_2 X_{2i} + \cdots + \beta_k X_{ki}),$$

then $\beta_j \exp(\beta_j X_{ji})$ measures how much the dependent variable is expected to change when X_j changes by one unit, holding all other explanatory variables constant.

Some computer packages also produce the *incidence rate ratio*. This calculates $E(Y)$ for some values of $X_1, X_2, \ldots, X_k$ and then changes one of the explanatory variables by one unit, calculates a new $E(Y)$ and then takes the ratio of the latter to the former. Derivations using the exponential function show that this is

$$\frac{\exp(\alpha + \beta_1 X_1 + \cdots + \beta_j(X_j + 1) + \cdots + \beta_k X_k)}{\exp(\alpha + \beta_1 X_1 + \cdots + \beta_j X_j + \cdots + \beta_k X_k)} = \exp(\beta_j).$$

The incidence rate ratio is not exactly the same as the marginal effect we have discussed for the multiple regression model, but it is a way of measuring the effect of a one-unit change in an explanatory variable on the dependent variable (holding all other explanatory variables constant). In the count data model it is a useful measure since it just depends on the coefficient and not on the explanatory variables.

Note also that, if the explanatory variable is logged to begin with (as it is in many applications), the interpretation simplifies. That is, if

$$E(Y_i) = \lambda_i = \exp(\beta \ln(X_i))$$
$$= X_i \exp(\beta),$$

then $\exp(\beta)$ is the conventional marginal effect. As a final general comment, the issues surrounding how to interpret marginal effects in the count data model are similar to those discussed in Chapter 4 (i.e. where we discussed how to interpret regression coefficients when dependent and/or explanatory variables are logged).

Testing for overdispersion in the Poisson regression model

The Poisson regression model has one restrictive assumption that does not occur in the regression model with normal errors. A property of the Poisson distribution is that its mean and variance are the same. With the normal distribution, the mean (often denoted μ) and variance (often denoted σ^2) are completely different things. In terms of the Poisson regression model, we said

$$E(Y_i) = \lambda_i,$$

but now we know this also implies

$$var(Y_i) = \lambda_i.$$

Is this a good assumption? The answer to this question depends on the particular dataset. In some applications it may be reasonable, in others it may not be. But this reasoning does suggest that it is important to test the hypothesis

$$H_0: E(Y_i) = var(Y_i).$$

There are several tests of this hypothesis (and relevant econometrics computer packages can calculate them for you). However, one test, which we will call the Cameron–Trivedi test after its originators, is easy to do in practice. Such tests are referred to as *tests of overdispersion*. To motivate this terminology, note that variance is a measure of 'dispersion', and, if H_0 is false, then the variance tends to be above (or 'over') what the Poisson regression model says it should be.

The Cameron–Trivedi test involves first estimating the Poisson regression model (using maximum likelihood methods) and obtaining the fitted values of the dependent variable. Let us call these fitted values $\widehat{\lambda}_i$ for $i = 1, \ldots, N$. The data and these fitted values can be used to construct a new variable:

$$Z_i = \frac{\left(Y_i - \widehat{\lambda}_i\right)^2 - Y_i}{\widehat{\lambda}_i \sqrt{2}}.$$

For reasons we will not explain, if H_0 is true, this variable should have mean zero. A simple way of testing this hypothesis is to run a regression of Z on an intercept and see if the intercept is significant using the familiar t-statistic. If the intercept is found to be insignificant, this suggests that H_0 is true and the Poisson regression model is an appropriate model to use. However, if the intercept is found to be significant, then the Poisson regression model should not be used.

What should you do if you use a test of overdispersion and it indicates the Poisson regression model should not be used? There are many alternatives. Perhaps the most popular one is the *negative binomial regression model*. We will not explain in detail what this is, but note only that it allows for $E(Y_i)$ and $var(Y_i)$ to be different from one another and is available in some econometrics software packages. The interpretation of regression coefficients is the same as for the Poisson regression model.[6]

Example: The demand for medical care

Suppose we are interested in explaining the factors that influence the demand for medical care by the elderly. We have data from $N = 4\,406$ Americans aged 66 and older, based on a survey taken in 1987.[7] The dependent and explanatory variables are:

- $Y =$ number of doctor visits in the past year;
- $INCOME =$ family income (in tens of thousands of dollars);
- $MALE = 1$ if the individual is male ($= 0$ if female);
- $EXHLTH = 1$ if the individual claims to be in excellent health ($= 0$ otherwise);
- $POORHLTH = 1$ if the individual claims to be in poor health ($= 0$ otherwise);
- $AGE =$ age in years (divided by ten);
- $MARRIED = 1$ if the individual is married ($= 0$ if unmarried);
- $INSURE = 1$ if the individual has private health insurance ($= 0$ otherwise).

Empirical results using the Poisson regression model are presented in Table 9.5. With the possible exception of $INCOME$ (which is significant at the 10 % level, but not at the 5 % level), all of the explanatory variables are strongly significant. This is something you often see with large datasets (such as this one with $N = 4\,406$).

Table 9.5 Poisson regression results for demand for medical care data.

Variable	Coefficient	P-value for $\beta_j = 0$	95 % confidence interval	Incidence rate ratio
Intercept	1.78	0.00	[1.62, 1.94]	—
$INCOME$	0.004	0.08	[−0.001, 0.008]	1.004
$MALE$	−0.09	0.00	[−0.11, −0.06]	0.92
$EXHLTH$	−0.49	0.00	[−0.54, −0.43]	0.62
$POORHLTH$	0.53	0.00	[0.49, 0.56]	1.69
AGE	−0.03	0.00	[−0.05, −0.01]	0.97
$MARRIED$	−0.06	0.00	[−0.03, −0.09]	0.94
$INSURE$	0.29	0.00	[0.26, 0.32]	1.33

As an example of how you might interpret these results, note that the coefficient on *EXHLTH* is negative. This means (unsurprisingly) that individuals who are in excellent health are less likely to visit their doctor. The incidence rate ratio is 0.62, which implies that individuals in excellent health visit their doctors 62 % as often as individuals who are not in excellent health. As another example, note that the incidence rate ratio for *INSURE* is 1.33. This means that individuals with private insurance visit their doctors 33 % more than those without private insurance, holding the other explanatory variables constant.

However, tests for overdispersion provide strong evidence that the Poisson regression model is not appropriate for this dataset. If you are doing a serious empirical application with these data, you should try the negative binomial regression model.

9.3.3 Extensions

Throughout this chapter, we have worked with cross-sectional data. It is worth noting that all of the models in this chapter can be extended to handle panel data. We will not describe how to do this in detail, other than to note that many of the models of Chapter 8 (e.g. the random effects model) can be adapted (e.g. there exist random effects probit models, etc.). Most relevant econometrics software packages will allow you to estimate the panel versions of qualitative choice and limited dependent variable models automatically.

Many other kinds of model exist for use when the dependent variable is restricted in specific ways. It is not possible to cover every possible limited dependent variable or qualitative choice model. However, we will briefly mention that *duration models* are used when the dependent variable is a duration (e.g. in a labor economics application the dependent variable might be the number of months an individual has been unemployed). It is also worth noting that, within the general classes of logit and probit models, there are many specialized variants (e.g. we previously briefly mentioned ordered probit and nested logit, but others do exist).

Another type of model that can be interpreted as a limited dependent variable model is the *treatment effects model*. To motivate this model, note that, in medical statistics, there are many cases where interest centres on the effect of a treatment on a health outcome. Models have been developed to estimate such *treatment effects*. In economics there are also many cases where interest centres on the effect of 'treatments' (e.g. participating in a training programme) on 'outcomes' (e.g. the salary achieved). In many economic and medical applications, statistical analysis is complicated by the fact that individuals are not randomly assigned to treatments. A related problem is non-compliance, where an individual allocated to a certain treatment may not take up the treatment. Thus, this is an area where the medical statistics and econometrics literatures have a lot in common. In an ideal world, if you could observe the outcome for each individual in both the treated and untreated state, you could clearly see the effect of the treatment. Suppose, for instance,

you could find out an individual's salary if he or she had participated in the training programme as well as the salary the individual would have obtained if he or she had not participated. The difference between these two salaries would then be a measure of the
benefit provided by the training programme. Of course, in practice you would not be
able to observe such counterfactual outcomes. So, in this sense, the dependent variable
is limited and falls in the general category of models discussed in this chapter. Treatment
effects models are becoming increasingly popular with researchers interested in estimating
the benefits of various programmes or policies.

We mention all these models here so you will know that they exist should you ever
come across an empirical problem that calls for them. At least knowing the names of
the models should allow you to know where to look in an advanced econometrics textbook.

9.4   Chapter summary

This chapter describes models for use when the dependent variable is limited to
take on a restricted range of values. The following is a summary of the main points
covered.

1. All of the models discussed in this book are similar to the multiple regression
   model in that they have a dependent variable depending on explanatory variables. However, the limited nature of the dependent variable implies that standard OLS or GLS methods should not be used.

2. Qualitative choice models involve data where individuals choose between various alternatives. Binary choice models involve two alternatives, and thus the
   dependent variable is a dummy variable. Multinomial choice models involve
   more than two alternatives.

3. Probit and logit are the two most popular binary choice models. Estimation of
   the coefficients in these models can be done using maximum likelihood methods. Computer software packages will provide standard statistical information
   (e.g. P-values for testing whether each coefficient equals zero, confidence intervals for each coefficient, etc.).

4. The interpretation of coefficients in logit and probit models is not as straightforward as in the multiple regression model. Coefficients cannot be interpreted
   simply as marginal effects. This chapter illustrated some other ways empirical
   information could be presented (e.g. predicted probabilities of making a choice,
   odds ratios, etc.).

5. Multinomial logit and multinomial probit are the two most popular multinomial choice models. Estimation of the coefficients in these models can be
   done using maximum likelihood methods. Computer software packages will

provide standard statistical information (e.g. *P*-values for testing whether each coefficient equals zero, confidence intervals for each coefficient, etc.).

6. Multinomial logit and probit models have multiple regression-like equations, with each equation relating to the choice between an alternative and a benchmark alternative.

7. Coefficients in these models cannot be interpreted directly as marginal effects, but this chapter discussed some alternative ways of presenting empirical results.

8. The multinomial logit model involves an independence of irrelevant alternatives assumption that may be a drawback in some applications. The multinomial probit model does not involve this assumption, but can be hard to estimate if the number of alternatives is large.

9. The conditional logit model can be used if you have more than two alternatives, but your explanatory variables relate to the alternatives (i.e. they vary across the alternatives and are not solely characteristics of the individual making the choice).

10. There are many other types of model where the dependent variable is limited (and at the end of the chapter, we offered a brief introduction to some of them). In this chapter we discussed two important ones: the tobit model and the Poisson regression model.

11. The tobit model is an example of a censored regression model. It has the dependent variable being censored at zero.

12. Estimation of the coefficients in the tobit model can be done using maximum likelihood methods. Computer software packages will provide standard statistical information (e.g. *P*-values for testing whether each coefficient equals zero, confidence intervals for each coefficient, etc.). Coefficients can be interpreted in the usual marginal effects manner.

13. The Poisson regression model is commonly used when the dependent variable is a count.

14. Estimation of the coefficients in the Poisson regression model can be done using maximum likelihood methods. Computer software packages will provide standard statistical information (e.g. *P*-values for testing whether each coefficient equals zero, confidence intervals for each coefficient, etc.).

15. Interpretation of coefficients in the Poisson regression model is very similar to interpretation of coefficients with multiple regression. However, this chapter discussed some interpretational issues that arise and introduced the concept of an incidence rate ratio.

16. The Poisson regression model has a restrictive assumption in that the mean and variance of the dependent variable (for given values of the explanatory variables) are the same. Tests of overdispersion can be done to see if this assumption is violated. If it is violated, another model such as the negative binomial regression model should be used.

Exercises

The data for these questions are provided on the website associated with this book.

1. In the body of the chapter, we wrote out the form of the likelihood function for the probit and logit models. Write out the likelihood function for the tobit model in a similar form.

2. Assume you have the same binomial choice set-up as in the chapter. That is, you have a simple regression model

$$Y_i^* = \beta X_i + \varepsilon_i,$$

where the errors are assumed to satisfy the classical assumptions, but Y_i^* is unobservable. Instead you observe $Y_i = 1$ if individual i makes choice 1 and $Y_i = 0$ if choice 0 is made.

   (a) What are the properties of the errors in the regression of Y on X? That is, if you work with

$$Y_i = \beta X_i + u_i,$$

   what are the properties of u_i? This regression is called the *linear probability model*.

   (b) In light of your answer to part (a), would OLS be an appropriate estimator? Explain why.

   (c) Would GLS be an appropriate estimator? Explain why.

3. Dataset COMMUTING.XLS contains data on $N = 390$ individuals on their commuting choice between bicycle, bus, and car. The data take the form
   - $Y = 0$ if the individual bicycles to work, $= 1$ if the individual takes the bus to work, and $= 2$ if the individual takes the car to work;
   - $INCOME =$ income (in thousands of dollars);
   - $DISTANCE =$ distance to work (in miles);
   - $COMCAR =$ commuting time by car (in hours);
   - $COMBUS =$ commuting time by bus (in hours);
   - $COMBIKE =$ commuting time by bicycle (in hours).

   (a) Estimate a multinomial logit model using these data and interpret your results (e.g. using various sorts of marginal effect, predicted probability, and odds ratio).

   (b) Estimate a multinomial probit model using these data and interpret your results (e.g. using various sorts of marginal effect, predicted probability, and odds ratio).

   (c) This is a supplementary question that goes beyond textbook material. But you should be able to do it either with a good computer software package and manual or through reading in an advanced econometrics textbook. Carry out hypothesis tests to decide whether the multinomial logit or probit model is to be preferred with this dataset. Is the independence of irrelevant alternatives assumption satisfied?

4. The Poisson regression example in this chapter uses the number of doctor visits as the dependent variable. The dataset, deb.trivedi.xls contains several other possible dependent variables and many more explanatory variables. The first six columns of this dataset are potential dependent variables, the remaining columns are potential explanatory variables. The paper 'Demand for medical care by the elderly: a finite mixture approach' by P. Deb and P. Trivedi, published in the *Journal of Applied Econometrics* in 1997, provides a full description of these data (see Table 1 of their paper for a full listing of variables). The general idea of this question is to get you experimenting with count data models with different dependent and explanatory variables, as you would if you were writing an empirical project on this topic. Here are a few precise questions to get you started.

   (a) Using as a dependent variable the number of hospital visits (labeled #hospvisit in the dataset), estimate a Poisson regression model using all the explanatory variables.
   (b) Interpret the coefficient estimates obtained in part (a).
   (c) Discuss the significance of the explanatory variables.
   (d) Calculate incidence rate ratios for the explanatory variables.
   (e) Do an overdispersion test. Does this indicate that the Poisson regression model is an appropriate one?
   (f) Estimate and interpret results from a negative binomial regression model. Note: this is an ambitious question that involves going beyond material in this textbook. So only do this question if you have good computer software that can estimate this model and a manual that explains the model.

5. Use the data from exercise 4 for this exercise. Take the variable that counts the number of hospital visits (labeled #hospvisit in the dataset) and create a new variable that is a dummy variable equaling 1 for individuals who have had at least one hospital visit and equaling 0 for individuals who did not go to the hospital. Use this new dummy variable as the dependent variable when answering the following questions.

   (a) Estimate a logit model using the explanatory variables in the dataset and interpret your results as described in the chapter (e.g. using various sorts of marginal effect, predicted probability, and odds ratio).
   (b) Estimate a probit model using the explanatory variables in the dataset and interpret your results as described in the chapter (e.g. using various sorts of marginal effect, predicted probability, and odds ratio).

Endnotes

1. The terminology for this is that with the simple regression model there is an *analytical solution* to the problem of how to maximize the likelihood function. However, for probit and logit an analytical solution does not exist and we have to resort to *numerical optimization algorithms*.
2. The advanced textbook *Econometric Analysis* by William Greene (published by Prentice-Hall) has a good chapter on qualitative choice models.
3. This paper by R. Fair is called 'A theory of extramarital affairs' and was published in the *Journal of Political Economy* in 1978.
4. Another complication with multinomial probit is that calculating probabilities with the multi-variate normal distribution can take the computer a lot of time. For the standard normal distribution, statistical tables (or their computer equivalent) exist and calculations are easy. However, comparable things do not exist with the multivariate normal distibution, and computationally demanding simulation methods are required.
5. The interested reader is referred to the paper by Paap and Franses called 'A dynamic multinomial probit model for brand choice with different long-run and short-run effects of marketing mix variables' published in the *Journal of Applied Econometrics* in 2000. The data we use are obtained from the *Journal of Applied Econometrics* data archive at http://econ.queensu.ca/jae/.
6. Advanced econometrics textbooks will discuss this model (and others). Alternatively, the book *Regression Analysis of Count Data* by C. Cameron and P. Trivedi (published by Cambridge University Press) is an excellent one with a sole focus on count data.
7. This example uses data from the paper 'Demand for medical care by the elderly: a finite mixture approach' by P. Deb and P. Trivedi, published in the *Journal of Applied Econometrics* in 1997. This paper provides more details about the data.

CHAPTER 10

Bayesian Econometrics

10.1 An overview of Bayesian econometrics

Throughout this book, we have discussed econometric methods using the classical approach to statistics.[1] However, there is another popular way of doing statistical inference, known as *Bayesian statistics*. Bayesian statistical methods are very popular in many applied fields (e.g. medical and biological statistics). In econometrics, Bayesian methods are used by a (growing) minority of researchers. Thus, the student simply interested in learning the dominant approach to econometrics could skip the current chapter altogether. Nevertheless, the Bayesian approach is an attractive and growing one. The well-educated econometrician should at least know the basic ideas of Bayesian econometrics, and the purpose of this chapter is to provide them. The reader interested in learning more about the Bayesian approach is referred to Geweke (2005), Koop (2003), Koop, Poirier, & Tobias (2007), Lancaster (2004), Poirier (1995), or Zellner (1971), listed in the bibliography at the end of this book. This chapter offers only a brief introduction to the field. It is organized so that the first half provides the basic ideas of Bayesian econometrics and the second half shows how they work in the context of a particular model you should be very familiar with by now: the simple regression model.

Bayesian theory

Bayesian econometrics is based on a few simple rules of probability. This is one of the chief advantages of the Bayesian approach. All of the things that an econometrician would wish to do, such as estimate the parameters of a model, compare different models, or obtain predictions from a model, involve the same rules of probability. Bayesian methods are, thus, universal and can be used any time a researcher is interested in using data to learn about a feature of interest.

To motivate the simplicity of the Bayesian approach, let us consider two random variables, A and B.[2] *Bayes rule* (see Appendix B, Theorem B.1) can be used to write

$$p(B|A) = \frac{p(A|B)p(B)}{p(A)},$$

where $p(B|A)$ is the probability of B occurring conditional on A having occurred (i.e. the *conditional probability* of B given A) and $p(B)$ is the *marginal probability* of B (i.e. the probability of B occurring without regard to what has happened to A). $p(A|B)$ and $p(A)$ are similar conditional and marginal probabilities for A.

Bayesian econometrics repeatedly uses Bayes rule – replacing A and B with appropriate arguments. To see what these 'appropriate arguments' are, let us return to the basic ideas of econometrics. Econometrics is concerned with using data to learn about something the researcher is interested in. Just what the 'something' is depends on the context. However, in economics we typically work with models that depend on parameters. For instance, in the simple regression model, the parameters are β and σ^2. In Chapter 3, we discussed using OLS to learn about β.

Let y be a compact notation for the data and θ be a compact notation for all the parameters in a model that seeks to explain y. We are interested in learning about θ based on the data y. Bayesian econometrics uses Bayes rule to do so. The Bayesian would replace B with θ and A with y in the previous equation to obtain

$$p(\theta|y) = \frac{p(y|\theta)p(\theta)}{p(y)}.$$

Bayesians treat $p(\theta|y)$ as being of fundamental interest. That is, it directly addresses the question 'Given the data, what do we know about θ?'. The treatment of θ as a random variable is controversial among some econometricians. Classical econometrics assumes that θ is not a random variable. For instance, in Chapter 3, we used the OLS estimator, $\widehat{\beta}$, to estimate the slope coefficient in the regression, β. It was $\widehat{\beta}$ that was the random variable, and we worked out that it had a normal distribution with a certain mean and variance. β was not a random variable. It was implicitly assumed that there was some true value of β. We did not know what β was, but this true value was not random.

In contrast to this view, Bayesian econometrics is based on a view of probability that argues that our uncertainty about anything unknown can be expressed using the rules of probability. In the linear regression model, the Bayesian would say: 'Even if there is a true value for β, the fact that it is unknown means we should treat it as a random variable'. Bayesian econometrics involves learning about something unknown (e.g. coefficients in a regression) given something known (e.g. data), and the conditional probability of the unknown given the known is a way of summarizing what we have learned.

Having established that $p(\theta|y)$ is of fundamental interest for the econometrician interested in using data to learn about parameters in a model, let us now return to Bayes rule. In so far as we are only interested in learning about θ, we can ignore the term $p(y)$ since it does not involve θ. We can then write

$$p(\theta|y) \propto p(y|\theta)p(\theta).$$

The term $p(\theta|y)$ is referred to as the *posterior density*. The p.d.f. for the data given the parameters of the model, $p(y|\theta)$, is the *likelihood function* and $p(\theta)$ is the *prior density*. You often hear this relationship referred to as 'posterior is proportional to likelihood times prior'. At this stage, this may seem a little abstract and the manner in which priors and likelihoods are developed to allow for the calculation of the posterior may be unclear. Things should become clearer when we return to the simple regression model.

The concept of a likelihood function was defined in Chapter 3. For the linear regression model, we denoted it by $L(\beta)$, and here we will adopt a similar notation and rewrite the posterior as

$$p(\theta|y) \propto L(\theta)p(\theta),$$

where $L(\theta) = p(y|\theta)$. Formally, the likelihood is the probability density function of the data conditional on the parameters of the model, viewed as a function of the parameters. We have made this clear by writing it as a function only of the parameters as $L(\theta)$.

The prior, $p(\theta)$, does not depend on the data (i.e. there is no y anywhere in it). Accordingly, it contains any non-data information available about θ. In other words, it summarizes what you know about θ prior to seeing the data. As an example, suppose θ is a parameter that reflects returns to scale in a production process. In many cases it is reasonable to assume that returns to scale are roughly constant. Thus, before you look at the data, you have prior information about θ, in that you would expect it to be approximately 1. Prior information is a controversial aspect of Bayesian methods. As we will see in the case of the regression model, it is possible to use both informative and non-informative priors for the parameters in any model. Non-informative priors are often used by researchers who do not wish to incorporate any prior information.

The posterior, $p(\theta|y)$, is the p.d.f. that is of fundamental interest. It summarizes all we know about θ after (i.e. posterior to) seeing the data. $p(\theta|y) \propto L(\theta)p(\theta)$ can be thought of as an updating rule whereby the data allow us to update our prior views about θ. The result is the posterior which combines both data and non-data information.

In addition to learning about parameters of a model, an econometrician might be interested in comparing different models. The classical analogue to this is hypothesis testing, although there are significant differences between classical hypothesis testing and Bayesian model comparison. A model is formally defined by a likelihood function and a prior.

Suppose we have m different models, M_i for $i = 1, \ldots, m$, that all seek to explain y (e.g. m regression models that all have the same dependent variable, but differ in their explanatory variables). M_i depends on parameters θ_i. In cases where many models are being entertained, it is important to be explicit about which model is under consideration. Hence, the posterior for the parameters calculated using M_i is written as

$$p(\theta_i | y, M_i) = \frac{p(y|\theta_i, M_i)p(\theta_i|M_i)}{p(y|M_i)} = \frac{L(\theta_i, M_i)p(\theta_i|M_i)}{p(y|M_i)}$$

and the notation makes clear that we now have a posterior, likelihood, and prior for each model (i.e. all probabilities above are written as being conditional on model M_i).

The logic of Bayesian econometrics suggests that we use Bayes rule to derive a probability statement about what we do not know (i.e. whether a model is a correct one or not) conditional on what we do know (i.e. the data). This means the *posterior model probability* can be used to assess the degree of support for M_i. Using our original expression for Bayes rule for random variables A and B, we can set $B = M_i$ and $A = y$:

$$p(M_i | y) = \frac{p(y|M_i)p(M_i)}{p(y)}.$$

Of the terms in this formula, $p(M_i)$ is referred to as the *prior model probability*. Since it does not involve the data, it measures how likely we believe M_i to have generated the data before seeing the data. $p(y|M_i)$ is called the *marginal likelihood*. The marginal likelihood can be calculated using the equation

$$p(y|M_i) = \int L(\theta_i, M_i)p(\theta_i|M_i)\, d\theta_i.$$

For the reader unfamiliar with integration, note that it is the extension of the summation operator to continuous variables. A consideration of the case where θ_i is a discrete random variable (see Appendix B, Definition B.6) provides some intuition. Suppose θ_i can take on two values, 1 or 2. Then the marginal likelihood becomes

$$p(y|M_i) = L(\theta_i = 1, M_i)p(\theta_i = 1|M_i) + L(\theta_i = 2, M_i)p(\theta_i = 2|M_i),$$

where $L(\theta_i = 1, M_i)$ is the likelihood function for model M_i evaluated at $\theta_i = 1$ and $p(\theta_i = 1|M_i)$ is the prior for model M_i evaluated at $\theta_i = 1$ (and analogous definitions apply for $\theta_i = 2$). Thus, the marginal likelihood is a weighted average of the likelihood function. In fact, it is the expected value of the likelihood function. In Chapter 3, we discussed the maximum likelihood estimator. The marginal likelihood introduced here involves similar concepts but is the expected value of the likelihood function instead of the maximum.

The proof of why the marginal likelihood takes this form uses Bayes theorem and the fact that probabilities sum to 1. The reader unfamiliar with integration may find the proof slightly difficult and can skip to the next paragraph without losing the thread of the argument. Previously, Bayes theorem gave us

$$p(\theta_i|y, M_i) = \frac{L(\theta_i, M_i)p(\theta_i|M_i)}{p(y|M_i)}.$$

If we integrate both sides of this equation with respect to θ_i, use the fact that $\int p(\theta_i|y, M_i)\, d\theta_i = 1$ (since probability density functions integrate to 1), note that $p(y|M_i)$ does not have θ_i in it (and hence can be taken outside the integral sign) and rearrange, we can obtain the formula for the marginal likelihood given above.

Remember that the marginal likelihood is a key component in the posterior model probability:

$$p(M_i|y) = \frac{p(y|M_i)p(M_i)}{p(y)}.$$

Since the denominator, $p(y)$, is often hard to calculate directly, it is common to compare two models, i and j, using the *posterior odds ratio* which is simply the ratio of their posterior model probabilities:

$$PO_{ij} = \frac{p(M_i|y)}{p(M_j|y)} = \frac{p(y|M_i)p(M_i)}{p(y|M_j)p(M_j)}.$$

Note that, since $p(y)$ is common to both models, it cancels out when we take the ratio. If we calculate the posterior odds ratio comparing every pair of models and we assume that our set of models is exhaustive (in that $p(M_1|y) + p(M_2|y) + \cdots + p(M_m|y) = 1$), then we can use posterior odds ratios to calculate the posterior model probabilities for every model. For instance, if we have $m = 2$ models, then we can use the two equations

$$p(M_1|y) + p(M_2|y) = 1$$

and

$$PO_{12} = \frac{p(M_1|y)}{p(M_2|y)}$$

to work out

$$p(M_1|y) = \frac{PO_{12}}{1 + PO_{12}}$$

and

$$p(M_2|y) = 1 - p(M_1|y).$$

Thus, knowledge of the posterior odds ratio allows us to figure out the posterior model probabilities.

To introduce some more jargon, econometricians may be interested in model comparison when equal prior weight is attached to each model. That is, $p(M_i) = p(M_j)$ or, equivalently, the *prior odds ratio*, which is $\frac{p(M_i)}{p(M_j)}$, is set to 1. In this case, the posterior odds ratio becomes simply the ratio of marginal likelihoods and is given a special name, the *Bayes factor*, defined as

$$BF_{ij} = \frac{p(y|M_i)}{p(y|M_j)}.$$

Let us now compare the Bayesian approach to model comparison with the classical approach to hypothesis testing. The Bayesian approach simply involves calculating $p(M_j|y)$ which can be interpreted as being 'the probability that model M_j generated the data'. This is a simple and intuitive concept about which little more needs to be said. It does not matter whether the researcher is comparing two models or 20 or whether the models are nested or non-nested:[3] the same basic idea is used. As we have seen in previous chapters, classical hypothesis tests have a different motivation. Standard approaches only allow for the comparison of two hypotheses (e.g. $H_0: \beta = 0$ versus $H_1: \beta \neq 0$). Furthermore, most hypothesis tests (and all tests in this book) involve only nested models. Although classical methods for non-nested hypothesis testing do exist, they are more sophisticated and typically are not covered in introductory econometrics textbooks. Classical hypothesis tests do not provide a number with a simple interpretation as reflecting the probability H_0 is true. Rather, classical hypothesis testing proceeds by assuming H_0 is true and deriving the distribution for a test statistic under this assumption. Then the researcher calculates the observed value for the test statistic. If the calculated value of the test statistic is very implausible (e.g. if there is less than a 5 % chance it could have occurred if the null hypothesis is true), then H_0 is rejected (and H_1 is accepted). Otherwise, H_0 is accepted. Of course, one cannot say 'the Bayesian approach is the correct one' or 'the classical approach is the correct one'. Both approaches are correct, but they are different and it is important to remember these differences when learning econometrics.

Another important distinction between Bayesian and classical econometrics can be made by introducing the concept of *Bayesian model averaging*. Classical econometricians (and some Bayesians) typically present empirical results based on a single model. For instance, in Chapter 2 we saw how the researcher might begin a multiple regression exercise by including many potential explanatory variables. Then, using hypothesis testing procedures, the researcher would drop out insignificant variables, leading to a final regression containing only significant variables. Since different choices of explanatory variables define different regression models, such a strategy can be interpreted as *model selection*. In contrast, many Bayesians prefer to average across models. To see why, suppose the researcher has many different models that shed light on a parameter of interest, θ (e.g. in a cross-country growth study we might have many regression models that all can be used to estimate the effect of education on economic growth). The Bayesian will be interested in the posterior, $p(\theta|y)$, which summarizes all that is known about θ given the data. As we have seen, the Bayesian can calculate the posterior model probability, $p(M_i|Data)$, for each of these models. A straightforward application of the rules of conditional probability tell us that

$$p(\theta|y) = \sum_{i=1}^{m} p(M_i|y)p(\theta|y, M_i).$$

In words, the Bayesian would work with the posterior in every model, $p(\theta|y, M_i)$, but then take a weighted average (with weights given by $p(M_i|y)$) in order to construct final results based on $p(\theta|y)$. This strategy is referred to as Bayesian model averaging.

On one level, our discussion of Bayesian econometrics could end right here. These few pages have outlined all the basic theoretical concepts required for the Bayesian to learn about parameters and compare models. We stress what an enormous advantage this is. Once you accept that unknown things (i.e. θ and M_i) are random variables, the rest of the Bayesian approach is non-controversial. It simply uses the rules of probability, which are mathematically true, to do econometrics. A benefit of this is that, if you keep these simple rules in mind, it is hard to lose sight of the big picture. When facing a new model, just remember that Bayesian econometrics requires selection of a prior and a likelihood. These can then be used to form the posterior, $p(\theta|y)$, which forms the basis for all inference about unknown parameters in a model. If you have many models and are interested in comparing them, you can use posterior model probabilities $p(M_i|y)$ for $i = 1, \ldots, m$ or the related concepts of the posterior odds ratio or Bayes factor. These few concepts can be used to carry out statistical inference in *any* application you may wish to consider. However, it is useful to see how these concepts work in the context of a particular model, and hence we turn to the linear regression model.

10.2   The normal linear regression model with natural conjugate prior and a single explanatory variable

10.2.1   The likelihood function

As in Chapter 3, we will work with the simple regression model

$$Y_i = \beta X_i + \varepsilon_i$$

under the classical assumptions:

1. $E(Y_i) = \beta X_i$.
2. $var(Y_i) = \sigma^2$.

3. $cov(Y_i, Y_j) = 0$ for $i \neq j$.
4. Y_i is normally distributed
5. X_i is fixed. It is not a random variable.

In Chapter 3, we showed how these assumptions implied

$$Y_i \text{ is independent } N(\beta X_i, \sigma^2)$$

for $i = 1, \ldots, N$ and that the formula for the p.d.f. of the normal distribution could be used to write the likelihood function as

$$L(\beta, \sigma^2) = \frac{1}{(2\pi\sigma^2)^{\frac{N}{2}}} \exp\left[-\frac{1}{2\sigma^2} \sum_{i=1}^{N} (Y_i - \beta X_i)^2\right],$$

where we have made explicit that the likelihood function depends on the parameters β and σ^2.

For future derivations, it proves convenient to rewrite the likelihood in a slightly different way. It can be shown that[4]

$$\sum_{i=1}^{N} (Y_i - \beta X_i)^2 = vs^2 + (\beta - \widehat{\beta})^2 \sum_{i=1}^{N} X_i^2,$$

where

$$v = N - 1,$$

$$\widehat{\beta} = \frac{\sum X_i Y_i}{\sum X_i^2},$$

and

$$s^2 = \frac{\sum \left(Y_i - \widehat{\beta} X_i\right)^2}{N - 1}.$$

In other words, we have written $\sum_{i=1}^{N} (Y_i - \beta X_i)^2$ in terms of $\widehat{\beta}$ (the OLS estimator for β) and s^2 (the OLS estimator of σ^2).

Using these results, we can write the likelihood function as

$$L(\beta, \sigma^2) = \frac{1}{(2\pi)^{\frac{N}{2}}} \left\{ \frac{1}{\sqrt{\sigma^2}} \exp\left[-\frac{1}{2} \frac{\left(\beta - \widehat{\beta}\right)^2}{\sigma^2 \left(\sum_{i=1}^{N} X_i^2\right)^{-1}} \right] \right\} \left\{ \frac{1}{\sqrt{\sigma^2}^v} \exp\left[-\frac{vs^2}{2\sigma^2} \right] \right\}.$$

For future reference, note that the first term in curly brackets is the p.d.f. of a normal density. The second term in curly brackets is a bit more complicated (we will discuss it in the appendix to this chapter). But suffice it to note that, if we are focusing on β and treating σ^2 as known, it can be ignored. That is, only terms that involve β will determine the shape of the likelihood function. Thus, we can suppress constants not involving β and (for the case where σ^2 is known) write the likelihood function as

$$L(\beta) \propto \frac{1}{\sqrt{\sigma^2}} \exp\left[-\frac{1}{2} \frac{\left(\beta - \widehat{\beta}\right)^2}{\sigma^2 \left(\sum_{i=1}^{N} X_i^2\right)^{-1}} \right].$$

10.2.2 The prior

Priors are meant to reflect any information the researcher has before seeing the data that she wishes to include. Hence, priors can take any form. However, it is common to choose particular classes of priors that are easy to interpret and/or make computation easier. *Natural conjugate priors* typically have both such advantages. A conjugate prior distribution is one that, when combined with the likelihood, yields a posterior that falls in the same class of distributions. A natural conjugate prior has the additional property that it has the same functional form as the likelihood function. These properties mean that the prior information can be interpreted in the same way as likelihood function information. In other words, the prior can be interpreted as arising from a fictitious dataset from the same process that generated the actual data.

As we did in Chapter 3, let us begin by assuming σ^2 is known. Thus, we must choose a prior for β which we denote by $p(\beta)$. Remember that the fact that we are not conditioning on the data means that $p(\beta)$ is a prior density, and the posterior density will be denoted by $p(\beta|y)$. The form of the likelihood function suggests that the natural conjugate prior will involve a normal distribution for β. This is indeed the case. As we will see, the natural conjugate prior has the form

$$\beta \sim N(\underline{\beta}, \sigma^2 \underline{V}),$$

where $\underline{\beta}$ and $\underline{V}$ are so-called *prior hyperparameters* chosen by the researcher to reflect the prior information. Bayesians refer to this process of choosing a distributional form and prior hyperparameters as *prior elicitation*. The exact interpretation of the hyperparameters becomes clearer once you have seen their role in the posterior, and hence we defer a deeper discussion of how $\underline{\beta}$ and $\underline{V}$ might be chosen until the next section. In this chapter, we will follow a common convention and use bars under parameters (e.g. $\underline{\beta}$) to denote parameters of a prior density, and bars over parameters (e.g. $\overline{\beta}$) to denote parameters of a posterior density.

10.2.3   The posterior

The posterior density summarizes all the information, both prior and data based, that we have about the unknown parameter, β. As we have seen, it is proportional to the likelihood times the prior density. Before beginning, one fact should be mentioned: when deriving results relating to the p.d.f. of a random variable, we can ignore constants that do not involve the random variable. So, for instance, Appendix B, Definition B.10 says that, if X is a random variable with a normal distribution (i.e. $X \sim N(\mu, \sigma^2)$), its p.d.f. is given by

$$p(X) = \frac{1}{\sqrt{2\pi\sigma^2}} \exp\left[-\frac{1}{2\sigma^2}(X - \mu)^2\right].$$

Thus, if we find that a random variable has a p.d.f. of this form, we can say it is $N(\mu, \sigma^2)$. However, we can go further and say that, if we find a random variable, X, with p.d.f. proportional to this form, then we can say it is $N(\mu, \sigma^2)$. That is, if

$$p(X) \propto \exp\left[-\frac{1}{2\sigma^2}(X - \mu)^2\right],$$

then $X \sim N(\mu, \sigma^2)$. We can ignore multiplicative terms that do not involve the random variable, X, in our derivations. Here, $\frac{1}{\sqrt{2\pi\sigma^2}}$ does not have an X in it, so we can ignore it.

To return to the simple regression model, we can use the form for the likelihood derived above and the normal p.d.f. for the prior to obtain the posterior:

$$p(\beta|y) \propto L(\beta)p(\beta)$$

$$\propto \left\{\frac{1}{\sqrt{\sigma^2}}\exp\left[-\frac{1}{2}\frac{\left(\beta - \hat{\beta}\right)^2}{\sigma^2\left(\sum_{i=1}^{N} X_i^2\right)^{-1}}\right]\right\}\left\{\frac{1}{\sqrt{\sigma^2\underline{V}}}\exp\left[-\frac{1}{2}\frac{\left(\beta - \underline{\beta}\right)^2}{\sigma^2\underline{V}}\right]\right\}$$

$$\propto \exp\left[-\frac{1}{2}\frac{\left(\beta - \hat{\beta}\right)^2}{\sigma^2\left(\sum_{i=1}^{N} X_i^2\right)^{-1}} - \frac{1}{2}\frac{\left(\beta - \underline{\beta}\right)^2}{\sigma^2\underline{V}}\right],$$

$$\propto \exp\left[-\frac{1}{2}\frac{\left(\beta - \overline{\beta}\right)^2}{\sigma^2\overline{V}}\right]$$

where

$$\overline{V} = \frac{1}{\underline{V}^{-1} + \sum X_i^2},$$

$$\overline{\beta} = \overline{V}\left(\underline{V}^{-1}\underline{\beta} + \widehat{\beta}\sum X_i^2\right).$$

But this is in the form of a normal p.d.f., and thus we can say that $\beta|y \sim N\left(\overline{\beta}, \sigma^2\overline{V}\right)$. Since the posterior, prior, and likelihood are all normal, the prior is a natural conjugate one. As a digression, to obtain the natural conjugate form, it is necessary to have the prior variance for β depend on the error variance, σ^2 (remember the prior variance is $\sigma^2\underline{V}$). We could have worked with a prior simply being $\beta \sim N(\underline{\beta}, \underline{V}_1)$ (and, indeed, such a prior is often used). However, when we move to the case where σ^2 is unknown, such a prior would no longer be natural conjugate.

In the previous equations, we have skipped a few (tedious but straightforward) steps in the derivations. Should you try and work through the complete derivations, note that we have dropped multiplicative terms that do not involve β and used the fact (which is not hard to prove) that

$$\left(\sum_{i=1}^{N} X_i^2\right)\left(\beta - \widehat{\beta}\right)^2 + \underline{V}^{-1}\left(\beta - \underline{\beta}\right)^2 = \left(\widehat{\beta} - \underline{\beta}\right)^2\left(\sum_{i=1}^{N} X_i^2\right)\left(\underline{V}^{-1} + \sum X_i^2\right)^{-1}\underline{V}^{-1}$$
$$+ \left(\underline{V}^{-1} + \sum X_i^2\right)\left(\beta - \overline{\beta}\right)^2,$$

where only the last term at the end of this equation involves β.

Notice the similarities (and differences) with the classical result we derived in Chapter 3. There we said $\widehat{\beta}$ is $N(\beta, \frac{\sigma^2}{\sum X_i^2})$. Here we have a Bayesian posterior saying $\beta \sim N\left(\overline{\beta}, \sigma^2\overline{V}\right)$. Both are statements involving the normal distribution. However, for the classical econometrician it is $\widehat{\beta}$ that is the random variable. For the Bayesian it is the unknown parameter β that is the random variable. This contrast arises since the classical econometrician treats the data as the random variable. The Bayesian proceeds conditionally on the dataset at hand and treats the unknown parameters as the random variables.

The posterior summarizes everything that is known about β, and this p.d.f. could simply be presented in an empirical analysis. However, econometricians often prefer numerical summaries. For instance, we have seen in Chapter 3 how the classical econometrician would present a point estimate, $\widehat{\beta}$, as well as a confidence interval. The Bayesian can do something similar. The posterior is, by definition, a distribution, and the mean of any distribution is a common measure of its location. This motivates use of the posterior mean as a point estimate (in any Bayesian analysis, not just for the regression model). Similarly, the posterior variance is a commonly used metric for the uncertainty associated with the point estimate. In the simple regression model, the posterior mean is

$$E(\beta|y) = \overline{\beta}$$

and the posterior variance

$$var(\beta|y) = \sigma^2 \overline{V}.$$

Thus, whereas a classical econometrician might present the OLS estimate $\widehat{\beta}$ along with its standard error (i.e. $\sqrt{\frac{\sigma^2}{\Sigma X_i^2}}$), the Bayesian would present $\overline{\beta}$ and $\sigma^2 \overline{V}$ (or the posterior standard deviation, $\sqrt{\sigma^2 \overline{V}}$).

The formulae for the posterior mean and variance of β provide insight into how Bayesian methods combine prior and data information in the simple regression model, and hence it is worthwhile discussing them in some detail. The common Bayesian point estimate in the simple regression model, $\overline{\beta}$, is a weighted average of the OLS estimate and the prior mean, $\underline{\beta}$. The weights are proportional to ΣX_i^2 and $\underline{V}^{-1}$ respectively. The latter of these reflects the confidence in the prior. Remember that a variance of any random variable describes how dispersed its distribution is; how wide a range of outcomes could plausibly happen. So, for instance, if the prior variance you select is high (large $\underline{V}$), you are saying you are very uncertain about what likely values of β are (before seeing the data). As a result, $\underline{V}^{-1}$ will be small and little weight will be attached to $\underline{\beta}$, your best prior guess at what β is. The term ΣX_i^2 plays a similar role with respect to data-based information. Loosely speaking, it reflects the degree of confidence that the data have in its best guess for β, the OLS estimate $\widehat{\beta}$. This intuition arises since, as we have seen in Chapter 3, $(\Sigma X_i^2)^{-1}$ is proportional to the variance of $\widehat{\beta}$.

Alternative intuition can be obtained by considering the simplest case where $X_i = 1$ for $i = 1, ..., N$. This would be the case where the simple regression model involves only an intercept. Then $\Sigma X_i^2 = N$ and the weight attached to $\widehat{\beta}$ will simply be the sample size, a reasonable measure for the amount of information in the data. Thus, the posterior mean attaches weight proportional to how precise the prior and data information is (i.e. 'precision' is measured by the inverse of their variances). Hence, Bayesian methods combine data and prior information in a sensible way. The posterior variance of β, like the posterior mean, incorporates both prior and data information. Its formula can be informally interpreted as saying 'posterior precision is an average of prior precision ($\underline{V}^{-1}$) and data precision (ΣX_i^2)'.

The fact that the natural conjugate prior implies prior information enters in the same manner as data information helps with prior elicitation. For instance, when choosing particular values for $\underline{\beta}$ and $\underline{V}$ it helps to know that $\underline{\beta}$ is equivalent to the OLS estimate from an imaginary dataset with an imaginary ΣX_i^2 equal to $\underline{V}^{-1}$. However, econometrics is a public science where empirical results are presented to a wide variety of readers. In many cases, most readers may be able to agree on what a sensible prior might be (e.g. economic theory often specifies what reasonable coefficient values might be). However, in cases where different researchers can approach a problem with very different priors, a Bayesian analysis with only a single prior can be criticized. There are two main Bayesian strategies for surmounting such a criticism. Firstly, a *prior sensitivity analysis* can be carried out. This means that empirical results can be presented using various priors. If empirical results are basically the same for various sensible priors, then the reader is reassured that researchers with different beliefs can, after looking at the data, come to agreement. If results are sensitive to choice of prior, then the data are not enough to force agreement on researchers with different prior views. The Bayesian approach allows for the scientifically honest finding of such a state of affairs. There is substantive literature that finds bounds on, for example, the posterior mean of a parameter. We will not discuss this so-called *extreme bounds analysis* literature in any detail. A typical result in this literature is of the form: 'For any possible choice of $\underline{V}$, $\overline{\beta}$ must lie between specified upper and lower bounds'. Poirier (1995, pp. 532–536) provides an introduction to this literature and further references.

A second strategy for prior elicitation in cases where wide disagreement about prior choice could arise is to use a *non-informative prior*. Loosely speaking, in many cases it is desirable for data information to be predominant over prior information. In the context of the natural conjugate prior above, it is clear how one can do this: one can set $\underline{V}$ to a large value (relative to $\frac{1}{\sum X_i^2}$). A large prior variance implies that there is a large degree of prior uncertainty over what β is. This accords well with the idea that the prior should be 'non-informative'. Another way of making this point is to note that, if $\underline{V}$ is large, then $\underline{V}^{-1}$ will be small. If you look at the formulae for the posterior mean and variance, you can see that a small $\underline{V}^{-1}$ implies that prior information plays little role. We refer to such a prior as a *relatively non-informative prior*.

Taking the argument in the previous paragraph to the limit suggests that we can create a purely non-informative prior by letting $\underline{V}$ go to infinity and, thus, $\underline{V}^{-1} \to 0$. Such a choice is commonly made and can be seen to imply a posterior $\beta|y \sim N(\overline{\beta}, \sigma^2 \overline{V})$, where

$$\overline{V} = \frac{1}{\sum X_i^2},$$
$$\overline{\beta} = \widehat{\beta}.$$

With this non-informative prior, these formulae involve only data information and, in fact, are equal to ordinary least-squares results.

In one sense, this non-informative prior has very attractive properties and, given the close relationship with OLS results, provides a bridge between the Bayesian and classical approaches. That is, the Bayesian with a non-informative prior will use the OLS estimate as a point estimate and use a variance of $\frac{\sigma^2}{\sum X_i^2}$ to summarize uncertainty about the point estimate. This is exactly what the classical econometrician would do. The Bayesian and classical econometricians would offer a somewhat different interpretation of their results, since the Bayesian views β as a random variable whereas the classical econometrician would view $\widehat{\beta}$ as the random variable. However, in practice, in the simple regression model the non-informative Bayesian and classical econometrician would obtain very similar estimation results. This pattern holds in many (but not every) model with regards to estimation. However, as we will see, the Bayesian approach to hypothesis testing is quite different from the classical one.

The non-informative prior obtained by letting $\underline{V}$ go to infinity is a popular one. However, it has one undesirable property: this prior 'density' is not, in fact, a valid probability density function in that it does not integrate to 1. Such priors are referred to as *improper*. The Bayesian literature has many examples of problems caused by the use of improper priors.

10.2.4   Model comparison in the simple regression model

Suppose we have two simple regression models, M_1 and M_2, that purport to explain the dependent variable. These models differ in their explanatory variables. We will distinguish the two models by adding subscripts to the variables and coefficients. That is, M_j for $j = 1, 2$ is based on the simple linear regression model

$$Y_i = \beta_j X_{ji} + \varepsilon_{ji}$$

for $i = 1, \ldots, N$. We will assume the classical assumptions about ε_{ji} and X_{ji} hold (i.e. ε_{ji} is i.i.d. $N(0, \sigma_j^2)$ and X_{ji} is not random for $j = 1, 2$).

For the two models, we write the natural conjugate priors as

$$\beta_j | M_j \sim N\left(\underline{\beta}_j, \sigma_j^2 \underline{V}_j\right),$$

which (using the results derived in the previous section) implies posteriors of the form

$$\beta_j | y, M_j \sim N\left(\overline{\beta}_j, \sigma_j^2 \overline{V}_j\right),$$

where

$$\overline{V}_j = \frac{1}{\underline{V}_j^{-1} + \sum X_{ji}^2},$$

$$\overline{\beta}_j = \overline{V}_j \left(\underline{V}_j^{-1} \underline{\beta}_j + \widehat{\beta}_j \sum X_{ji}^2\right).$$

That is, everything is as in the formulae derived in the previous section, except that we have added j subscripts to distinguish between the two models.

As described earlier in this chapter, a chief tool of Bayesian model comparison is the posterior odds ratio

$$PO_{12} = \frac{p(y|M_1)p(M_1)}{p(y|M_2)p(M_2)}.$$

The prior model probabilities, $p(M_i)$ for $i = 1, 2$, must be selected before seeing the data. The non-informative choice, $p(M_1) = p(M_2) = \frac{1}{2}$, is commonly made. The marginal likelihood for the linear regression model with known variance, $p(y|M_j)$, can be shown to be

$$p(y|M_j) = \prod_{i=1}^{N} \phi\left(Y_i|\underline{\beta}_j X_i, \sigma^2 + \underline{V}_j X_i^2\right)$$

for $j = 1, 2$, where $\phi(Y_i|a, b)$ denotes the p.d.f. of the normal with mean a and variance b, evaluated at Y_i (see Appendix B, Definition B.10). We will not provide the details of this calculation, since it involves integration and, in practice, you will usually use the marginal likelihood for the case where σ^2 is unknown (which has a different formula). The key thing to note is that the marginal likelihood for each model can be calculated in a simple fashion. The posterior odds ratio comparing M_1 with M_2 becomes

$$PO_{12} = \frac{\prod_{i=1}^{N} \phi\left(Y_i|\underline{\beta}_1 X_i, \sigma^2 + \underline{V}_1 X_i^2\right) p(M_1)}{\prod_{i=1}^{N} \phi\left(Y_i|\underline{\beta}_2 X_i, \sigma^2 + \underline{V}_2 X_i^2\right) p(M_2)}.$$

This posterior odds ratio could either be used to select M_1 or M_2 as the preferred model or be used to construct posterior model probabilities to be used in a Bayesian model averaging exercise.

In this section, we have shown how a Bayesian would compare two models. If you have many models, you can compare any or all pairs of them or calculate posterior model probabilities for each model (e.g. for use in a Bayesian model averaging exercise).

In this section, we have tried to give the reader a flavor of how the Bayesian econometrician would approach a simple class of models. There are two important extensions we have not presented so far. The first of these is the case where the error variance, σ^2, is unknown. The interested reader is referred to the appendix of this chapter for details. The second important extension is to the multiple regression model. This is not provided here. The interested reader is referred to one of the many Bayesian econometrics textbooks listed at the beginning of this chapter. To provide complete details of Bayesian inference in the multiple regression model (or any of the other models considered in this book) would be to take us too far from the main purpose of this book: to give the student an adequate understanding of the dominant approach to econometrics and the associated computer software necessary to do empirical work in practice.

Example: Empirical illustration

The simple regression model is probably too simple to be used for any serious empirical work. For one thing, to simplify the algebra, we have not included an

Table 10.1 Prior and posterior properties of β.

	Prior	Posterior	
	Informative	Using non-informative prior	Using informative prior
Mean	1.50	2.06	1.96
Standard deviation	0.50	0.24	0.22

intercept in the model. Furthermore, virtually any serious application will involve several explanatory variables. Hence, to illustrate the basic concepts discussed in this chapter, we will work with a dataset artificially generated by the computer. That is, we set $N = 50$. We begin by generating values of the explanatory variable, X_i, which are i.i.d. draws from the $N(0, 1)$ distribution for $i = 1, \ldots, 50$. We then generate values for the errors, ε_i, which are $N(0, \sigma^2)$. Finally, we use the explanatory variables and errors to generate the dependent variable $Y_i = \beta X_i + \varepsilon_i$. We set $\beta = 2$ and $\sigma^2 = 1$. We use two priors, the non-informative one and the informative natural conjugate prior with $\underline{\beta} = 1.5$ and $\underline{V} = 0.25$. The choices of data generating process and prior hyperparameter values are purely illustrative.

Table 10.1 presents prior and posterior properties of β. Figure 10.1 plots posteriors for β under the informative and non-informative priors as well as the informative prior itself (the non-informative prior for β is simply a flat line). As we have seen, posterior properties based on the non-informative prior reflect only likelihood function information and use OLS quantities. For this reason, the posterior for β under the non-informative prior is labeled 'Likelihood' in Figure 10.1.

The table and figure show how Bayesian inference involves combining prior and data information to form a posterior. For instance, in Figure 10.1 it can be seen that the posterior based on the informative prior looks to be an average of the prior density and the likelihood function. Table 10.1 shows that the posterior mean of the coefficient, $E(\beta|y)$, using the informative prior lies between the prior mean and the likelihood-based quantity (where the latter is also the posterior mean using the non-informative prior). The prior we have selected contains less information than the data. This can be seen either in the figure (i.e. the prior p.d.f. is more dispersed than the likelihood) or in the tables (i.e. the prior standard deviation is larger than the likelihood-based quantity).

Remember that, since the dataset has been artificially created, we know that the coefficient value is $\beta = 2$. You would, of course, never expect a point estimate like a posterior mean or an OLS quantity to be precisely equal to the true value. However, the posterior means are quite close to the true value of 2 relative to their posterior standard deviations. Note also that the posterior standard deviation using the informative prior is slightly smaller than that using the non-informative prior. This reflects the intuitive notion that, in general, more information allows for more precise estimation. That is, it is intuitively sensible that a posterior that

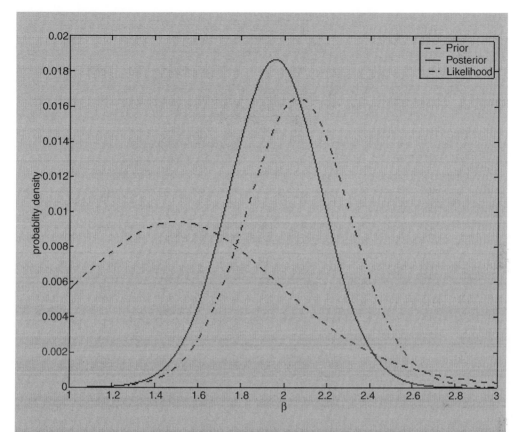

Figure 10.1 Prior and posterior for β.

combines both prior and data information will be less dispersed than one that uses a non-informative prior and is based only on data information.

To illustrate model comparison, let us suppose we are interested in comparing the model we have been discussing with another linear regression model that contains only an intercept (i.e. in this second model $X_i = 1$ for $i = 1, \ldots, 50$). For both models, we use the same informative prior described above (i.e. both priors are $N(1.5, 0.25)$). Assuming a prior odds ratio equal to 1, the equation for PO_{12} in the previous section can be used to calculate the posterior odds ratio comparing these two models. Of course, we know our first model is the correct one, and hence we would expect the posterior odds ratio to indicate this. This does turn out to be the case, since we find a posterior odds ratio of 8 697.5. In other words, we are finding overwhelming support for our correct first model. It is over 8 000 times more likely to be true than the second model. In terms of posterior model probabilities, the posterior odds ratio implies that $p(M_1|y) = 0.99988$ and $p(M_2|y) = 0.00012$. If we were to do Bayesian model averaging using these two models, we would attach 99.988 % weight to results from the first model and only 0.012 % weight to results from the second.

10.3   Chapter summary

This chapter began by covering all the basic issues in Bayesian econometrics at a high level of abstraction. We have stressed that the ability to put all the general theory in a few pages, involving only basic concepts in probability, is an advantage of the Bayesian approach. The basic building blocks of the Bayesian approach are the likelihood function and the prior, and the product of these defines the posterior which forms the basis for inference about the unknown parameters in a model. Different models can be compared using *posterior model probabilities* which require the calculation of *marginal likelihoods*.

The second half of this chapter involves a complete Bayesian analysis (i.e. likelihood, prior, posterior, and model comparison) for the normal linear regression model with a single explanatory variable with a known error variance and a so-called natural conjugate prior (i.e. a normal prior is used for β). The natural conjugate nature of the prior means that the posterior also has a normal distribution. For this prior, posterior inference and model comparison can be done analytically using a few simple formulae. The case where the error variance is unknown is treated in the appendix to this chapter. Other themes introduced in this chapter include the concept of a non-informative prior and Bayesian model averaging.

With this chapter we have illustrated the basic methodological ideas underlying Bayesian econometrics and shown how they work in one particular model. Of course, Bayesian methods can be used with any statistical model and are enjoying an increased popularity in many fields. For the reader interested in learning more about Bayesian methods, the introduction to this chapter provides a set of readings. Koop, Poirier, & Tobias (2007) is a book of solved exercises useful for learning Bayesian theory and computation.

Exercises

To do Bayesian econometrics requires either specialized software or some knowledge of computer programming (e.g. to write computer code to evaluate the formulae for the posterior mean and variance or the marginal likelihood). Since the rest of this textbook does not require these skills, we do not include any empirical questions in this chapter. The ambitious student may be interested in redoing the empirical questions at the end of Chapter 2 using Bayesian methods or look at Koop, Poirier, & Tobias (2007). Here, we provide some theoretical questions to familiarize you with the working of the rules of conditional probability and the way Bayesian methods combine prior and likelihood to yield a posterior in models other than the regression model.

1. A laboratory blood test is 95 % effective in detecting a certain disease when it is, in fact, present. However, the test also yields a 'false positive' result for 1 % of the healthy persons tested. If 0.1 % of the population actually has the disease, what is the probability that a person has the disease given that the test result for that person is positive?

2. Consider the television game show 'Let's Make a Deal' in which host Monty Hall asks contestants to choose the prize behind one of three curtains. Behind one curtain lies the grand prize; the other two curtains conceal only relatively small gifts. Monty knows what is behind every curtain. Once the contestant has made a choice, Monty reveals what is behind one of the two curtains that were not chosen. Having been shown one of the lesser prizes, the contestant is offered a chance to switch curtains. Should the contestant switch?

3. Suppose you have N i.i.d. random variables Y_i for $i = 1, 2, \ldots, N$ that can take either the value 1 or 0 (e.g. ' success' or 'failure' in an experiment). The p.d.f. is defined by

$$p(Y_i = 1) = p,$$
$$p(Y_i = 0) = 1 - p,$$

where p is the probability of success. p is the unknown parameter you wish to estimate.

(a) Show that the likelihood function is

$$L(p) = p^m (1 - p)^{N-m},$$

where $m = \sum_{i=1}^{N} Y_i$ is the number of successes (i.e. the number of cases where $Y_i = 1$) in the N experiments.

(b) Suppose prior beliefs concerning p are represented by the so-called beta distribution which has p.d.f.

$$p(p) \propto p^{\underline{\alpha}-1} (1 - p)^{\underline{\delta}-1},$$

where $\underline{\alpha} > 0$ and $\underline{\delta} > 0$ are known prior hyperparameters selected by the researcher. Find the posterior density of p .

(c) Is the prior in part (b) a conjugate prior?

(d) Show how this prior can be made non-informative and derive the resulting posterior.

4. Suppose you have a random sample, Y_i $(i = 1, 2, \ldots, N)$ from the $N(\mu, 1)$ distribution and you wish to estimate μ. Suppose prior beliefs for μ are represented by the normal distribution

$$\mu \sim N(\underline{\mu}, \underline{V}),$$

where $\underline{\mu}$ and $\underline{V}$ are prior hyperparameters selected by the researcher.

(a) Find the posterior density of μ.

(b) Show how this prior can be made non-informative and derive the resulting posterior.

5. Suppose Y_i for $i = 1, 2, \ldots, N$ is a random sample from the uniform distribution defined over the interval $(0, \theta)$, where θ is unknown. The p.d.f. of this distribution is

$$p(Y_i) = \frac{1}{\theta} \text{ if } < 0 < Y_i < \theta.$$

(a) Show that the likelihood function is given by $L(\theta) = \theta^{-N}$ for $\theta \geq \max\{Y_1, Y_2, \ldots, Y_N\}$ (i.e. the latter qualification says θ must be greater than the largest value of Y).

(b) Suppose the prior distribution for θ is Pareto with prior hyperparameters $\underline{\gamma} > 0$ and $\underline{\lambda} > 0$. That is, the prior density for θ is

$$p(\theta) = \frac{\underline{\lambda}\underline{\gamma}^{\underline{\lambda}}}{\theta^{\underline{\lambda}+1}} \text{ for } \theta > \underline{\gamma}.$$

Find the posterior distribution of θ and show that it is also a Pareto distribution, and hence that this prior is conjugate.

Appendix: Bayesian analysis of the simple regression model with unknown variance

The simple linear regression model with unknown variance involves two unknown parameters: β and σ^2. It turns out that it is easier to work with the *error precision* which is the inverse of the error variance. We denote the error precision by $h = \frac{1}{\sigma^2}$. This has no implications for the econometrics. We can, for instance, simply estimate h and then use the inverse of this as an estimate of σ^2. However, the natural conjugate prior can be written in a slightly simpler form involving the gamma distribution when we work in terms of h. The gamma distribution is a generalization of the familiar chi-square distribution and is defined in Appendix B, Definition B.15.

The likelihood function is provided in the body of the chapter, except that now it is written as $L(\beta, h)$ to emphasize that both β and h are the unknown parameters. We must elicit a prior for β and h which we denote by $p(\beta, h)$. It proves convenient to use the rules of conditional probability to write $p(\beta, h) = p(\beta|h)p(h)$ and think in terms of a prior for $\beta|h$ and one for h. If you examine the form of the likelihood function, you can see that it involves a normal distribution for $\beta|h$ and a gamma distribution for h. This suggests that the natural conjugate prior will involve normal and gamma parts.

The name given to a distribution such as this, which is a product of a gamma and (conditional on h) a normal, is the *normal–gamma* distribution. Appendix B, Definition B.17 provides further details on this distribution. Using notation introduced in Appendix B, if

$$\beta|h \sim N(\underline{\beta}, h^{-1}\underline{V})$$

and

$$h \sim G(\underline{s}^{-2}, \underline{v}),$$

then the natural conjugate prior for β and h is denoted by

$$\beta, h \sim NG\left(\underline{\beta}, \underline{V}, \underline{s}^{-2}, \underline{v}\right).$$

The posterior can be obtained by multiplying the prior by the likelihood function. For the sake of brevity, we do not provide all the algebraic details here. Koop, Poirier, & Tobias (2007, Ch. 10) or Poirier (1995, p. 527) or Zellner (1971, pp. 60–61) provide closely related derivations (the derivations are similar to those provided in the body of the chapter). The posterior can be shown to be of the normal–gamma form, confirming that the normal–gamma prior is indeed a natural conjugate one.

Formally, we have a posterior of the form

$$\beta, h|y \sim NG\left(\overline{\beta}, \overline{V}, \overline{s}^{-2}, \overline{v}\right),$$

where

$$\overline{V} = \frac{1}{\underline{V}^{-1} + \sum X_i^2},$$
$$\overline{\beta} = \overline{V}\left(\underline{V}^{-1}\underline{\beta} + \widehat{\beta}\sum X_i^2\right),$$
$$\overline{v} = \underline{v} + N,$$

and $\overline{s}^{-2}$ is defined implicitly through

$$\overline{v}\overline{s}^2 = \underline{v}\underline{s}^2 + vs^2 + \frac{\left(\widehat{\beta} - \underline{\beta}\right)^2}{\underline{V} + \left(\frac{1}{\sum X_i^2}\right)}.$$

In the body of the chapter, we motivated the posterior mean, $E(\beta|y)$, as a commonly used point estimate and $var(\beta|y)$ as a commonly used metric for the uncertainty associated with the point estimate. Using the basic rules of probability, the posterior mean can be calculated as

$$E(\beta|y) = \iint \beta p(\beta, h|y)\, dh\, d\beta = \int \beta p(\beta|y)\, d\beta.$$

This equation motivates interest in the marginal posterior density, $p(\beta|y)$. Fortunately, this can be calculated analytically using the properties of the normal–gamma distribution (see Appendix B, Theorem B.5). In particular, these imply that, if we integrate out h (i.e. use the fact that $p(\beta|y) = \int p(\beta, h|y)\, dh$), the marginal posterior distribution for β is a t-distribution. In terms of the notation of Appendix B, Definition B.16

$$\beta|y \sim t\left(\overline{\beta}, \overline{s}^2\overline{V}, \overline{v}\right),$$

and it follows from the definition of the t-distribution that

$$E(\beta|y) = \overline{\beta}$$

and

$$var(\beta|y) = \frac{\overline{v}\overline{s}^2}{\overline{v}-2}\overline{V}.$$

The error precision, h, is usually of less interest than β, but the properties of the normal–gamma imply that

$$h|y \sim G(\overline{s}^{-2}, \overline{v}),$$

and hence

$$E(h|y) = \overline{s}^{-2}$$

and

$$var(h|y) = \frac{2\overline{s}^{-4}}{\overline{v}}.$$

These formulae can be used to carry out Bayesian inference on β and h (or σ^2). As described in the body of the chapter, the Bayesian can either choose values for prior hyperparameters (which are, in this case, $\underline{\beta}, \underline{V}, \underline{s}^2$, and $\underline{v}$) or use a non-informative prior. For this model, the non-informative prior is obtained by setting $\underline{V}^{-1} = 0$ and $\underline{v} = 0$, and in this case we obtain a posterior that involves only OLS quantities:

$$\overline{V} = \frac{1}{\sum X_i^2},$$
$$\overline{\beta} = \widehat{\beta},$$
$$\overline{v} = N,$$

and

$$\overline{v}\overline{s}^2 = vs^2.$$

To show how model comparison can be done, we return to the same set-up as in the body of the chapter. That is, we have two simple regression models, M_1 and M_2, that purport to explain y. These models differ in their explanatory variables. We distinguish the two models by adding subscripts to the variables and parameters. That is, M_j for $j = 1, 2$ is based on the simple linear regression model

$$y_i = \beta_j X_{ji} + \varepsilon_{ji}$$

for $i = 1, \ldots, N$. The marginal likelihood, $p(y|M_j)$, is calculated as

$$p(y|M_j) = \iint p(y|\beta_j, h_j) p(\beta_j, h_j) \, d\beta_j \, dh_j.$$

Poirier (1995, pp. 542–543) or Zellner (1971, pp. 72–75), provides details of how this integral is calculated. It turns out to be

$$p(y|M_j) = c_j \left(\frac{\overline{V}_j}{V_j} \right)^{\frac{1}{2}} \left(\overline{v}_j \overline{s}_j^2 \right)^{-\frac{\overline{v}_j}{2}},$$

for $j = 1, 2$, where

$$c_j = \frac{\Gamma\left(\frac{\overline{v}_j}{2}\right) \left(v_j s_j^2 \right)^{\frac{v_j}{2}}}{\Gamma\left(\frac{v_j}{2}\right) \pi^{\frac{N}{2}}},$$

and $\Gamma(.)$ is the gamma function.[5] The posterior odds ratio comparing M_1 with M_2 becomes

$$PO_{12} = \frac{c_1 \left(\frac{\overline{V}_1}{V_1} \right)^{\frac{1}{2}} \left(\overline{v}_1 \overline{s}_1^2 \right)^{-\frac{\overline{v}_1}{2}} p(M_1)}{c_2 \left(\frac{\overline{V}_2}{V_2} \right)^{\frac{1}{2}} \left(\overline{v}_2 \overline{s}_2^2 \right)^{-\frac{\overline{v}_2}{2}} p(M_2)}.$$

A discussion of the posterior odds formula offers insight into the factors that enter a Bayesian comparison of models. Firstly, the greater the prior odds ratio, $\frac{p(M_1)}{p(M_2)}$, the higher is the support for M_1. Note, secondly, that $\overline{v}_j \overline{s}_j^2$ contains the term $v_j s_j^2$ which is the standard OLS sum of squared residuals. The sum of squared residuals is a common measure of the model fit, with lower values indicating a better model fit. Hence, the posterior odds ratio rewards models that fit the data better. Thirdly, other things being equal, the posterior odds ratio will indicate support for the model where there is the greatest coherency between prior and data information (i.e. $(\widehat{\beta}_j - \underline{\beta}_j)^2$ enters $\overline{\nu}_j \overline{s}_j^2$). Fourthly, $\left(\frac{\overline{V}_1}{\underline{V}_1}\right)$ is the ratio of posterior to prior variances. This term can be interpreted as saying, all else being equal, the model with more prior information (i.e. smaller prior variance) relative to posterior information receives most support.

It is worth mentioning that, in general, posterior odds ratios also contain a reward for parsimony in that, all else being equal, posterior odds favor the model with fewer parameters. The two models compared here have the same number of parameters (i.e. β_j and h_j), and hence this reward for parsimony is not evident. However, in general, this is an important feature of posterior odds ratios.

Under the non-informative variant of the natural conjugate prior (i.e. $\underline{\nu}_j = 0$, $\underline{V}_j^{-1} = 0$), the marginal likelihood is not defined and, hence, the posterior odds ratio is undefined. This is one problem with the use of noninformative priors for model comparison. However, in the present context, a common solution to this problem is to set $\underline{\nu}_1 = \underline{\nu}_2$ equal to an arbitrarily small number and do the same with $\underline{V}_1^{-1}$ and $\underline{V}_2^{-1}$. Also, set $\underline{s}_1^2 = \underline{s}_2^2$. Under these assumptions, the posterior odds ratio is defined and simplifies and becomes

$$PO_{12} = \frac{\left(\frac{1}{\sum X_{1i}^2}\right)^{\frac{1}{2}} \left(\nu_1 s_1^2\right)^{-\frac{N}{2}} p(M_1)}{\left(\frac{1}{\sum X_{2i}^2}\right)^{\frac{1}{2}} \left(\nu_2 s_2^2\right)^{-\frac{N}{2}} p(M_2)}.$$

In this case, the posterior odds ratio reflects only the prior odds ratio, the relative goodness of fit of the two models, and the ratio of terms involving $\frac{1}{\sum X_{ji}^2}$ which reflect the precision of the posterior for M_j.

Endnotes

1. Sometimes the classical approach to statistics is referred to as *frequentist*, since it is based on the so-called *frequency theory* of probability where probability is defined as the frequency with which each outcome would occur if an experiment were repeated an infinite number of times.
2. This chapter involves extensive use of the basic rules of probability. Appendix B provides a brief introduction to probability for the reader who does not have such a background or would like a reminder of this material.
3. Model A is nested inside model B if it can be written as a restricted version of model B. For instance, if model B is the simple regression model, then the simple regression model with $\beta = 0$ is nested within it.
4. To prove this, take $Y_i - \beta X_i$ and add $\widehat{\beta} X_i$ to it and then subtract $\widehat{\beta} X_i$ from it, leaving it unchanged. That is, write: $\Sigma(Y_i - \beta X_i)^2 = \Sigma\{(Y_i - \widehat{\beta} X_i) - (\beta - \widehat{\beta})X_i\}^2$ and then expand out the right-hand side.
5. See Poirier (1995, p. 98) for a definition of the gamma function. All that you need to know here is that the gamma function can be calculated by relevant computer software packages.

Appendix A: Mathematical Basics

The level of mathematics used in this book is not high, mostly involving the manipulation of equations. The typical reader of this book should have learned the relevant mathematical concepts in coursework at the pre-university or university level. However, for the reader without this background (or for the reader wanting a brief review), in this appendix a summary of the mathematical concepts used in this book is provided. There are many mathematical economics textbooks that provide much more detail for the reader wishing to learn more about the mathematical techniques used by economists. Examples include 'Mathematics for Economics and Business' by Ian Jacques and 'Mathematics for Economics and Business' by Jean Soper.

Functions and the equation of a straight line

Economists are often interested in the relationship between two (or more) variables. Let us use the notation Y and X for these variables. A very general way of denoting a relationship is through the concept of a function. A common mathematical notation for a function of X is $f(X)$. So, for instance, if economists are interested in the factors that explain why some houses are worth more than others, they may think that the price of a house depends on the size of the house. In mathematical terms, they would then let Y denote the variable 'price of the house' and X denote the variable 'size of the house', and the fact that Y depends on X is written using the notation: $Y = f(X)$. This notation should be read 'Y is a function of X' and captures the idea that the value for Y depends on the value of X.

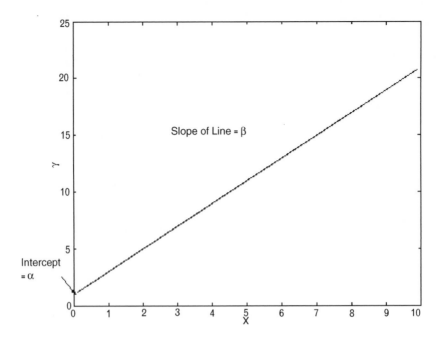

Figure A.1 A straight line.

There are many functions that one could use. The linear function is a common one. Any straight line can be written in terms of an equation:

$$Y = \alpha + \beta X$$

where α and β are coefficients that determine a particular line. So, for instance, setting $\alpha = 1$ and $\beta = 2$ defines one particular line, while $\alpha = 4$ and $\beta = -5$ defines a different line.

These concepts can be understood in terms of Figure A.1. Any line can be defined by its intercept and slope. In terms of the equation of a straight line, α is the intercept and β is the slope. The intercept is the value of Y when $X = 0$ (i.e. the point at which the line cuts the Y axis). The slope is a measure of how much Y changes when X is changed. The slope is the first derivative:

$$\beta = \frac{\mathrm{d}Y}{\mathrm{d}X}.$$

Figure A.1 has an intercept of 1 ($\alpha = 1$) and a slope of 2 ($\beta = 2$).

Logarithms

For various reasons (which are explained in this textbook), in some cases the researcher does not work directly with a variable but with a transformed version of it.

Many transformations are straightforward. For instance, in comparing the incomes of different countries, the variable GDP per capita is used. This is a transformed version of the variable GDP. It is obtained by dividing GDP by population.

One particularly common transformation is the logarithmic one. The logarithm (to the base B) of a number, A, is the power to which B must be raised to give A. The notation for this is $\log_B(A)$. So, for instance, if $B = 10$ and $A = 100$, then the logarithm is 2 and we write $\log_{10}(100) = 2$. This follows since $10^2 = 100$. In econometrics, it is common to work with the so-called natural logarithm which has $B = e$, where $e \approx 2.71828$. We will not explain where e comes from or why this rather unusual looking base is chosen. The natural logarithm operator is denoted by ln (i.e. $\ln(A) = \log_e(A)$).

In this book, you do not really have to understand the material in the previous paragraph. The key things to note are that the natural logarithmic operator is a common function (for reasons explained in the book) and it is denoted by $\ln(A)$.

The inverse of the natural logarithm function is the exponential function, denoted by exp. It is defined as

$$\exp(A) = e^A.$$

There are many properties involving the logarithm and exponential functions that any basic mathematics for economists textbook will list. Here we give only a few of the key properties that are used in this textbook:

$$\ln(AB) = \ln(A) + \ln(B);$$
$$\ln(A^B) = B \ln(A);$$
$$\ln[\exp(A)] = A;$$
$$\exp[\ln(A)] = A;$$
$$\exp(A + B) = \exp(A)\exp(B);$$
$$\ln(1 + A) \approx A \text{ if } A \text{ is small.}$$

Summation and product notation

Subscripts are typically used to denote different observations of a variable. For instance, labor economists might be interested in the wage of every one of 100 people in a certain industry. If the economists use Y to denote this variable, then they will have a value of Y for the first individual, a value of Y for the second individual, etc. A compact notation for this is to use subscripts so that Y_1 is the wage of the first individual, Y_2 the wage of the second individual, etc. In some contexts it is useful to speak of a generic individual and refer to this individual as the *i*th. We can then write Y_i for $i = 1, \ldots, 100$ to denote the set of wages for all individuals.

With the subscript notation established, summation notation can now be introduced. In many cases we want to add up observations (e.g. when calculating an average, you add up all the observations and divide by the number of observations). The Greek symbol, Σ, is the summation (or 'adding up') operator, and superscripts and subscripts on Σ indicate the observations that are being added up. So, for instance,

$$\sum_{i=1}^{100} Y_i$$

adds up the wages for all of the 100 individuals. As other examples,

$$\sum_{i=1}^{3} Y_i$$

adds up the wages for the first three individuals and

$$\sum_{i=47}^{48} Y_i$$

adds up the wages for the 47th and 48th individuals. Sometimes, where it is obvious from the context (usually when summing over all individuals), the subscript and superscript are dropped and we write

$$\sum Y_i.$$

A commonly used notation is to let the observations on a variable be denoted as Y_i for $i = 1, \ldots, N$, where N is the number of observations. A collection of observations of a variable is referred to as a *sample*, and thus N is called the *sample size*. The summation operator is used to construct the average, also known as the *sample mean*:

$$\overline{Y} = \frac{\sum_{i=1}^{N} Y_i}{N}.$$

The summation operator can also be used with any function of the observations. That is, if $f(.)$ is a function,

$$\sum_{i=1}^{N} f(X_i) = f(X_1) + \ldots + f(X_N).$$

Here are some useful properties of the summation operator, where we use the notation that X_i and Y_i for $i = 1, \ldots, N$ are observations on two variables and c is a constant:

$$\sum_{i=1}^{N} cX_i = c\sum_{i=1}^{N} X_i,$$

$$\sum_{i=1}^{N} (X_i + Y_i) = \sum_{i=1}^{N} X_i + \sum_{i=1}^{N} Y_i,$$

$$\sum_{i=1}^{N} c = cN.$$

The product operator has the same format and notational conventions as the summation operator, except that it multiplies observations together instead of adding them together. That is, if Y_i for $i = 1, \ldots, N$ are observations on a variable, then

$$\prod_{i=1}^{N} Y_i = Y_1 \times Y_2 \times \ldots \times Y_N.$$

There are several properties of the product operator we could give. However, these are not used in this textbook so will not be provided. In this textbook, the product operator is used largely for deriving the likelihood function. If $p(.)$ is a function (in the case of the likelihood function, it is a probability density function, a concept explained in the next appendix), then the likelihood function has the form

$$\prod_{i=1}^{N} p(Y_i) = p(Y_1) \times \cdots \times p(Y_N).$$

It is often easier to work with the log of the likelihood function (often shortened to log-likelihood function) than the likelihood function itself. Remember, however, a property of the log operator is that $\ln(AB) = \ln(A) + \ln(B)$. Using this rule, we can write the log-likelihood function as

$$\ln\left[\prod_{i=1}^{N} p(Y_i)\right] = \sum_{i=1}^{N} \ln[p(Y_i)].$$

Thus, although the likelihood function involves the product operator, the log-likelihood function involves the summation operator. In short, in this textbook the product operator is only rarely used. And even when it is used (as with the likelihood function), the problem is often transformed into one involving the summation operator (as with the log-likelihood function).

Appendix B: Probability Basics

This appendix presents only the elements of probability that are used in this book. There are a myriad of probability and statistics books that will cover this material in more detail (e.g. the book by Wonnacott and Wonnacott listed in the bibliography at the end of this book). Most of this appendix is simply a listing of definitions and theorems. However, some notes have been added below to help the reader by providing intuition and motivation or by highlighting issues of importance. Proofs of theorems are not provided.

Basic concepts of probability

Definition B.1: Experiments and events
An *experiment* is a process whose outcome is not known in advance. The possible outcomes (or *realisations*) of an experiment are called *events*. The set of all possible outcomes is called the *sample space*.

Definition B.2: Discrete and continuous variables
A variable is *discrete* if the number of values it can take on is finite (or countable). A variable is *continuous* if it can take on any value on the real line or in a specified interval.

Definition B.3: Random variables and probability (informal definition)
Usually (and everywhere in this book) issues relating to probability, experiments, and events are represented by a variable (either continuous or discrete). Since the outcome of

an experiment is not known in advance, such a variable is known as a *random variable*. The precise definition and interpretation of *probability* are sources of dispute. In this book, it is enough to have an intuitive grasp of probability (perhaps as reflecting the likelihood that each event will occur) and know its properties as described below. The probability of event A occurring will be denoted by $\Pr(A)$. The following example will serve to clarify these basic concepts.

Suppose an experiment involves rolling a single fair die (i.e. each of the six faces of the die is equally likely to come up when the die is tossed). Then the sample space is $\{1, 2, 3, 4, 5, 6\}$ and the discrete random variable, X, takes on values 1,2,3,4,5,6 with probabilities given by $\Pr(X = 1) = \Pr(X = 2) = \ldots = \Pr(X = 6) = \frac{1}{6}$ Alternatively, the random variable X is a function defined at the points 1,2,3,4,5,6. The function is implicitly defined through the probabilities $\Pr(X = 1) = \Pr(X = 2) = \ldots = \Pr(X = 6) = \frac{1}{6}$.

Note: It is important to distinguish between the random variable, X, which can take on values 1,2,3,4,5,6, and the *realization* of the random variable which is the value that actually arises when the experiment is run (e.g. if the die is rolled, a 4 might appear which is the realization of the random variable in a particular experiment). It is common to denote random variables by upper-case letters (e.g. X), with associated realizations denoted by lower-case letters (e.g. x). In this textbook, we do not adopt this notational convention and sometimes are informal in distinguishing between a random variable and its realization. It is clear from the context which is being referred to.

Definition B.4: Independence
Two events, A and B, are *independent* if $\Pr(A, B) = \Pr(A)\Pr(B)$, where $\Pr(A, B)$ is the joint probability of A and B occurring. If A and B are independent then $g(A)$ and $g(B)$ are independent, for any function $g(\cdot)$.

Definition B.5: Conditional probability
The conditional probability of A given B, denoted by $\Pr(A|B)$, is the probability of event A occurring given event B has occurred.

Theorem B.1: Rules of conditional probability including Bayes theorem
Let A and B denote two events. Then

$$\Pr(A|B) = \frac{\Pr(A, B)}{\Pr(B)}$$

and

$$\Pr(B|A) = \frac{\Pr(A, B)}{\Pr(A)}.$$

These two rules can be combined to yield *Bayes theorem*:

$$\Pr(A|B) = \frac{\Pr(B|A)\Pr(A)}{\Pr(B)}.$$

Note: Theorem B.1 and definitions B.4 and B.5 are expressed in terms of two events, A and B. However, they also can be interpreted as holding for two random variables, A and B, with probability or probability density functions (see below) replacing the $\Pr(\cdot)$s in the previous formulae.

Definition B.6: Probability and distribution functions
The *probability function* associated with a discrete random variable X with sample space $\{x_1, x_2, x_3, \ldots, x_N\}$ is denoted by $p(x)$, where

$$p(x) = \begin{cases} \Pr(X = x_i) & \text{if } x = x_i \\ 0, \text{otherwise} \end{cases}$$

for $i = 1, 2, \ldots, N$. The *distribution function*, denoted by $P(x)$, is defined as

$$P(x) = \Pr(X \leq x) = \sum_{j \in J} \Pr(x_j),$$

where J is the set of js with the property that $x_j \leq x$.
   Probability and distribution functions satisfy the following conditions:

- $p(x_i) > 0$ for $i = 1, 2, \ldots, N$;
- $\sum_{i=1}^{N} p(x_i) = P(x_N) = 1$.

Notes: N can be infinite in the previous definition. In words, a probability function simply gives the probability of each event occurring and the distribution function gives the cumulative probability of all events up to some point occurring.

Definition B.7: Probability density and distribution functions
The distribution function of a continuous random variable, X, is $P(x) = \Pr(X \leq x) = \int_{-\infty}^{x} p(t)dt$, where $p(\cdot)$ is the *probability density function* or *p.d.f.* Probability density and distribution functions satisfy the following conditions:

- $p(x) \geq 0$ for all x;
- $\int_{-\infty}^{\infty} p(t)dt = P(\infty) = 1$;
- $p(x) = \frac{dP(x)}{dx}$.

Notes: With discrete random variables, the definition of a probability function is clear—it is simply the probability of each event in the sample space occurring. With continuous random variables, such a definition is not possible since there are an infinite number of events. For instance, there are an infinite number of real numbers in the interval [0,1], and, hence, if this is the sample space in an experiment, we cannot simply attach a probability to each point in the interval. With continuous random variables, probabilities are thus defined only for intervals and represented as areas under (i.e. integrals of) p.d.f.s.

For instance, definition B.7 implies that $\Pr(a \leq x \leq b) = P(b) - P(a) = \int_a^b p(x)\mathrm{d}x$. For the student who does not know integration, this intuition that areas under the p.d.f. provides you with probabilities (see, for example, Figure 3.2 in Chapter 3) is adequate for the purposes of this textbook. An alternative way of thinking about integrals is that they are summation operators for the case of continuous variables.

The concepts of the expected value and variance operators were intuitively explained in Chapter 1. Here we provide the formal definition and some key properties.

Definition B.8: Expected value, variance, covariance, and correlation

The *expected value* of X, denoted $E(X)$, is defined by

$$E(X) = \sum_{i=1}^{N} x_i p(x_i)$$

if X is a discrete random variable with sample space $\{x_1, x_2, x_3, \ldots, x_N\}$, and by

$$E(X) = \int_{-\infty}^{\infty} x p(x)\mathrm{d}x$$

if X is a continuous random variable (provided $E(X) < \infty$).

The expected value can be intuitively interpreted as an average or typical value that might occur. The expected value of a random variable is also called the *mean*, which is often denoted by the symbol μ. Thus, $\mu \equiv E(X)$. The *variance* can be defined using the expected value operator as $var(X) = E[(X - \mu)^2] = E(X^2) - \mu^2$. The *standard deviation* is the square root of the variance. The variance and standard deviation are commonly used measures of dispersion of a random variable.

The *covariance* between two random variables, X and Y, can also be defined using expected values as

$$cov(X, Y) = E(XY) - E(X)E(Y).$$

The covariance is the key component of the *correlation* between X and Y. The correlation, which was intuitively motivated in Chapter 1, has a formal definition:

$$corr(X, Y) = \frac{cov(X, Y)}{\sqrt{var(X)var(Y)}}.$$

Notes: If $X = Y$, then covariance is simply variance. Correlation can be interpreted as the degree of association between two random variables. It satisfies $-1 \leq corr(X, Y) \leq 1$, with larger positive/negative values indicating stronger positive/negative relationships between X and Y. If X and Y are independent, then $corr(X, Y) = 0$ (although the converse does not necessarily hold).

Theorem B.2: Properties of expected value and variance operator

If X and Y are two random variables and a and b are constants, then:

1. $E(aX + bY) = aE(X) + bE(Y)$.
2. $var(aX) = a^2 var(X)$.
3. $var(a + X) = var(X)$.
4. $var(aX + bY) = a^2 var(X) + b^2 var(Y) + 2ab cov(X, Y)$.
5. $E(XY) \neq E(Y)E(Y)$ unless $cov(X, Y) = 0$.

Note: These properties generalize to the case of many random variables.

Definition B.9: Joint probability density functions

The concept of joint probability (as being the probability that more than one event, say, A and B, both occur) was discussed in definition B.4. The definition of joint probability can be formalized and extended to the case of continuous random variables. We do not provide a general definition here. Instead we provide a definition for the important case (used in this textbook) where the random variables are independent of one another. If $X_1, \ldots, X_N$ are N independent random variables, each with p.d.f. $p(X_i)$ for $i = 1, \ldots, N$, then the joint probability density function for $X_1, \ldots, X_N$ is

$$p(X_1, \ldots, X_N) = p(X_1) \times p(X_2) \times \cdots \times p(X_N) = \prod_{i=1}^{N} p(X_i).$$

Note: The intuition underlying the joint probability density function is similar to that underlying the probability density function. For instance, suppose we have two random variables X_1 and X_2. Their joint p.d.f. is $p(X_1, X_2)$. We also have the p.d.f.s of each random variable individually: $p(X_1)$ and $p(X_2)$. These are known as *marginal* p.d.f.s. The area under the curve defined by $p(X_1)$ (over some interval) provides us with probabilities that X_1 will be in the interval (e.g. we can use the p.d.f. to calculate $\Pr(X_1 \leq 0)$ or $\Pr(-1.96 \leq X_1 \leq 1.96)$ or the probability of any other interval). The joint probability density function, $p(X_1, X_2)$, allows us to calculate probabilities involving both random variables in a similar fashion. A plot of $p(X_1, X_2)$ will be three-dimensional, so things get a bit more complicated. However, we can extend the previous intuition to say that the volume under the three-dimensional curve defined by $p(X_1, X_2)$ (over some region) provides us with probabilities that both X_1 and X_2 will be in the region (e.g. we can use the joint p.d.f. to calculate $\Pr(X_1 \leq 0 \text{ and } X_2 \leq 0)$ or $\Pr(-1.96 \leq X_1 \leq 1.96 \text{ and } -1.64 \leq X_1 \leq 1.64)$ or the probability of any other region). In this textbook, we will not often use joint p.d.f.s to calculate probabilities in this manner. However, in the context of maximum likelihood estimation we often use the

$p(X_1, \ldots, X_N) = \prod_{i=1}^{N} p(X_i)$ definition of the joint probability density function for independent variables.

Definition B.10: The normal distribution

A continuous random variable, X, has a *normal distribution* with mean μ and variance σ^2, denoted $X \sim N(\mu, \sigma^2)$, if its p.d.f. is given by

$$p(X) = \frac{1}{\sqrt{2\pi\sigma^2}} \exp\left[-\frac{1}{2\sigma^2}(X - \mu)^2\right].$$

It is common to use the symbol ϕ to denote the p.d.f. of the normal distribution. That is, $p(X) = \phi(X|\mu, \sigma^2)$ if $X \sim N(\mu, \sigma^2)$. A property of the normal distribution, which we will use, is that, if you have several normal random variables, any linear combination of them will be a normal random variable.

Note: The normal distribution is the familiar bell-shaped distribution that arises in many scientific disciplines. It is symmetric about the mean (i.e. the curve defined by the p.d.f. to the left of μ is the mirror image of the curve to the right). The special case where $\mu = 0$ and $\sigma^2 = 1$ is referred to as the *standard normal* distribution. Tables providing percentiles of the standard normal can be used to calculate probabilities of any interval. If X is not a standard normal, then we can create a new random variable $Z = \frac{X-\mu}{\sigma}$ which is standard normal. Thus, standard normal statistical tables can be used to calculate probabilities for any $N(\mu, \sigma^2)$ random variable.

Example: Using normal statistical tables

To illustrate how normal statistical tables can be used to calculate the probability associated with any interval, suppose $X \sim N(10, 400)$ and we are interested in calculating the probability that X lies in the interval $[5, 40]$. Firstly, we must rewrite the problem in terms of $Z = \frac{X-\mu}{\sigma}$ which is standard normal since we only have statistical tables for this case. This is done as follows:

$$\Pr(5 \leq X \leq 40)$$

$$= \Pr\left(\frac{5 - \mu}{\sigma} \leq \frac{X - \mu}{\sigma} \leq \frac{40 - \mu}{\sigma}\right)$$

$$= \Pr\left(\frac{5 - 10}{\sqrt{400}} \leq Z \leq \frac{40 - 10}{\sqrt{400}}\right)$$

$$= \Pr(-0.25 \leq Z \leq 1.50).$$

Secondly, we must use the standard normal statistical tables to calculate this probability. Statistical tables come in different formats. But the table in this textbook provides $\Pr(0 \leq Z \leq c)$ for any positive number c. We can turn our problem into this format as follows:

$$\Pr(-0.25 \leq Z \leq 1.50)$$
$$= \Pr(-0.25 \leq Z \leq 0) + \Pr(0 \leq Z \leq 1.50)$$
$$= \Pr(0 \leq Z \leq 0.25) + \Pr(0 \leq Z \leq 1.50),$$

where the first equals sign arises since we can break any area into two parts (i.e. the interval $[-0.25, 1.50]$ can be broken into two parts: $[-0.25, 0]$ and $[0, 1.50]$) and we can calculate the areas under the p.d.f.s for these two regions separately. The second equals sign arises since the normal distribution is symmetric. Thus, $\Pr(-c \leq Z \leq 0) = \Pr(0 \leq Z \leq c)$ for any value of c.

Finally, we can use the standard normal table to find $\Pr(0.00 \leq Z \leq 0.25) = 0.0987$ and $\Pr(0 \leq Z \leq 1.50) = 0.4332$. Adding these numbers together gives us the answer $\Pr(-0.25 \leq Z \leq 1.50) = 0.5319$. Thus, there is a 53.19 % chance that X will be in the interval $[5,40]$.

Definition B.11: *The chi-square distribution*

We will never use the precise formula for the p.d.f. of a chi-square random variable, so we will not provide it here. If X has a chi-square distribution with k degrees of freedom, then we write it as $X \sim \chi_k^2$. As with the normal distribution, probabilities for intervals (e.g. $\Pr(X \leq 1)$) can be obtained from statistical tables. For the purposes of this textbook, it is not important that you understand the concept of 'degrees of freedom', other than to note that it tells you what row in the statistical tables to look at. The chi-square distribution is not bell shaped like the normal distribution. It is defined only for positive values for X.

Example: *Using chi-square statistical tables*

To illustrate how the chi-square statistical tables are used, suppose you have a test statistic, X, that under a certain hypothesis, H_0, has a chi-square distribution with 60 degrees of freedom. In your dataset, the test statistic is calculated to be 50. Do you reject H_0 at the 5 % level of significance? To answer this question, note that, if you look in the chi-square statistical tables in the row for 60 degrees of freedom, you will find $\Pr(X \leq 79.08) = 0.95$. Thus, 79.08 is the critical value for this test. That is, there is only a 5 % chance (i.e. $1 - 0.95 = 0.05$) that X is greater than 79.08 if H_0 is true. Since the value for the test statistic, which is 50, is less than the critical value of 79.08, you accept H_0.

Definition B.12: *The Student t distribution*

As with the chi-square distribution, we will never use the precise formula for the p.d.f. of a Student t random variable, so we will not provide it here. If X has a Student t distribution with k degrees of freedom, then we write it as $X \sim t_k$. As with the normal and chi-square distributions, probabilities for intervals (e.g. $\Pr(-1 \leq X \leq 1)$) can be obtained from statistical tables. As with the chi-square distribution, the degrees of freedom tell you what row in the statistical tables to look at. The Student t is bell shaped like the normal and is symmetric.

Example: Using Student t statistical tables

To illustrate how the Student t statistical tables are used, suppose you have a test statistic, X, that under a certain hypothesis, H_0, has a t_{25} distribution. Using your dataset, the test statistic is calculated to be 3.0. Do you reject H_0 at the 1 % level of significance? To answer this question, note that, if you look in the Student t statistical tables in the row for 25 degrees of freedom, you will find $\Pr(X \geq 2.787) = 0.005$. Since the Student t is a symmetric distribution, we can also say $\Pr(X \leq -2.787) = 0.005$. Thus, if H_0 is true, the probability of obtaining a value of X that is greater than 2.787 (in absolute value) is 1 %. This means 2.787 is the 1 % critical value for this test. Since the value for the test statistic, which is 3.0, is greater than the critical value of 2.787, you reject H_0 at the 1 % level of significance.

Definition B.13: The F-distribution

As with the chi-square and Student t distributions, we will never use the precise formula for the p.d.f. of an F random variable, so we will not provide it here. If X has an F-distribution with k_1 degrees of freedom in the numerator and k_2 degrees of freedom in the denominator, then we write it as $X \sim F_{k_1, k_2}$. For the purposes of this textbook, it is not important that you understand the concepts of 'degrees of freedom in the numerator' and 'degrees of freedom in the denominator', other than to note that they tell you what row and column in the statistical tables to look at. To save space, F statistical tables usually only provide values for a with the property that $\Pr(X \leq a) = 0.95$. This is the number required to figure out the critical value for an F-test using the 5 % level of significance. Like the chi-square distribution, F random variables are always positive.

Example: Using F statistical tables

To illustrate how the F statistical tables are used, suppose you have a test statistic, X, that, under a certain hypothesis, H_0, has an $F_{6,40}$ distribution. In your dataset, the test statistic is calculated to be 5.0. Do you reject H_0 at the 5 % level of significance? To answer this question, note that, if you look in the 5 % F statistical tables in the column for six degrees of freedom and the row for 40 degrees of freedom, you will find $\Pr(X \geq 2.34) = 0.05$. Thus, 2.34 is the 5 % critical value for this test. Since the value for the test statistic, which is 5.0, is greater than the critical value of 2.34, you reject H_0 at the 5 % level of significance.

Definition B.14: Other statistical terminology

Let $X_1, \ldots, X_N$ be random variables that are independent of each other and all have the same p.d.f. $p(X)$. Then $X_1, \ldots, X_N$ is referred to as a *random sample* and $p(X)$ is referred to as the p.d.f. of the underlying *population*. This distribution will have a mean and variance which are called the *population mean* and *population variance*. The actual data (i.e. the realisation of random variables $X_1, \ldots, X_N$) is referred to as a *sample*. The sample can be used to estimate the population mean and variance, and these estimates are called the *sample mean* and *sample variance*. Since $X_1, \ldots, X_N$ are independent of one another and all have the same distribution, they are referred to as being *independent and identically distributed* or *i.i.d.* for short.

Advanced material used only in the appendix to Chapter 10

Definition B.15: The gamma distribution

A continuous random variable Y has a *gamma* distribution with mean $\mu > 0$ and degrees of freedom $v > 0$, denoted by $Y \sim G(\mu, v)$, if its p.d.f. is

$$f_G(y|\mu, v) \equiv \begin{cases} c_G^{-1} y^{\frac{v-2}{2}} \exp\left(-\frac{yv}{2\mu}\right) & \text{if } 0 < y < \infty \\ 0 & \text{otherwise,} \end{cases}$$

where the integrating constant is given by $c_G = \left(\frac{2\mu}{v}\right)^{\frac{v}{2}} \Gamma\left(\frac{v}{2}\right)$, where $\Gamma(a)$ is the gamma function (see Poirier, 1995, p. 98). For most purposes it suffices to know that the gamma function is a function that can be calculated in relevant computer packages (like the log or the exponential functions).

Theorem B.3: Mean and variance of the gamma distribution

If $Y \sim G(\mu, v)$, then $E(Y) = \mu$ and $var(Y) = \frac{2\mu^2}{v}$.

   Notes: The gamma distribution is a very important one in Bayesian econometrics as the error precision (i.e. the inverse of the error variance) usually has a gamma distribution. Further properties of the gamma distribution are given in Poirier (1995), pp. 98–102. Distributions related to the gamma include the chi-square distribution, which is a gamma distribution with $v = \mu$. The *exponential distribution* is a gamma distribution with $v = 2$. The *inverted gamma distribution* has the property that, if Y has an inverted gamma distribution, then $\frac{1}{Y}$ has a gamma distribution. In some other Bayesian books, the authors work with error variances (instead of error precisions) and the inverted gamma is used extensively.

Definition B.16: The t-distribution

A continuous random variable, Y, has a *t-distribution* with parameters μ, Σ, and v (a positive scalar referred to as a *degrees of freedom* parameter), denoted $Y \sim t(\mu, \Sigma, v)$, if its p.d.f. is given by

$$f_t(y|\mu, \Sigma, v) = \frac{1}{c_t \sqrt{\Sigma}} \left[v + \frac{(y - \mu)^2}{\Sigma}\right]^{-\frac{v+1}{2}},$$

where

$$c_t = \frac{\pi^{\frac{k}{2}} \Gamma(\frac{v}{2})}{v^{\frac{v}{2}} \Gamma(\frac{v+k}{2})}.$$

Notes: The case with $\mu = 0$ and $\Sigma = 1$ is referred to as the *Student t distribution* and is discussed in definition B.12.

Theorem B.4: Mean and variance of the t-distribution

If $Y \sim t(\mu, \Sigma, v)$, then $E(Y) = \mu$ if $v > 1$ and $var(Y) = \frac{v}{v-2}\Sigma$ if $v > 2$.

Notes: The mean and variance only exist if $v > 1$ and $v > 2$ respectively. Σ is not exactly the same as the variance and, hence, is given another name: the *scale*.

Definition B.17: The normal–gamma distribution

Let Y and h be random variables. If the conditional distribution of Y given h is normal and the marginal distribution for h is gamma, then (Y, h) is said to have a *normal–gamma distribution*. Formally, if $Y|h \sim N(\mu, \sigma^2)$ and $h \sim G(m, v)$, then (Y, h) has a normal–gamma distribution denoted $NG(\mu, \sigma^2, m, v)$.

Theorem B.5: Marginal distributions involving the normal–gamma

If $(Y, h) \sim NG(\mu, \Sigma, m, v)$, then the marginal distribution of Y is given by $Y \sim t(\mu, m^{-1}\Sigma, v)$. Of course, by definition, the marginal for h is given by $h \sim G(m, v)$.

Appendix C: Basic Concepts in Asymptotic Theory

Asymptotic theory derives results as $N \to \infty$. In empirical practice, we have finite N (e.g. $N = 100$). Thus, we use asymptotic results as approximations of what might happen with finite N. Provided N is not too small, asymptotic approximations can be a reasonable guide.

Convergence in probability

Let Z_i for $i = 1, \ldots, N$ be random variables, independent of one another and all having an identical distribution (i.i.d. for short) with

$$E(Z_i) = \mu,$$
$$var(Z_i) = \sigma^2.$$

The mean (average) is

$$\bar{Z} = \frac{\sum_{i=1}^{N} Z_i}{N}.$$

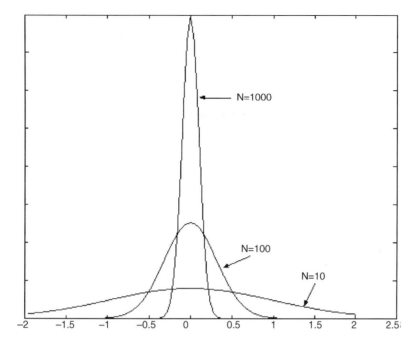

Figure C.1 Distribution of sample mean for different values of N.

Using the properties of the expected value and variance operators, we can derive the mean and variance of $\overline{Z}$ as

$$E(\overline{Z}) = \mu,$$

$$var(\overline{Z}) = \frac{\sigma^2}{N}.$$

Note that, as $N \to \infty$, $var(\overline{Z}) \to 0$. But the variance is a measure of the dispersion of a variable. If $var(\overline{Z}) \to 0$, then the dispersion of $\overline{Z}$ is going to zero. Figure C.1 plots the distribution of $\overline{Z}$ for various values of N (assuming $\mu = 0$ and $\sigma^2 = 10$). It can be seen that the distribution becomes more and more concentrated about its mean as sample size gets larger. Figure C.1 only considers sample sizes up to 1 000. As N gets larger and larger, the distribution of the sample mean becomes more and more concentrated and, eventually, would appear simply to be a spike at the mean of zero.

The idea of a distribution collapsing to a spike, as illustrated by Figure C.1, is the intuition behind *convergence in probability*. We will not provide a formal definition. Intuition plus the following definitions and properties will be enough for you to understand and work with convergence in probability in practice.

Convergence in probability is written as

$$\mathrm{plim}(\overline{Z}) = \mu$$

or

$$\overline{Z} \to \mu.$$

In Chapter 3, we saw how an estimator (e.g. $\widehat{\beta}$) is a random variable. Thus, an estimator has a distribution. If this distribution converges in probability to the thing it is estimating (e.g. β), then we say it is *consistent*. This is a desirable property for any estimator. Informally it is saying that, although any estimate may not be exactly correct, if we had enough data then it would eventually be correct. Above we have written $\text{plim}(\overline{Z}) = \mu$ (which is true, although we have not proved it yet). Thus, $\overline{Z}$ (the sample mean) is a consistent estimator of μ (the population mean).

Econometricians are often interested in checking whether estimators are consistent and, hence, require tools for proving convergence in probability. There are two main tools the econometrician can use:

- Look at the mean and variance of your estimator (e.g. $\overline{Z}$). If, as $N \to \infty$, $E(\overline{Z}) \to \mu$ and $var(\overline{Z}) \to 0$, then $\text{plim}(\overline{Z}) = \mu$.
- Look at the mean and variance of the data going into your estimator (e.g. Z_i for $i = 1, \ldots, N$) and use a *law of large numbers* (LLN).

There are many laws of large numbers. Instances are given below.

A basic law of large numbers

If Z_i for $i = 1, \ldots, N$ are i.i.d. random variables with $E(Z_i) = \mu$, then

$$\text{plim}(\overline{Z}) = \mu.$$

An easy way of remembering the general format of an LLN is through the phrase 'averages converge to expected values' (e.g. the sample mean, $\overline{Z}$, is an average and it converges in probability to the population mean, μ, which is the expected value of Z_i). There are many different LLNs which are derived under different assumptions about the sample (i.e. Z_i for $i = 1, \ldots, N$). Note that the LLN above assumes that the variance of Z_i is the same for every element in the sample (i.e. the i.i.d. assumption implies an *identical* distribution for each of $i = 1, \ldots, N$ and, hence, an identical variance). In some proofs relating to least-squares estimators, this assumption is violated, and hence another LLN is used.

Another law of large numbers

If Z_i for $i = 1, \ldots, N$ are uncorrelated random variables with $E(Z_i) = \mu$ and $var(Z_i) = \sigma_i^2$ (where σ_i^2 are finite for $i = 1, \ldots, N$), then

$$\text{plim}(\overline{Z}) = \mu.$$

This LLN allows for the variances of the elements in the sample to be different, but we still get the same 'averages converge to expected values' result.

Convergence in distribution

Sometimes, our estimators do not converge in probability. That is, their distributions do not degenerate to a single number as we had when plim $(\overline{Z}) = \mu$. Sometimes, though, they converge to a distribution (usually the normal distribution). *Central limit theorems* (CLTs) are a tool used to figure out what distribution they converge to. There are many CLTs, the most common of which is as follows.

A basic central limit theorem

Let Z_i for $i = 1, \ldots, N$ be i.i.d. random variables with

$$E(Z_i) = \mu,$$
$$var(Z_i) = \sigma^2.$$

Then $\sqrt{N}(\overline{Z} - \mu)$ converges in distribution to $N(0, \sigma^2)$ as $N \to \infty$.

Note: This rather remarkable theorem says that, no matter what your random variables are (provided they are i.i.d.), if you take an average of them and multiply by $\sqrt{N}$, you will obtain a normal random variable. Your original random variables (i.e. Z_i for $i = 1, \ldots, N$) could be chi-square or Student t or anything else; the CLT says you end up with a normal distribution for $\sqrt{N}(\overline{Z} - \mu)$.

Other useful theorems

Often our estimators involve two different random variables (usually averages such as the sample mean) or various functions of random variables. There exist several theorems that are relevant for these cases. In the following material, we assume we have two random variables $\overline{Z}$ and $\overline{W}$, the first of which converges in probability and the second in distribution. That is,

$$\text{plim}(\overline{Z}) = \mu_Z$$

and

$$\overline{W} \text{ converges to } N(\mu_W, \sigma_W^2).$$

Slutsky's theorem
If $g(\cdot)$ is a function, then

$$\text{plim}[g(\overline{Z})] = g(\mu_Z).$$

Examples: $\text{plim}(\overline{Z}^2) = \mu_Z^2$ or $\text{plim}(a\overline{Z}) = a\mu_Z$ or $\text{plim}(a + \overline{Z}) = a + \mu_Z$, where a is a constant. Note that this theorem also holds if you have many variables. For instance, if we have $\overline{U}$ with $\text{plim}(\overline{U}) = \mu_U$, then

$$\text{plim}(\overline{ZU}) = \mu_U\mu_Z.$$

With expected values, such a theorem does not work. That is, in general

$$E(\overline{ZU}) \neq \mu_U\mu_Z.$$

Cramer's theorems

1. $\overline{Z} + \overline{W}$ converges in distribution to $N(\mu_Z + \mu_W, \sigma_W^2)$.
2. $\overline{ZW}$ converges in distribution to $N(\mu_Z\mu_W, \mu_Z^2\sigma_W^2)$.
3. $\dfrac{\overline{W}}{\overline{Z}}$ converges in distribution to $N(\frac{\mu_W}{\mu_Z}, \frac{\sigma_W^2}{\mu_Z^2})$ provided $\mu_Z \neq 0$.

Appendix D: Writing an Empirical Project

This appendix offers general guidelines on writing an empirical paper or project. This discussion is followed by two project topics (including data) which you may wish to work on in order to gain a deeper understanding of the techniques described in this book. Some of the exercises (especially in Chapters 6 and 7) are substantial enough almost to be empirical projects in and of themselves. Hence, if you want additional project topics, look through the exercises at the end of each chapter.

Description of a typical empirical project

Economists are engaged in research in a wide variety of areas. Undergraduate and graduate students, academic economists, policymakers working in the civil service and central banks, and professional economists working in private sector banks or industry may all need to write reports that involve analysing economic data. Depending on the topic and intended audience, the form of these reports can vary widely, so that there is no one correct format for an empirical paper. With this in mind, we provide common elements of economic reports below as a guideline for future empirical work. Note, however, that, in the context of your own undergraduate projects or careers, it may not be necessary for you to include all of these elements in your reports.

1. *Introduction.* Most reports begin with an introduction that briefly motivates and describes the issue being studied and summarizes the main empirical findings. The introduction should be written in simple non-technical language, with statistical and economic jargon kept to a minimum. A reader who is not an expert in the field should be able to read and understand the general issues and findings of the report or paper.

2. *Literature Review.* This should summarize related work that others have done. It should list and very briefly describe other papers and findings that relate to yours.

3. *Economic Theory.* If the report is academic in nature and involves a formal theoretical model, then it is often described in this section. For policy reports you may not need to include a formal mathematical model, but this section allows you to describe the economic or institutional issues of your work in more detail. This section can be more technical than the preceding ones and will typically include some mathematics and economic jargon. In short, you can address this section to an audience of experts in your field.

4. *Data.* In this section you should describe your data, including a detailed discussion of their sources.

5. *The Model to be Estimated.* In this section you should discuss how you plan on using the data to investigate the economic theory outlined in section 3. The exact form of this section might vary considerably, depending on the topic and on the intended audience. For instance, you may want to argue that a particular regression is of interest for the study, that a certain variable will be the dependent variable, and that other variables will be the explanatory variables. Similarly, in a macroeconomic time series exercise, you may wish to argue that your economic theory implies that your variables should be cointegrated and that, for this reason, a test of cointegration will be carried out. In short, it is in this section that you should justify the techniques used in the next section.

6. *Empirical Results.* This section is typically the heart of any report. At this stage you should describe your empirical findings and discuss how they relate to the economic issue(s) under investigation. It should contain both statistical and economic information. By 'economic' information we refer, for example, to coefficient estimates or to a finding of cointegration between two variables, and what these findings may imply for economic theory. In contrast, 'statistical' information may include: results from hypothesis tests that show how coefficient estimates are significant; a justification for choice of lag length; an explanation for deleting insignificant explanatory variables; a discussion of model fit (e.g. the R^2); heteroskedasticity tests; etc. Much of this information can be presented in tables or graphs. It is not uncommon for papers to begin with some simple graphs (e.g. a time series plot of the data) and then follow with a table of descriptive statistics (e.g. the mean, standard deviation, and minimum/maximum of each variable, and a correlation matrix). Another table might include results from a more formal statistical analysis, such as OLS coefficient estimates, together with t-statistics (or P-values), R^2s, and F-statistics for testing the significance of the regression as a whole.

7. *Conclusion.* This should briefly summarize the issues addressed in the paper, specifically its most important empirical findings.

General considerations

The following contains a discussion of a few of the issues that you should keep foremost in your mind while carrying out an empirical project. In particular, it discusses what constitutes good empirical science and how you should present your results.

The first thing worth stressing is that there are no right or wrong empirical results. Empirical results are what they are, and you should not be disappointed if they do not show what you had hoped they would. In an ideal world, a researcher comes up with a new theory, then carries out empirical work that supports this new theory in a statistically significant way. The real world very rarely approaches this ideal. In the real world, explanatory variables that you expect to be statistically significant often aren't significant. Variables you expect to be cointegrated often aren't cointegrated. Coefficients you expect to be positive often turn out to be negative. Such results are obtained all the time – even in the most sophisticated of studies. They should not discourage you. Instead, you should always keep an open mind. A finding that a theory does not seem to work is just as scientifically valid as a finding that a theory does work.

Furthermore, empirical results are often unclear or confusing. For instance, one statistical test might indicate one thing while another might indicate the opposite. Likewise, an explanatory variable that is significant in one regression might be insignificant in another regression. There is nothing you can do about this, except to report your results honestly and try (if possible) to understand why such conflicts or confusions are occurring.

It would be rare for economists to falsify their results completely. Often, however, they may be tempted to do slightly dishonest things in order to show that results are indeed as economic reasoning anticipated. For instance, it is common for researchers to run a large number of regressions with many different explanatory variables. On the whole, this is a very wise thing; a sign that the researchers are exploring the data in detail and from a number of angles. However, if the researchers present only the regression that supports a particular theory and not the other regressions that discredit it, they are intentionally misleading the reader. Always avoid this temptation to misrepresent your results. In general, you might want to present results for a few regressions (or, in a time series context, a few different VARs) rather than select a single model and only present results from it.

On the issue of how results should be presented, the importance of clarity and brevity cannot be stressed enough. Whether it is a good thing or a bad thing, it is undoubtedly the case that professors, civil servants, policymakers, and employers are busy people who do not want to spend a lot of time reading long, poorly organized, and verbose reports.

One key skill that writers of good reports show is selectivity. For example, you may have many different coefficient results and test statistics from your various regression runs. An important part of any report is to decide what information is important and what is unimportant to your readership. Select only the most important information for inclusion in your report and – as always – report honestly and openly the results that you obtain.

Project topics

The following are two project topics that you may wish to undertake. The first relates to basic regression methods (see Chapters 1 to 5), the other to time series methods (see Chapters 6 and 7).

Project 1: *The equity underpricing puzzle*

Investors and financial economists are interested in understanding how the stock market values a firm's equity (i.e. shares). In a fundamental sense, the value of a firm's shares should reflect investors' expectations of the firm's future profitability. However, data on expected future profitability are non-existent. Instead, empirical financial studies must use measures such as current income, sales, assets, and debt of the firm as explanatory variables.

In addition to the general question of how stock markets value firms, a second question has also received considerable attention from financial economists in recent years. By way of motivating this problem, note that most of the shares traded on the stock market are old shares in existing firms. However, many old firms will occasionally issue some new shares in addition to those already trading – what are referred to as 'seasoned equity offerings' or SEOs. Furthermore, some firms that have not traded shares on the stock market in the past may decide now to issue such shares (e.g. a computer software firm owned by one individual may decide to 'go public' and sell shares in order to raise money for future investment or expansion). Such shares are called 'initial public offerings' or IPOs. Some researchers have argued on the basis of empirical evidence that IPOs are undervalued relative to SEOs (although other work has suggested the opposite).

In this project, you are asked empirically to investigate these questions using the dataset EQUITY.XLS. This contains data on $N = 309$ firms who sold new shares in the year 1996 in the USA. Some of these are SEOs and some are IPOs. Data on the following variables are provided. All variables except SEOs are measured in millions of US dollars:

- VALUE = the total value of all shares (new and old) outstanding just after the firm issued the new shares (this is calculated as the price per share times the number of shares outstanding);
- DEBT = the amount of long-term debt held by the firm;
- SALES = total sales of the firm;
- INCOME = net income of the firm;

- ASSETS = book value of the assets of the firm (i.e. what an accountant would judge the firm's assets to be worth);
- SEO = a dummy variable that equals 1 if the new share issue is an SEO and equals 0 if it is an IPO.

Project 2: *What moves the stock and bond markets?*

An influential paper in the *Journal of Finance* in 1991 ('What moves the stock and bond markets? A variance decomposition for long-term asset returns' by Campbell and Ammer) investigated the factors that influenced the stock and bond markets in the long run. Without going into the theoretical derivations, suffice it to note here that the authors develop a model where, at a given point in time, unexpected movements in excess stock returns should depend on changes in expectations (i.e. news) about future dividend flows, future excess stock returns, and future real interest rates. Similarly, current unexpected movements in excess bond returns should depend on news about future inflation, future interest rates, and future excess bond returns. The question of interest is which of these various factors is most important in driving the stock and bond markets. The authors conclude that news about future excess stock returns is the most important factor in driving the stock market, and news about future inflation is the most important factor in driving the bond market.

A key part of this model (and many similar models) is that the researcher has to distinguish between 'expected' and 'unexpected' values of variables. To show how this distinction is operationalized, let er_t be the excess return on the stock market at time t. Consider the investors at time $t - 1$ trying to make investment decisions. At time $t - 1$, they will not know exactly what er_t will be. However, they will have some expectation about what it might be. Let us denote the expectation at time $t - 1$ of what the excess stock return at time t will be by $E_{t-1}(er_t)$. As discussed in the previous paragraph, unexpected movements in stock and bond markets are crucial to the underlying financial theory. These are defined as $er_t - E_{t-1}(er_t)$ (i.e. unexpected things are defined as the difference between what actually happened and what was expected).

Even though we have not spelled out all the details, we hope the previous paragraph has motivated why expectations such as $E_{t-1}(er_t)$ appear in financial models. VARs or VECMs are frequently used to model such expectations. That is, since the right-hand side of an equation in a VAR only contains variables dated $t - 1$ or earlier, it can be thought of as reflecting information available to the investor at time $t - 1$. So if we have an equation where er_t is the dependent variable, we can use the fitted value from this regression as an estimate of $E_{t-1}(er_t)$. Using this informal motivation for why VARs are useful, and noting that some variables (e.g. dividend–price ratios) have been found useful for long-run prediction of stock and bond markets, the authors of the paper end up working with a VAR involving the following six variables:

- *er* is the excess stock return;
- *r* is the real interest rate;
- d*y* is the change in the return on a short-term bond;

- s is the yield spread (difference in yields between a 10 year and a 2 month bond);
- dp is the log of the dividend–price ratio;
- rb is the relative bill rate (a return on a short term bond relative to the average returns over the last year).

Monthly observations from December 1947 to February 1987 on all of these variables are available in the dataset VAR.XLS.

In this project you are asked to justify and estimate an appropriate VAR or VECM and use it to carry out Granger causality tests (i.e. to see which variables have the predictive power required to calculate features such as $E_{t-1}(er_t)$). You should use tools such as unit root tests (and, if unit roots are found, cointegration tests) and information criteria (or sequential testing procedures) in order to justify your chosen model.

Table 1. Area under the standard normal distribution $Pr(0 \leq Z \leq z)$.

z	0.00	0.01	0.02	0.03	0.04	0.05	0.06	0.07	0.08	0.09
0.0	0.0000	0.0040	0.0080	0.0120	0.0160	0.0199	0.0239	0.0279	0.0319	0.0359
0.1	0.0398	0.0438	0.0478	0.0517	0.0557	0.0596	0.0636	0.0675	0.0714	0.0753
0.2	0.0793	0.0832	0.0871	0.0910	0.0948	0.0987	0.1026	0.1064	0.1103	0.1141
0.3	0.1179	0.1217	0.1255	0.1293	0.1331	0.1368	0.1406	0.1443	0.1480	0.1517
0.4	0.1554	0.1591	0.1628	0.1664	0.1700	0.1736	0.1772	0.1808	0.1844	0.1879
0.5	0.1915	0.1950	0.1985	0.2019	0.2054	0.2088	0.2123	0.2157	0.2190	0.2224
0.6	0.2257	0.2291	0.2324	0.2357	0.2389	0.2422	0.2454	0.2486	0.2517	0.2549
0.7	0.2580	0.2611	0.2642	0.2673	0.2704	0.2734	0.2764	0.2794	0.2823	0.2852
0.8	0.2881	0.2910	0.2939	0.2967	0.2995	0.3023	0.3051	0.3079	0.3106	0.3133
0.9	0.3159	0.3186	0.3212	0.3238	0.3264	0.3289	0.3315	0.3340	0.3365	0.3389
1.0	0.3413	0.3438	0.3461	0.3485	0.3508	0.3531	0.3554	0.3577	0.3599	0.3621
1.1	0.3643	0.3665	0.3686	0.3708	0.3729	0.3749	0.3770	0.3790	0.3810	0.3830
1.2	0.3849	0.3869	0.3888	0.3907	0.3925	0.3944	0.3962	0.3980	0.3997	0.4015
1.3	0.4032	0.4049	0.4066	0.4082	0.4099	0.4115	0.4131	0.4147	0.4162	0.4177
1.4	0.4192	0.4207	0.4222	0.4236	0.4251	0.4265	0.4279	0.4292	0.4306	0.4319
1.5	0.4332	0.4345	0.4357	0.4370	0.4382	0.4394	0.4406	0.4418	0.4429	0.4441
1.6	0.4452	0.4463	0.4474	0.4484	0.4495	0.4505	0.4515	0.4525	0.4535	0.4545
1.7	0.4554	0.4564	0.4573	0.4582	0.4591	0.4599	0.4608	0.4616	0.4625	0.4633
1.8	0.4641	0.4649	0.4656	0.4664	0.4671	0.4678	0.4686	0.4693	0.4699	0.4706
1.9	0.4713	0.4719	0.4726	0.4732	0.4738	0.4744	0.4750	0.4756	0.4761	0.4767
2.0	0.4773	0.4778	0.4783	0.4788	0.4793	0.4798	0.4803	0.4808	0.4812	0.4817
2.1	0.4821	0.4826	0.4830	0.4834	0.4838	0.4842	0.4846	0.4850	0.4854	0.4857
2.2	0.4861	0.4864	0.4868	0.4871	0.4875	0.4878	0.4881	0.4884	0.4887	0.4890
2.3	0.4893	0.4896	0.4898	0.4901	0.4904	0.4906	0.4909	0.4911	0.4913	0.4916
2.4	0.4918	0.4920	0.4922	0.4925	0.4927	0.4929	0.4931	0.4932	0.4934	0.4936
2.5	0.4938	0.4940	0.4941	0.4943	0.4945	0.4946	0.4948	0.4949	0.4951	0.4952
2.6	0.4953	0.4955	0.4956	0.4957	0.4959	0.4960	0.4961	0.4962	0.4963	0.4964
2.7	0.4965	0.4966	0.4967	0.4968	0.4969	0.4970	0.4971	0.4972	0.4973	0.4974
2.8	0.4974	0.4975	0.4976	0.4977	0.4977	0.4978	0.4979	0.4979	0.4980	0.4981
2.9	0.4981	0.4982	0.4983	0.4983	0.4984	0.4984	0.4985	0.4985	0.4986	0.4986
3.0	0.4987	0.4987	0.4987	0.4988	0.4988	0.4989	0.4989	0.4989	0.4990	0.4990

Note: This table was generated using the SAS® function PROBNORM

Source: Hill, R.C., Griffiths, W.E. and Judge, G.G., *Undergraduate Economics* (2001), John Wiley & Sons, Inc., New York. Reproduced by permission of John Wiley & Sons, Inc.

Table 2. Area under the Student t distribution for different degrees of freedom (DF), $\Pr(Z \geq z) = \alpha$.

DF	$\alpha = .05$	$\alpha = .025$	$\alpha = .005$
1	6.314	12.706	63.657
2	2.920	4.303	9.925
3	2.353	3.182	5.841
4	2.132	2.776	4.604
5	2.015	2.571	4.032
6	1.943	2.447	3.707
7	1.895	2.365	3.499
8	1.860	2.306	3.355
9	1.833	2.262	3.250
10	1.812	2.228	3.169
11	1.796	2.201	3.106
12	1.782	2.179	3.055
13	1.771	2.160	3.012
14	1.761	2.145	2.977
15	1.753	2.131	2.947
16	1.746	2.120	2.921
17	1.740	2.110	2.898
18	1.734	2.101	2.878
19	1.729	2.093	2.861
20	1.725	2.086	2.845
21	1.721	2.08	2.831
22	1.717	2.074	2.819
23	1.714	2.069	2.807
24	1.711	2.064	2.797
25	1.708	2.060	2.787
26	1.706	2.056	2.779
27	1.703	2.052	2.771
28	1.701	2.048	2.763
29	1.699	2.045	2.756
30	1.697	2.042	2.750
40	1.684	2.021	2.704
50	1.676	2.009	2.678
60	1.671	2.000	2.660
70	1.667	1.994	2.648
80	1.664	1.990	2.639
90	1.662	1.987	2.632
100	1.660	1.984	2.626
110	1.659	1.982	2.621
120	1.658	1.980	2.617
∞	1.645	1.960	2.576

Note: This table was generated using the SAS® function TINV
Source: Hill, R.C., Griffiths, W.E. and Judge, G.G., *Undergraduate Economics* (2001), John Wiley & Sons, Inc., New York. Reproduced by permission of John Wiley & Sons, Inc.

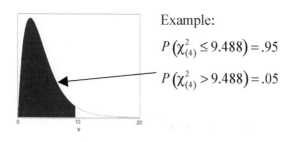

Example:

$$P\left(\chi^2_{(4)} \le 9.488\right) = .95$$

$$P\left(\chi^2_{(4)} > 9.488\right) = .05$$

Table 3. Percentiles of the chi-square distribution.

df	$\chi^2_{(df,.90)}$	$\chi^2_{(df,.95)}$	$\chi^2_{(df,.975)}$	$\chi^2_{(df,.99)}$	$\chi^2_{(df,.995)}$
1	2.706	3.841	5.024	6.635	7.879
2	4.605	5.991	7.378	9.210	10.597
3	6.251	7.815	9.348	11.345	12.838
4	7.779	9.488	11.143	13.277	14.860
5	9.236	11.070	12.833	15.086	16.750
6	10.645	12.592	14.449	16.812	18.548
7	12.017	14.067	16.013	18.475	20.278
8	13.362	15.507	17.535	20.090	21.955
9	14.684	16.919	19.023	21.666	23.589
10	15.987	18.307	20.483	23.209	25.188
11	17.275	19.675	21.920	24.725	26.757
12	18.549	21.026	23.337	26.217	28.300
13	19.812	22.362	24.736	27.688	29.819
14	21.064	23.685	26.119	29.141	31.319
15	22.307	24.996	27.488	30.578	32.801
16	23.542	26.296	28.845	32.000	34.267
17	24.769	27.587	30.191	33.409	35.718
18	25.989	28.869	31.526	34.805	37.156
19	27.204	30.144	32.852	36.191	38.582
20	28.412	31.410	34.170	37.566	39.997
21	29.615	32.671	35.479	38.932	41.401
22	30.813	33.924	36.781	40.289	42.796
23	32.007	35.172	38.076	41.638	44.181
24	33.196	36.415	39.364	42.980	45.559
25	34.382	37.652	40.646	44.314	46.928
26	35.563	38.885	41.923	45.642	48.290
27	36.741	40.113	43.195	46.963	49.645
28	37.916	41.337	44.461	48.278	50.993
29	39.087	42.557	45.722	49.588	52.336
30	40.256	43.773	46.979	50.892	53.672
35	46.059	49.802	53.203	57.342	60.275
40	51.805	55.758	59.342	63.691	66.766
50	63.167	67.505	71.420	76.154	79.490
60	74.397	79.082	83.298	88.379	91.952
70	85.527	90.531	95.023	100.425	104.215
80	96.578	101.879	106.629	112.329	116.321
90	107.565	113.145	118.136	124.116	128.299
100	118.498	124.342	129.561	135.807	140.169
110	129.385	135.480	140.917	147.414	151.948
120	140.233	146.567	152.211	158.950	163.648

Note: This table was generated using the SAS® function CINV

Source: Hill, R.C., Griffiths, W.E. and Judge, G.G., *Undergraduate Economics* (2001), John Wiley & Sons, Inc., New York. Reproduced by permission of John Wiley & Sons, Inc.

Table 4a. Area under the F-distribution for different degrees of freedom, ν_1 and ν_2, $\Pr(Z \geq \zeta) = 0.05$.

Upper 5% Points

ν_2 / ν_1	1	2	3	4	5	6	7	8	9	10	12	15	20	24	30	40	60	120	∞
1	161.45	199.50	215.71	224.58	230.16	233.99	236.77	238.88	240.54	241.88	243.91	245.95	248.01	249.05	250.1	251.14	252.2	253.25	254.31
2	18.51	19.00	19.16	19.25	19.30	19.33	19.35	19.37	19.38	19.40	19.41	19.43	19.45	19.45	19.46	19.47	19.48	19.49	19.50
3	10.13	9.55	9.28	9.12	9.01	8.94	8.89	8.85	8.81	8.79	8.74	8.70	8.66	8.64	8.62	8.59	8.57	8.55	8.53
4	7.71	6.94	6.59	6.39	6.26	6.16	6.09	6.04	6.00	5.96	5.91	5.86	5.80	5.77	5.75	5.72	5.69	5.66	5.63
5	6.61	5.79	5.41	5.19	5.05	4.95	4.88	4.82	4.77	4.74	4.68	4.62	4.56	4.53	4.50	4.46	4.43	4.40	4.37
6	5.99	5.14	4.76	4.53	4.39	4.28	4.21	4.15	4.10	4.06	4.00	3.94	3.87	3.84	3.81	3.77	3.74	3.70	3.67
7	5.59	4.74	4.35	4.12	3.97	3.87	3.79	3.73	3.68	3.64	3.57	3.51	3.44	3.41	3.38	3.34	3.30	3.27	3.23
8	5.32	4.46	4.07	3.84	3.69	3.58	3.50	3.44	3.39	3.35	3.28	3.22	3.15	3.12	3.08	3.04	3.01	2.97	2.93
9	5.12	4.26	3.86	3.63	3.48	3.37	3.29	3.23	3.18	3.14	3.07	3.01	2.94	2.90	2.86	2.83	2.79	2.75	2.71
10	4.96	4.10	3.71	3.48	3.33	3.22	3.14	3.07	3.02	2.98	2.91	2.85	2.77	2.74	2.70	2.66	2.62	2.58	2.54
11	4.84	3.98	3.59	3.36	3.20	3.09	3.01	2.95	2.90	2.85	2.79	2.72	2.65	2.61	2.57	2.53	2.49	2.45	2.40
12	4.75	3.89	3.49	3.26	3.11	3.00	2.91	2.85	2.80	2.75	2.69	2.62	2.54	2.51	2.47	2.43	2.38	2.34	2.30
13	4.67	3.81	3.41	3.18	3.03	2.92	2.83	2.77	2.71	2.67	2.60	2.53	2.46	2.42	2.38	2.34	2.30	2.25	2.21
14	4.60	3.74	3.34	3.11	2.96	2.85	2.76	2.70	2.65	2.60	2.53	2.46	2.39	2.35	2.31	2.27	2.22	2.18	2.13
15	4.54	3.68	3.29	3.06	2.90	2.79	2.71	2.64	2.59	2.54	2.48	2.40	2.33	2.29	2.25	2.20	2.16	2.11	2.07
16	4.49	3.63	3.24	3.01	2.85	2.74	2.66	2.59	2.54	2.49	2.42	2.35	2.28	2.24	2.19	2.15	2.11	2.06	2.01
17	4.45	3.59	3.20	2.96	2.81	2.70	2.61	2.55	2.49	2.45	2.38	2.31	2.23	2.19	2.15	2.10	2.06	2.01	1.96
18	4.41	3.55	3.16	2.93	2.77	2.66	2.58	2.51	2.46	2.41	2.34	2.27	2.19	2.15	2.11	2.06	2.02	1.97	1.92
19	4.38	3.52	3.13	2.90	2.74	2.63	2.54	2.48	2.42	2.38	2.31	2.23	2.16	2.11	2.07	2.03	1.98	1.93	1.88
20	4.35	3.49	3.10	2.87	2.71	2.60	2.51	2.45	2.39	2.35	2.28	2.20	2.12	2.08	2.04	1.99	1.95	1.90	1.84
21	4.32	3.47	3.07	2.84	2.68	2.57	2.49	2.42	2.37	2.32	2.25	2.18	2.10	2.05	2.01	1.96	1.92	1.87	1.81
22	4.30	3.44	3.05	2.82	2.66	2.55	2.46	2.40	2.34	2.30	2.23	2.15	2.07	2.03	1.98	1.94	1.89	1.84	1.78
23	4.28	3.42	3.03	2.80	2.64	2.53	2.44	2.37	2.32	2.27	2.20	2.13	2.05	2.01	1.96	1.91	1.86	1.81	1.76
24	4.26	3.40	3.01	2.78	2.62	2.51	2.42	2.36	2.30	2.25	2.18	2.11	2.03	1.98	1.94	1.89	1.84	1.79	1.73
25	4.24	3.39	2.99	2.76	2.60	2.49	2.40	2.34	2.28	2.24	2.16	2.09	2.01	1.96	1.92	1.87	1.82	1.77	1.71
26	4.23	3.37	2.98	2.74	2.59	2.47	2.39	2.32	2.27	2.22	2.15	2.07	1.99	1.95	1.90	1.85	1.80	1.75	1.69
27	4.21	3.35	2.96	2.73	2.57	2.46	2.37	2.31	2.25	2.20	2.13	2.06	1.97	1.93	1.88	1.84	1.79	1.73	1.67
28	4.20	3.34	2.95	2.71	2.56	2.45	2.36	2.29	2.24	2.19	2.12	2.04	1.96	1.91	1.87	1.82	1.77	1.71	1.65
29	4.18	3.33	2.93	2.70	2.55	2.43	2.35	2.28	2.22	2.18	2.10	2.03	1.94	1.90	1.85	1.81	1.75	1.70	1.64
30	4.17	3.32	2.92	2.69	2.53	2.42	2.33	2.27	2.21	2.16	2.09	2.01	1.93	1.89	1.84	1.79	1.74	1.68	1.62
40	4.08	3.23	2.84	2.61	2.45	2.34	2.25	2.18	2.12	2.08	2.00	1.92	1.84	1.79	1.74	1.69	1.64	1.58	1.51
60	4.00	3.15	2.76	2.53	2.37	2.25	2.17	2.10	2.04	1.99	1.92	1.84	1.75	1.70	1.65	1.59	1.53	1.47	1.39
120	3.92	3.07	2.68	2.45	2.29	2.18	2.09	2.02	1.96	1.91	1.83	1.75	1.66	1.61	1.55	1.50	1.43	1.35	1.25
∞	3.84	3.00	2.60	2.37	2.21	2.10	2.01	1.94	1.88	1.83	1.75	1.67	1.57	1.52	1.46	1.39	1.32	1.22	1.00

Note: This table was generated using the SAS® function FINV. ν_1 = numerator degrees of freedom; ν_2 = denominator degrees of freedom

Source: Hill, R.C., Griffiths, W.E. and Judge, G.G., *Undergraduate Economics* (2001), John Wiley & Sons, Inc., New York. Reproduced by permission of John Wiley & Sons, Inc.

Table 4b. Area under the F-distribution for different degrees of freedom, ν_1 and ν_2, $\Pr(Z \geq z) = 0.01$.

Upper 1% Points

ν_2/ν_1	1	2	3	4	5	6	7	8	9	10	12	15	20	24	30	40	60	120	∞
1	4052.18	4999.50	5403.35	5624.58	5763.65	5858.99	5928.36	5981.07	6022.47	6055.85	6106.32	6157.28	6208.73	6234.63	6260.65	6286.78	6313.03	6339.39	6365.86
2	98.50	99.00	99.17	99.25	99.30	99.33	99.36	99.37	99.39	99.40	99.42	99.43	99.45	99.46	99.47	99.47	99.48	99.49	99.50
3	34.12	30.82	29.46	28.71	28.24	27.91	27.67	27.49	27.35	27.23	27.05	26.87	26.69	26.60	26.50	26.41	26.32	26.22	26.13
4	21.20	18.00	16.69	15.98	15.52	15.21	14.98	14.80	14.66	14.55	14.37	14.20	14.02	13.93	13.84	13.75	13.65	13.56	13.46
5	16.26	13.27	12.06	11.39	10.97	10.67	10.46	10.29	10.16	10.05	9.89	9.72	9.55	9.47	9.38	9.29	9.20	9.11	9.02
6	13.75	10.92	9.78	9.15	8.75	8.47	8.26	8.10	7.98	7.87	7.72	7.56	7.40	7.31	7.23	7.14	7.06	6.97	6.88
7	12.25	9.55	8.45	7.85	7.46	7.19	6.99	6.84	6.72	6.62	6.47	6.31	6.16	6.07	5.99	5.91	5.82	5.74	5.65
8	11.26	8.65	7.59	7.01	6.63	6.37	6.18	6.03	5.91	5.81	5.67	5.52	5.36	5.28	5.20	5.12	5.03	4.95	4.86
9	10.56	8.02	6.99	6.42	6.06	5.80	5.61	5.47	5.35	5.26	5.11	4.96	4.81	4.73	4.65	4.57	4.48	4.40	4.31
10	10.04	7.56	6.55	5.99	5.64	5.39	5.20	5.06	4.94	4.85	4.71	4.56	4.41	4.33	4.25	4.17	4.08	4.00	3.91
11	9.65	7.21	6.22	5.67	5.32	5.07	4.89	4.74	4.63	4.54	4.40	4.25	4.10	4.02	3.94	3.86	3.78	3.69	3.60
12	9.33	6.93	5.95	5.41	5.06	4.82	4.64	4.50	4.39	4.30	4.16	4.01	3.86	3.78	3.70	3.62	3.54	3.45	3.36
13	9.07	6.70	5.74	5.21	4.86	4.62	4.44	4.30	4.19	4.10	3.96	3.82	3.66	3.59	3.51	3.43	3.34	3.25	3.17
14	8.86	6.51	5.56	5.04	4.70	4.46	4.28	4.14	4.03	3.94	3.80	3.66	3.51	3.43	3.35	3.27	3.18	3.09	3.00
15	8.68	6.36	5.42	4.89	4.56	4.32	4.14	4.00	3.89	3.80	3.67	3.52	3.37	3.29	3.21	3.13	3.05	2.96	2.87
16	8.53	6.23	5.29	4.77	4.44	4.20	4.03	3.89	3.78	3.69	3.55	3.41	3.26	3.18	3.10	3.02	2.93	2.84	2.75
17	8.40	6.11	5.19	4.67	4.34	4.10	3.93	3.79	3.68	3.59	3.46	3.31	3.16	3.08	3.00	2.92	2.83	2.75	2.65
18	8.29	6.01	5.09	4.58	4.25	4.01	3.84	3.71	3.60	3.51	3.37	3.23	3.08	3.00	2.92	2.84	2.75	2.66	2.57
19	8.18	5.93	5.01	4.50	4.17	3.94	3.77	3.63	3.52	3.43	3.30	3.15	3.00	2.92	2.84	2.76	2.67	2.58	2.49
20	8.10	5.85	4.94	4.43	4.10	3.87	3.70	3.56	3.46	3.37	3.23	3.09	2.94	2.86	2.78	2.69	2.61	2.52	2.42
21	8.02	5.78	4.87	4.37	4.04	3.81	3.64	3.51	3.40	3.31	3.17	3.03	2.88	2.80	2.72	2.64	2.55	2.46	2.36
22	7.95	5.72	4.82	4.31	3.99	3.76	3.59	3.45	3.35	3.26	3.12	2.98	2.83	2.75	2.67	2.58	2.50	2.40	2.31
23	7.88	5.66	4.76	4.26	3.94	3.71	3.54	3.41	3.30	3.21	3.07	2.93	2.78	2.70	2.62	2.54	2.45	2.35	2.26
24	7.82	5.61	4.72	4.22	3.90	3.67	3.50	3.36	3.26	3.17	3.03	2.89	2.74	2.66	2.58	2.49	2.40	2.31	2.21
25	7.77	5.57	4.68	4.18	3.86	3.63	3.46	3.32	3.22	3.13	2.99	2.85	2.70	2.62	2.54	2.45	2.36	2.27	2.17
26	7.72	5.53	4.64	4.14	3.82	3.59	3.42	3.29	3.18	3.09	2.96	2.82	2.66	2.58	2.50	2.42	2.33	2.23	2.13
27	7.68	5.49	4.60	4.11	3.78	3.56	3.39	3.26	3.15	3.06	2.93	2.78	2.63	2.55	2.47	2.38	2.29	2.20	2.10
28	7.64	5.45	4.57	4.07	3.75	3.53	3.36	3.23	3.12	3.03	2.90	2.75	2.60	2.52	2.44	2.35	2.26	2.17	2.06
29	7.60	5.42	4.54	4.04	3.73	3.50	3.33	3.20	3.09	3.00	2.87	2.73	2.57	2.49	2.41	2.33	2.23	2.14	2.03
30	7.56	5.39	4.51	4.02	3.70	3.47	3.30	3.17	3.07	2.98	2.84	2.70	2.55	2.47	2.39	2.30	2.21	2.11	2.01
40	7.31	5.18	4.31	3.83	3.51	3.29	3.12	2.99	2.89	2.80	2.66	2.52	2.37	2.29	2.20	2.11	2.02	1.92	1.80
60	7.08	4.98	4.13	3.65	3.34	3.12	2.95	2.82	2.72	2.63	2.50	2.35	2.20	2.12	2.03	1.94	1.84	1.73	1.60
120	6.85	4.79	3.95	3.48	3.17	2.96	2.79	2.66	2.56	2.47	2.34	2.19	2.03	1.95	1.86	1.76	1.66	1.53	1.38
∞	6.63	4.61	3.78	3.32	3.02	2.80	2.64	2.51	2.41	2.32	2.18	2.04	1.88	1.79	1.70	1.59	1.47	1.32	1.00

Note: This table was generated using the SAS® function FINV. ν_1 = numerator degrees of freedom; ν_2 = denominator degrees of freedom

Source: Hill, R.C., Griffiths, W.E. and Judge, G.G., *Undergraduate Economics* (2001), John Wiley & Sons, Inc, New York. Reproduced by permission of John Wiley & Sons, Inc.

Bibliography

Geweke, J. (2005) *Contemporary Bayesian Econometrics and Statistics*, John Wiley & Sons, Inc., New York, NY, USA.

Koop, G. (2003) *Bayesian Econometrics*, John Wiley & Sons, Inc., New York, NY, USA.

Koop, G., Poirier, D., & Tobias, J. (2007) *Bayesian Econometric Methods. Volume 7 in the Econometrics Exercises Series* (eds K. Abadir, J. Magnus, & P.C.B. Phillips), Cambridge University Press, Cambridge, UK.

Lancaster, A. (2004) *An Introduction to Modern Bayesian Econometrics*, Blackwell, Oxford, UK.

Poirier, D. (1995) *Intermediate Statistics and Econometrics: A Comparative Approach*, (The MIT Press, Cambridge, MA, USA).

Wonnacott, T. & Wonnacott, R. (1990) *Introductory Statistics for Business and Economics*, 4th edition, John Wiley & Sons, Inc., New York, NY, USA.

Zellner, A. (1971) *An Introduction to Bayesian Inference in Econometrics*, John Wiley & Sons, Inc., New York, NY, USA.

Index

Note: Page references in *italics* refer to Figures; those in **bold** refer to Tables